EUNUCHS for HEAVEN

Uta Ranke-Heinemann

EUNUCHS for HEAVEN

The Catholic Church and Sexuality

Translated by
John Brownjohn

ANDRE DEUTSCH

To my husband

First published in Great Britain in 1990
by André Deutsch Limited
105–106 Great Russell Street London WC1B 3LJ

Published in West Germany by Hoffmann und Campe Verlag, Hamburg

British Library Cataloguing in Publication Data

Ranke-Heinemann, Uta
  Eunuchs for heaven.
  1. Sex relations. Attitudes, history of Catholic Church
  I. Title II. Eunuchen für das Himmelreich. *English*
  261.8'357

ISBN 0 233 98553 0

Typeset by CentraCet, Cambridge
Printed in Great Britain by
St Edmundsbury Press, Bury St Edmunds, Suffolk

CONTENTS

INTRODUCTION

The Lawyers' Jesus

On 14 July 1981, Division 144 of Hamburg's District Court imposed a fine equivalent to forty days' salary on Herr X, the editor of a satirical magazine, for having publicly impugned religious beliefs and ecclesiastical institutions. The court stated its reasons as follows: 'The Christian faith, being founded on the person of Jesus Christ in his capacity as the essential constituent of the Christian Church's profession of faith, consists in God's having revealed himself to mankind in the person of Jesus Christ. He is defined as the Redeemer whose life was devoid of all sin and pleasure.' Although the court's judgment suffered from a certain theological and syntactical obscurity, it had quite clearly ruled – 'in the name of the people' – that Jesus was a thoroughly joyless Redeemer.

One can only presume that the court did not mean quite what it said. Devoid of all sin, fair enough, but devoid of all pleasure? To call Jesus that would be to make a sorry creature of him, and any such assertion might have rendered the judges, in their turn, guilty of offending religious sensibilities. In acquitting Jesus of all forms of pleasure it was doubtless referring to one in particular, namely, physical, sensual pleasure as distinct from the spiritual pleasure also known as joy. This can occur on several levels. It ranges from musical appreciation and the enjoyment of food and drink (Jesus's enemies called him a glutton and a winebibber [Matt. 11: 19; Luke 7: 34]), to its last and lowest form, sexual pleasure. The court, having clearly leapt to this worst of conclusions, had formally laid it down that Jesus never experienced anything of the kind. Simultaneously, by linking sexual pleasure closely with the term 'sin', it clarified another juridical point: sexual pleasure is a Bad Thing. In so doing, it seems to have endorsed the early

Catholic view that sexual pleasure cannot be devoid of sin. But sexual joylessness, coupled with a negative view of pleasure in general, betokens an active hostility to pleasure, and in the eyes of celibate theologians Jesus has never been anything but a sexually austere and pleasure-hating Saviour.

This attitude has had repercussions, and not only on the blasphemous editor referred to above, who got away with the loss of forty days' salary. Its consequences for many people in the course of history have been abundant and usually far more serious, sometimes lifelong, sometimes fatal. Under Article 133 of Emperor Charles V's 'Peinliche Gerichtsordnung' (penal code) of 1532, the use of contraceptive devices – a practice implying a quest for sexual gratification proscribed by the Church – became a capital offence. Even in our own century, for instance during the Nazi period, devout hostility to pleasure has played a major role in decisions affecting the fate of human beings, *inter alia* the question of how to treat the hereditarily sick and 'how such *Schädlinge* [a common term for 'pests' and 'vermin'] are to be removed from the community in the legitimate interests of self-defence' (thus Cardinal Faulhaber to Hitler in 1936). It was the same old hostility to pleasure, ostensibly based on the teachings of Jesus, that prompted Faulhaber to oppose the Führer's plans for compulsory sterilisation and argue in favour of internment (alias concentration) camps, but more of that later.

To revert to our starting point, the joyless Jesus. His alleged abhorrence of pleasure affected his mother's married life: even before his birth, he laid down conditions whose non-fulfilment would have precluded her from becoming his mother at all. Church doctrine holds that Jesus would not have undertaken the Redemption – that he would have either refrained from becoming man in the first place or picked himself another mother – had Mary been desirous of bearing children in addition to himself. This was stated as long ago as the fourth century by Pope Siricius, who wrote that, under such circumstances, Jesus would never have accepted Mary as his mother. 'Jesus would not have chosen to be born of a virgin had he been compelled to regard her as so incontinent that the womb in which the body of the Lord took shape, that hall of the Everlasting King, would be defiled by the presence of male seed. Anyone who says so is simply endorsing Jewish unbelief' (letter to Bishop Anysius dated 392). In other words, the bearing of children denoted incontinence and self-abandonment to sexual pleasure;

to conceive a child, otherwise than by the Holy Spirit, was self-defiling and impure. That this was not just the personal opinion of one particular pope is confirmed by the Catholic dogmatist Michael Schmaus, who states that, in making these assertions, Siricius bore witness to 'the Church's unanimous doctrine'.

For theologians, Jesus's alleged disapproval of pleasure affected the image of other women as well. Unless they virginally pursued their own self-sanctification like Mary, they presented a picture of inferiority: their only function was the bearing of children, but childbearing presupposed sexual activity and 'defilement with male seed'. Thus Jesus's hostility to pleasure had repercussions on Christian marriage: sexual enjoyment was excluded from it as far as possible and not infrequently made subject to threats of eternal damnation.

The same disapproval of pleasure affected the priestly way of life, which had to be remote from the moral slums of everyday existence. The logical consequence of hostility to marriage was a celibate priesthood, so it is hardly surprising to find Pope Siricius, that great Mariologist and despiser of matrimony, in the forefront of the campaign against married priests. He decisively influenced the growth of celibacy by describing it as a *crimen*, or crime, for priests to have intercourse with their wives after ordination. His letter to Himerius, the Spanish bishop of Tarragona (385), further condemned such conduct as *obscoena cupiditas*, or 'vile lechery'. (The majority of priests were married when the practice of celibacy began to develop, and it was not until 1139 that matrimony was formally denied them.)

In 390 the same sexual neurotic fired off a broadside at Jovinian, who had contended that married and celibate life were of equal merit. Having two years earlier evolved some almost Lutheran ideas on the subject of marriage and celibacy, Jovinian came to Rome during Siricius's pontificate and persuaded several devout virgins and men of ascetic habits to get married. His argument: 'Are you any better than Sarah, Susanna, Anna, and many of the holy women and men in the Bible?' Where the mother of Jesus was concerned, Jovinian held that she had conceived him as a virgin but not borne him as one, her physical virginity having been terminated by parturition. He thus disputed the doctrine of 'virginity in birth', in other words, he denied that Mary had preserved her hymen intact while giving birth. Then as now, however, this biological truism was an abomination to pious ears. A number of respected lay ascetics went to Pope Siricius and urged him to condemn the heretic, whereupon (in 391) Siricius excommunicated Jovinian and eight of his followers.

Even at this early stage, then, we find Siricius embodying much that is still typically Catholic: a disapproval of pleasure conducive to hostility toward marriage; a hostility toward marriage conducive to celibacy; and – a corollary of the foregoing – the doctrine of the virgin birth and Mary's continuing biological virginity. Only seven of Pope Siricius's letters have survived, but almost all of them demonstrate his sexual pessimism. This antimarital, antiphysical nonsense, as purveyed by Siricius and many others, has attained such dominance within the Catholic Church that it is widely regarded as the essence of Christian doctrine and can even be reflected in the findings of a German district court.

Siricius is one of many milestones in a long historical process that has transformed Christianity as it once was or should have been – a religion founded on personal experience of the universally accessible love of God, in which the body has its natural and God-given place – into a regime imposed by an unmarried oligarchy on a subordinate and largely married majority. This has perverted the work of him from whom the Christians take their name. Confronted by a Church that has ceased to manifest God's mercy and intimate connection with humankind – that has converted Christ into a grim and joyless adjunct to the policing of bedrooms and marital intercourse – men and women can no longer see themselves as beloved of God, only as impure and reprehensible.

ONE

The Non-Christian Roots of Christian Sexual Pessimism

It is untrue that Christianity introduced self-control and asceticism into a licentious and hedonistic heathen world. Sexual pessimism and hostility toward the pleasures of the flesh are a legacy from the ancient world which Christianity has preserved in special measure to this day. It was not the Christians who taught self-denial and continence to immoral and intemperate heathens, but the heathens who were forced to acknowledge that Christians were much like themselves. Galen (second century), a heathen Greek and personal physician to Emperor Marcus Aurelius, found it commendable that, despite their philosophical deficiences, the Christians practised such genuine and, in his view, estimable virtues as lifelong sexual continence. He wrote:

> Most people are unable to follow any demonstrative argument consecutively, hence they need parables and benefit from them, just as now we see the people called Christians drawing their faith from parables and miracles and yet sometimes acting in the same way [as those who philosophise] . . . For their contempt of death and of its sequel is patent to us every day, and likewise their restraint in cohabitation. For they include not only men but also women who refrain from cohabiting all through their lives; and they also number individuals who in self-discipline and self-control in matters of food and drink and in their keen pursuit of justice have attained a pitch not inferior to that of genuine philosophers.
> (Richard Walzer, 'Galen on Jews and Christians', pp. 57, 65)

Unlike that of Christianity, the sexual pessimism of the ancient world did not derive from the concept of sin and atonement, but was based

1

primarily on medical considerations. Pythagoras (sixth century BC) is reported as saying that men should devote themselves to sex in winter, not summer, and in moderation only during the spring and autumn, but that it was injurious to the health at every season of the year. The best time to make love, he stated, was when a man wished to weaken himself (Diogenes Laertius, 'Lives of the Philosophers', VIII). Sexual intercourse was harmless to women because they sustained no loss of energy resulting from the emission of semen. The sexual act was represented as dangerous, difficult to control, detrimental to health, and debilitating. This view was shared by Xenophon (d. after 355 BC), Plato, Aristotle, and the physician Hippocrates (fourth century BC). Plato (d. 348 or 347 BC), describing the Olympic victor Issos of Tarentum in 'The Laws', stated that he was ambitious and possessed a skill and strength born of moderation. Once in training, 'he never, so it is said, touched woman nor boy'. Hippocrates described the fate of a young man who died insane after an illness lasting twenty-four days. It began as a simple stomach upset, but he had previously overindulged in sexual intercourse ('Epidemics', III, 18). Hippocrates believed that the retention of semen was the key to physical strength, and that excessive loss of semen wasted the spinal marrow and resulted in death. Sexual activity was thought to be a dangerous squandering of energy. Soranus of Ephesus (second century AD), Emperor Hadrian's personal physician, asserted that permanent celibacy was health-giving, and that the generation of offspring was the sole justification for sexual activity. He also listed the harmful effects of all sexual excesses superfluous to the needs of procreation.

These voices from the ancient world were investigated by Michel Foucault (d. 1984) in his 'History of Sexuality'. According to him, sexual activity was more and more harshly judged during the first two centuries of our era. Physicians recommended abstinence and celibacy, the philosophers of the Stoa condemned all sexual activity outside marriage and demanded marital fidelity of both spouses, and pederasty was less highly regarded than before. The same period witnessed a reinforcement of marital ties, sexual relations being considered permissible only between spouses. Sex and marriage became one. The Greek historian Plutarch (d. c. 120), one of the most influential and widely read authors in literary history, extolled Laelius for having cohabited with one partner only, the first and only woman he ever married ('Cato the Younger', in 'Lives', 7).

This growing derogation and disparagement of sexual activity during the first two centuries AD was spearheaded by the Stoa, the great school of philosophy that existed *c.* 300 BC–AD 250. The word stoic connotes impassivity to this day. Although most Greek philosophers had accorded the pursuit of pleasure an important place in the scale of human values, the Stoics in particular – and particularly during the first two centuries of our era – ceased to do so. They rejected the pursuit of pleasure. The salutary effect of this rejection was to concentrate sexual activity on marriage. As the pursuit of pleasure and the gratification of carnal desire became suspect, however, so marriage itself was called into question and celibacy more highly esteemed. Matrimony was regarded as a concession to those incapable of continence, a sop to the carnal desire of those to whom carnal desire seemed indispensable. The rigorist elevation of celibacy and abstinence above marriage, foreshadowed in the Stoa, attained its consummation in the Christian ideal of virginity. Thus the Stoa's aversion to the pursuit of pleasure led, on the one hand, to a preference for marriage over promiscuous sexual activity, and, on the other, to the subordination of marriage to total abstinence from carnal desire and passion.

The Stoic Seneca, appointed tutor to Nero in AD 50 when the future emperor was eleven years old, wrote as follows in his treatise on marriage:

> All love for the wife of another is shameful, but it is also shameful to love one's own wife to excess. The wise man causes reason, not emotion, to prevail when loving his wife. Let him resist the onset of passion and not be rashly impelled to the conjugal act. Nothing can be more depraved than to make love to one's wife as if she were an adulteress. Those men who claim to have coupled with their wives in order to beget children for the sake of the state or the human race should at least emulate the beasts and, when their wives' bellies swell, refrain from destroying their progeny. They should treat their wives, not like lovers, but like husbands.

This passage so appealed to that austere Father of the Church, St Jerome (d. 419 or 420), that he cited it in his attack on Jovinian ('Adversus Jovinianum', I, 49). Even John Paul II speaks of 'adultery' with one's own wife. 'Nothing for pleasure's sake' was Seneca's fundamental tenet (Epistolae 88, 29). His younger contemporary Musonius, a Stoic whose philosophical teachings influenced numerous members of the Roman ruling class, pronounced copulation for purposes other than begetting children immoral. In his view, only sexual intercourse aimed at procreation accorded with the proper scheme of things, and any man solely intent on pleasure was to be condemned, even if he kept within the bounds of matrimony. Musonius expressly rejected contraception and condemned homosexuality for the same reason: the sexual act had to be generative.

Over and above its generative purpose, however, marriage was esteemed by the Stoics as a union formed in the interests of mutual assistance (Musonius, 'Reliquiae', XIII). Aristotle (d. 322 BC) stated that no bond is closer than that existing between parents and their children, whereas Musonius (ibid., XIV) regarded love between husband and wife as the strongest tie of all. Aristotle stressed the subjection of wife to husband and described women as inferior in virtue to men, whereas Musonius regarded both sexes as equally virtuous. Musonius further advocated equal rights for women and female education, an idea too seldom adopted by Catholic hierarchs who see the female mentality as restricted to childbearing and cooking. Although Christianity, too, speaks of marriage as 'reciprocal help', it really regards the wife as her husband's helpmate: Eve was created to assist Adam, not vice versa. This underlines woman's subordinate role. Aristotle has been an ex officio Father of the Church ever since Thomas Aquinas. Whether 'mutual assistance' be construed in terms of equal rights, as it was by Musonius, or of subordination, as it is by the Church, what is common to both Stoics and Christians is a certain 'dephysicalisation' of marriage in that its sexual aspect is set apart and viewed solely from the aspect of procreation or self-gratification. Marital intercourse remains confined to the realm of carnal desire and incapable of integration because it is still branded by the suspicion that attaches to the pursuit of pleasure in general. Christianity has been lastingly influenced by the idea that marital intercourse must be either a procreative act or classified under the pejorative heading of lust.

Seneca broached an idea whose disastrous consequence it was to focus Christian morality on the sexual domain. 'When you consider,' he wrote to his mother Helvia, 'that the sexual urge is bestowed on man, not for his enjoyment, but for the reproduction of his own kind, then, provided you remain untouched by the noxious breath of sensual pleasure, every other form of craving, too, will pass you by without touching you. Reason fells all vices at a stroke, not just some of them. Its victory occurs only once and is universal.' In other words, the essence of morality is sexual morality. To be vigilant in that respect is to be vigilant absolutely.

The celibatarian ideal is far from being a uniquely Christian ideal. According to his biographer Philostratus, the wonder-worker Apollonius of Tyana (first century AD) took a vow of celibacy and kept it throughout his life. Pliny the Elder, the Roman naturalist who met his end during the eruption of Vesuvius in AD 79, commended the example of the elephant, which mates only once every two years ('Historia naturalis', VIII, 5). In so doing, he subscribed to a contemporary ideal. Pliny's chaste pachyderm was destined to enjoy a great and enduring future among Christian theologians and in Christian devotional literature. It was extolled by Richard of St Victor (d.c. 1173), by Alanus ab Insulis (d. 1202), by an anonymous 'summa' or treatise of the thirteenth century (Codex latinus monacensis 22233), and by the Dominican Giulielmus Peraldus (d. prior to 1270). It also reappeared in 'Philothea' (1609) by the Genevese bishop Francis of Sales (d. 1622). In every case, the elephant was held up as an example to married couples.

'Though naught but an ungainly beast,' wrote Francis of Sales, 'it is the most dignified and intelligent on earth . . . It never changes its mate and tenderly loves the one it has chosen, with which it mates only once every three years, and then for no longer than five days and so secretly that it is never seen in the act. It shows itself on the sixth day, when it goes at once to the river and bathes its entire body, not returning to the herd before it has cleansed itself. Is not that a good and righteous mode of conduct?' ('Philothea', 3, 39). Faithful to the Christian obsession with continence, Francis of Sales credited Pliny's chaste elephant with an extra year's abstinence. Pliny had written: 'Out of modesty, elephants never mate except in secret . . . They do so only once every two years, and even then, so it is said, never for longer than five days. On the sixth they bathe in the river. They do not return to the herd beforehand. Adultery is unknown among them' ('Historia naturalis', VIII, 5).

We re-encounter the elephant in 'The Dolorous Passion of Our Lord according to the Meditations of Catherine Emmerich' (1833), a work still sold by Catholic bookshops and much read by certain devout persons. Here it figures, and more than once, in what Jesus is supposed to have said to the nun Catherine Emmerich, for instance thus: 'Jesus spoke also of the great depravity besetting human procreation and said that abstinence must be practised after conception, adducing the chastity and abstinence of the elephant as proof of how far inferior human beings are in this regard to the nobler beasts' (dictated to the poet Clemens von Brentano on 5 November 1820). The young couple at the wedding in Cana were deeply impressed by these remarks. 'At the end of the meal the bridegroom came alone to Jesus and spoke with him in all humility, telling him that he felt devoid of carnal desire and would gladly live in abstinence with his bride, were she to permit this; and the bride, too, came alone to Jesus and said the same, and Jesus called the two of them together and spoke with them of marriage and the purity that is pleasing to God' (dictated on 2 January 1822). A visionary and stigmatic, Catherine Emmerich died in 1824. Writing of her in 1978, the Catholic 'Offertenzeitung' declared: 'There can scarcely be a greater contrast to the enjoyment of this world by our unprayerful contemporaries than the love, suffering, and atonement of this follower of Christ, who lived entirely in God.' The newspaper went on to hope that 'this great servant of God' would soon be beatified.

The disparagement of sexual pleasure that prevailed in the Stoa and characterised the first two centuries AD was intensified shortly before the beginning of our era by an irruption of oriental pessimism, probably of Persian provenance, which invaded the West and became Christianity's most formidable competitor. This movement, which styled itself 'Gnosis' (knowledge), claimed to have perceived the worthlessness and evil of everything in existence and preached abstinence from marriage, meat, and wine. Gnosticism and its contempt for life is assailed in the New Testament. The First Epistle to Timothy ends: 'O Timothy . . . [avoid] profane and vain babblings, and oppositions of science [*gnosis* in the original Greek] falsely so called.' To Gnostics, the body was 'the sense-endowed corpse, the grave, which you carry about with you'. The world owed its existence, not to a righteous god, but to demons. Only the soul of man, his true self or ego, hailed like a luminous spark from the world of light, but it was captured by demonic forces and banished to our own world of darkness. Thus the human soul dwelled in an alien, hostile environment, chained to the gloomy prison of the body. Seduced by the clamour and the pleasures of this world, the soul was in danger of failing to find its way back to the god of light from whom it came.

The demons sought to stupefy it because the world, their demonic creation, would relapse into chaos and darkness if deprived of these luminous particles.

A vehement rejection of the idea that existence is good, Gnosticism was dominated by a profound pessimism opposed to the view of life prevailing toward the end of classical antiquity. Although disparagement of the material world was common among the Greeks – Plato himself called the body the dungeon of the soul ('Gorgias', 493A) – the *kosmos* (the well-ordered world or universe) was a coherent, integrated structure that led upwards from matter to mind with no intervening hiatus. But the negative influx of Gnosticism was powerful enough to effect a transformation in the old view of life. Research into Gnosticism has invalidated our once bright and cheerful picture of the ancient world. Neoplatonist philosophy, which evolved during the first half of the third century AD and characterised the thinking of the late classical era (it held great significance for Augustine), was influenced by Gnosticism in its conception of life and general tenor. Although Plotinus (d. 270), Neoplatonism's leading light, wrote a work opposing the Gnostics, he was heavily infected with Gnostic pessimism and escapism. 'He seemed ashamed of possessing a body', wrote his biographer Porphyrius (d.*c.* 305; 'Life of Plotinus', I). Neoplatonism demanded an abstinent, indeed, ascetic life of its adherents. Hard though it fought against Gnosticism from the first, it became – like Catholicism – infected with the Gnostic abhorrence of things physical.

Judaism, in particular, was a stranger to asceticism until the advent of Gnosticism as manifested, for example, in the Qumran sect. The Jews did not consider it devout to overcome the world and deny life, and Judaism's steadfast belief in a single, righteous god, the creator of everything in existence, diluted the pessimism and negation inherent in the Gnostic influence on the Qumran sect but could not overcome it. Although sexual pessimism had no place in the Judaism of the Old Testament, many Catholics consider it to be rooted in the Book of Tobit, which originated *c.* 200 BC. St Jerome was the Father of the Church responsible for biblically justifying sexual asceticism. In his Latin translation of the Bible (the Vulgate), which the Catholic Church still accepts as the authentic translation to this day, he amended the text to accord with his own, celibatarian, ideal. According to Wetzer-Welte's Catholic encyclopedia (1899), Tobias survived his wedding night 'because of the newly-weds' abstinence'. His bride, Sarah, had already been married to seven men, but the demon Asmodeus had slain them all on their wedding night. Tobias' grave was already dug, but he escaped with his life. The original version stated that the couple slept together that first night. According to Jerome, however, Tobias waited three nights (later called 'Tobias nights') before consummating their union. In approaching Sarah after these three prayerful nights, Tobias utters the words of Jerome, not of Judaism, when he says: 'And now, O Lord, thou knowest that I take not my sister for lust, but only for love of posterity' (Tobit, 8: 9). Tobias's falsified statement is still adduced by all rigorist theologians as an argument in favour of the exclusively procreative purpose of marriage. His original words, which came from Genesis 2: 18 – 'It is not good that the man should be alone' – were simply omitted by Jerome for fear that they might cast doubt on that exclusive purpose.

More recent Catholic biblical translations have restored Jerome's cuts and omitted his additions. Long gone, too, are the days when the bishop of Amiens and the parish priest of Abbeville demanded a dispensation fee from engaged couples reluctant to observe the three 'Tobias nights' and intent on having intercourse on their wedding night. Voltaire (d. 1778), incidentally, discerned a connection between these dues payable to the bishop of Amiens and the so-called *ius primae noctis*, a seigneur's right to the maidenhead of his female inferiors when they married. There may indeed be a relationship between the bridegroom's abstinence for God's sake, as Jerome described it in the case of Tobias, the bridegroom's abstinence in favour of his temporal ruler, as expressed by the *ius primae noctis*, and the bishop's relinquishment of this *droit de seigneur* in return for a financial consideration. The same idea obtains in both instances: precedence on the wedding night belongs either to 'the lord' or to 'the Lord'. It should be added that Protestants exclude the Book of Tobit from the Old Testament and assign it to the Apocrypha, or non-canonical texts.

The Qumran finds made beside the Dead Sea in 1947 have provided us with a clearer picture of the Essenes, a desert-dwelling sect contemporary with Jesus. The influence of Gnosticism and its sexual asceticism, which was alien to Judaism, is manifest in this sect. Although it was not a purely monastic community and included married couples, the extensive burial ground on the eastern side of Qumran shows that monks enjoyed full membership and a dominant status. The very arrangement of the graves testifies to the pre-eminence of the celibate and the inferior standing of women and children. The settlement was completely destroyed by the Romans in AD 68.

The Jewish idea of a good world fashioned by a righteous Creator was gravely undermined by Gnostic influence at Qumran, whose inhabitants believed in a world of darkness ruled by Satan. Language of a similar nature can be found in St John, for notwithstanding all the polemics against Gnosticism the sect's influence on the New Testament was considerable.

The Jewish historian Josephus (d.c. AD 100) wrote of the Essenes:

> Jews by birth . . . these Essenes reject life's pleasures as an evil and esteem continence a virtue. They take a derogatory view of marriage, yet they adopt the children of others provided these are still of educable age. They are chary of the inconstancy of women and convinced that none of them remains faithful to her husband . . . No clamour or other commotion ever disturbs the solemn hush that reigns in their homes . . . but to those outside the silence within seems awesomely mysterious. This silence results from their perpetual sobriety and their habit of eating and drinking a sufficiency only . . . They are firmly persuaded that the body perishes and that matter is ephemeral, but that souls are immortal in perpetuity . . . They believe that souls derive from the finest of air . . . Once liberated from the bonds of the flesh, they feel as if released from long imprisonment and soar upwards once more in blissful joy . . . But there is another group of Essenes . . . They believe that anyone who renounces marriage neglects an important function in life, to wit, the generation of offspring; in other words, they believe that, if everyone thought the same, the human race would speedily come to an end. But they test their future wives for the space of three years, and once they . . . have proved their ability to bear children the marriage is contracted. They do not engage in intercourse during pregnancy, whence it follows that they marry, not for reasons of sensual pleasure, but for procreation's sake.
>
> ('The Jewish War', 8, 2–13)

Whereas the Jewish Qumran sect espoused an extremely negative view of marriage in conformity with non-Jewish Gnostic influence, Philo of Alexandria, a Judaeo-Hellenistic philosopher and contemporary of Jesus, represented a synthesis of Jewish and Hellenistic ideas. Active at the beginning of the Christian era, this erudite Jew formed a bridge between Judaism and Hellenism, the Jewish religion and Greek philosophy, and strove, strongly influenced by the Greek philosophers, to familiarise his non-Jewish contemporaries with the Jewish bible (the Old Testament). Reading Philo's blend of Judaeo-Hellenistic (predominantly Stoic) elements, one is tempted to mistake him for the first Christian Father of the Church, at least where his view of marriage is concerned. He remained a Jew in his non-endorsement of the celibatarian ideal that was developing among the early Christians.

According to Philo, Joseph tells his temptress, Potiphar's wife: 'We descendants of the Hebrews have very particular customs and usages. At marriage we come in purity to pure virgins, making it our purpose to beget legitimate children, not to indulge in sensual pleasure' ('On Joseph', 9, 43). In his exposition of the Mosaic law concerning adultery Philo speaks of 'lecherous men who, in their frenzied passion, have excessively lustful intercourse, not with the wives of others; but with their own' ('De legibus specialibus', 2, 9). Philo believed that married couples should have intercourse only in the hope of having children, not for sexual enjoyment's sake. He extolled Abraham's polygamy on the ground that it was motivated by his determination to multiply, not by sexual desire. Indeed, Philo went further than the Greeks and Jews before him in pursuing his idea that the sole purpose and function of marriage is the generation of offspring: if a man knew that a woman was infertile in her previous marriage but married her nonetheless, he was 'tilling barren and stony ground' for sensual pleasure's sake alone, and his conduct was reprehensible. If the wife's infertility did not manifest itself until after marriage, the man might be forgiven for not divorcing her. The latter-day ramifications of the view that marriage is a generative partnership were not removed from Catholic marriage law until 1977: for a marriage to be valid, the husband no longer needs to be capable of procreation, only of copulation.

Philo fiercely inveighed against contraception: 'Those who, when copulating, simultaneously effect the destruction of their seed, are indisputably enemies of Nature' (ibid., 3, 36). He also strongly condemned homosexuals because their sexual acts were unproductive. 'Like a bad husbandman, the homosexual leaves fertile soil to lie fallow and busies himself day and night with soil from which no crop at all can be expected.' Philo, who thought like a Greek in so many ways, was thoroughly Jewish in his aversion to homosexuality. 'Ruthless action must be taken against these people in conformity with the law which prescribes that the effeminate man who distorts his natural characteristics shall be slain without compunction and not left alive for another day, nay, another hour, because he brings dishonour upon himself, his family, his country, and the whole human race . . . because he pursues unnatural lusts and contributes to the desolation and depopulation of cities . . . by destroying his seed' (ibid., 3, 37–42).

TWO

Female Blood: The Ancient Taboo
and its Christian Consequences

Intercourse with a menstruating woman was a particular taboo in the ancient world, and one to which Christianity, too, subscribed. Like the physician Soranus of Ephesus (second century AD), Philo believed that conception could not occur during menstruation and that, consequently, intercourse with a menstruating woman was impermissible. The womb being moist with fresh menstrual blood, 'the moisture not only saps the vitality of the semen but entirely neutralizes it' ('De legibus specialibus', 3, 6, 32). Philo was thus justifying the Old Testament prohibition contained in Leviticus 20: 8 – the Lord had told Moses that, if a man slept with a menstruating woman, they should both be 'cut off from among their people'. Leviticus gives no reason for this draconian decree, though it does tell us (15: 19f.) that a menstruating woman remains unclean for seven days: all that she touches is unclean, likewise anyone who touches her or touches anything touched by her or anything touched by anyone who has been in contact with her. In the ancient world, Jews and heathens were equally convinced of the noxious properties of menstrual blood. Whereas Philo believed that the virulent effects of menstrual blood on semen were such that conception could not occur, the Roman naturalist Pliny (d. AD 79) condemned sexual intercourse with a menstruating woman because any children conceived during menstruation were sickly, afflicted with purulent blood serum, or stillborn ('Historia naturalis', 7, 15, 87).

In the opinion of such Fathers of the Church as Clemens Alexandrinus and Origen (*c.* 200) and Jerome (*c.* 400), children conceived during menstruation were born handicapped. Jerome: 'If a man has intercourse with his wife at this time, leprous, hydrocephalic children are born of

12

this conception, and the effect of the tainted blood is such that the contaminated bodies of both sexes become either too small or too large' ('Commentary on Ezekiel', 18, 6).

'He that has intercourse with his wife during her period', warned Archbishop Caesarius of Arles (d. 542), 'will father children that are leprous, epileptic, or possessed by the Devil' (Peter Browe, 'Beiträge zur Sexualethik des Mittelalters', p. 48). Isidore of Seville (d. 636), whose encyclopedic 'Origines' was widely read for centuries, wrote of menstrual blood: 'After contact with it fruits cannot germinate, flowers wilt, grasses wither . . . iron rusts, bronze turns black, and dogs that partake of it develop rabies' (ibid., p. 2). Like Philo, he believed it so 'corrupted' semen that menstruation precluded conception. Abbot Regino of Prüm (d. 915) and Burchard of Worms (d. 1025) laid it down that priests in the confessional should question penitents on the subject of intercourse during menstruation.

Great theologians of the thirteenth century such as Albertus Magnus, Thomas Aquinas and Duns Scotus condemned intercourse with a menstruating woman as a mortal sin because of its detrimental effect on children. Berthold of Ratisbon (d. 1272), the thirteenth century's most celebrated preacher, made this abundantly clear: 'As for the children that are conceived at such times, you will delight in none of them, for they will be either possessed by the Devil, or leprous, or epileptic, or hunchbacked, or blind, or malformed, or feeble-minded, or club-headed . . . Even if you have been absent for four weeks, nay more, for two years, beware of desiring her . . . Being honest folk, you know full well that the stinking Jew takes great pains to eschew the time in question' (F. Göbel, 'Die Missionspredigten des Franziskaners Berthold von Regensburg', p. 354f.). Berthold mentions the Jews ('stinking' Jews in accordance with Christian anti-Semitism) because the fact that so few of them contracted leprosy was often ascribed during the Middle Ages to their careful observance of the ban on intercourse with menstruating women. The contrary circumstance – that leprosy and other ailments were especially rife among the peasantry – is attributed by Berthold to their habit of copulating with their wives at such times (Browe, op. cit., p. 4). John Hus (d. 1415) held that children born of intercourse with menstruating women were likely to be hunchbacked, one-eyed, epileptic, lame, and possessed by the Devil (ibid., p. 5).

Over the ensuing centuries, the belief that handicapped children had been conceived during menstruation was gradually ousted by advances in medical science. Cardinal Cajetan (sixteenth century), an opponent of Luther's, classified menstrual intercourse merely as a 'minor sin' ('Matrimonium' in 'Summula peccatorum', 1526). Thomas Sanchez (d. 1610), a leading authority on marital matters and one whose influence endured for centuries, wrote that many theologians had ceased to regard menstrual intercourse as a sin proper, but that most of them held it to be a venial sin on the grounds that it was 'unseemly' and denoted a lack of self-control. He no longer believed that it harmed children because its detrimental effects of menstrual intercourse could very seldom be proved. Indeed, intercourse with a menstruating woman could sometimes be entirely sinless when justified by a sufficient reason, e.g. inordinate carnal temptation or a domestic quarrel ('De sancto matrimonii sacramento', *lib.* 9, disp. 21, n. 7).

A different view was espoused by one or two theologians of the Jansenist sect (a seventeenth-century revival of strict Augustinianism). The Belgian Laurentius Neesen (d. 1679) regarded intercourse with a menstruating wife as a mortal sin on the part of the spouse who initiated it (Heinrich Klomps, 'Ehemoral und Jansenismus', p. 190), though most Jansenists classified it as venial. Alfonso de' Liguori (d. 1787), the eighteenth century's leading moral theologian and one whose influence persisted through into the early years of the twentieth, took his cue from Thomas Sanchez. Until the beginning of our own century, therefore, menstrual intercourse was generally regarded as a venial sin on account of its 'impropriety' and deficient self-control (Dominikus Lindner, 'Der Usus matrimonii', p. 218).

As to whether menstruating women should be permitted to receive Communion, this was regularly disputed until well into the Middle Ages, the Eastern Church being even more hidebound than the Western. Patriarch Dionysus of Alexandria (d. 264 or 265), a pupil of Origen, declared that it was unnecessary even to pose the question of permissibility 'for it would never occur to pious, devout women to touch the sacred Communion table or the Lord's body and blood' (Epistolae can. 2, PG10, 1281A). Cardinal Humbert, the papal legate who formally consummated the Great Schism between the Eastern and Western Churches at Constantinople in 1054, reproached the Greek Church for discriminating against women in this respect. Theodore of Balsamon (d. after 1195), a celebrated Greek Orthodox canonist and patriarch of Antioch, supported the practice of discrimination, as did Cyril III, the

Coptic patriarch of Alexandria (d. 1243). The Maronites did not abolish it until 1596.

The West adopted a milder stance. Although Pope Gregory the Great (d. 604) did not forbid menstruating women to enter churches and receive Communion, he commended those that refrained from communicating at such times. He regarded menstruation as the consequence of guilt: a woman should not be 'prohibited during these same days from receiving the mystery of holy communion. If, however, out of great reverence, she does not presume to receive, she is to be commended. The menstruous habit in women is no sin, seeing that it occurs naturally; yet that nature itself has been so vitiated as to seem polluted even without human volition' (Letter in reply to Bishop Augustine of England, 10th answer).

This inconsistency gave rise to ambiguous canonical legislation in the West. Menstruating women were forbidden to communicate in some places and permitted to do so in others. Canon Matthew of Janov (d. 1394), for instance, inveighed against priests who barred such women from Communion and declared that they should refrain from inquiring about such things in the confessional, this being 'neither needful nor useful nor proper' (Browe, op. cit., p. 14). As late as 1684, however, the parish records of Deckenpfronn, a village in the Black Forest, recorded that menstruating women lingered outside the church door and 'do not truly go in, but stand there as though in the pillory' (ibid.).

Menstruation proved particularly disastrous to women wishing to hold ecclesiastical office. Theodore of Balsamon wrote: 'The order of deaconesses was once known to canon law and had access to the altar. In consequence of their monthly pollution, however, their order was ousted from the ritual domain and the sacred altar. Although deaconesses are still chosen in the venerable Church of Constantinople, they are no longer admitted to the altar' ('Responsa ad interrogationes Marci' [Interr. 35]; cf. Ida Raming, 'Der Ausschluss der Frau vom priesterlichen Amt', p. 39).

The blood of women in childbirth was regarded as even more noxious than menstrual blood. New mothers presented the antisexual Christian Church with additional problems, for instance in respect of burial. Unlike menstruating women, they could be presumed to have indulged in carnal pleasure, and carnal pleasure – almost invariably according to Augustine and invariably according to many of his successors – had sinful associations. It was even stated by the Synod of Treves (c. 8; 1227) that women who had given birth required 'reconciliation with the Church', and that they could not be readmitted to a place of worship until the said reconciliation had taken place. This 'churching', to use the modern term, combines Jewish purification laws (it was forty days before Mary herself could re-enter the Temple after ritual lustration [cleansing]) with Christian denunciation of carnal pleasure and disparagement of the female sex. Mothers who died in childbed 'unreconciled' with the Church were often denied burial in churchyards. Several synods, notably those of Rouen (1074) and Cologne (1279), opposed this practice and argued that they should be buried like other Christians (Browe, op. cit., p. 20). Writing to John, Elector of Saxony, in connection with the Diet of Augsburg (1530), Luther mentions that in the papal Church women who died in childbed were buried with 'a ceremony of their own': instead of being placed in the middle of the church like those of other parishioners, their coffins were left just inside the door (Correspondence 7, Calw/Stuttgart, 1897, p. 258). In the diocese of Ghent, a deanery conference of 1632 prescribed that women who died in childbirth prior to churching should be buried in secret (Browe, op. cit., p. 21).

But new mothers had to fight longer for the right of readmission to church than for that of normal burial. On 13 January 1200, Pope Innocent III placed France under an interdict because the French king's marriage to his mistress Agnes of Meran was declared invalid. This interdict ordained that all the churches in France remain shut except for baptisms. The pope 'sternly' forbade women who had just given birth to enter them for purposes of purification, nor, being still unclean, were they allowed to attend their children's christening. They remained debarred from admission until the king sent Agnes away and the interdict was lifted a year or more later. This betrayed a certain inconsistency. In 1198, when asked by the Archbishop of Armagh if the Mosaic law concerning women in childbirth still held good, Innocent III had replied in the negative, 'but if women desire to absent themselves from church for a while out of reverence, we believe that we cannot censure them' (Ep. I, 63; Browe, op. cit., p. 26). Where discrimination against women is concerned, it has always been expedient to straddle the fence.

The practice of churching women has endured almost to the present day. Wetzer-Welte's Catholic encyclopedia (1886) describes it thus:

'Like catechumens and penitents, the puerpera [woman who has recently given birth] must initially stand or even kneel outside the church door. Not until she has been lustrated with holy water and priestly prayer does the priest conduct her into church after the manner of catechumens prior to baptism and, in former times, of public penitents on Holy Thursday' (Wetzer-Welte, I, p. 1711). Churching was strictly observed as late as the 1960s. In 1987 a woman wrote to me: 'My mother, I recall, was very embarrassed on one occasion. My youngest sister was born in 1960. My mother could not be present at her christening because she had not yet been "churched". One afternoon some time later she slunk into the church on her own. The priest churched her. Only then could she once more attend divine service.'

THREE

New Testament Misconceptions: Virgin Birth, Celibacy, Remarriage after Divorce

Foremost among the immediate influences on the development of the Christian sexual ethic were Judaism and Gnosticism: Judaism as we have encountered it in Philo of Alexandria, a contemporary of the early Christians; and Gnosticism in so far as it espoused the ideal of celibacy and proclaimed the superiority of the unmarried over the married state. Although the Christians resisted the influx of Gnostic pessimism and regarded the Gnostics as their chief opponents during the early centuries AD, it was from those opponents that they borrowed the idealisation of virginity, which was thought to be nearer to God than its contrary condition, and which even, though only to a minor extent, infiltrated the New Testament.

Thus we find the Revelation of St John referring to 'the hundred and forty and four thousand' that sang 'a new song before the throne': 'These are they which were not defiled with women; for they are virgins. These are they which follow the Lamb withersoever he goeth.' Here in the New Testament, Gnosis triumphed over the Jewish legacy of the Old. The Old Testament never talks in such terms. Although Revelation goes on to cite Isaiah 53: 9 – 'And in their mouth was found no guile: for they are without fault' – the relevant Old Testament passage makes no mention of virgins.

Elsewhere in the New Testament, however, Gnosticism and its hostility toward marriage and sex are rejected. I Timothy 4: 2–3 warns against those who speak 'lies in hypocrisy' and forbid marriage, a passage which Luther levelled at the papacy in 'To the Christian Nobility of the German Nation' (1520): 'It occurred to the See of Rome, of its own iniquity, to forbid the priesthood to marry. That was commanded of the Devil, as St Paul proclaims in I Timothy 4: "There shall come teachers bringing devilish doctrines and forbidding marriage." This resulted in much distress and was the reason why the Greek Church cut itself off. I recommend that each man be left free to decide whether to marry or no.' Luther's 'On the Babylonian Captivity of the Church of God' (1520) states: 'I see that Paul commands that "the bishop shall be the husband of one wife." . . . Perish then those accursed man-made ordinances that seem to have crept into the church only to augment the dire peril, sin and evil thereof! Why should I be deprived of my freedom by someone else's ignorance or superstition?' ('Reformation Writings of Martin Luther', I, pp. 302, 304). Finally, in the 'Schmalkaldic Articles' of 1537 he says:

> They had no right whatever to forbid marriage and burden the divine estate of the priesthood with an insistence on permanent celibacy. By so doing they acted like foul, tyrannical, anti-Christian scoundrels and provided the occasion for all manner of terrifying, atrocious and numberless sins of [im]purity, in which they are still embroiled today. We and they are as little empowered to make male of female or female of male as they have been to part those creatures of God or to forbid them to live together in honourable matrimony. Wherefore we shall neither consent to their evil celibacy nor tolerate it, but desire to know marriage as untrammelled as God ordained and instituted it. For St Paul, in I Tim. iv, calls this a devilish doctrine.

The New Testament's account of a virgin birth was increasingly misconstrued as inimical to sex and marriage. The Old Testament made no promise of a biological virgin birth, nor did the New Testament seek to represent such a birth as a historical occurrence. Rather, Matthew 1 and Luke 1 employ virgin birth as a metaphor like others found in the New Testament. The prophet Isaiah (eighth century BC) made no mention whatever of a virgin birth. His alleged prediction of a virgin birth is at variance with the original Hebrew text. Accurately translated, Isaiah 7: 14 states: 'A young woman [*alma*] shall become pregnant and bear a son and call him Immanuel.' The fact that the word 'virgin' appears in Matthew 1: 23 can be traced back to the Greek translation of the Hebrew scriptures (Septuagint), which originated in the third century BC and rendered the word *alma* by *parthenos* (virgin). The former *can* mean 'virgin' but need not do so any more than every young woman *must* have preserved her virginity. Even if Isaiah really was speaking of a virgin, however, this would still not mean that she conceived as one. Thus, even if we assume that the translation of *alma* as 'virgin' accords with Isaiah's meaning, the relevant passage merely states that the mother of the child was a virgin before its conception; it does not imply that conception left her intact and was effected in a supernatural manner. Whatever young woman or virgin Isaiah meant when he conferred with King Ahaz at Jerusalem during the Syro-Ephraimitic War of 734 BC and told him of the birth that was to be a 'sign', he was in any case referring to an imminent event, not one that lay seven hundred years in the future. Speaking of the child Immanuel, he says: 'Butter and honey shall he eat, that he may know to refuse the evil, and choose the good. For before the child shall know to refuse the evil, and choose the good, the land that thou abhorrest shall be forsaken of both her kings' (Isaiah 7: 15f.). In 733 and 732 BC the Assyrians conquered the kingdoms of Damascus and Northern Israel, thereby relieving King Ahaz of the danger that had threatened him from both quarters. Immanuel, the young woman's child, was by then still a baby feeding on milk and honey and incapable of discrimination between good and evil, just as the prophet had foretold.

The Old Testament does not, therefore, foreshadow a virgin birth on Mary's part. Even in the New Testament itself, the earliest New Testament writer, St Paul, is as silent on the subject as the earliest gospel, St Mark. The Gospel according to St John expressly describes Jesus as 'the son of Joseph' (1: 45 and 6: 42) and invokes the Old Testament: 'Philip [one of the twelve Apostles] findeth Nathanael, and saith unto him, We have found him, of whom Moses in the law, and the prophets, did write, Jesus of Nazareth, the son of Joseph' (1: 45). The legend of the virgin birth is to be found only in Matthew and Luke, but even in these two gospels the notion of a virgin birth occurs only in the later, not the earliest, sections. Jesus's genealogies in Matthew 1 and Luke 3, which date from a time when Joseph's paternity was taken for granted, seek to prove that Jesus was descended via Joseph from David. The presumption here, therefore, is that Joseph was Jesus's father, a description employed as a matter of course by Mary herself (Luke 2: 48).

It is only in the later sections of these two gospels that we encounter the idea of the virgin birth as a metaphorical expression of God's special initiative in the process of redemption. It is as little intended to be taken literally as the Old Testament account of Adam's creation from 'the dust of the ground'. Both are vivid metaphors conveying that the creation of the first man and the creation of 'the second man', as Paul calls Jesus (I Cor. 15), were the work of God. The virgin birth metaphor accords with the legends and figurative language of the ancient world, in which famous persons were credited with divine ancestry. Suetonius (b.*c*. 70) fathered Augustus on Apollo, Plutarch attributed Alexander's conception to a shaft of lightning. It has been the Christians' peculiarity, even as late as the twentieth century, to take such metaphors literally – not, of course, in respect of heathen deities, but of their own Christian god. This is not to deny that many heathens, too, believed in the reality of such apotheoses in the ancient world, but the educated and enlightened among them did not. The general attitude is probably best conveyed by one of Plutarch's anecdotes: 'There lived a woman in Pontus who claimed to be with child by Apollo, an assertion which many doubted, as was only natural, but which many believed' ('Lysander', in 'Lives', 26).

David Friedrich Strauss, one of the most eminent Protestant theologians of the nineteenth century, showed how the progressive historicisation of an ancient metaphor could produce a concrete history of chastity complete with sequels. He refers in his 'Leben Jesu' to Plato's nephew Speusippus, who mentions a legend, widespread in Athens, to the effect that Plato had been begotten by the god Apollo, and that Plato's father had abstained from intercourse with his wife Perictione until Plato's birth (Diogenes Laertius, 'Lives', 3, 1, 2). According to Strauss, the legend of Jesus's virgin birth is similarly restricted to Mary's virginity prior to her confinement: 'And he [Joseph] knew her not till she had brought forth her firstborn son: and he called his name Jesus' (Matt. 1: 25). Like Plato, Jesus had brothers and sisters. These are mentioned by Mark (6: 3) and Matthew (13: 55f.). If the New Testament and Matthew himself (13) record that Jesus had brothers and sisters, this indicates that the virgin birth metaphor was not at first construed in the sexually pessimistic sense in which it came more and more to be understood in the course of its historicisation over the centuries.

In post-New Testament times, or from the second century onwards, Jesus's brothers and sisters became stepbrothers and stepsisters from the widower Joseph's first marriage (Protevangelium Jacobi ix, *c.* AD 150). Eventually, in the year 400 or thereabouts, Jerome transmogrified these stepbrothers and sisters into cousins and proclaimed it a 'godless, apocryphal daydream' to believe that Joseph had had children by a first marriage: in his view, only a virginal Joseph was fit for a virginal Mary ('Ad Matthaeum', 9). Thus, Mary was a virgin both before and after the birth of Jesus. Even that last window of virginal vulnerability, the hymen that would have been ruptured in childbirth, was closed during the second century. In the Protevangelium Jacobi (xixf.) a midwife states that Mary's hymen remained intact during Jesus's birth. Thus the New Testament metaphors of the virgin birth developed into a serialised account of Mary's personal chastity and biological integrity.

To recapitulate: the prophet Isaiah referred in the eighth century BC to a young woman who would conceive. The New Testament began by moulding this statement into the metaphor of a virgin birth as an expression of God's special initiative in the creation and existence of Jesus. In ensuing centuries this metaphor was elaborated into a detailed account of Mary's abiding virginity before, during, and after Jesus's birth. Coincidentally, this development of the virgin birth metaphor also established – and this is the gravest consequence of the historicisation process – that God is a kind of man, for his dealings with Mary were quasi-masculine. To cite the noted Catholic dogmatician Michael Schmaus: 'What is usually accomplished through the agency of man [that is to say, of *a* man] was affected in Mary's case by the omnipotence of God' ('Mariologie', p. 107).

The growing tendency to place an antisexual construction on passages from the New Testament with no antiphysical, antisexual connotations was not confined to the metaphor of the virgin birth. This sexually pessimistic process of reinterpretation is clearly apparent in another passage still regarded as the mainstay of celibacy and as Jesus's own verdict on the unmarried state. In his 'Letter to All the Priests of the Church on the Occasion of Holy Thursday 1979' John Paul II refers to a 'celibacy "for the sake of the kingdom of heaven"' of which Jesus is supposed to have said: 'He that is able to receive [i.e. accept] it, let him receive it.' Although Jesus was not here referring to celibacy at all, this passage has been restyled in favour of celibacy and has become the *locus classicus* of all its champions up to and including John Paul II.

We need only take account of the subject on which Jesus was being questioned to perceive the gist of his response. He was neither being questioned about celibacy nor alluding to it. The Pharisees having inquired into his attitude to divorce, he advanced a theory that sounded scandalous at a time when a man could divorce his wife for spoiling a meal (thus Rabbi Hillel). He said: 'Whosoever shall put away his wife, except it be for fornication, and shall marry another, committeth adultery.' Even his disciples jibbed at this new doctrine. 'All men cannot receive [i.e. accept] this saying,' he replied, and added: 'For . . . there be eunuchs, which have made themselves eunuchs for the kingdom of heaven's sake' (Matt. 19: 11–12). This statement, which was, of course, figuratively intended, is grammatically linked (by the conjunction 'for') with the foregoing discussion of divorce: it refers to voluntary renuncia-tion of remarriage, or adultery. 'Unmarried' or 'incapable of marriage' (thus the New English Bible) are common but erroneous translations of the Greek word *eunuchoi*, meaning simply eunuchs. Admittedly, Jesus's reference to eunuchs for the kingdom of heaven's sake – to psychical self-castration in the context of adultery and remarriage – was a turn of phrase that has nonplussed many besides his disciples. Indeed, Jesus himself left it to the individual to decide whether or not he was able to accept it. But whatever one's attitude – whether it be one of acceptance or non-acceptance – the words refer to the renunciation of adultery, not to celibacy or incapacity for marriage, and have nothing whatever to do with a duty to remain celibate. All else apart, this would base the whole argument in favour of celibacy – as it still does, in practice – on a foolish objection lodged by the disciples, whose implication was that a man would do better not to marry at all rather than forfeit his sexual freedom and the possiblity of unloading his wife.

So Jesus condemned adultery and divorce and his disciples protested that it would be better (given the impossibility of divorce) not to marry at all. Being among those who were unable to accept his words, they thought it better to live with a woman in the absence of any firm, indissoluble ties if the bonds of matrimony implied what Jesus had said, namely, that they could never have another woman. In adding 'He that is able to receive it, let him receive it' Jesus was not making a gospel of their objection, for it was simply a macho objection, and it is a great pity that the advocates of celibacy have always invoked it. Jesus was upholding his own gospel. He meant what *he* had said and was not endorsing a protest inspired by the polygamous inclinations of his disciples, who found his demand hard to stomach.

What nonplussed the disciples and is patently hard to grasp was not Jesus's attitude to the unmarried state, which was not the subject of his remarks, but his teaching in regard to marriage and divorce, which was new to his listeners. When they invoked Moses, who had sanctioned 'a writing of divorcement', Jesus replied: 'Moses because of the hardness of your hearts suffered you to put away your wives: but from the beginning it was not so.' In saying this he was going back to the beginning as a fundamental idea. He quoted the story of the Creation: 'Have ye not read . . . for this cause shall a man leave father and mother and cleave to his wife: and they twain shall be one flesh? What therefore God hath joined together, let not man put asunder.' To Jesus, becoming one flesh meant complete and irrevocable integration, not just a temporary relationship, and it is upon that integration that the indissolubility of marriage is founded. Thomas Aquinas (d. 1274) was later to base the indissolubility of marriage on concern for its offspring, whereas Jesus makes no mention of children and does not restrict the purpose of conjugal union to procreation. His new doctrine, which has its roots in an old verity, is the doctrine of the indissoluble oneness of husband and wife.

Jesus's doctrine, which harked back to the time before Moses, struck his listeners as outrageous. To them the only alternative to the view of Rabbi Hillel was that of Rabbi Shammai, who made stricter demands on husbands but did not dispute the possibility of divorce. Jesus's words completely overturned his disciples' conception of marriage. 'Thou shalt not commit adultery . . .' To the Jews, this prohibition from the Ten Commandments meant two different things when applied to men and women: in the man, only intercourse with another man's wife constituted adultery; in the woman, adultery was any act of infidelity. The man could only violate another's marriage, the woman could violate her own as well. In the man, adultery was only the invasion of another's marriage, in the woman it was any evasion of her own. This was because a wife was regarded as her husband's chattel, not his partner. By committing adultery a woman diminished her husband's property, whereas a man only diminished the property of another. Adultery being a species of offence against property, intercourse with an unmarried woman did not constitute adultery in the man. This privileged male

24

view of adultery was revoked by Jesus's doctrine of the importance of becoming one flesh – of the inseparable union. Also revoked was male polygamy, which Judaism then thought sanctioned by God. If a married man fell for an unmarried woman, he was free to marry her in addition to his existing wife. The Judaism of Jesus's day – the Qumran sect excepted – sanctioned polygamy. A wife belonged to her husband, not vice versa, so a man could not commit adultery against his own marriage. Jesus's way of interpreting the story of Creation destroyed the whole patriarchal edifice. No wonder the disciples said: 'If the case of the man be so with his wife, it is not good to marry' (Matt. 19: 10). Marriage of that kind was not to their taste.

The same gospel contains a corollary to this passage on adultery in the Sermon on the Mount (Matt. 5: 27f.), in which Jesus, as everyone knows, spoke on other subjects as well. But because of its increasing emphasis on sexual infractions as opposed to all other forms of human misconduct, the Catholic Church singled out the divorced and remarried for special treatment and left the sowers of discord to their own devices. Then as now, the cardinal sins of mankind are committed in the bedroom – not, for example, on the battlefield. The Sermon on the Mount, that most exalted blueprint for a Christian utopia, has been dichotomised. The greater part of it is, in practice, regarded as unattainable and unachievable. Only the remarriage of divorcees has been singled out by the Catholic Church for special punishment, although Jesus himself said, twice over, that not everyone could accept the implications of his doctrine. It would betoken the bankruptcy of human coexistence to deny the possibility and the ideal of radical solidarity, in other words, to reject the indissolubility of marriage as an ideal, but to believe that human failure in this sphere is more heinous than any other type of human shortcoming is a product of the Church's sexual pessimism. This celibatarian rigorism in respect of divorce and the remarriage of divorced persons quite wrongly invokes Jesus. Jesus was well disposed toward marriage and women on principle – indeed, well disposed toward mankind at large – whereas here it is hostility toward marriage, if not sheer inhumanity, that sacrifices mankind to a principle instead of affirming a principle for mankind's sake.

That exceptions to the ban on the remarriage of divorcees were already made at the period when the New Testament originated is evident from the two so-called 'Matthew provisos' (Matt. 5: 32 and 19: 9). The tenor of the longer passage, in Matthew 19 makes Jesus's meaning quite plain: while stressing the indissolubility of marriage, he also stresses that not everyone can accept it. Practical exceptions were made from the first in cases of adulterous fornication, so the thread of his remarks was broken by the subsequent insertion of a loophole. The Protestant Church and the Orthodox Church translate this proviso correctly as a weakening of Jesus's firm contention that divorce and remarriage are contrary to the will of God, so they write 'except it be for fornication'. The Catholic Church, by contrast, translates this as 'not even in the case of adultery' and disregards the practice of the early Church, which inserted this proviso. The Orthodox and Protestant Churches countenance the remarriage of divorcees, therefore, whereas the Catholic Church firmly rejects it.

But not even the Catholic Church has always practised the stringency that prevails today. The Spanish Synod of Elvira (early fourth century) and the Synod of Arles (314) treated men and women differently: women were excommunicated for life on account of remarriage, whereas men were not; they were merely advised not to marry again and admitted to Communion. Among the Fathers of the Church who spoke in favour of exceptions to the ban on the remarriage of divorcees were Origen (d. 253 or 254), Basil (d. 379) and Epiphanius (d. 403). Basil and Epiphanius sanctioned the remarriage of men only, and only under certain circumstances. Augustine (d. 430), too, upheld the interests of the man:

> He that divorces a wife taken in adultery and marries another is plainly not be compared with those that divorce their wives for some reason other than adultery and marry again. In the divine scriptures it is far from clear [obscurum est] whether he that is unhesitatingly permitted to divorce his wife if she commits adultery should himself be deemed an adulterer if he later marries another woman. I, at all events, consider that he commits a venial sin in such a case.
>
> ('De fide et operibus', 19)

Theodore, Archbishop of Canterbury (d. 690), the Frankish Synods of Verberie (756) and Compiègne (757) and the collection of authorities compiled by Burchard of Worms (d. 1025) all laid down exceptional rules for the remarriage of divorcees. The reformist pope Gregory VII (d. 1085), who inculcated celibacy and campaigned against married clergy, also – and for similarly sexophobic reasons – opposed remarriage after divorce. Even in the wake of the Gregorian reforms, however, many theologians advocated exceptions to the rule of indissolubility, among them the anti-Lutheran Cardinal Cajetan (d. 1534), Luther himself and Erasmus of Rotterdam (d. 1536).

It was left to the Council of Trent to state categorically in 1563, on behalf of the Catholic Church, that the remarriage of divorced persons was impermissible for any reason whatever. Canon 7, which lays this down, was nonetheless redrafted in somewhat milder language at the request of the Venetians. Being a colonial power, Venice was apprehensive of difficulties with its Greek Orthodox subjects in the Eastern Mediterranean – in Crete, Cyprus and Corfu. 'It is common knowlege,' the Venetian petition to the council pointed out, 'that the Greeks have preserved the custom of divorcing an adulterous wife and marrying another. In this, they say, they are observing a very ancient custom of their forefathers. They were never condemned on that account by any council, although their custom was well known to the Roman Church.' The Council of Trent's original wording ran more or less as follows: 'If anyone asserts that a person may remarry in the case of adultery, let him be excluded.' Thanks to the Venetian intervention, Canon 7 now reads: 'If anyone says that the Church errs in teaching' that a person may not remarry, let him be excluded. Pius XI expressed himself similarly, in deference to the Greek Orthodox Church, in his encyclical 'Casti connubii' (1930). In other words, condemnation attaches, not to the Greek practice of remarriage, but only to those who say that the Catholic Church is in error. The popes set greater store by their infallibility than they do by their rigorism toward the remarried.

Jesus never pronounced upon celibacy – on the contrary, he dismayed his disciples by correcting the tendency of a polygamous society to look down on women and painted an ideal picture of marriage as a union and a process of coalescence. Despite this, celibate theologians later reinterpreted his doctrine as a call for celibacy and his remarks on the importance of becoming one flesh as a celibatarian encomium on eunuchs for the kingdom of heaven's sake.

But there is another point on which the New Testament is misconstrued in an antisexual sense. John Paul II wrongly regards the compulsory celibacy of the Catholic priesthood, not only as recommended by Jesus himself but as an 'apostolic' doctrine ('Letter to All the Priests of the Church on the Occasion of Holy Thursday 1979', 8). In reality, all the apostles were married men. It is interesting to trace the centuries-long process whereby translators and interpreters of the New Testament transmuted the wives of the apostles into quasi-housekeepers, seeking more and more to represent the apostles as celibatarians until finally, on Holy Thursday 1979, our own Pope promoted them into advocates and teachers of compulsory celibacy.

The doctrine of compulsory celibacy within the priesthood is *not* an apostolic doctrine. On the contrary, apostolic doctrine teaches the right of all ecclesiastical office-holders to marriage. Paul states (I Cor. 9: 5) that all the apostles including Peter, who rates as the first pope, were married and took their wives with them on their missionary tours. He states that he, too, possessed that right. Since it was the question of priestly marriage that substantially contributed to the secession of the Eastern Church, in which ordinary priests (though not bishops) may marry, and later of the Protestant Church (sixteenth century), in which ordinary priests *and* bishops may marry, it is worth taking a closer look at the words in I Cor. 9: 5 whose mistranslation has for four hundred years prevented Catholic seminarists from stumbling on their apostolically attested right to marry – especially if their Greek is sketchy. The passage states that the apostles were entitled to take their wives with them on their travels, as Peter and the others actually did. Literally: 'Have we not authority to lead about [travel accompanied by] a sister [a female fellow Christian] as a wife . . . like the rest of the apostles and Peter?'

By degrees, the apostles' right to be escorted by a Christian wife was transmuted into the right to take along a sisterly helpmate. How? First, by rendering the Greek word *gyne* as 'woman' rather than 'wife', and secondly, from 1592 onwards, by reversing the order of the words 'sister as woman' and writing 'woman as sister'. This successfully obliterated all traces of the apostles' wives. Jerome (d. 419 or 420), who oversaw the Vulgate, or official version of the Latin Bible, and was a first-class philologist, began in 383 by correctly rendering *gyne* as *uxor* (wife). From 385 onwards, however, he favoured *mulier* (any woman, a wife included) and construed the passage as meaning that the apostles were entitled to travel accompanied by a 'sister as a woman' (*mulier*). He had concluded in the interim that the women concerned were serving-women, not wives. What prompted his change of mind was the aforementioned letter (see p.xi) from Pope Siricius, who in 385 informed the bishop of Tarragona that he considered it 'lechery', indeed, 'a crime', for priests to have intercourse with their wives and beget children after ordination.

28

From 1592 onwards, transposition of the words that spoke *against* compulsory celibacy entirely robbed the passage in I Cor. 9: 5 of its original meaning: the apostles' right of companionship was thereafter restricted to 'a woman (*mulier*) as sister' (i.e. a serving-woman) by the official version of the Latin Bible, the Vulgata Clementina. In this it is at variance not only with the original Greek text, but with twenty-eight Vulgate manuscripts in which the correct sequence was observed, taking its cue instead from two inferior Vulgate manuscripts whose transposed word order ('woman as sister') had garbled the original Greek text. (For a review of this subject see H.-J. Vogels, 'Pflichtzölibat'.)

Other passages can be adduced to prove that compulsory celibacy is not an apostolic doctrine, e.g. I Tim. 3: 2 and Titus 1: 6. These state that a bishop must be 'the husband of one woman', meaning that he must not marry a second time, but they are not too popular with the champions of celibacy, who find Peter's mother-in-law (Mark 1: 30) an equally distasteful subject.

Although Paul refers (I Cor. 7) to the celibate's greater dedication to the service of God, this cannot be enlisted in support of compulsory celibacy, given that the same epistle (I. Cor. 9: 5) expressly mentions his *right* to take his wife on missionary journeys like the other apostles. We can gauge the extent to which the Pope, an unmarried successor of the married Peter, has distanced himself from Peter and Paul if we reflect how unimaginable it would be to hear *him* speak of his right to a wife and his right to take her with him on his pilgrimages. It would nonetheless be quite in keeping with the New Testament were he to voice that right. As Clemens Alexandrinus wrote (*c.* 200): 'Paul, too, did not scruple to address his wife in one of his epistles [Phil. 4: 3], though he forbore to take her about with him so as not to be hampered in the fulfilment of his ministry. Thus he says in an[other] epistle: "Are not we, too, free to take with us a sister as spouse like the other apostles?"' ('Stromateis', III, 53).

It is not uninteresting to note that Paul was still known to have been married, even in the year 200. Paul was a Pharisee (Phil. 3: 5) and, as such, a strict observer of Jewish traditions. He mentions the fact with pride, incidentally, for the word 'Pharisaism' had yet to be regrettably transmuted by self-righteous, hypocritical, anti-Semitic Christians into a synonym for self-righteous hypocrisy. According to the German Protestant theologian Joachim Jeremias (b. 1900), Paul was a qualified Pharisaic scholar in middle age at the time of his conversion. He would also, since Jews of Jesus's day customarily married between the ages of eighteen and twenty, have been a married man. The scribes' attitude to marriage and celibacy was quite unequivocal: it was a man's bounden duty to marry. Rabbi Eliezer (*c.* AD 90) stated: 'He that does not devote himself to procreation is like a man that sheds blood' (Yebamoth 63b; H. L. Strack and P. Billerbeck, 'Kommentar zum Neuen Testament aus Talmud und Midrasch', II, p. 373). Jeremias believes that Paul was a widower when he wrote I Corinthians ('Zeitschrift für d. Ntl. Wissenschaft', 28, 1929, pp. 321–3).

As well as I Cor. 9: 5, another passage in the New Testament has been similarly misconstrued as an argument in favour of celibacy. Christians influenced by Gnostic asceticism asked Paul if 'It is good for a man not to touch a woman' (I Cor. 7: 1). To this day, the majority of celibatarian exegetes treat this verse as Paul's reply, though he was only restating the question that had been put to him. That was how the Gnostics' misguided doctrine became an apostolic mainstay of the ideals of celibacy and virginity. Contrary to its true meaning, the New Testament was enlisted in the service of growing sexual pessimism.

Paul examines the Corinthians' question. Their Gnostic proposition was that a man would do well 'not to touch a woman'. Contrasting this with his own view of marriage, Paul states that every man should have his own wife and every woman her own husband. He emphasises that spouses should not bow to those who preach continence in the Gnostic sense; on the contrary, each has a duty to respect the other's desire for sexual union. He does not, therefore, make common cause with the advocates of marital continence: 'Defraud [deny] ye not one the other, except it be with consent for a time, that ye may give yourselves to fasting and prayer; and come together again, that Satan tempt you not for your incontinency' (I Cor. 7: 5). Then comes verse 6, which Augustine misconstrued and used to buttress his fateful theory that marital intercourse needed to be 'excused' because he held that it was reprehensible and in need of a mitigating factor, to wit, the desire for progeny. Paul continues (v. 6): 'But I speak this by permission [by way of concession], not command.' To what does 'this' refer? It could apply either to the statement that spouses are not to deny each other save for prayer, or to the injunction to 'come together' again, for both these alternatives occur in the preceding verse. Is Paul conceding (Augustine has 'excusing') the right of marital intercourse or the right to deny it for reasons of prayer? Probably the latter. In that case, while not commanding them to do so, he leaves the Corinthians free to abstain for prayer. Even if he means marital intercourse or 'coming together', he does not wish his words to be interpreted as an order to engage in it; he instructs the Corinthians to regard it as their right and leaves the decision to them. Either way, the leitmotif of the entire passage is supplied by 'to avoid fornication, let every man have his own wife, and let every woman have her own husband! (v. 2) and 'defraud [deny] ye not one the other' (v. 5).

At all events, the gist of Paul's exposition did not favour the Gnostic advocates of continence. Rather, he rebuked those whose misconceived piety prompted them to deny their partners in marriage. He defined the motive for matrimony and marital intercourse as the avoidance of fornication. Although this sounds somewhat crude, given that it represents marriage as a remedy for sexual desire and Satanic temptation (v. 5), Paul recommended marital intercourse on that very account. His attitude may strike us as a trifle insensitive today, but it was a clear and unequivocal response to the Gnostics who had asked him if sexual intercourse was a good thing. One noticeable feature is the total absence of any allusion to the begetting of children, which Augustine regarded as the most important 'excuse' for marital intercourse. Paul's remarks are thus at odds with the Church's continuing belief that procreation should be the predominant purpose of the conjugal act.

The passage (I Cor. 7: 25) in which Paul refers to the greater spirituality of the unmarried opens with the words: 'Now concerning virgins [male and female] I have no commandment of the Lord: yet I give my judgement . . .' The disciples' objection to Jesus's remarks on divorce (Matt. 19) – 'If the case of the man be so with his wife, it is not good to marry' – and Jesus's reply – 'All men cannot receive this saying' (meaning his *own* remarks on marriage, not his disciples' objection to them) – have been regarded by almost all Catholic theologians, down to and including John Paul II, as the supreme vindication of celibacy and monasticism. Unlike them, Paul concedes that he knows of no 'commandment of the Lord' – no injunction from Jesus – in regard to celibacy. The celibatarian imagination has since been at pains to plug such crucial gaps in Jesus's message to mankind.

As far as Paul himself is concerned, there are certain indications that, unlike Jesus, he was not entirely free from Gnostic tendencies. Although Jesus did not pronounce upon celibacy, he writes, he proposes to advance his personal opinion. There follow sentences such as 'Art thou loosed from [rid of] a wife? Seek not a [second] wife' (I Cor. 7: 27). It is probable, however, that such remarks were prompted by a strong belief in the imminence of the Second Coming and the end of the world. Paul himself says: 'I suppose therefore that this is good for the present distress [in the present time of stress]' (ibid., 7: 26). Seen in this light, his 'Art thou loosed of a wife? Seek not a wife' should be judged no differently from other remarks made with the same prospect in mind, for instance: 'Let every man abide in the same calling wherein he was called. Art thou called being a servant [slave]? Care not for it: but if thou mayest be made free, use it rather' (ibid., 7: 20f.). If we take account of Paul's expectations – he was convinced that the Second Coming would occur during his lifetime (I Thess. 4: 17) – we can no more regard him as an advocate of celibacy than an upholder of slavery.

The third New Testament passage to deal in detail with marriage (in addition to Matt. 19 and I Cor. 7) occurs in the Epistle to the Ephesians (v. 22f.). Although Paul's authorship of Ephesians is disputed, it is noteworthy that I Cor. 7 never employs the word 'love' in connection with marriage, whereas the Epistle to the Ephesians makes striking use of it: 'Husbands, love your wives, even as Christ also loved the church, and gave himself for it . . . So ought men to love their wives as their own bodies. He that loveth his wife loveth himself . . . For this cause shall a man leave his father and mother, and shall be joined unto his wife, and they two shall be one flesh. This is a great mystery . . .'

It is worth mentioning that all three New Testament passages dealing with marriage are silent on the subject of procreation, which steadily gained in importance until Catholic sexual morality promoted it above every other function of, and motive for, marital intercourse. This is not to say that Jesus (Matt. 19), Paul (I Cor. 7) and Ephesians 5 deliberately excluded the subject, but it shows that marriage can be meaningfully discussed without immediate reference to children.

New Testament scholars attach great importance to the Jewish Qumran sect and its Gnostic tendencies because Jesus, John the Baptist and the apostles lived next door to it, so to speak, for decades. The baptismal site where the Jordan flows into the Dead Sea was little more than ten miles from the Qumran settlement. Jesus was no ascetic, but there are many indications that John the Baptist was influenced by Qumran and 'may even at one time have been a member of it' ('Religion in Geschichte und Gegenwart', vol. 5, 1961, p. 751). Even their contemporaries were struck by the differences between them. Jesus said: 'For John came neither eating nor drinking, and they say, He hath a devil. The Son of Man came eating and drinking, and they say, Behold a man gluttonous, and a winebibber, a friend of publicans and sinners' (Matt. 11: 18–19). Not only did Jesus fail to practise Qumran asceticism, but we cannot, despite his proximity to the place, discover any tendency in him to glorify celibacy for its greater godliness. Jesus was rooted in the Old Testament tradition, to which any such idea was alien. He sought to guide Judaism back to its origins: to the Creation story of one man and one woman who become one flesh and are thus inseparable.

Jesus's relation to Old Testament and Judaic tradition also bears upon an important question recently revived by the Jewish theologian Ben-Chorin, who subscribes to the theory that Jesus was married. It is quite conceivable that the early Gnostic-ascetic influence on Christianity not only helped to shape Jesus's doctrine, as interpreted by its promulgators, but coloured the accepted image of Jesus himself, so that – in the absence of even the smallest New Testament allusion to the subject – it now strikes us as axiomatic that he was unmarried.

Ben-Chorin posits the contrary by adducing 'a chain of indirect evidence' in favour of Jesus's married state:

> When Luke (2: 51f.) notes that Jesus was 'subject' to his parents as a boy, this clearly implies that he adapted himself to the rhythm of middle-class life ... The next stage in life is of crucial importance: an eighteen-year-old beneath the 'nuptial canopy' (La-Khupa). If, as is expressly reported, the young Jesus suppressed all his peculiarities until he emerged into active public life and bowed to his parents' wishes, it is a very fair assumption that they chose him a suitable bride and that, like any youth who studied the Torah [Mosaic law], he entered into the state of matrimony. The Talmud remarks: 'A twenty-year-old youth who lives without a wife is visited by sinful thoughts' (bKiddushin 29b), for 'a man is ever in the power of the urge from which marriage alone delivers him' (bYebamoth 63a). A *tosephta* [explanatory gloss] on Yebamoth 88 records a harsh remark by

33

Rabbi Eleasar Ben-Asai: 'He that abstains from marriage trans-
gresses the law of procreation and is to be regarded as a murderer
who diminishes the number of beings created in the image of
God.'

'Of the many hundreds of teachers of the Talmudic period
known to us by name, only one, Ben-Asai (second century AD),
was unmarried. According to one version, even this confirmed
bachelor was briefly married to a daughter of his teacher Rabbi
Akiba, but later practised celibacy in order to devote himself
exclusively to the study of the Torah. He was fiercely rebuked on
that account by his colleagues: 'Many a man preaches well and
acts well, many a man acts well and preaches badly, but you
preach well and act badly.' Ben-Asai replied: 'What am I to do?
My soul cleaves to the Torah, but the world can be received by
others.' (bYebamoth 63b). Ben-Asai's good preaching and bad
conduct consisted in his teaching all the commandments but
defying the fundamental precept 'Be fruitful and multiply' by
remaining unmarried . . .

One should bear this in mind when reviewing Jesus's career . . .
Had he disdained marriage his Pharisaic opponents would have
rebuked him for this sin of omission and his disciples would have
questioned him about it . . . It should not surprise us to be told
nothing of this, for we are told equally little of the boy's schooling
or his professional training and professional activities as a young
man. We learn only that he returned to Nazareth to lead the
entirely normal life of a Jew. We are told nothing, either, about
the wives of the later disciples, nor, with very few exceptions,
about the wives of most of the rabbis of Jesus's day, so this matter
remains within the bounds of the self-evident. The only women
mentioned in the subsequent course of the narrative are those
who were prominent in Jesus's public life.

(Shalom Ben-Chorin, 'Mutter Mirjam', p. 92f.)

Ben-Chorin's theory is additionally supported by the following consideration: Paul's statement that he had no knowledge of any pronouncement on celibacy by Jesus and could offer a personal opinion
only (I Cor. 7: 25) is difficult to reconcile with an unmarried Jesus. If
Paul, although he knew of no such pronouncement, had been intent on
Jesus's celibatarian example, he would scarcely have confined himself
to pointing out that Jesus had said nothing on the subject. It is hard to
believe that he would have neglected to draw attention to Jesus's
exceptional and exemplary way of life.

FOUR

Fathers of the Church
before Augustine

Although Jesus was no ascetic or eulogist of virginity, the ideal of virginity spread throughout Christendom. Bishop Ignatius of Antioch, who was thrown to the wild beasts at Rome (*c.* 110), it being the Romans' privilege to import persons under sentence of death from the provinces for their circuses, wrote seven letters while being transported to the capital. These seven letters are regarded as an important source of information about the period immediately succeeding the events described in the New Testament. In his letter to Bishop Polycarp of Smyrna Ignatius mentions people who 'live chastely in honour of the flesh of Our Lord'. Far from commending them, however, he warns against 'self-exaltation' and goes on: 'He that vaunts himself is lost, and he that esteems himself more than his bishop is a prey to perdition.' It is clear that the superiority of the celibate, at least in their own estimation, had already become too blatant to disregard and was creating problems for their bishops, who were still married at this stage.

Writing *c.* 150, Justin the Martyr states: 'Either we have entered into wedlock from the first for the sole purpose of rearing children, or we have abstained from matrimony and remain entirely continent' ('1st Apology', 29). Justin goes on to speak with unqualified approval of a young Christian who had sought permission from the Roman governor to be castrated. Emperor Domitian (d. 96) had made castration a penal offence, and Emperor Hadrian (d. 138) had expressly extended this sanction to those who acquiesced in their own mutilation. In so doing, he opposed the rigorist, predominantly Gnostic, antimarital and anti-sexual tendencies of the time. Hadrian made castration without official consent a capital offence for physician and castrate alike. Justin writes:

To satisfy you that unbridled debauchery is not a secret constituent of our religion, I would add this: one of our people in
Alexandria once addressed a petition to Governor Felix requesting him to permit his physician to remove his testicles, the local
physicians having said that they could not do this without the
governor's consent. When Felix refused to sanction this under
any circumstances, the youth remained single and declared himself content with his own attitude and that of those who shared
his beliefs.

(ibid.)

The young man of whom Justin spoke wished his castration to signalise
the Christians' high standard of morality and asceticism and rebut the
charge that they were morally inferior. Justin's 'Apologies' (writings in
defence of Christianity) sought to characterise the Christians, who were
then a reviled minority, as politically reliable, morally superior persons.
His reference to the Christian youth from Alexandria denotes that the
contemporary world could be impressed by virginity and celibacy. He
meant his story of the young man's attempt at emasculation to
commend Christianity – to excite approbation, not disapproval.

The Christians did not yet regard themselves as enlighteners of a
world that had dwelt in darkness without them, nor as persons called
to instil propriety into heathens and atheists. It was the other way
round: the Christians – who were, incidentally, called 'atheists' by the
heathens – wished to demonstrate that they measured up to the lofty
ideals of the heathen world. Justin was canvassing on Christianity's
behalf. Contemporary public opinion was dominated by the idea
stressed by the Stoics of the first and second centuries AD – that the
sole purpose of marriage is procreation – and by the Gnostically
pessimistic and antiphysical idealisation of virginity. But, as we have
seen, prizing of virginity was not a Christian invention, nor did it derive
from Jesus at all. Having begun by adapting itself to its environment,
the Church seized upon the ideal of virginity as the hallmark of genuine,
pristine Christianity and has clung to it ever since – the end is still not
in sight – when almost everyone else including many from its own
ranks, i.e. the Protestants, renounced this ancient heathen shibboleth
long ago.

Although the post-apostolic period witnessed a bitter and centuries-
long struggle between the Church and the Gnostics, the two camps also

interacted. Justin's would-be castrate from Alexandria and his approval of the young man's spirit of piety indicate the extent to which Christianity had already been infiltrated by Gnostic contempt for the flesh. On the other hand, many Gnostics had incorporated Christ in their system as a saviour from the material world who, clad only in the semblance of a body (the body, being matter, was evil), had taught the human soul how to flee the material world by escaping from the prison of the flesh and entering the pure realm of light after death. The resurrection of the body was rejected by these Gnostics, who considered themselves Christians on a plane superior to that occupied by ordinary believers. The Church, in its turn, called them archheretics, but the frontiers of belief were fluid even among the early Fathers. Justin the Martyr extolled marriage, albeit only for generative purposes, whereas his pupil Tatian drifted off into the Gnostic camp and became the leader of the 'continent' for whom marriage was 'lechery' (Clemens Alexandrinus, 'Stromateis', III, 12, 89). Many Christians, particularly in Rome and Alexandria, were in danger of submersion in or absorption by Gnosticism.

Clemens Alexandrinus or Clement of Alexandria, 'the most learned of the Fathers', as Jerome later called him, devoted considerable effort to the campaign against Gnosis. Alexandria was the centre of Christian as well as Gnostic scholarship in the years around 200, and Clement's principal target was the Basilidian sect founded by Basilides, a Gnostic who had taught in Alexandria c. 120–40. According to Clement, the aforementioned and generally accepted distortion of Jesus's words into an argument in favour of the unmarried state – the 'eunuchs' passage in Matthew 19 forms the favourite plank in John Paul II's campaign for the preservation of obligatory celibacy – stemmed from the archheretics, that is to say, from the Gnostics. Clement wrote: 'The Basilidians say that our Lord, when asked by the apostles whether it is better not to marry, replied: "Not all can accept this saying" . . . and they interpret this saying more or less thus . . . : "Those who have rendered themselves incapable of marriage for the kingdom of heaven's sake take this decision on account of the consequences accruing to them from marriage, because they shrink from the effort involved in procuring the necessities of life"' (ibid., II, 1, 1). Clement went on to interpret the passage correctly, and it is high time that the Pope and all other celibatarians realised, after eighteen hundred years of error, that they can justifiably drop their pet argument in favour of the unmarried state and recognise it for what it is: a false and tendentious interpretation of Jesus's words by the Gnostics. Priestly celibacy is founded on a misconception. Clement rightly contended that the passage in Matthew 19 referred to divorce: 'However, as regards Jesus's dictum "Not all can accept this saying" . . . they [the Basilidians] do not know that, after he had pronounced upon the letter of divorcement, some said: "If that is the case with a wife, it is better for a man not to marry", and that Our Lord thereupon said: "All men cannot receive this saying, save they to whom it is given." For his questioners were desirous of knowing precisely this: whether, when a wife has been condemned for fornication and put away, it is permissible to marry another' (ibid., III, 50, 1–3).

Clement was here defending Jesus's original words against appropriation by the antimarital Gnostics, and anyone reading the passage with an open mind will agree with him that they refer to divorce, not celibacy. Although he opposed the Gnostics in holding that marriage accords with the will of God and is good, however, his total adherence to the Stoic ideal of emotionlessness and the Stoic idea that procreation is the sole end of marriage made him a true forerunner of the papal 'Pill encyclicals'. He even misconstrued Paul (I Cor. 7), who makes no mention of procreation, in a Stoic sense: ' "Deny ye not one another," says the Apostle, "except it be by consent for a while." In saying "Deny ye not one another" he is drawing attention to the generative duty of marriage, as he had already made clear above with the words: "Let the husband fulfil his conjugal duty toward the wife and, similarly, the wife toward the husband" ' (Stromateis', III, 107, 5). Clement did hint that Paul (I Cor. 7: 2) saw marriage as a means of appeasing the sexual urge, but this had little bearing on his own conception of marriage ('Stromateis', III, 15).

Clement employed the Stoics' favourite comparison with rural life. 'Thus it is wrong to indulge in the pleasures of love and be lewdly intent on the gratification of one's lust, and just as wrong to yield to excitement by irrational passions and crave to become impure. As for the farmer, so for the married man, it is permissible to scatter seed only when the season favours sowing' ('Paidagogos', II, 10, 102, 1). He also cited the idea of adultery with one's own wife, that stock item in the repertoire of every rigorist from Philo the Jew down to and including the present Pope. Thus Clement: 'He that has intercourse in marriage as he would with a whore commits adultery with his own wife.' (ibid., II, 10, 99, 3). It accorded with his Stoic aversion to carnal pleasure that he also condemned intercourse with a pregnant wife (ibid., II, 92, 2) and between elderly spouses (ibid., II, 95 3) as inconsistent with the Christian ideal.

On 16 September 1968, Cardinal Frings of Cologne summoned all the deans and university teachers in his diocese and solicited their support for the Pill encyclical by invoking, among others, Clement of Alexandria. Clement had even rejected intercourse with an elderly wife, he pointed out, so it was clear that the Church had aspired to and supported the precepts of Pill encyclicals from earliest times. From earliest times, perhaps, but not, as we have seen, from the very first, i.e. from Jesus or Paul. Disapproval of sensual pleasure is a Gnostic-Stoic legacy that has overshadowed the Christian gospel since Clement's day and branded such pleasure as a contaminant. Clement went on to cite the 'Stoic finger' to which Augustine would later attribute so much importance: 'For if reason, which the Stoics taught, fails even to permit the wise man to move his finger at will, how much more must those who aspire to wisdom strive to gain mastery over the generative member?' (ibid., II, 10, 90, 1).

While Clement correctly construed Jesus's pronouncement on self-castration for the kingdom of heaven's sake (Matt. 19), the same dictum was misapprehended twice over by his celebrated successor as head of the catechetical school at Alexandria, Origen (d. 253 or 254), the leading theologian of the Greek Church. Origen not only interpreted it as a summons to remain celibate but took it quite literally: at the age of eighteen or thereabouts he became so carried away by his quest for Christian perfection that he castrated himself, invoking the example of Christians who had done likewise before him ('Commentary on Matthew', 15, 3). Although he later conceded that he had been wrong to take the passage on self-castration literally, he stuck to his belief that celibacy was superior in the eyes of God. Regarded even during his lifetime as the most eminent theologian of his day, he acquired a wealthy pupil and grateful patron in the person of Ambrosius, whom he had converted from Gnosticism to Christianity, and who provided him with sufficient funds to employ seven stenographers, seven copyists, and several female calligraphers. Origen was a strict lifelong ascetic who never touched meat, wine, or women. Hard to classify but undoubtedly the most important patristic writer prior to Augustine, he was also early Christianity's most controversial theologian. Although the Church posthumously condemned him (in 553) for advancing false doctrines, his influence on the leading theologians of East and West was very considerable.

Origen combined the Judaeo-Christian belief in a single, righteous god as the author of body and matter, marriage and procreation, with a Gnostic contempt for the flesh. He held that, although the body and matter stemmed from a single, righteous god (and not, as the early Gnostics believed, uninfluenced by Christian ideas, from an evil creator), the body was not that righteous god's primary consideration; it was more of a 'fetter' and 'prison' – the penalty for a prior fall from grace by souls originally pure. Such were the ideas that earned Origen his condemnation by the Church.

Origen influenced the theology of marriage with other trains of thought as well. For example, he warned against condemning Lot's daughters out of hand because they had, for want of husbands, provided themselves with children by copulating with their father. This form of incest, he declared, was more chaste than the chastity of many. He urged wives to examine their consciences. Did they truly 'go in unto' their husbands for the sake of children and then, like Lot's daughters, desist when conception had occurred? Many women were constant slaves to lust and worse than the beasts, for the latter want no more to do with sexual intercourse once fertilised. Apostolic doctrine prescribed that the conjugal act, too, should be performed for the glory of God. This was so when it took place only for the sake of offspring ('In Genesim homiliae', 5, 4). The notion that it is better to make children with one's own father than to avoid making them with one's husband was destined to enjoy a long post-Augustinian career.

Greatly influenced by Origen was Gregory of Nyssa (d. 395), younger brother of Basil the Great (known to modern tourists because of the many cathedrals that bear his name). Although he rejected the theory that men's souls had fallen from grace before clothing themselves in flesh – a belief at odds with the Old Testament – he adhered to Origen's Gnostic disdain for the body. Gregory – who was, incidentally a married bishop – devoted himself to a question that was later to exercise those two great pillars of Catholic sexual morality, Augustine and Thomas Aquinas: did Adam and Eve have intercourse in the Garden of Eden? (For a discussion of what follows, v. Michael Müller, 'Die Lehre des heiligen Augustinus von der Paradiesehe und ihre Auswirkung in der Sexualethik des 12. und 13. Jahrhunderts bis Thomas von Aquin'.)

Gregory answered, no. Rather, life before the Fall was angelic in character. Had the Fall not occurred, Adam and Eve would have multiplied in an angelic fashion, without recourse to marriage and sexual reproduction. Although we cannot imagine what form this celibatarian and angelic generative process would have taken, 'it is a fact' ('De hominis opificio', op. 17). Having foreseen the Fall, however, God knew that man would renounce his parity with the angels and seek the company of inferior beings. That was why, when creating man, he gave him the sexuality, in other words, the generative capacity, of the beasts, 'which in no wise accords with the nobility of our creation'. These twin decisions regarding the creation of man, who was essentially angelic but endowed with animal sexuality in view of the coming Fall, Gregory believed to be implicit in the Bible's account of the Creation: 'God created man in his own image' is followed by the statement: 'male and female created he them' (Gen. 1: 27). According to Gregory, the process of sexual differentiation was a subsequent addition to the true nature of man. Only human nature resembled God's image, not the distinction between the sexes. That was merely an appendage to the finished likeness, an animal element really intended for animals alone ('De hominis opificio', 16f., 22).

Augustine and the medieval theologians, too, would later discern man's resemblance to God only where sexual distinctions did not obtrude ('*ubi sexus nullus est*'): sexuality had no bearing on true humanity (Augustine, 'De trinitate', XII, VII, 12). These celibate theologians wondered why 'God created man in his own image' should be immediately followed by 'male and female created he them' since, in their opinion, the second sentence bore no relation to the first. They never grasped that the full sexuality of the one, whole, spiritually individual person is more than his or her gender, more than his or her mere biological capacity for physical procreation. Sexuality is not a limited, purely functional designation but a peculiarity of the nature of a person from his or her very earliest physico-spiritual origins forward – a peculiarity that codetermines, and is codetermined by, all the delimitable dimensions of each person in a particular way. Sexuality is not something human beings *have* in addition to many other attributes; it is a fundamental mode affecting all that they *are*, and, thus, an inseparable part of their existence and individuality. It is this all-embracing aspect of sexuality that makes it so difficult to arrive at a truly definitive description of masculinity and femininity. They must be redefined afresh in accordance with the dimensions of each individual.

That is why such attempts are for ever exposed to accusations of social casting and sexual stereotyping along historically determined lines, of confusing generative capacity with the essence of sexuality, or of absolutising one sex and using it to define the other in a one-sided way.

Despite his antiphysical and antisexual approach, Christianity's Judaic heritage prevented Gregory from lapsing wholly into Gnostic body-hatred. Gender, he said, had been created by God – if only with an eye to the forthcoming Fall – and was consequently good. The sexual organs were valuable because man used them (when generating) to combat death ('Oratio catechetica magna', 28). The bestial propensities of man, that is to say, his sexual differentiation into male and female, did not come into play in the Garden of Eden. There he was 'liberated from the threat of death, looking freely upon the face of God, not yet judging the beautiful by taste and sight, but delighting only in the Lord and using the helpmate given him for this purpose'. He had still to conceal himself in 'leaves and shadows' and, later, to 'cover himself with skins' ('De virginitate', 12).

It was only after the Fall, according to Gregory, that the present way of life began and man's bestial propensities came into effect. Human beings multiplied like animals, and their bestial mode of reproduction brought out the bestial passions residing in them. Man, originally created in the likeness of God, was without passion. The passions do not form part of his true nature but were in the beginning peculiar to animals. These bestial emotions were adopted by man, together with the bestial mode of reproduction, from the nature of animals, not of God. Carnivorous animals survive by means of anger, weaker animals by means of fear, and the preservation of the species is assured by the desire for pleasure (ibid., 18). As God's likeness, man would have remained free from passion. He would have devoted himself to that which he freely chose, but only in accordance with the dictates of reason (ibid., 12). 'We look forward with yearning to that time of perfection when human life shall be redeemed and restored to its blessed primeval state' ('De hominis opificio', op. 22). The resurrection will be a 'return' to the first, angelic mode of existence, a 'restoration' of that pristine state; for Christ says; at the resurrection 'they neither marry, nor are given in marriage' (ibid., op. 17).

John Chrysostom (d. 407), the greatest preacher of the Eastern Church (hence the surname he has borne since the sixth century: Chrysostom means 'Gold-Mouth'), was more biblically oriented than

Gregory of Nyssa. He did, however, subscribe to many of Gregory's antiphysical, antisexual ideas, – for instance, that no sexual intercourse had occurred between Adam and Eve in Paradise. 'In accordance with God's will, people dwelt in Paradise like angels, uninflamed by any lustfulness ... There was no desire for intercourse, neither was there conception nor birth-pangs nor parturition nor any form of corruption.' They dwelt in pure virginity, 'as in Heaven, and were blessed in their intercourse with God'. The woman had been created by God as a 'help-meet' for Adam – as a being who possessed the same nature, was endowed with speech and intelligence and could 'offer him much solace' ('In gen. hom.', 15, 3, 4). Augustine, being convinced to an exceptional degree of woman's inferiority, declared that man meant more to man as an antidote to solitude than woman, whereas Chrysostom had personal experience of feminine consolation: he addressed seventeen letters from exile to his most faithful adherent, the widow Olympias in Constantinople.

For Chrysostom, the Fall put paid to Adam and Eve's virginal idyll in Paradise. 'In addition to that happy existence, our progenitors lost the adornment of virginity ... Once they had put off that kingly robe and forfeited that celestial adornment, receiving in exchange the perdition of death, the curse, the pains, the tribulations of life, these things were accompanied by marriage, that mortal and slavish garment' ('De virginitate', 14; 'In gen. hom.', 18, 1). So marriage derived from disobedience, accursedness and death. Virginity went hand in hand with immortality, marriage with death ('De virginitate', 14; 'In gen. hom.', 18, 4).

Like Gregory of Nyssa, Chrysostom took the view that an asexual form of procreation occurred in Paradise, but he did not know its nature: 'What marriage engendered Adam, what birth-pangs Eve? Many myriads of angels worship God, yet none of them came into being through generation or birth, pains or conception.' Similarly, God could have multiplied the human race without marriage – 'Whether in the same way as Adam and Eve, or whether in some other way, I cannot say' ('De virginitate', 14, 17). God's command 'Be fruitful and multiply' (Gen. 1: 28), which he uttered immediately after creating man and woman in Paradise, is treated by Chrysostom as if it postdated their expulsion: ' "Be fruitful and multiply," said the divine physician when nature raged, when they could no longer control their tumultuous passions and, in the midst of such a tempest, could flee to no other haven' ('De virginitate', 17, 19).

It is surprising that Chrysostom should have clung, at odds with the Old Testament text, to the notion of Adam and Eve's abiding virginity in Paradise. Even he, with his characteristic respect for biblical texts, was deeply influenced by the superimposition on the Jewish bible of the Gnostic tendency to belittle marriage and glorify virginity. Compared to the latter, marriage was no more than 'the child's apparel' which adults who have attained the maturity of Christ remove in order to don the shining robe of virginity (ibid., 16).

Where the purpose of marriage was concerned, Chrysostom adhered more closely to the Pauline text than any other patristic writer. He held that marriage, though also instituted 'for the generation of children', was far more a means of assuaging natural passions. Paul, he pointed out, had said that each man should take a wife to avoid fornication, not for the purpose of generating offspring. He had further enjoined spouses to have intercourse, not in order to become the parents of numerous progeny, but to avoid being tempted by Satan. Now that the earth was populated with human beings 'there remains but one purpose: the avoidance of debauchery and lasciviousness' (ibid., 17, 19). 'For this reason alone must we take a wife, that we escape sin and deliver ourselves from all fornication' (*quales ducendae sint uxores* 5; similarly *hom. in illud: propter fornicationes* [I Cor. 7: 3]). In Chrysostom's view, therefore – a view to which he held more strongly than any Father of the Church before him – marriage was a concession to human weakness.

Thus, Chrysostom differed from Augustine and his successors in the same tradition, who represented the generation of offspring as the sole legitimate purpose of marriage. Although his terminology is insufficiently personal – like Paul's in I Corinthians 7 – he nonetheless believed, like Paul, that marriage was in the interests of married couples and should not be regarded simply as a means of having children. He made no mention of any ban on coitus with a pregnant or post-menopausal woman, and his knowledge of the scriptures prevented him from giving priority to procreation as Catholic canon law continued to do until a few years ago: 'The primary purpose of marriage is the generation of children' (thus the CIC of 1917, which remained valid until 1983).

More than any Father of the Church before him, Chrysostom

regarded marriage – to use the subsequent definition – as a *remedium concupiscentiae* or remedy for lust, and he gave that function precedence over the purely generative. His great patristic contemporaries, Ambrose, Jerome, and Augustine, were dominated by the Stoic view of children as the supreme and only legitimate purpose of marriage. That Chrysostom, at variance with his own view of marriage, should have strongly condemned contraception, as we shall see below, was a Stoic legacy from which even he dissociated himself as little as he did from the Gnostic ideal of celibacy. As he remarked toward the end of his sermon on Ephesians 5: 22–3, in which he found some wonderful things to say about love: 'He that marries in such a manner and for such purposes will, in the estate of matrimony, be little inferior to monks and celibate persons.' But inferior he will be nonetheless: of that, every Father of the Church was as firmly convinced as is every senior member of the present Catholic hierarchy.

According to Ambrose, bishop of Milan (d. 397), voluntary renunciation of the flesh was a virtue first introduced into the world by Christianity. We find it almost impossible today to appreciate the importance attached to the ideal of virginity during the fourth and fifth centuries and the extent to which it influenced contemporary thought and religious imaginings. Virginity was *the* Christian virtue *par excellence*. Ambrose saw it as the essentially novel feature of the Christian religion and the object of the promises contained in the Old Testament.

> This virtue is, indeed, our exclusive possession. It is lacking in heathens and unpractised among savage, primitive peoples. Nowhere else are there living creatures in which it occurs. Although we breathe the same air as all others, partake in all the conditions of an earthly body, and do not differ from them even in birth, we are exempt from the defects of an otherwise similar nature, if only because virginal chastity, which is seemingly prized by the heathens but really infringed and persecuted by the primitive, albeit under the aegis of religion, is quite unknown among all other creatures.
>
> ('De virginibus', I, 3f.)

Ambrose demanded that priests desist from intercourse with their wives ('De officiis ministrorum', 1, 50, 248). Many of his writings glorify virginity and, in particular, the status of virgins consecrated to God, who did not at that time – in the West, at least – live in convents but formed a class of their own within the community. These virgins were expected to live in seclusion with their families, devoting themselves to prayer, fasting, and sanctification.

Ambrose played a leading part in the condemnation of Jovinian (see p. xi), who had not only declared that virginity was no more pleasing to God than matrimony but disputed that Mary had preserved her virginity when giving birth to Jesus. Having excommunicated Jovinian and his eight followers in Rome, Pope Siricius informed Ambrose of his decision. A great opponent of Jovinian's, Ambrose convened a special synod at Milan and passed his own sentence of excommunication on Jovinian and his adherents. Emperor Theodosius, who was on friendly terms with Ambrose, proceeded to have Jovinian scourged with leaden whips and exiled to the island of Boa. The only report of Jovinian's death comes from Jerome in the year 406: instead of giving up the ghost, he had apparently 'belched it forth 'twixt pheasant and pork' ('Adversus Jovinianum', 1).

Ambrose held that marriage, though not to be eschewed like a sin, should where possible be avoided like a burden ('De viduis', 13, 81). Although he referred to the remedial nature of marriage in connection with I Corinthians – 'In stating that it is better to marry than to burn, the Apostle clearly recommended marriage as a remedy for the preservation of all who might otherwise be imperilled' (ibid., 2, 12) – he nonetheless regarded procreation as its true purpose. His condemnation of intercourse with a pregnant wife was correspondingly severe. Like the Stoics before him, he cited the animal world as an example to humanity:

> Even the beasts convey, by the mute language of their behaviour, that they are animated by the urge to preserve their kind, not by the desire for sexual union. For, as soon as they perceive that the womb is gravid, they cease to indulge in sexual intercourse and lovers' lasciviousness and assume the cares of parenthood. Men, on the other hand, show no such consideration, neither toward the child in the body, nor toward God. They defile the former and anger the latter. Control your lust and look upon the hands of your Creator, who fashions a human being within the maternal body. If he be at work, will you profane the peaceful sanctuary of the maternal body with carnal desire? Either emulate the beasts or fear God.
>
> ('In Lucam', 1, 44)

Ambrose also forbade intercourse between older married couples:

> Everything has its season ... Especially within marriage, too,
> have certain seasons been appointed at which the generation of
> offspring is proper. For as long as the full vigour of the years
> endures, [and] for as long as the prospect of children exists ...
> the desire for sexual intercourse may also be sanctioned. In older
> spouses, however, age itself sets a limit on their performance of
> the conjugal act and dissuades them from incurring the justifiably
> shameful suspicion of incontinence. Even young spouses custom-
> arily feign a desire for children in the belief that a wish for
> progeny can excuse their youthful ardour. How much more
> shameful in older persons would be an act which even the young
> are embarrassed to admit! Moreover, even young spouses who
> mortify their hearts out of devotion to God frequently abstain
> from those youthful acts as soon as they conceive offspring.
>
> (ibid., 1, 43)

Theology became more and more of a bachelors' province and sin
more and more restricted to the sexual domain. With its growing sexual
neurosis and commitment to the monasticising of the laity, the Church
increasingly diverged from its Jewish, Old Testament origins and from
Judaism in general. Virginal Christianity anathematised carnal Judaism.
In 387 Chrysostom delivered eight slanderously anti-Jewish sermons at
Antioch in which he described the Jews as 'carnal', 'lascivious', and
'accursed'. These sermons were an 'arsenal of all the weapons [that
have ever been used] against the Jews to this day' (Friedrich Heer,
'Gottes erste Liebe. Die Juden im Spannungsfeld der Geschichte', p. 67).
In 388, at the instigation of their bishop, the Christians of Kallinikon
on the Euphrates burned down the local synagogue. When Emperor
Theodosius decreed that the synagogue should be rebuilt at the bishop's
expense, Ambrose protested: 'I declare that I set fire to the synagogue –
yes, that I gave them the order, so that there would be no place left in
which Christ is denied ... Which is superior, the concept of order or
the welfare of religion?' (Epistolae 40, 11). When Theodosius balked,
Ambrose broke off divine service and informed him in the presence of
the assembled congregation that he would not continue saying Mass
until the decree had been revoked. By securing total immunity for the
Christian arsonists, as he eventually did, Ambrose went down in
ecclesiastical history as a righteous Christian who stood his ground,
even in defiance of an emperor.

It is erroneous to believe that anti-Semitism came from below; it came from above, from bishops and Fathers of the Church as eminent as Ambrose of Milan. 'We must never lose sight of this, since the contrary assertion is mistakenly hazarded to this day, even by distinguished theologians: in Christian Europe, anti-Semitism emanates from above, not from below, not from the people, not from humble folk. It comes from above, from theologians and theological conceptions of the world and history. It was fashioned on high, the Jewish stereotype and image that was to be so terribly acted upon below' (Heer, op. cit., p. 80).

No Father of the Church wrote of marriage more offensively or despised sex more profoundly than Jerome (d. 419 or 420), yet none was so loved by women, lived in closer spiritual (and physical) proximity to them, or loved them more in his own desexualised way. He moved to Rome in 382, when he was in his mid-thirties, and became the spiritual adviser and focal point of an ascetic circle of wealthy ladies belonging to the Roman aristocracy. Jerome's feminine coterie included a widow in her early thirties named Paula, who came of an old Roman family and was the mother of five children. Her daughter Eustochium, an intelligent girl, learned Greek and Hebrew from Jerome for purposes of biblical study and became, under his guidance, the first female member of the Roman aristocracy to consecrate her virginity to God. When Blaesilla, another of Paula's daughters, died in 384, Jerome was accused of having starved her to death with his injunctions to fast, and her funeral in Rome gave rise to a loud outcry against 'the loathsome tribe of monks' (Eph. 39: 6). In 386 Jerome moved with his female soulmates to Bethlehem, where he used his own considerable fortune and that of Paula, who was wealthier still, to finance a school and a monastic settlement complete with several pilgrims' hostels. Paula supervised the women's convent and Jerome the adjoining monastery. He was so disconsolate when Paula died in 404 that he found it impossible to work for some time, and he survived the death of his 'daughter' Eustochium in 419 by only a year. His last letters convey the grief he felt at having lost her.

While still in Rome, Jerome became embroiled in a controversy with Helvidius, a layman who had cited the New Testament (Mark 6; Matt. 13) in support of his assertion that Jesus had had brothers and sisters.

In 383 Jerome wrote a treatise entitled 'Adversus Helvidium de perpetua gloriosae Virginis Mariae virginitate'. The arguments and exegetic factors he adduced against Helvidius were the same, in essence, as those still endorsed by the Catholic Church, so its notion of Mary's virginity bears Jerome's impress to this day. Jerome held that Mary had furnished both sexes with grounds for preserving their virginity, and that the moral superiority of the virginal state was manifest in her person. This stood the truth on its head: it was not that people prized virginity because Mary had been a virgin, but that they transformed Mary into a perpetual virgin because they prized virginity.

Also involved in the above controversy was Bishop Bonosus of Sardica, who supported Helvidius in his contention that Mary had led a normal married life with Joseph after Jesus's birth and had borne other children. Thus, Bonosus denied the doctrine of Mary's virginity *after the birth of Jesus*. That Mary could have led a normal married life was then considered – as it still is, by most celibatarians – to be an immoral and impermissible idea, so Bishop Bonosus, too, was excommunicated by Pope Siricius.

At Bethlehem in 393 Jerome wrote his two books attacking the heretic Jovinian, who had disputed that Mary remained intact *while giving birth*. He not only declared that virginity was superior to marriage in the eyes of God but decried marriage so fiercely that Paula's son-in-law, a senator named Pammachius, tried to withdraw all the copies that had gone into circulation. Seizing upon the words 'It is good for a man not to touch a woman' (I Cor. 7: 1), which he wrongly attributed to Paul himself and not to the Corinthians who had questioned him on the subject, he wrote as follows: 'So it is good not to touch a woman. To touch a woman must, therefore, be an evil thing. If the conjugal act be treated with indulgence notwithstanding, it is only for the avoidance of something far worse. But what value can be placed on a thing permitted only with a view to avoiding something worse?' ('Adversus Jovinianum', 1, 7). In this tirade against the heretic Jovinian, who had dared to put marriage on a par with virginity, Jerome cited a maxim by one Sextus (he at first identified him with the martyred Pope Sixtus II [d. 258]), which had originally appeared in a heathen compilation.

Sextus' maxim, which medieval theologians attributed to Jerome himself, was to become a stock argument and leitmotif of the whole antisexual Catholic tradition down to John Paul II. As modified and honed to an even finer point by Jerome, the aphorism read thus: 'He that is too passionate (*ardentior*) a lover of his wife is an adulterer.' Jerome went on to buttress this statement by citing the passage from the Stoic Seneca which we ourselves encountered when examining the non-Christian sources of sexual hostility (ibid., 1, 49), and which was likewise attributed to Jerome during the Middle Ages. Thomas Aquinas reiterated the same idea: marriage being directed toward the generation of offspring, any man who loves his wife too passionately offends against the good of matrimony and may be termed an adulterer ('Summa theologica', II/II, q. 54, a. 8). John Paul II broached and endorsed the idea of adultery with one's own wife at a general audience on 8 October 1980 ('Der Spiegel', No. 47, 1980, p. 9).

The only 'good' he could discover in marriage, Jerome declared in a letter to Eustochium, was that 'it brings forth virgins; I glean the rose from the thorns, the gold from the earth, the pearl from the shell' (Ep. 22, 20). According to him, therefore, 'The generation of children in marriage is permitted, but feelings of sensual pleasure such as are experienced by whores when embracing are, in a wife, to be condemned' ('Commentary on Ephesians', III, 5, 25). Jerome stressed that, once conception had occurred, married couples should devote themselves to prayer rather than physical intimacy. Human beings should freely accept what the law of nature prescribes in the animal world, namely, that animals desist from mating after fertilisation. By abstaining from sensual pleasure in this way, they earn themselves a heavenly reward (ibid., III, 5, 25).

Jerome had some words of consolation to offer wives: 'I do not deny that holy women are to be found among wives, but only when they have ceased to be spouses, and when they themselves, in the predicament which the married state brings in its train, imitate virginal chastity' ('Adversus Helvidium', 21). Blaesilla, who was widowed after seven months of marriage, measured up to this ideal of virginity: under Jerome's guidance she consecrated herself wholly to God, alias the unmarried state. In his letter of condolence to Paula, written a month after Blaesilla's death, Jerome approvingly points out that 'the loss of her virginity occasioned her more sorrow than the death of her husband' (Ep. 39, 1).

FIVE

Family Planning in the Ancient World: Infanticide, Abortion, Contraception

Ever since Augustine, contraception has played an uninterrupted part in the policing of marital intercourse by celibatarians hostile to sexual pleasure. Because Christian doctrine on this subject evolved against the background of pre- and non-Christian family planning, a brief account of the ancient world's family-planning methods would be in order here. They were: (i) infanticide; (ii) abortion; and (iii) contraception (v. John T. Noonan, 'Contraception: A History of its Treatment by the Catholic Theologians and Canonists').

It was not until 374 that infanticide was, under Christian influence, legally defined as murder. Seneca (d. 65) had described the drowning of malformed or puny Roman children as a sensible everyday proceeding ('De ira', 1, 15). Suetonius (b.c. 70, date of death unknown) referred to the exposure of new-born children as a measure left to the discretion of parents ('Caius Caligula', 5). The eminent Greek historian Plutarch (d.c. 120) tells us in his biography of the Spartan legislator Lycurgus (dates uncertain; eleventh-eighth centuries BC) that in Sparta new-born babies were inspected by the elders of the community. The puny and malformed among them were then thrown from a rock in the Taygetus Mountains to prevent them from becoming a charge on the state. Plutarch further states that Spartan mothers bathed their new-born babies in wine, not water, because sickly and epileptic infants could not withstand such treatment and died ('Lycurgus' in 'Lives', 16).

Also informative in this context is a passage from Tacitus (d. 120), Judaism's foremost opponent in heathen antiquity, whose anti-Jewish polemic is among the most acrimonious pieces he ever wrote. One of his long series of charges against the Jews, 'that race abhorred by the gods', was that they refrained from killing off their surplus children – a practice of which he evidently approved. This passage is indicative of how natural it seemed in Tacitus' day to dispose of unwanted or physically handicapped babies, and also of the fact that the Jews were, in this respect as in so many others, alien and undesirable exceptions to the general rule. Tacitus wrote:

> In order to secure the allegiance of his people in the future, Moses prescribed for them a novel religion quite different from those of the rest of mankind. Among the Jews all things are profane that we hold sacred; on the other hand they regard as permissible what seems to us immoral ... The bull is also offered up, because the Egyptians worship it as Apis. They avoid eating pork in memory of their tribulations, as they themselves were once infected with the disease to which this creature is subject.

Tacitus was here referring to the skin disease which the Egyptian priest Manetho (third century BC) claimed to be the reason why his compatriots had expelled the Jews from their country – an Egyptian counterblast to the Jews' account of their God-assisted escape from Egyptian oppression. Tacitus went on to talk of their stubborn loyalty and ready benevolence towards fellow Jews.

> But the rest of the world they confront with the hatred reserved for enemies ... Though a most lascivious people, the Jews avoid sexual intercourse with women of alien race. Among themselves nothing is barred. [It is interesting to note that Tacitus accuses the Jews of an inordinate sex drive just as the Fathers of the Church did when contrasting their own ideal of virginity with the Jews' carnality – that is to say, with the Jewish aversion to celibacy. The Christians adopted their celibatarian ideal from the heathens of the first two centuries AD, not from the Jews.] They have introduced the practice of circumcision to show that they are different from others. Proselytes to Jewry adopt the same practice, and the very first lesson they learn is to despise the gods, shed all feelings of patriotism, and consider parents, children and brothers as readily expendable. However, the Jews see to it that their numbers increase. It is a deadly sin to kill an unwanted child, and they think that eternal life is granted to those who die in battle or execution – hence their eagerness to have children

and their contempt for death . . . The Egyptians worship a variety of animals and half-human, half-bestial forms, whereas the Jewish religion is a purely spiritual monotheism . . . For this reason they erect no images in their cities, still less in their temples. Their kings are not so flattered, the Roman emperors not so honoured . . . King Antiochus [second century BC] made an effort to get rid of their primitive cult and hellenise them, but his would-be reform of this degraded nation was foiled by the outbreak of war with Parthia.

Tacitus further called the Jews 'a nation which is the slave of superstition and the enemy of true beliefs' ('Histories', V, 3–13). What he scorned in the Jews, he extolled in the Germanic tribes: 'To restrict the number of children, or to kill any of those born after the heir, is considered wicked. Good morality is more effective in Germany than good laws are elsewhere' ('Germania', 19). Tacitus found the Jews an inconsistent race: on the one hand, they relished war because they believed in the resurrection of those killed in battle; on the other, they preached protection for the new-born.

Interviewed in 1984 by the 'Frankfurter Allgemeine', the Polish Catholic priest Henryk Jankowski, Lech Walesa's confessor and companion on the occasion of his audience with John Paul II, was asked what qualities he most admired in a man. His answer: manliness and courage. And in a woman? Religious devotion and a readiness to bear children. Manly courage, meaning primarily courage in battle, and maternal fecundity – what else are these but a Christian version of the old Jewish ideal which Tacitus rejected? Appalling though it is that Tacitus should have taken the killing of unwanted children for granted, and grateful though we must be to Judaism and Christianity for changing the world's moral outlook in this respect, it is nonetheless noteworthy that Tacitus found it odd that the Jews should sanction killing and being killed in battle while opposing curbs on the survival of unwanted children. Today, after two thousand years of Christianity, few Christians would call their bishops schizophrenic for campaigning against the Pill and abortion while favouring rearmament, or for being far more protective of the unborn than of the already born. Tacitus the heathen would probably have accused them of the same inconsistency that so surprised him in the Jews.

Thus the Jews anticipated the Christians in their concern for all new-born children and their corresponding disapproval of abortion. Philo of

Alexandria (d. 40–50), a Jew whose pronouncements on the subject might have been those of an early Father, expressly linked abortion and infanticide: 'The same prohibition [on abortion] applies to another, greater, form of wrongdoing, namely, the exposure of infants, an outrage that has become common practice among many other peoples in consequence of their innate misanthropy' ('De legibus specialibus', 3, 20, 110). Philo complained that infanticide was rife. There were parents who strangled their infants, weighted them down and drowned them, or left them in the wilds to be devoured by beasts and birds of prey. Such parents were guilty of murder. Their crime was associated with lechery, 'for they are lechers if, instead of having intercourse with their wives for the perpetuation of the human race, they merely assuage their lust by copulating like boars or he-goats' (ibid., 3, 20, 113).

It is noticeable that Philo the Jew accused heathen infanticides of lechery while Tacitus the heathen levelled the same charge at the Jews for preserving human life ('nothing was barred' among members of that 'most lascivious' race). That morality means predominantly sexual morality was a Stoic or Gnostic idea widespread among the heathens, Jews and Christians of the first two centuries of our era, and the same notion continues to be a favourite theme among Christians anxious to disqualify those of other persuasions. Philo the Jew and Tacitus the Roman were at one in accusing their opponents of lechery because they either killed or forbore to kill their new-born children. This was because the first two centuries AD witnessed the growth of a two-caste idea based on differing philosophical systems whose common feature was contempt for the flesh. Tacitus and Philo, being remote from 'lechery' in their own estimation, compared themselves favourably with the 'lecherous' persons and peoples who continued to procreate whether or not they let their children live. Neither Philo nor Tacitus, Jew nor heathen, made the transition from contempt for 'lechery' to total asceticism and the veneration of celibacy. It was left to the Christians to draw the conclusion that all married persons and producers of children should be regarded as a lower, more sinful form of humanity – in other words, to downgrade the married state and exalt the celibate into a higher, holier caste.

Early Christianity took over its condemnation of infanticide or exposure from the Jews. Justin the Martyr (d.c. 165) wrote of the latter practice: 'We are further taught that the exposure of new-born infants is wicked because we perceive that almost all of them, not only girls but boys as well, are led into debauchery' ('1st Apology', 27). Many children, it seems, were found alive and taken home by strangers. 'Moreover, it is to be feared that one of the exposed children, if not taken in, will perish and thus make murderers of us' (ibid., 29). Lactantius, a Christian apologist whom Emperor Constantine appointed tutor to his son, wrote of the heathens in 'Divinarum institutionum libri septem' (304–13): 'They strangle their own children, or, if too pious to do so, expose them' (5, 19, 15).

Infanticide and abortion were frequently mentioned together and placed on a par. The Epistle of Barnabas (first half of the second century AD) states: 'Thou shalt kill neither the foetus by means of abortion nor the new-born child' (xix, 5). The Christian philosopher Athenagoras, author of an apology addressed to Emperor Marcus Aurelius in the year 177, informed him that the Christians branded 'those women who take medicines to induce an abortion as murderesses of men' and prohibited the exposure of children 'because to expose a child is tantamount to murdering it'. Tertullian, writing in 198, stated that it was customary among the heathen to kill new-born children 'either by drowning, or by exposing them to cold or death by starvation or dogs . . . But we, since murder is forbidden us once and for all, may not destroy . . . the foetus in the maternal body . . . It makes no difference whether one destroys a life already born or one in the process of birth' ('Apologeticus', 9, 7f.). Minucius Felix, a Roman advocate and Christian apologist writing at the end of the second century, addressed himself to the heathens thus: 'I see you sometimes exposing new-born children to wild beasts and birds, sometimes doing away with them by strangling them in a deplorable manner. Many women destroy the seed of future life by taking medicines and thus commit infanticide before giving birth' ('Octavius', 30, 2). Ambrose (d. 397), too, speaks of murder in both cases: 'The poor abandon their children; the wealthy kill the fruit of their own bodies in the womb lest their fortune be divided among several, destroying their own children in the maternal body by means of parricidal potions. Thus, before life is transmitted, it is extinguished' ('Hexaemeron', 5, 18, 58).

On 16 January 318, Emperor Constantine forbade fathers to kill their adult children, as it had hitherto been within their paternal power to do, but it was not until 7 February 374, half a century after Christianity had been recognised as the state's supreme religion, that the killing of new-born children was legally defined as murder.

Although Christians campaigned from the first on behalf of the unborn child and against abortion, this early phase in the Christian era saw no changes in the official abortion laws, which, as we shall see, were protective solely of a husband's rights and the mother's life, not of the foetus.

One of the Cornelian Laws promulgated by Sulla in 81 BC penalised those who procured and administered poisonous draughts, but it was applied as much to aphrodisiacs and fertility drugs as to contraceptives and abortifacients, the administering of which became a capital offence if the man or woman who took them died in consequence. It was thus designed to protect the adult, not the foetus. The legislation enacted by Emperors Septimius Severus (d. 211) and Caracalla (d. 217), which prescribed exile for a wife who aborted herself on the ground that it was 'dishonourable for a wife to deprive her husband of children with impunity', was similarly protective of the husband's interests. Unmarried women who procured abortions were not penalised, so this law, too, was unrelated to the preservation of the foetus as such.

Little by little, fierce Christian hostility to abortion carried the day on behalf of the unborn child. One indication of how frequently abortion was practised in the Roman Empire may be gleaned from the fact that Seneca praised his mother because, unlike so many other women, she had not 'destroyed the prospect of children in her womb' ('Ad Helviam', 16, 1).

The Christians followed Jewish tradition in fiercely condemning abortion from the outset. The 'Didache' or 'Teaching of the Twelve Apostles', an apocryphal work dating from the first half of the second century AD, speaks of 'infanticides who go the way of death, who destroy the likeness of God in the womb' (v, 2). The Spanish Synod of Elvira at the beginning of the fourth century forbade abortion on pain of excommunication or even death, and the Synod of Ancyra (314) prescribed ten years' penance for women who fornicated and then destroyed the fruit of their intercourse. These synodal decrees were often cited by conciliar resolutions subsequently passed in both East and West alike. The Apostolic Constitutions, a fourth-century compilation, condemned the killing of a foetus that had already taken shape (7, 3, 2). The Canons of St Basil (d. 379), which substantially influenced the canon law of the Greek Church, condemned any woman who underwent an abortion irrespective of foetal development. The penalty was the same as that laid down by the Synod of Ancyra: ten years' penance.

The earliest extant documents relating to contraceptive techniques come from Egypt. These papyri, which date from between 1900 and 1100 BC, prescribe the use of vaginal tampons designed to exclude sperm or neutralise it by means of substances such as acacia gum, honey and crocodile dung in which they were to be steeped. The Graeco-Roman science of contraception was based primarily on three works: the 'Historia animalium' by Aristotle (d. 322 BC); 'Historia naturalis' by Pliny (d. AD 79), the best and most comprehensive ancient encyclopedia of the natural sciences; and 'Gynaecologia' by Soranus of Ephesus, who practised at Rome under Emperors Trajan and Hadrian (early second century). The 'Gynaecologia', the Roman Empire's most important source of information about contraceptive methods, was handed down to medieval Europe by the Arabs.

The contraceptives mentioned by these three writers were mainly to be drunk. Pliny gave only one: a decoction of rue (which was also an abortifacient), oil of roses and aloe juice ('Historia naturalis', 20, 51, 142–3). Soranus wrote of contraceptive potions under the heading: 'Ought one to use abortifacient and contraceptive medicines, and how?' He prescribed three contraceptive potions: panax sap, rue seed and 'Cyrenaic sap' coated with beeswax and administered in wine; wallflower seed, myrtle, myrrh, and white pepper stirred in wine and taken on three successive days; and, lastly, a mixture of oxymel, rocket seed, and cow parsnip. Soranus warned his readers to be careful because 'these preparations not only impede conception but destroy what is already conceived'. Although they could cause a woman to abort, their primary purpose was contraceptive. Soranus also pointed out that they could cause heavy-headedness, indigestion, and vomiting '('Gynaecologia', 1, 19, 60–3).

The second ancient method consisted in preventing sperm from reaching the uterus. Aristotle stated that conception was hampered by a smooth cervix, 'which is why some anoint that part of the womb on which the semen falls with oil of cedar, ointment of lead, or a salve compounded of frankincense and olive oil' ('Historia animalium', 7, 3, 583a). Soranus recommended the introduction into the womb of a mixture of old olive oil, honey, and balsam mastic or cedar gum. Soft wool inserted into the uterine orifice could also be effective if moistened with wine in which pine bark and the dyewood of the smoke tree had previously been steeped ('Gynaecologia', 1, 19, 61f.).

The third method of contraception entailed smearing the male member with an ointment intended either to neutralise sperm or, like a pessary, to seal the uterus when the vagina was penetrated. Pliny recommended cedar gum ('Historia naturalis', 24, 11, 18).

In addition to the above methods, advantage could be taken of the woman's sterile periods. The Hippocratic school (fifth century BC) had come to the conclusion that a fertile period occurred just after menstruation ('Diseases of Woman', I, 38). Soranus was of the same opinion. 'The uterus, being much congested with blood during menstruation, can very readily discharge this accumulated blood but is incapable of absorbing and retaining semen.' Although he held that women occasionally conceived while menstruating, 'scientific considerations' indicated that the menstrual period was not the proper time for conception. The period preceding menstruation was also unfavourable to conception, he believed, because the uterus was already 'receiving material' and thus had difficulty in absorbing semen. The best time for conception, in his view, was immediately after menstruation ('Gynaecologia', 1, 10, 36).

Euteknia, or a 'goodly brood' of children, was a topic frequently discussed in the ancient world. Of prime importance to *euteknia* was the age of the parents. Plato held that men produced their finest offspring between the ages of thirty and thirty-five, women between sixteen and twenty. Aristotle recommended that 'marriage be set for girls at eighteen, for men at thirty-seven or somewhat less'. Xenophon (d. after 355 BC) extolled the laws enacted by Lycurgus (author of the Spartan code) and the measures he took to ensure that parents produced fine, healthy offspring. Pregnant women were forbidden to drink wine, except when diluted with water, and encouraged to take part in athletics. Lycurgus introduced 'races and trials of strength, as for men, so for women'. The best time to beget and conceive 'goodly' children, according to Soranus, was immediately after menstruation, the worst immediately beforehand. Just as the stomach, when replete with food, tended to vomit up its contents, so did the uterus when congested with blood. After menstruation, on the other hand, the uterus regained its 'appetite'. In women, this was apparent from the special predilection for engaging in the sexual act as soon as menstruation ceased.

It is interesting to note, incidentally, how often women have been persuaded, or persuaded themselves, that their libido reaches a peak consistent with the current state of knowledge about fertility. On 16 September 1968, when Cardinal Frings called a meeting of deans and university teachers at Cologne in an attempt to 'sell' them the encyclical letter 'Humanae vitae' (the first Pill encyclical), one of his arguments in favour of the doctrine that marital intercourse is primarily a generative act was precisely this: that a woman's libido is at its strongest during her time of greatest fertility. To that extent, the cardinal's statement agreed with that of Soranus. Scientists having relocated the fertility phase since Soranus's day, however, the maximal female libido has had, despite its alleged obedience to the law of nature, to undergo a similar change of timing. A woman's libido evidently varies according to the state of scientific research. It seems either that the maximal libido is a moralists' invention, or that women locate their libido wherever fertility renders it most desirable, or, if they have no wish to become pregnant, positively *un*desirable. Prohibitions, too, can be sexually stimulating.

Amulets form the last category of contraceptive devices known to the ancient world. Although Soranus strongly decried their use ('Gynaecologia', 1, 19, 63), his views failed to eradicate the widespread belief in the efficacy of such charms. Pliny advised prolific mothers 'whose fecundity is to be remedied somewhat' to wear an amulet made from a certain kind of spider, which had to be wrapped in a piece of deerskin and placed on one's person before sunrise ('Historia naturalis', 29, 27, 85).

None of the Greek or Roman authors mentioned above refers to coitus interruptus, either because the method required no explanation or because, even in those days, there was a preference for devices used by the woman.

The fact that contraceptive draughts had abortifacient properties presented the physicians of antiquity with certain problems. Soranus, the leading writer in this field, wrote of the dilemma that confronted him whenever he prescribed such a potion. He was heavily influenced by the Stoa, so his criteria for permitting abortion were correspondingly strict: he sanctioned it only when childbirth would put the mother's life in danger and held that contraception was preferable to abortion ('Gynaecologia', 1, 19, 60f.).

Soranus continued to enjoy high esteem during the Christian era of the Roman Empire. Tertullian quoted from one of his treatises, and even Augustine, that great campaigner against contraception, called him 'a most noble writer on medicine' ('Contra Julianum', 5, 14, 51). As for Aëtius, a senior official and Christian court physician to the Christian emperor and legislator Justinian (sixth century), he went so far as to list some of the contraceptive medicines recommended by Soranus. This suggests that Christians were freer during the first few centuries of our era than the Catholics of today. The married physician Aëtius took a less hidebound view than celibatarian Fathers of the Church such as Chrysostom and Jerome, who were against contraception.

Chrysostom inveighs against married couples who want no children and consequently 'slay the new-born' or 'inhibit the beginnings of life' ('Homilia 28 in Matthaeum v'), though it is uncertain whether he identifies the latter act with abortion or contraception. He is definitely speaking of contraception elsewhere, when addressing Christian husbands who 'scorn their wives and consort with harlots':

> Why do you scatter your seed where the field is at pains to destroy the harvest, where pregnancies are avoided by all and any means, where murder is committed prior to birth? Even a harlot you do not suffer to remain a harlot; you make her a murderess as well ... There is indeed something worse than murder, and I know not what to call it, for such women do not kill what has taken shape, they prevent it from taking shape at all. Why do you despise God's gift and oppose his laws? Why do you make the antechamber of birth the antechamber of slaughter? Woman, created for procreation, becomes through you an instrument of murder. So that she may continue to be used and desired by her lovers, and so that she may bleed them of more money, she becomes adept at such an act and prepares your damnation, for, even though the damnation stems from her, the blame for it is yours. Idolatry, too, arises from the same source. To look fair of face, many of these woman employ incantations, libations, love potions, poisonous draughts, and countless other devices. Even after such infamy, after murder and sorcery, the matter still seems harmless to many men, even to many men that have wives. And among the latter there arises a whole source of mischief, for poisons are prepared, not against the harlot's womb, but against the injured wife ... And there are wars without end, battles without cease, and conflict is commonplace.
>
> ('Homilia 24 in Rom.')

Chrysostom allowed rhetoric to carry him away when painting this battle scene, for he described contraception as 'murder . . . worse than murder', and no other writer in the Graeco-Roman world ever equated semen with a human being.

The predominant view in antiquity was that of Aristotle, who held that the foetus did not develop a human soul for some time after conception, the male after forty days, the female after ninety. Prior to that it possessed a vegetable and then an animal soul ('Historia animalium', 7, 3, 583b). This discrepancy between the origination of the male and the female soul was more than a span of time; it was also a measure of human quality because it indicated that the soul belonged to the man before the woman. The soul, meaning the essence of humanity, was something male rather than female.

Leviticus 12: 1–5 defined a woman as unclean for forty days after giving birth to a son and eighty days in the case of a daughter. Mary herself was unclean for forty days after the birth of Jesus (Luke 2: 22). Aristotle's ninety days for the making of a female soul and the Old Testament's eighty days of uncleanliness, probably based on a similar notion of woman's inferiority to that of Aristotle, became fused in the Christian tradition, which credited the female foetus with a soul after eighty days.

According to this view of successive ensoulment, 'murder' was an incorrect definition, not only for contraception, but for early abortion as well. Augustine followed Aristotelian biology in holding that no soul can reside in an unformed body ('In Exodum', 21, 80), so there could be no talk of murder in either case. Jerome, too, wrote to Aglasia (one of his spiritual pupils): 'The seed takes gradual shape in the uterus, and it does not count as killing until the various elements have acquired their outward appearance and their members' (Ep. 121, 4). He did, however, write in inconsistent and exaggerated terms of 'homicide' when referring to contraception in a letter of admonition to Eustochium on the subject of certain virgins consecrated to God: 'But others take a potion to make themselves sterile and thus murder a human being not yet conceived. Some, when they perceive that they are with child in consequence of their lapse, seek to induce a miscarriage with poisonous potions, often perishing themselves and going to Hell as threefold murderesses: as suicides, as adulteresses in respect of Christ, their heavenly bridegroom, as murderesses of a child yet unborn' (Ep. 22, 13).

SIX

Augustine

St Augustine (d. 430), the greatest of all the Fathers of the Church, was the man responsible for welding Christianity and hostility to sexual pleasure into a systematic whole. His influence on the development of the Christian sexual ethic is undisputed, and the papal condemnations of the Pill by Paul VI (1968) and John Paul II (1981) were heavily coloured by it. To speak of sexual hostility, therefore, is to speak of Augustine. He was the theological thinker who blazed a trail for the ensuing centuries – indeed, for the ensuing millennium-and-a-half. The history of the Christian sexual ethic was shaped by him. The binding nature of Augustine's pronouncements was accepted by the great theologians of the Middle Ages, notably Thomas Aquinas (d. 1274), and by the Jansenists, who championed a revival of stringent prudery in France during the seventeenth and eighteenth centuries. Augustine's authority in the field of sexual morality was so supreme that his views merit closer examination. Like many neurotics, he divorced love from sex. 'The disastrous process of desexualisation ... was decisively promoted in the West, in Europe, by Augustine' (Heer, 'Gottes erste Liebe', pp. 69 and 71).

Principal author of the still widely accepted Christian conception of God, the world, and mankind, Augustine not only shared the disdain for sex characteristic of his contemporaries and predecessors among the early Fathers but allied it with a new factor: sexual angst, both personal and theological. Theologically, he established a relationship between original sin, which played so great a part in his redemptive system, and enjoyment of the sexual act. To him, original sin betokened eternal death and damnation for all who had not been saved, that is to say, delivered by God's grace from 'the multitude of the damned' to which all human beings belonged. Salvation was, however, denied to many – even, in Augustine's view, to unbaptised children.

Augustine was so obsessed with the damnation of unbaptised infants that his Pelagian opponent Bishop Julian of Eclanum took him to task: 'You, Augustine, are far removed from religious sentiments, from civilized thought, far removed even from common sense, if you think your God capable of committing crimes against justice of which even barbarians find it hard to conceive.' He called Augustine's God 'a persecutor of the new-born who casts tiny infants into the eternal fire' ('Opus imperfectum contra Julianum', I, 48).

Augustine once regaled his congregation with the story of a child that had died while still undergoing instruction prior to baptism. Driven to despair by the prospect of her child's eternal damnation, the mother carried its corpse to the shrine of St Stephen. There it revived just long enough to be baptised and then relapsed into death, satisfied that it had escaped the 'second death' known as Hell ('Sermones' 323 and 324).

Johannes Beleth (d.c. 1165), a respected theologian who taught at Paris, forbade the coffins of women who died while pregnant to be brought into church because their unborn children had not been baptised. Before any expectant mother could be buried in consecrated ground, her child had to be surgically removed and interred outside the graveyard. This pious practice was not in vogue everywhere – Norwegian canon law, for example, expressly forbade such operations (Browe, 'Sexualethik', p. 23) – but its mere existence proves how widespread were the gruesome consequences of Augustine's doctrine of original sin.

Pelagius (d.c. 420) and Julian of Eclanum have passed into ecclesiastical history as great heretics. Augustine remains a spiritually formative influence to this day, even though theologians are gradually beginning, in defiance of his inhumane doctrine, to grant unbaptised children admission to heaven. 'Was it all wrong,' Karl Rahner asked not long ago, 'what Pelagius and Julian of Eclanum alleged against Augustine, their seeming vanquisher, or have they not in many respects been vindicated by a gradual process of development lasting into our own day?' ('Theologie der Gegenwart', 1977, 2, p. 76).

Augustine's erroneous and superstitious belief in the damnation of unbaptised children, which the Church officially endorsed until very recent times (and largely still does), is not the only catastrophe for which he was responsible. Disastrous consequences have also flowed from his doctrine concerning the way in which original sin is transmitted to children, in other words, to the whole human race. Augustine held that, when the first human beings disobeyed God and ate of the forbidden fruit, 'they were ashamed and covered their genitals with fig leaves'. He concluded 'from this, therefore' (*ecce unde*) that what the couple tried to conceal was the vehicle of original sin ('Sermones', 151, 8). According to Augustine, it is sexual intercourse, or rather, sexual pleasure, that has transmitted original sin from generation to generation. 'Christ was begotten and conceived without carnal lust, and thus remained free from all pollution by original sin' ('Enchiridion', 13, 41).

Living as we do in an age when the advent of AIDS has bred fear of infection by sexual contact, we can well imagine what it meant to be told that a child was infected with original sin by the sexual act. The linking of original sin with sexual pleasure was not finally abandoned until the last century, when the 'immaculate conception' of Mary was dogmatised by papal bull in 1854. The dogma of the immaculate conception is often confused with the virgin birth by many who believe that it relates to the moment when Mary conceived Jesus by the Holy Ghost. It does, in fact, relate to the moment when Mary herself was sinlessly conceived by her mother. As long as the Church subscribed to Augustine's belief in the transmission of original sin by the sexual act, there could be no talk of Mary's sin-free conception. In Augustine's view, only Jesus was devoid of original sin because he alone came into the world without the necessity for any sexual act. Conversely, according to the Augustinian construction, it was only because he had been borne to a virgin that Jesus could be accounted devoid of original sin.

Bernard of Clairvaux, an ardent Marian, strongly opposed the introduction of a Feast of the Immaculate Conception at Lyon in 1140. To assert that Mary had been preserved from original sin, he argued, would mean that she was not the product of a normal sexual union, and that she too had emanated from a virgin birth.

Augustine, who engendered a fear of sex that has endured for fifteen hundred years and a sexual hostility whose effects persist to this day, dramatised fear of sexual pleasure and identified it with lust to such an extent that any attempt to follow his train of thought induces a sense of nightmare. He encumbered marriage with such a moral mortgage that it should not surprise us if many human beings weighed down by so unnatural a burden have since reacted strongly against the whole of the Christian sexual ethic.

Despite its major theological significance, Augustine's conversion in the year 387, when he was twenty-nine, was hard luck on the married. It was prefaced by his repudiation of the woman with whom he had lived since he was sixteen or seventeen ('she had sensed my unthinking ardour, albeit she was my only mistress'), and on whom he had fathered a son, Adeodatus (God-given). Augustine retained custody of the boy, by then eleven. His mistress, whose name he never mentions in his 'Confessions', swore to remain eternally faithful to him when he sent her away. He called his relations with her 'a loose bond of impure love in which children are most unwelcome, even if they subsequently constrain us to love them' ('Confessiones', IV, 2).

His strict observance of contraceptive methods and attention to his partner's infertile days, foiled by the miscalculation that resulted in the birth of Adeodatus, was succeeded after his conversion by a fanatical campaign against contraception of all kinds. He had not wanted to get the girl pregnant, during his affair with her, partly because her social inferiority made him reluctant to marry her. His mother, St Monica, was chiefly responsible for undermining their relationship and persuading him to send the woman back to Africa. She was making preparations for a suitable marriage, but the wealthy prospective bride of her choice had yet to attain marriageable age. Rather than wait another two years, Augustine took another mistress.

> Since the one whose bed I used to share was wrested from my side, being, as it were, an impediment to my marriage, my heart, because it clung to her, was deeply wounded and bled. That woman had returned to Africa, vowing to Thee, O God, to belong to no other man. The son I had from her remained behind with me. But I, wretch that I was, could not even emulate that woman. Since I was not for two years to obtain her whose hand I sought, I would brook no delay, being no lover of marriage but a slave to lust. Consequently, I procured myself another woman . . . Far from healing, however, the wound inflicted on me by my separa-

tion from the first woman began, after fever and severe pain, to fester. It pained me less but was all the more irremediable.

(Ibid. VI, 15)

After his conversion, the pangs of conscience he felt at his own disloyalty to his abandoned mistress transformed themselves into a growing contempt for all sexual love. Guilty though he felt, he was less to blame than the evil pleasure deriving from the sexual act. Augustine's sexual pessimism was one long endeavour to suppress his own sense of guilt, his fear of women an endless search for the guilty cause of his failure.

The vehemence with which Augustine opposed conception was not merely a reaction against his reluctance to marry his mistress. (That he *could not* marry her 'for legal reasons' is untrue, and is one of the many posthumous justifications bestowed on him by sympathetic theologians.) It stemmed principally from the fact that, during his affair with her, he belonged to the Gnostic Manichaean sect, which had many adherents among the intelligentsia and had been banned by the Roman state because it advocated childlessness. Founded by a Persian named Mani (b.c. 216), Manichaeism was the last great religious development in the East before Islam. Mani described himself as the Holy Ghost promised by Jesus. According to him, the earth was 'a realm of boundless darkness' created by the Devil. Procreation was a diabolical act because every human being was a particle of light imprisoned in a body begotten by a demon. Like all strict Gnostics before and after them, the Manichaeans rejected the Old Testament because it associated the creation of the world with a righteous god, whereas the world and carnality were of evil, demonic origin. They demanded complete asceticism of their full members, the 'elect', but very few of them were capable of such renunciation. Most belonged to a second, inferior class of Manichaeans and were, like Augustine, merely 'hearers' (*auditores*). This meant that they cohabited with wives or mistresses but pledged themselves not to imprison a human soul by having children. After Augustine's conversion, his Manichaean acceptance of sexual pleasure and denial of procreation became transposed: the Manichaean turned into a Christian. In a certain sense, Augustine had graduated from the lower to the higher Manichaean caste, for Christians and Manichaeans were at one in regarding the celibate as superior to ordinary, married believers. Manichaeism enjoyed wide popularity in Augustine's day precisely because it resembled Christianity in idealising virginity and was, indeed, considered by many to be a superior form of Christianity.

Augustine's unsatisfying affair with his second mistress coincided with his study of the Neoplatonic philosophers and Plotinus in particular. Plotinus combined Gnostic escapism and contempt for material things with a perception of the one, true, righteous God. He did not, like the Manichaeans and the Gnostics proper, attribute evil to an independent evil principle, but regarded it as a departure from truth and goodness. Augustine's ascetic, Neoplatonist tendency to renounce all worldly objects of affection and devote himself to the one true God was ultimately directed toward an escapist form of Christianity by a chance visitor. An African compatriot of his, Pontician, called on him one day and drew his attention to the first monk, Antonius the Egyptian (c. 300; later St Anthony), whose biography by Athanasius (d. 373) was gaining an ever wider readership in the West and had already prompted many to follow the hermit's example. Augustine was deeply impressed. When Pontician had gone, he told his friend Alypius: 'Did you hear? Unlearned men are rising up and storming the kingdom of heaven while we, with all our knowledge, unfeelingly wallow in flesh and blood' (ibid., VIII, 8). There followed the celebrated scene in a Milan garden in 386: Augustine's instantaneous conversion to Christianity. It was quite in keeping with the process whereby he had suppressed his sense of guilt by turning to asceticism, or, in concrete terms, to the depreciation of marriage as compared with celibacy.

While walking in the garden Augustine heard a child's voice chanting: 'Take it, read it!' again and again. He picked up a bible that was lying open there and read the following passage: 'Let us walk honestly, as in the day; not in rioting and drunkenness, not in chambering and wantonness, not in strife and envying. But put ye on the Lord Jesus Christ, and make not provision for the flesh, to fulfil the lusts thereof' (Rom. 13: 13). The scales fell from his eyes: the ultimate foe was concupiscence, evil lust, sexual desire, carnal longing. 'All the darkness of doubt had fled', wrote Augustine. 'Thou didst turn me unto Thee, so that I sought no wife nor any ambition for this world' ('Confessiones' VIII, 12).

The effect of Augustine's conversion to Christianity, which made him an enemy of the pleasures he had once enjoyed, was to lead him to classify women not as partners but as means to self-gratification, the role in which celibatarians still cast them to this day. On Holy Saturday in the year 387, he and his son Adeodatus were baptised by Ambrose, the eulogist of virginity, whom he greatly venerated. The motherless Adeodatus, who was very dear to Augustine even though he had been 'begotten in sin' (ibid., IX, 6), died three years later at the age of eighteen.

Although the vast majority of Catholic textbooks state that Augustine, once converted, championed 'the sanctity of marriage' against the Manichaeans, this is inaccurate: he merely championed marital *procreation* against them. None of the Fathers of the Church grasped the true meaning of marriage and Augustine least of all, neither while cohabiting with a mistress during his Manichaean phase, nor – to put it mildly – during the monastic, episcopal phase of his career as a Christian convert.

The contraceptive method favoured by the Manichaeans, the rhythm method – on which Augustine poured scorn after his conversion – is the only method that can now be employed with the blessing of the Catholic Church. It was the one method sanctioned by supreme authority at the Synod of Bishops in Rome in 1980, which firmly rejected contraception as such. Prominently featured in the television news broadcasts and current events programmes of the time were a Catholic man and wife (a model couple of the Knaus-Ogino-cervical-smear variety) whom Pope John Paul II had enlisted as his personal consultants. It is not uninteresting to note that Augustine, far from regarding this married couple as papal paragons, would have characterised them as 'adulterous' and 'whorish'. 'Did you not formerly advise us,' he thundered, writing of the Manichaeans, 'to pay the greatest possible heed to the period ensuing upon the monthly purification, when a woman may be expected to conceive, and to abstain from intercourse at that time lest a soul become imprisoned in flesh? It follows therefrom that, in your opinion, marriage exists to appease desire, not to generate children' ('De moribus Manichaeorum', 18, 65).

Augustine's Manichaean avoidance of the immediately post-menstrual period had accorded with the current medical belief that this was a woman's most fecund time of the month. He expressed himself in even stronger terms elsewhere: 'What you most abominate in marriage is that children should be born, and so you make your hearers [*auditores*] adulterers with their own wives if they ensure that the wives with whom they have intercourse fail to conceive . . . They desire no children, for whose sake alone marriages are contracted. Why, then, are you not among those that forbid marriage ... if you seek to deprive marriage of that which constitutes it? For, if that be taken away, husbands become vile lovers, wives whores, marriage beds brothels, and fathers-in-law procurers' ('Contra Faustum', 15, 7).

Speaking at a general audience on 8 October 1980, the Pope broached the subject of adultery with one's own wife in terms that were wholly Augustinian, Thomasian, Jeromian, Stoic, Philonian – in short, opposed to the pleasures of the flesh. Unlike Augustine, however, he was not referring to those who practise the rhythm method of birth-control; his targets were those who employ 'unnatural' methods, so called. The Pope excepts and approves the rhythm method as 'natural', but he cannot invoke Augustine, who attacked that method with particular vehemence after employing it himself. Augustine called it a 'procurer's method', whereas John Paul II, in his apostolic exhortation of 1981, 'Familiaris consortio', no longer included it under the heading of contraception but divorced it from other, evil, methods and praised it to the skies: 'The choice of the natural rhythms involves accepting the cycle of the person, that is, the woman, and thereby accepting dialogue, reciprocal respect, shared responsibility and self-control.' It meant 'living personal love with its requirement of fidelity'.

It was only when he turned to other contraceptive methods that the Pope rejoined Augustine in stating that those who practise them 'act as "arbiters" of the divine plane and ... manipulate and degrade human sexuality'. In 'Familiaris consortio' John Paul II extended 'a pressing invitation' to theologians 'to study further the difference, both anthro-pological and moral, between contraception and recourse to the rhythm of the cycle'. Theologians must feel unequal to this papal request, and the Pope will doubtless have to work out the difference for himself. To cite Franz Böckle, Germany's best-known Catholic moral theologian: 'One should not be surprised if harassed priests, still less the overtaxed laity, fail to perceive the metaphysical distinction between "natural" and "unnatural" methods.'

Contraception was simply contraception to Augustine, whereas John Paul II's 'Familiaris consortio' of 1981 called upon theologians to discover differences where none exist, theologically speaking, and the sole distinction is medical. Although the sanctioning of the rhythm method is to be welcomed – the Greek Orthodox Church is still thoroughly Augustinian in this respect and even less progressive than the Roman Catholic – progress in relation to Augustine should not consist of a hair-splitting process whereby a pope selects one particular method and gives it his blessing; it should mean that, at long last, he leaves this whole vexed question to the married couples concerned.

John Paul II has, in fact, changed tack a little since his encomium on the rhythm method in 1981. At another of his weekly general audiences on 6 September 1984, during the eighth of a series of twelve addresses on birth-control, he warned the faithful against 'abusing' the Church-approved method of birth-control. This abuse occurred whenever married couples sought 'for dishonest reasons' to keep their number of children 'below the birth-rate morally proper to their family'. However, no pope should meddle in the question of method, nor speak of a 'morally proper' birth-rate, nor impugn the motives of married couples.

Unlike the present head of the Church, therefore, Augustine did not divide contraceptive methods into two categories, one permissible and the other not: all contraception was impermissible to him – in fact he assailed the present Pope's favoured method with particular vehemence because of the particular use he himself had made of it. There is, however, one passage in which he also referred to the so-called artificial methods of birth-control: 'Sometimes [*Aliquando*] this lustful cruelty or cruel lust is such that they even procure poisons of infertility [*sterilitatis venena*] . . . so that the wife actually becomes her husband's whore or he an adulterer with his own wife' ('De nuptiis et concupiscentia', 1, 15, 17). This dictum, known as 'Aliquando' for short, was destined to play a major part in the Church's campaign against contraception. It was heard, for instance, during the Second Vatican Council in 1962, when Cardinal Ernesto Ruffini, archbishop of Palermo, cited it in condemnation of the Pill.

Another of Augustine's pronouncements on contraception was to play at least as fateful a part in the long-standing debate. 'It is impermissible and vile,' he wrote, 'to have intercourse with one's wife and avoid the conception of progeny; Onan, the son of Judah, did this and was slain by God in consequence' ('De conjugiis adulterinis', 2, 12). That Onan should have met his end after displeasing the Almighty by practising *coitus interruptus* has contributed in no small measure to the neuroses of many married couples to whom the Old Testament passage has repeatedly been cited as a warning, even in our own century. 'Small wonder, therefore,' Pius XI wrote in 1930, 'if Holy Writ bears witness that the Divine Majesty regards with supreme detestation this horrible crime and at times has punished it with death. As St Augustine notes,

"Intercourse even with one's legitimate wife is unlawful and wicked where the conception of offspring is prevented. Onan, the son of Judah, did this, and the Lord killed him for it"' ('Casti connubii', II). God's 'supreme detestation' of those who employ contraceptive methods was used by Pius XI to reinforce an already alarming story. He added it from his own store of papal invention, deliberately overlooking the fact that Onan's was not a marital misdemeanour but connected with the right of inheritance. Onan, the multipurpose whipping boy, became one of those who wished 'to gratify their desires without the consequent burden'. 'Casti connubii', the first anti-contraception encyclical of our century, converted him into a married couples' bugbear.

Who was the real Onan, the man whose name is so commonly but unjustly associated with the masturbatory sense of onanism? Onan did not masturbate; he practised coitus interruptus for dynastic reasons. If a man died childless, it was the duty of his closest male relative, usually his brother, to have intercourse with the widow on her late husband's behalf and thus provide him with an heir to his name and possessions. Genesis relates that Er, Judah's first-born son, was 'wicked in the sight of the Lord', who duly slew him. 'And Judah said unto Onan, Go in unto thy brother's wife, and marry her, and raise up seed to thy brother. And Onan knew that the seed should not be his; and it came to pass, when he went in unto his brother's wife, that he spilled it on the ground, lest that he should give seed to his brother. And the thing which he did displeased the Lord: wherefore he slew him also.' It suited Augustine's anticontraception campaign to enlist this passage as a deterrent. Others were more cautious. Neither Jerome nor Thomas Aquinas used it to reinforce the ban on contraception.

Although the Manichaeans aspired to halt procreation because they wanted no more particles of light imprisoned in devilish matter, they did permit their second-class adherents, the *auditores*, to contract childless marriages. Augustine, the ex-Manichaean and Christian convert, regarded procreation as the sole significance and purpose of marriage and condemned sexual pleasure as evil. The Manichaeans tolerated sexual pleasure and condemned procreation. Once converted, Augustine tolerated the former only as a means to the latter. 'I am persuaded that nothing so turns a man's spirit from the heights as a woman's caresses and those bodily contacts without which a man cannot possess his wife' ('Soliloquia', 1, 10). Like the Stoics, he now saw procreation as the sole excuse for the conjugal act.

That procreation was good and sexual pleasure evil constituted the twin premises that underpinned his stringent demands on the married. Since the second of those premises was false, the result was a disaster for all concerned. However right Augustine was to oppose the Manichaeans, his campaign against Julian, the Pelagian bishop of Eclanum, was largely unjustified. The Pelagians took a positive view of sexual pleasure, regarding it as a natural and in no way sinful aspect of married life. In Augustine's eyes, that made them gainsayers of original sin.

Julian, a bishop's son from an upper-class Apulian family, was a married priest and a learned man, meaning that he had studied Greek. His wife Titia was the daughter of Bishop Aemilius of Benevento. Installed as bishop of Eclanum by Pope Innocent I in 416, Julian was excommunicated and expelled from his diocese by Pope Zosimus in 418 as a result of the Pelagian controversy, in which Augustine was deeply involved. Julian, for whom Augustine was simply 'the African', died in Sicily some time after 450. He ended his chequered career as resident tutor to a Pelagian family. Although friends inscribed 'Here lies Julian, a Catholic bishop' on his tombstone, Augustine the celibatarian had defeated Julian the married man and, with him, married couples everywhere.

Like his patristic predecessors and contemporaries Augustine debated whether Adam and Eve had engaged in sexual intercourse in Paradise. 'It is asked with perfect justification,' he wrote in 389, 'how we are to conceive of the union between man and woman prior to sin, and whether the benediction "Be fruitful, and multiply, and replenish the earth" should be comprehended in a carnal or a spiritual sense. For we can also construe that benediction spiritually and assume that it was not transformed into carnal fertility until after the Fall' ('De Genesi contra Manichaeos', 1, 19). Augustine went on to imagine the nature of this spiritually construed fertility: 'To what end was the woman to assist the man? That he should, by means of a spiritual connection, bring forth spiritual fruits; that is to say, good works in praise of God' (ibid., 2, 11). Augustine's conclusion: the union between man and woman in Paradise was asexual (ibid., 1, 19).

Augustine subsequently wavered in this view. In 401 he hazarded three possibilities: either the Creator's benediction – 'Be fruitful and multiply' – should be construed 'mystically and metaphorically'; or Adam and Eve might have 'had children without intercourse, in some other manner, as a gift from the Almighty Creator who had, after all, created them without parents'; or, finally, the children of Adam and Eve might have been generated by physical union proper. In this particular treatise ('De bono conjugali', 2) Augustine refrained from passing judgment on such a knotty problem.

In another work begun just after the above in 401 but not completed until 415, he again broached the possibility that children might have been begotten in Paradise without the sexual act. Perhaps, he wrote, they had been generated by purely spiritual love 'uncorrupted by lust' ('De Genesi ad litteram', 3, 21). In the course of time, however, he came to the conclusion that, even in Paradise, procreation had entailed sexual intercourse. This conclusion derived from his low opinion of the female sex. Gregory of Nyssa and John Chrysostom had been wrong, he said, in their contention that no sexual intercourse occurred in Paradise. For their error he substituted a new one – a piece of nonsense whose scathing indictment of womankind was later cited with approval by Thomas Aquinas:

> I cannot see to what end woman was created as a helpmeet for man if the generative purpose be excluded, nor can I understand why this purpose is excluded notwithstanding. To what end is woman given to man, if not as an aid to the bearing of children? Perchance that they should till the soil together? If help had been needed to that end, a man would have been of more assistance to the man. The same may be said of consolation in solitude. How much more agreeable it is for life and conversation when two [male] friends dwell together than when man and woman cohabit.
>
> (Ibid., 9, 5–9)

According to Augustine, therefore, sexual intercourse took place in Paradise because Eve would have been no help to Adam in spiritual matters. At the same time, God had created her as Adam's helpmate in accordance with the biblical, male-conceived story of the Creation.

Women, to their great dismay, had been pronounced fit only for childbearing and unqualified for anything of a spiritual or intellectual nature. Augustine's perception of them was later, as we shall see, reformulated by Thomas Aquinas, thus: the wife is an aid to procreation (*adiutorium generationis*) and useful about the house but unimportant to her husband's spiritual life. The rearing of children entails cooking; as for churchgoing, that – to the Fathers of the Church – went without saying. Augustine was, therefore, the heavy-handed originator of what Germans refer to as 'the three Ks': *Kinder, Küche, Kirche*. That a woman's predominant concerns are her children and her kitchen continues to be the Catholic hierarchy's primary theological perception of the female sex.

In 'De civitate Dei', written during the years 413–36, Augustine went on to state that 'The difference in their physical conformation shows clearly that man and woman were so created as to grow and multiply and replenish the earth by generating offspring, and no purpose would be served by rejecting this literal interpretation [of the words "Be fruitful and multiply"]' (14, 22). He now described his previous view as absurd and expressly withdrew it in his 'Retractationes', a corrective work on which he embarked three years before his death.

So sexual intercourse had, after all, occurred in the Garden of Eden. This rebutted the Manichaean view that procreation was of devilish origin, but what of sexual desire? Had that, too, existed in Paradise? Augustine, being an anti-Pelagian, naturally replied in the negative. Before the Fall, sexual intercourse was unaccompanied by any sexual excitement of the kind that had characterised it since. In Paradise, will-power had controlled the sexual organs just as it now controlled the hands and feet. 'Why should we not believe that people before the Fall could control their sexual organs as they do their other limbs?' ('De Genesi ad litteram', 9, 10). 'After all, we move our hands and feet to their appropriate functions whenever we choose and with no rebellion on their part. Personal experience and observation prove that great facility can be obtained . . . Why then, should we refuse to believe that the organs of generation, in the absence of that lust which is a just penalty imposed because of the sin of rebellion, could have obeyed man's will as compliantly as do his other organs?' ('De civitate Dei', 14, 23). 'In Paradise, then, generative seed would have been sown by the husband and the wife would have conceived as need prescribed, and all would have been accomplished by deliberate choice, not uncontrollable lust' (ibid., 14, 24). 'Without the lascivious promptings of lust, with perfect serenity of soul and body, the husband would have seminated into his wife's womb' (ibid., 14, 26).

Augustine devoted a whole chapter of 'De civitate Dei' to proving his abstruse idea that the sexual organs of the paradisal or ideal couple were wholly subject to their volition.

> There are people who can move their ears, either separately or together, and people who can move the entire scalp, for as far as the hair extends, toward the brow and retract it again at will without moving their heads. Others, again, having swallowed an abundance of the most diverse objects, are able to bring them up at will unscathed, as though from a purse, by slightly contracting the stomach . . . What this proves is that, even at the present time, when we are living with all the afflictions of corruptible flesh, the human body can in certain cases be marvellously obedient in motions and conditions that transcend the normal course of nature, and which show that, before man sinned by rebellion and was punished with the rebellion of his passions, his human organs, without the excitement of lust, could have obeyed his human will for all the purposes of parenthood . . . Once man was disobedient to God he was bound to be disobedient to himself.
>
> (Ibid., 14, 24)

So the sexual organs were 'not moved by the will' but 'excited by lust'. Whence came this peculiar characteristic? Augustine's answer: 'In punishment for that sin, disobedience was requited with, in a word, disobedience' (ibid., 14, 15). The body refused to obey the mind so that man would be aware of his disobedience toward God (ibid., 14, 24). The penalty for the Fall was 'particularly and most properly' sexual (ibid., 14, 20). That sin declares itself mainly in the realm of sex remains the view of the celibatarian Catholic establishment and is rooted in Augustine's antisexual flights of fancy.

His observation of the fact that there are people who can waggle their ears was destined to be accepted, even in our own century, as proof that procreation was originally pleasureless. Many authorities seek to excuse his nonsensical remarks on the deliberate control of the orgasm by pleading his defective knowledge of the human nervous system, almost as if his line of argument had been prompted by a medical misapprehension. Since Augustine himself stressed that 'it is certain that man and woman were created in the beginning just as we see and perceive them now, as two human beings of different sex' (ibid., 14, 22), and since it was precisely this premiss that persuaded him to abandon the theory of purely spiritual generation, Augustine's defenders claim that a knowledge of the current state of medical research would have dissuaded him from postulating that the human sexual organs were controllable by will-power prior to the Fall.

They are mistaken. Augustine would have devised some other way of transforming sexual pleasure into a consequence of the Fall. His concern was not medical; he was determined to outlaw sexual pleasure by any and every means. The current state of medical research had no bearing on the matter. It was the Stoic ideal of equanimity and self-control, coupled with his own peculiar and characteristic horror of sex, that prompted his long-enduring discrimination against a major aspect of human existence. 'Far be it from us to believe that the kind of lust [*libido*] which made the couple in Paradise ashamed of their nakedness was meant to be the only means of fulfilling the command given them by God when He blessed them ... This passion had no place before they sinned; it was only after the Fall, when their nature had lost its power to exact obedience from the sexual organs ... that lust came into being' (ibid., 14, 21).

Where 'lust' or sexual desire was concerned, Augustine drew marginally closer to the Pelagians during the last decade of his life. He conceded the possibility that it had existed in Paradise, though only in a thoroughly restrained and regulated form. A polemic addressed to the Pelagians in 420 suggested either that sexual desire had been entirely absent from intercourse in Paradise, or, at most, that it had arisen at the behest of the will when intercourse was rationally deemed needful in the interests of procreation. 'If it pleases you to assume that the latter form prevailed in Paradise; if it seems right to you that children in that fortunate estate were generated by a carnal desire [*concupiscentia carnalis*] of that nature, which neither anticipated nor impeded nor exceeded the bidding of the will, I shall not contest that assumption' ('Contra duas epistolas Pelagianorum', I, 17).

Toward the end of his life, therefore, Augustine conceded the existence in Paradise of a species of sexual desire submissive to the human will and intellect. His last, uncompleted work, the 'Opus imperfectum contra Julianum' (429–30), re-examines the same problem, which seems to have plagued him to the very end. Julian had asserted that sexual desire was the body's sixth sense, a neutral form of energy that could be used for good or ill, and that the sexual urge had existed in Paradise as it was at present. Augustine, for his part, insisted that sexual intercourse in Paradise must have taken a different form: either sexual desire had been wholly absent, in which case it was a vice, or it had been present but subject to the will and later vitiated by sin, for the nature of sexual desire in Paradise was such that it 'arose only at the bidding of the soul' ('Opus imperfectum', 6, 22) and had not 'suppressed the thinking of the mind' in the form of 'inordinate lust' (ibid., 4, 39). Sexual desire in its present form was 'an evil' (ibid., 4, 23) – indeed, it could even be described as a sin 'because it was engendered by sin and strives after the same' (ibid., 1, 71). Thus, Augustine's sexual phobia accompanies him to the grave.

He believed that sexual desire, which clouded the mind and had ceased to obey the will, degraded human procreation to the level of the beasts. 'Of course, it does not follow that this power of propagation, which was left intact even after the Fall, is identical with what it would have been had man not sinned. For once man had departed his place of honour – once he had sinned and placed himself on a level with the beasts – then did he also become like them in the matter of procreation, even though that light of reason which makes man an image of God has not been extinguished altogether' ('De civitate Dei', 22, 24).

Married couples put the evil of sexual desire to good use only when each and every conjugal act served the sole purpose of marriage, namely, procreation; in other words, when their intention before and during the consummation of marriage was to have a child. 'That which cannot be done without lust,' Augustine emphasised in 422, 'must be done in such a way that it is not done for lust's sake' ('Contra Julianum', 5, 9). And again: 'Were there another means of generating offspring, all sexual intercourse would quite clearly imply a surrender to lust, and would thus be a reprehensible use of that evil.' Because no human being could be begotten in any other way, however, married couples who had intercourse with procreation in mind made 'a good use of that evil' (ibid., 5, 46). In other words, any form of manipulation engaged in for generative purposes would be better than the conjugal act itself.

Louise Brown, the world's first test-tube baby, was thus half-way to being Augustine's dream-child, her mother having conceived her without experiencing any sexual pleasure. The only feature that would have worried Augustine was the necessity for (pleasurable) masturbation on the father's part. Had his semen been obtained by surgical means, however, the paradisal state would have been more or less attained and all Augustine's requirements and conditions fulfilled. Discounting the anaesthetic, there would have been none of that sex-induced clouding of the mind which so deeply disturbed Augustine and was later so deplored by Thomas Aquinas.

The Virgin Mary exemplifies the esteem in which pleasureless conception was held. Augustine adjusted her image to suit the celibatarian standards of his day, most of which continue to hold good in our own century: she conceived Jesus as a virgin, exempted from the need to feel ashamed of sexual pleasure, and bore him without pain ('Enchiridion', 41). All other luckless women remained subject to the curse laid on them after the Fall: 'In sorrow thou shalt bring forth children' (Genesis 3: 16).

Since parthenogenesis and artificial insemination were not normal occurrences and sexual pleasure could not be excluded from ordinary, unprivileged procreation – Augustine wrote that he had yet to meet a married man who could claim to have had intercourse 'solely in the hope of conception' ('De bono conjugali', 13) – Augustine had a formula ready: where sexual pleasure was concerned, a distinction must be drawn between 'feeling' it and 'seeking' it. 'Distinguish clearly between these two', he adjured his readers. Carnal sensation was good, carnal desire evil. Thus, while the intercourse undertaken with the proper end in view (i.e. procreation) was good, it was sinful for man and wife to yield to lust ('Opus imperfectum', 4, 29).

This plea for marital schizophrenia occurs in Augustine's final polemic against Julian, which death prevented him from completing. For him it was the end, but for devout Christian couples it was only the start of an insoluble problem that repeatedly reared its head during every Augustinian revival, e.g. in Jansenism. At the age of forty-eight, Louis XIV complained to the father confessor of his second wife, Madame de Maintenon, that she showed scant enthusiasm for the conjugal act. The priest in question, the bishop of Chartres, Monseigneur Godet des Marais, thereupon assured her that it was a source of grace 'to do from pure virtue what so many women perform with passion and, thus, without merit'. In other words, the less you feel, the more you endear yourself to God.

Augustine believed that he had found apostolic confirmation of his precept that it was sinful to seek pleasure in the conjugal act. He rendered Paul's controversial words: 'But I speak this by permission [by way of concession], and not of commandment' (ibid., 7: 6) as 'I say this by way of excuse [*venia*]' and related it to the resumption of marital intercourse. He argued, again and again, that marital intercourse required Paul's pardon. 'By granting pardon, the Apostle manifestly branded [it as] a sin' ('De peccato originali', 42). Or again: 'Where pardon must be granted, the presence of guilt can on no grounds be denied' ('De nuptiis et concupiscentia', 1, 14). His last attack on Julian, too, states: 'The Apostle would not have granted pardon had he not perceived that a sin was in evidence' ('Opus imperfectum', 4, 29).

Now that generative intercourse was guiltless even in Augustine's eyes, however, the excusing of the conjugal act could apply only to intercourse engaged in for 'pleasure in pleasure', not for 'pleasure in generation' ('De nuptiis et concupiscentia', 1, 14). Augustine naturally stressed that Paul's readiness to excuse it should not be exaggerated. Excessive sexual pleasure could be a mortal sin, even in marital intercourse, when it became 'inordinate'. The apostle's indulgence and forgiveness did not cover any such loss of self-control, which made the husband 'an adulterer' with his own wife ('Contra Julianum', 2, 7, 20). The idea that pleasurable marital intercourse could be a mortal sin was to fascinate and preoccupy theologians and popes until our own century, as, for instance, when van de Velde's 'Ideal Marriage' was condemned and banned.

That marital intercourse could under certain circumstances be pardonable – i.e. only a venial sin and, given the wish to procreate, positively sinless despite the influence of sensual pleasure, which original sin had invested with so sinister a power over human beings – Augustine ascribed to the three 'goods' of marriage, which were later (from the time of the early Schoolmen onward) described as the 'saving graces' of marriage. These three 'goods' rendered the conjugal act tolerable, justified it morally, and offset the evil of attendant pleasure provided this was not 'inordinate'.

The three 'goods' are (i) progeny, (ii) fidelity, and (iii) indissolubility. 'The good of marriage is threefold: fidelity, progeny, and the sacrament. Fidelity does not permit sexual intercourse to occur outside marriage; the good of progeny ensures that children are accepted with love, well nourished, and dutifully reared; the sacrament ensures that marriage is not dissolved or that a divorced wife does not marry anew' ('De Genesi ad litteram', 9, 7). Thanks to these three compensating assets, marital intercourse could now – according to Augustine – be either excused (wholly guiltless) or pardonable (venially sinful). Intercourse was guiltless only when engaged in for procreative purposes. Marital intercourse prompted by lust, though pardoned by the Apostle because of the good of fidelity within marriage, was not guiltless, therefore, but only pardonable.

Marital intercourse being a joint activity, that left one question unanswered: what if one participant was prompted by lust and the other not? Having considered this point, too, Augustine drew a suitable distinction: persons who *demanded* intercourse with their spouses (for other than procreative purposes) committed a pardonable or venial sin; persons who *engaged in* intercourse at the request of their spouses, but neither felt nor sought sexual pleasure, were guiltless and in no need of apostolic forgiveness. Rather at odds with his theory that procreation was the sole legitimate purpose of marriage, Augustine defined even *debitum reddere* ('rendering what is due', or the performance of one's conjugal duty on request) as guiltless: 'To fulfil one's obligation entails no guilt, but to demand the fulfilment of that obligation over and above the requirements of procreation is a venial sin' ('Sermones', 51, 13). The married were under a strict obligation not to fail their partners lest the latter be tempted to commit an even graver sin, declared Augustine, so he did not deny the Pauline definition of marriage as a remedy for lust.

The archbishop of Chartres, Madame de Maintenon's confessor, gave her some thoroughly Augustinian advice after Louis XIV had complained to him of her distaste for the conjugal act. 'One is duty-bound,' he told her, 'to serve as a haven for the weakness of the husband, who would otherwise go astray.' In other words, the fact that she felt nothing, thanks to her frigidity, was all to her credit.

Given this scale of values, it need hardly be added that Augustine condemned intercourse with menstruating, pregnant, and post-menopausal wives: 'Proper conjugal chastity . . . obtains during menstruation and pregnancy, nor has it union with one no longer able to conceive on account of age' ('Contra Julianum', 3, 21).

Because of his blinkered view of marriage as a procreative institution, his total exclusion of personal factors from the conjugal act, and his attempt to suppress sexuality, Augustine made exorbitant demands on the faithful. Christians must permanently focus their gaze on eternal life, he declared. The greater their love for the immortal, the fiercer their hatred of the ephemeral. That was why the Christian husband abhorred the mortal bond of matrimony and concentrated on 'that which can accompany us into that kingdom'. He also sought to mould his wife accordingly. 'He loves her humanity and hates her femininity' ('De sermone Domini in monte', 1, 15 and 1, 41).

In view of this one-sided emphasis on the generative function, it is hardly surprising that Augustine thought polygamy in the male preferable to loving and desiring one woman for her own sake alone:

> I find it more commendable to use the fertility of many women for an unselfish end than to use the flesh of one woman for her own sake. For in the former instance man aspired to a good that befitted those Old Testament times, while in the latter his object is the assuaging of a desire aimed at earthly pleasure. For that reason, those in whom the Apostle in I Corinthians 7: 6 condoned carnal intercourse with a woman because of their incontinence stand lower on the road to God than those who, despite their many wives, had marital intercourse with the sole intention of begetting children.
>
> ('De doctrina christiana', 3, 18)

This does not, of course, mean that Augustine favoured the introduction of polygamy, which he restricted to the Old Testament era. It was polyandry rather than polygyny that conflicted with the system of Creation, according to him, because wives were their husbands' servants. 'Neither does one servant have many masters, as many servants have one master. Thus we read that none of the holy women served two or more living husbands, but that many holy women served one husband . . . That does not run counter to the nature of matrimony' ('De bono conjugali', 17, 20). Whereas the civil marriage contract of the contemporary Roman legal code made no mention of the wife's subjection to the husband (cf. Kari Elisabeth Borresen, 'Subordination et équivalence', 1968, p. 82f.), Augustine drew attention to the Christians' marriage contract, which carried their bishop's signature and stressed that the wife was subject to her husband ('Sermones', 37, 6, 7 and 332, 4). He cited a model adherent of the wife-slave ethic in the person of his mother Monica.

> When she had attained marriageable age she was given to a husband whom she served as if he were her master . . . She likewise endured his marital infidelity, with the result that she never quarrelled with him . . . While many women, although they

had gentler husbands, bore the marks of blows on their disfigured faces and blamed their husbands in conversation with their women friends, Monica laid the blame at their own door for neglecting to keep silent. She reminded them, jocularly yet earnestly, that they ought, ever since the reading of the marriage contract, to have been aware that it had made servants of them, and that, in consideration of their status, they should not rebel against their masters.

Augustine went on to state that the fact that Monica was never beaten by her irascible husband Patricius, his father, had prompted many women to emulate her example. 'The women who followed her example were grateful to her, whereas those who failed to do so continued to suffer ill-treatment' ('Confessiones', IX, 9). It is a long-enduring myth that the Christian religion spelled the liberation of women.

That Augustine's sexual hostility meant more to him than his emphasis on the generative purpose of every conjugal act is evident from his advocacy of the so-called Josephan, or Marian, marriage, a married life of absolute continence such as those described by many hagiographers in the course of ecclesiastical history. 'Your husband does not cease to be your spouse because you jointly abstain from carnal conjunction,' he assured a woman whose relations with her husband were wholly sexless. 'On the contrary: you will, as spouses, be all the holier the more holily you abide by your joint resolve' (Ep. 262, 4). Morally speaking, he esteemed virginity superior to matrimony and matrimony without sexual intercourse superior to matrimony with it. By jointly abstaining from intercourse, married couples furthered their moral development. 'Anyone who has attained to perfect love of God in our day must surely have but a spiritual desire for children' ('De bono conjugali', 3, 3; 8, 9; 17, 9).

In view of the soul-destroying potency of sexual desire, Augustine demanded continence on Sundays and feast days, during Lent, while preparing for baptism, and at times of prayer in general. Prayer, he declared, was more pleasing to God when spiritual, in other words, when man was free from carnal desire ('De fide et operibus', 6, 8). He was not alone in making such demands. His contemporary Jerome inferred them from I Corinthians 7: 5: 'Defraud [deny] ye not one the other, except it be with consent for a time, that ye may give yourselves to fasting and prayer; and come together again . . .' Jerome's interpretation: 'The Apostle denies the possibility of prayer at the time when a

man has intercourse with his wife. Thus, if prayer be rendered impossible by coitus, how much more so is the greater thing, the receiving of
the body of Christ ... I appeal to the conscience of those who
communicate on the very day on which they have had marital intercourse' (Ep. 48, 15). Origen (d. 253 or 254) had also banned intercourse
prior to Communion: 'Anyone who enters the sanctuary of the church
after the conjugal act and his own pollution, presumptuously intending
to receive the eucharistic bread, does so wantonly. He dishonours and
profanes that which is sacred' ('Select. in Ezech.', 7).

Paul's words had been turned upside down. Having begun by urging
his married readers not to deny each other, he went on to speak of
mutual consent. His joint agreement to abstain from intercourse for
prayer's sake was transformed by degrees into a strictly supervised ban
on intercourse before and after prayer, on Sundays and feast days,
during Lent, and at as many other times as possible. As to what happens
when one wishes to procreate on a Sunday, and what fate lies in store
for any child conceived on that day, more will be said of that in due
course.

SEVEN

The Growth of Celibacy

Catholic celibacy has heathen roots, as we have seen. Celibatarian rules of purity hail from the Stone Age of religious consciousness and originated in fear of the unapproachably numinous, the awe-inspiringly divine. They have no place in the gospel of God's love.

Many heathen priests castrated themselves to avoid pollution by sexual intercourse and render themselves pure, sanctified intercessors between mankind and the deity or deities they served. Cultic castration was common to Babylonia, Lebanon, Phoenicia, Cyprus, Syria, the Artemic cult at Ephesus, the Osiris cult in Egypt, and the Phrygian Cybele-Atys cult, which gained a wide following in both East and West (cf. Browe, 'Zur Geschichte der Entmannung', p. 13f.).

Deschner's 'Das Kreuz mit der Kirche: Eine Sexualgeschichte des Christentums' traces the history of the age-old belief that sexual abstinence brings one closer to the divine. According to Demosthenes (d. 322 BC) it was necessary to 'practise continence for a certain number of days' before entering a temple and touching its sacred appurtenances. Tibullus (d.*c.* 17 BC) wrote: 'I bid you keep your distance from the altar, all who have enjoyed the pleasures of love the previous night' (Eleg. II, 11). Plutarch (d.*c.* AD 120) likewise warned against entering a temple and making sacrifice after sex unless a night's sleep had intervened ('Quaest. conv.', 3, 6). A temple inscription at Pergamum insists on one day's purification after marital and two days' after extramarital intercourse.

The Catholic Church, which treasures celibatarian echoes from antiquity like a noble pedigree, has no hesitation in reinterpreting them to suit its book. Pius XI wrote of celibacy that 'The ancient Romans had already recognized the seemly nature of such conduct. One of their laws, which ran as follows: "One must approach the gods in purity", was cited by the greatest of their orators' ('The Catholic Priesthood', 1936). In other words, Pius did not shrink from representing Cicero as an advocate of celibacy. He did so by equating the purity to which the Roman referred ('De legibus', 2, 8) with celibacy and, by extension, marriage with impurity.

The compulsory celibacy of the Catholic priesthood as we know it today was born of the hostility toward marriage and sex, such as we explored in the last chapter, entertained by leading theologians, and by the popes in particular. Although the process of celibatarian desexualis- ation began during the early centuries of the Christian era, it was not juridically consummated until much later, and in two stages. The first of these came in 1139, when Pope Innocent II proclaimed that ordina- tion was an impediment to marriage. Under canon law, matrimony and priesthood were mutually exclusive, so any marriage contracted after ordination was invalid. Having thus equipped themselves with the means to prevent priests from marrying, the leaders of the Church fashioned another instrument of control at the Council of Trent (1545–63), which introduced an obligatory form for the solemnisation of matrimony. Marriage had hitherto been free from formal constraints, so secret but valid marriages could be entered into without a priest or witnesses. The new, obligatory form of marriage before a qualified priest and witnesses prevented persons who had married in secret from being ordained as priests. From 1139 onwards, therefore, it was impossible for priests to marry; from Trent onwards, married men were precluded from becoming priests. The age of the permitted priestly marriage was succeeded by that of the clandestine and persecuted priestly marriage. After Trent the only remaining alternative was concubinage, a sad but not uncommon last resort. The imposition of celibacy was an arduous process, less for its instigators and zealots than for those whom it affected. Many of them, especially the women, were destroyed by it.

The papal obsession with 'severing intercourse between priests and women by means of everlasting anathema', as that ardent champion of celibacy, Pope Gregory VII (d. 1085), demanded (v. Hefele, 'Konzilien- geschichte', vol. 5, p. 22), had been voiced in the Church long before him. The first appreciable and official step in that direction was taken, early in the fourth century, by Canon 33 of the Spanish Synod of Elvira.

This decreed that 'bishops, priests, deacons, and all clergy celebrating Mass are to be instructed to abstain from intercourse with their wives and beget no more children. All who act to the contrary are to be expelled from the priesthood.' This was not yet celibacy proper. There was no insistence that priests be unmarried or send their wives away, but the ban on further marital intercourse was the first chapter in a long history of suppression and oppression.

The Elviran demand had little effect on the Church as a whole, and it should at once be added that the Eastern Church did not join in the Western Church's enforcement of celibacy, which ultimately became a major cause of the Great Schism. Elvira was only the start, however. Increasing efforts to enforce celibacy were made by successive synods and Fathers of the Church, especially popes. Antimarital laws similar to those enacted by the Synod of Elvira were proposed at the First General Council of Nicaea (325), but the attempt to impose them on the entire Church failed. Bishop Hosius of Cordoba, who had played a leading role at Elvira, is assumed to have been the proposer of a ban on priestly marriages at Nicaea as well. We are told by the historian Socrates (d. 439) that Bishop Paphnutius of Egypt (fl. c. 300), himself an unmarried and much-venerated man who had lost an eye and a hamstring during the persecution of the Christians under Emperor Diocletian, declared that marriage was an honourable estate, and that priests should not be subjected to so heavy a burden. It was sufficient that those who entered the clergy unwed should remain so, and no priest should be parted from the wife he had married as a layman in years gone by. It is immaterial whether Paphnutius' intervention in the debate was historical or apocryphal, as some authorities – mainly Latin advocates of celibacy – were later to claim. Whatever the truth, it clearly illustrates Eastern practice and the contemporary opposition to celibacy.

The ensuing synods varied in their approach. The Synod of Gangra (340–41) defended married priests and censured those unwilling to attend Masses celebrated by them. The so-called Apostolic Canons (c. 380) prescribed the excommunication of any bishop or priest who repudiated his wife on the pretext of piety, whereas the Council of Carthage (390) placed clergy under the same obligation as Elvira (Canon 2), likewise a synod convened at Carthage in 401 (Canon 4). Even harsher demands were made. The Roman synod of Pope Innocent I (d. 417) declared in 402 that 'bishops, priests and deacons must be unmarried' (Canon 3). In practice, however, canon law remained unaffected. Married men continued to be ordained, and many subsequent synods, e.g. that of Arles in 443 (Canon 3f.) and the Third Synod of Orléans in 538 (Canon 2), confined themselves to insisting on marital continence. 'Priests and deacons may not share the same bed and the same room with their wives, lest they be suspected of carnal intercourse' (Fourth Synod of Orléans, 541, Canon 17). The Synod of Clermont (535) decreed that 'he that is ordained a deacon or priest may not continue in marital intercourse. He becomes the brother of his existing wife' (Canon 12).

The Synod of Tours (567) regulated the married life of bishops: 'A bishop may look upon his wife as a sister only. He must always, wherever he goes, be surrounded by clergy, and his own and his wife's apartments must be separated from each other so that the clergy attending him do not come into contact with the serving-women of the bishop's wife' (Canon 12). Furthermore: 'Because, in the country, very many archpriests, and likewise deacons and subdeacons, are suspected of persisting in intercourse with their wives, the archpriest is always to have with him a cleric who accompanies him everywhere and must have his bed in the same room with him.' Surveillance was total, for: 'Seven subdeacons, lectors, or laymen can take it in turn to do this' (Canon 19). Bed was thus controlled by ecclesiastical shift system. The bishop himself had to sleep alone. However, the Synod of Toledo presided over in 633 by St Isidore of Seville declared: 'Priests having occasioned no little scandal by their way of life, bishops shall, in order to divest the laity of all evil suspicion, keep witnesses to their conduct in their rooms' (Canon 22). Bishops did present something of a dilemma, however. The Synod of Paris (829) decreed that it was 'not permitted to a priest to betray the sins of his bishop because the latter is in authority over him' (Canon 20). It was somewhat safer if priests and their wives lived apart. Canon 1 of the Synod of Lyon (583) resolved that 'married clergy may not live with their wives', and Canon 5 of the Synod of Toledo (589) followed suit.

The Fathers of the Church were particularly committed to the cause of celibacy. Cyril of Jerusalem (d. 386) held that 'a good priest abstains from women' ('Catecheses', 12, 25), and Jerome attacked bishops who tolerated it 'that the wives of the clergy are with child and infants cry in their mothers' arms'. Ultimately, he said, 'we differ in no respect from swine' ('Adversus Vigilantium', 2). Ambrose declared that priests who continued to beget children 'pray for others with an impure mind as well as an impure body' ('De officiis ministrorum', 2, 249). Augustine gave practical effect to the idea of celibacy in North Africa. As soon as he was appointed Bishop of Hippo in 395, he built a monastery and prevailed on all the priests in the city to move into it. Every ordinand had likewise to undertake to live there under his supervision.

It was papal support for the cause that proved decisive. Pope Siricius, whom we encountered in the Introduction, deserves pride of place here. His previously cited letter to Bishop Himerius of Tarragona in 385 branded the conduct of priests who had intercourse with their wives as 'a disgrace to honourable religion' and 'a crime'. Such priests were 'tutors in sin' and 'slaves to their desires'. In another letter addressed to the bishops of Africa in 386, he again spoke of 'disgrace', charged the priests whom he was attacking with 'pollution by carnal lust', and quoted the Epistle to Titus: 'Unto them that are defiled and unbelieving is nothing pure.' Siricius or his predecessor Pope Damasus (d. 384) wrote a letter to the bisops of Gaul (its authorship is in doubt) which enjoined priests to marital continence and included an admonitory reference to Adam, who had been 'driven from Paradise' for having transgressed in that respect. Whoever wrote the letter, Siricius or Damasus, he evidently believed in a special version of the idea later discarded by Augustine, namely, that Paradise was devoid of sexual intercourse.

Leo I ('the Great'; d. 461) was the first pope to extend the ban on marital intercourse to subdeacons. Writing to Bishop Athanasius of Thessalonica in 446, he declared: 'Although persons outside the clerical state are permitted to engage in conjugal union and procreation, in order to exemplify the purity of absolute continence, carnal marriage is not permitted even to subdeacons, so that those who have wives are to be as if they had them not' (Ep. 14, 4). He expressed similar sentiments in a subsequent letter (458 or 459) addressed to Bishop Rusticus of Narbonne, though he forbade the repudiation of wives: 'The same law of chastity obtains for ministers of the altar as for bishops and priests. These, when they were laymen or lectors, could legitimately marry and beget children. Once they had attained to the aforesaid ranks, however, that which was formerly allowed them became illicit. Although they may not put away their wives in order that a carnal marriage become a spiritual one, they must have them as if they had them not, so that conjugal love be preserved while the conjugal functions cease' (Ep. 167,

q. 3). Pope Gregory I ('the Great'; d. 604) addressed a similar instruction to Bishop Leo of Catania: 'May you, my Brother, in respect of those who have already been ordained, take great pains to ensure that they do not presume to have intercourse with their wives, if wives they possess, but very strictly decree that all be done as is fitting in the sight of the Apostolic See.' He demanded that a priest, once ordained, should 'love his wife like a sister and shun her like an enemy' (Dial. IV, 11).

In this connection, Pope Gregory recounted how a priest from Nursia had given up the ghost, a story told him by the venerable Abbot Stephanus, 'who died here in Rome not long ago'. The said priest from Nursia had been a lifelong and exemplary subscriber to the principle that a priest's wife should be loved like a sister and shunned like an enemy. 'He consequently refused to allow his wife to wait on him in even the most necessary ways, lest she lead him into sin.' Having credited this holy man from Nursia with a heroic measure of sanctity far surpassing the perfection normal in the clergy, since the latter gladly permitted women to serve them in everything and were reluctant to serve themselves, Gregory went on: 'This venerable priest, having a long life behind him, was smitten in the fortieth year of his priesthood with a violent fever and drew near his end. When his wife saw that his limbs were becoming limp, and that he was stretching out as if dead, she desired to see if the breath of life was still in him and put her ear to his nose.' Perceiving this, the old paragon cried: 'Get thee away, woman. A little fire is left; away with the straw. Welcome, my Lords, welcome, my Lords . . . I come, I come.' On that note, he went off to join the celestial celibatarians' club. Gregory opined in conclusion that the holy apostles (unaccompanied by their wives, of course) had come to meet the holy priest from Nursia when he departed this life (ibid.).

The universal Church began to break up in consequence of Western celibatarian rigorism. The rift initiated by the First General Council of Nicaea (325) widened considerably at Trullanum II (691–2), a synod named after its venue, the *trullus* or domed hall in the imperial palace at Constantinople. This synod is still of crucial importance to the Orthodox Church, which styles it the Sixth General Council. Convened as an imperial synod by Emperor Justinian II, it opposed the pope but sought a partial compromise. Canon 13 read: 'In the Roman Church, those who desire to enter the deaconate or the priesthood must undertake to desist from intercourse with their wives. For our part, however, we suffer them to continue in matrimony pursuant to the Apostolic Canons [No. 6]. Anyone seeking to dissolve such marriages shall be dismissed, and any cleric who repudiates his wife on the pretext of piety shall be excommunicated. If he insists on so doing, he shall be dismissed.' Canon 48 may be construed as a sop to Rome: 'If a man be consecrated bishop, his wife shall withdraw to a somewhat remote convent, but the bishop must provide for her. If worthy thereof, she may also become a deaconess.'

So although Constantinople, too, subscribed to the notion that marital intercourse was impure and that a priest was defiled by marriage, the consequences of that idea were milder there than in the papal domain. It is not surprising, therefore, that Pope Sergius I refused to endorse these resolutions, which were signed by the emperor and 211 patriarchs, bishops, or episcopal delegates, declaring that he would rather die. Nearly two centuries of intricate manoeuvring had to elapse before Pope John VIII (872–82) acknowledged the Trullan resolutions with an elastic form of words: he accepted all the canons of Trullanum II which 'do not conflict with the true faith, good usages, and decretals of Rome' (Hefele, op. cit., III, p. 316f.). His implication was that married priests conflicted with all three. The Orthodox Church still bases its marital practice on the Trullan resolutions. Its priests may marry before ordination and remain married thereafter. The sole change applies to bishops: to avoid the repudiation of wives, only monks are appointed to the episcopate.

In the West, by contrast, developments continued to follow the harder line foreshadowed by the Synod of Elvira. Boniface (d. 754), known as 'the Apostle of Germany', saw it as his principal mission in life to campaign against the married clergy of his day. The rigour with which he pursued this vocation is apparent from the penalties he imposed on 'lecherous' priests, monks and nuns at the first German council, which he convened in 742. A guilty priest was to 'remain two years in prison, but first to be publicly flogged and scourged, whereafter the bishop may have the said punishment repeated'. Monks and nuns were to be 'conveyed to prison after the third scourging, there to do penance until the expiry of one year'. At the same time, nuns were to have 'all the hair of their head shorn off' ('Sämtliche Schriften des hl. Bonifatius', 1859, vol. 2, p. 7). Despite these drastic ecclesiastical measures, married clerics still seem to have predominated around the year 1000.

The Gregorian Reform, so named after the reformist pope Gregory VII, was initiated by Pope Leo IX (d. 1054). In addition to reinforcing papal authority, every reform movement in the Catholic Church served first and foremost to repress women and inculcate celibacy. At one Roman synod, Pope Leo IX had priests' wives enslaved for service in the Lateran Palace (cf. Kempf in Jedin, 'Handbuch der Kirchengeschichte', vol. III/I, 1966, p. 407f.). It was Leo IX's legate, Cardinal Humbert, who precipitated the break with the Eastern Church, which admits married priests to this day. That the Great Schism between the Eastern and Western Churches should have coincided with the Gregorian Reform, in which priestly marriage played a crucial part, was no mere quirk of history. Cardinal Humbert, who led the papal delegation to Constantinople and anathematised the Eastern Church on 16 July 1054, defined the difference between Rome and Byzantium thus: 'Young married men, exhausted but lately by carnal lust, minister at the altar. And immediately thereafter they embrace their wives once more with hands sanctified by the undefiled body of Christ. That is no mark of true faith, but an invention of Satan.' In the Latin Church, declared the cardinal, ordination was restricted to those who vowed to remain continent (C. Will, 'Acta et scripta quae de controversiis ecclesiae graecae et latinae saeculo undecimo composita extant', 1861, p. 126).

Patriarch Petrus of Antioch, sarcastically responding to the Western Church's insistence on celibacy, suggested that the Latins had lost the genuine records of the Nicene Council when the Vandals occupied Rome. He, too, defended the married clergy of his patriarchate (Denzler, 'Das Papsttum und der Amtszölibat', vol. 1, p. 54).

Another upholder of the Gregorian Reform was Petrus Damiani (d. 1072), a misogynistic preacher of penitential sermons. He held that, since Christ had been born of a virgin, he must be served during Communion by virginal souls. Only virginal hands could be permitted to touch the Lord's body ('De dignitate sacerdotii'). A devout and fanatical champion of celibacy, he brushed aside the awkward fact that Peter, the first pope, had been married by declaring that he had 'washed away the filth of marriage with the blood of martyrdom' ('De perfectione monachorum').

But the most rabid champion of celibacy was Gregory VII himself (1073–85). Although a priest could contract a valid marriage, even after ordination, he was stripped of his ecclesiastical office under existing canon law. For the most part, however, this remained a purely theoretical sanction, and it was common practice in many parts of the world for priests to have wives and continue to hold office. Gregory, for his part, made clear what he thought of priestly marriage in a letter to Bishop Bernold of Constance: he called it a *crimen fornicationis*. Calling for a general boycott, he forbade the laity on pain of excommunication to attend Masses or other ecclesiastical functions at which the officiating priests were married. To him, married priests were living in concubinage.

Gregory encountered open resistance on the part of the priests concerned. Lambert of Hersfeld recorded that many of them believed him to be a heretic who had forgotten the words of Christ ('All men cannot receive this saying') and of Paul ('To avoid fornication, let every man have his own wife'). He was seeking to compel men to live like angels, they said. By opposing the normal course of nature, however, he was only promoting unchastity. If he persisted in his view they would sooner abandon the priesthood than marriage, and then where would he find sufficient angels for divine service? (Hefele, op. cit., V, p. 23f.). Another chronicler, Sigebert of Gemblours, wrote: 'To forbid people to attend a Mass celebrated by a married priest was thought by many to be in patent conflict with the doctrine of the Fathers. This caused such great offence that the Church has never been divided by a greater schism. Continence is practised by very few' (ibid., p. 24).

Archbishop Siegfried of Mainz followed Gregory's lead, but only with extreme reluctance (ibid., p. 25f.). He enjoined his clergy to do 'voluntarily' what it was incumbent upon them to do, namely, to renounce either their wives or the priesthood, and simultaneously pleaded that he was acting under papal duress. The priests were so indignant that many of them called for his dismissal, and a few even advocated his murder in the hope that this would deter his successor from similar attacks on their marriages. The archbishop thereupon sent envoys to Rome asking Gregory to be less stringent. His request remained unfulfilled. Bishop Heinrich of Chur turned up at the Synod of Mainz in 1075, armed with full authority from the pope, and commanded the archbishop to compel his clergy to renounce their wives or quit the priesthood. The outcry was again so furious and the archbishop's position so perilous that he took no further action. Bishop Altmann of Passau, who had called priestly marriage 'a vice' deserving of eternal damnation (ibid., p. 27), aroused similar protests and was physically assaulted.

Bishop Otto of Constance did the precise opposite of what the pope had commanded: he not only suffered his married priests to remain married but permitted his unmarried priests to marry. The pope wrote an encyclical in which he called upon the priesthood and laity of Germany to withdraw obedience from anticelibate bishops. In 1078 he anathematised a letter by St Ulrich of Augsburg, favouring marriage among priests (ibid., p. 121).

Protests arose in other countries too, for instance at the Synod of Paris in 1074. Nearly all the bishops, abbots and other clergy present took the view that the pope was acting wrongly, and uproar broke out when Abbot Galter of St Martin, near Pontoise, declared that the flock must obey its shepherd. The abbot was spat upon, struck, and ejected (ibid., p. 28). Archbishop Jean of Rouen, who threatened married priests with excommunication at a synod convened at Rouen in 1074, was pelted with stones and likewise driven from the church. During the synod of 1119, the same controversy gave rise to an affray in the same church under his successor, Goisfred of Rouen.

The women concerned came off worst of all, as the following facts testify. As early as 1089, Pope Urban II, Gregory VII's successor, had ruled at the Synod of Melfi that, if a subdeacon refused to part with his wife, 'the prince may take his wife for a slave' ('Decretum Gratiani', pars. II, dist. XXXII, c. 10; Hefele, op. cit., V, p. 175). In 1099 Archbishop Manasse II of Rheims permitted the Count of Flanders to take the wives of clerics into custody (ibid., p. 231), and a synod held at London (1108) by the celebrated and sainted Anselm of Canterbury, a vigorous proponent of celibacy, declared the wives of clergy to be the property of their bishop (Canon 10).

It was at about this time that the popes became convinced that priestly marriages were invalid, even though this notion did not accord with existing canon law. Pope Innocent II (d. 1143) proclaimed at the Synod of Clermont in 1130 that 'since the priests of God's temple should be vessels of the Lord and sanctuaries of the Holy Ghost . . . it infringes their dignity to lie in marriage beds and live in uncleanliness' (Mansi, 'Sacr. conc. collectio', 21, 438). The corollary of this attitude was that priests' wives were merely 'concubines' devoid of rights.

Innocent II took the decisive canonical step at the Second Lateran Council of 1139. Not only was marriage forbidden to priests, but marriages contracted after ordination were officially declared invalid; in other words, the Church simply ceased to regard them as marriages at all. Priests were unmarriageable by definition, and those that had married after ordination must divorce. The reason: 'So that the purity pleasing to God shall become disseminated among ecclesiastical persons and orders of the priesthood.' Although marriages were ordinarily indissoluble in the Catholic Church, they were in this case declared retrospectively invalid and the partners separated in the interests of clerical 'purity'.

From 1139 onwards married men could not be ordained if the Church was aware of their marital status, though the latter condition was not always fulfilled prior to 1563 (introduction of the so-called obligatory form of marriage). Until 1563, therefore, priests could be validly married under canon law provided they had married in secret before being ordained. After 1139, however, the wives of such priests were referred to in ecclesiastical parlance – regardless of canon law – as 'concubines' or 'whores' (thus Pope Alexander III; d. 1181), or as 'adulteresses' (thus Pope Innocent III; d. 1216). In 1231 the provincial synod of Rouen resolved that priests' concubines should, during divine service, have their hair shorn and undergo severe punishment in the presence of the assembled congregation.

In 1227 Pope Gregory IX instructed the dreaded Conrad of Marburg to take effective measures to ensure that German priests dismissed their concubines. Conrad of Marburg, confessor to St Elisabeth of Thuringia and, from 1227 onwards, 'papal inquisitor for all Germany', was an instrument of papal centralism, visitator (inspector) of the clergy, and fund-raiser and organiser of the 1227 crusade. Murdered in 1233, he fell prey to those who resisted his introduction of the first great campaign against heretics in Germany.

The Danish clergy continued to protest against compulsory celibacy for centuries. It did not begin to be introduced into Sweden until the thirteenth century. In Italy the General Synod of Melfi (1284) attacked those who 'marry as minorists [clerics of the minor or lower orders] and then, after being received into the higher orders, retain their wives in the Greek manner'. In Spain the Synod of Salamanca (1335) strove to underline the ban on matrimony among the higher clergy. The widespread incidence of such unions is apparent from the frequency with which resolutions against them were passed by medieval synods. Among those that condemned priestly 'concubinage' were the synods of Saumur (1253), Albi (1254), Cologne (1260), Vienna (1267), Ofen (1279), Bourges (1280), St Pölten (1284), Würzburg (1287), Grado

(1296), Rouen (1299), Pennanfiel (1302), Cologne (1310), Bergamo (1311), Notre-Dame-du-Pré (1313), Bologna (1317), Valladolid (1322), Prague (1349, 1365, 1381), Padua (1350), Benevento (1378), and Palencia (1388). This list could be expanded.

The ecclesiastical authorities were capable of extreme callousness when it came to enforcing celibacy. This is illustrated by a synod held at Münster in 1280, which forbade priests to attend the weddings or funerals of their children (Canon 2), and by the widespread ban on the Christian burial of priests' wives, for instance under Canon 7 of the Synod of Valladolid (1322); while the Synod of St Pölten (1284) decreed that priests should engage in mutual denunciation.

The Synod of Bremen (1266), presided over by Clement IV's papal legate Cardinal Guido, testified to the general difficulties that persisted in Germany at this time.

> Subdeacons and higher clergy who take a concubine under the name of wife and actually join in wedlock with them shall for ever be deprived of all their ecclesiastical offices. The scions of such prohibited unions have no claim on the chattels of their fathers, and anything bequeathed by the latter when they die shall be divided between the bishop and the town. The sons of such priests are for ever infamous. But, since some prelates sanction this corruption in return for money, we excommunicate and anathematize all, clergy and laymen, prelates and subordinates, who openly or secretly protect such concubinarians, likewise any who abet the violation of this statute, which must be read out at all diocesan and provincial synods. But those clergy and laymen that give their daughters or sisters to clergy of the higher orders, whether in putative matrimony or for concubinage, are henceforth debarred from admission to church.
>
> (Hefele, op. cit., VI, p. 84)

Resistance to celibacy was maintained, however, and events gradually moved in the direction of a reform quite different in character from the Gregorian: the Reformation. At the Council of Basle (1435) the 'Reformatio Sigismundi', a reformist document named after Emperor Sigismund, championed the cause of those who wished to abolish celibacy and advocated that the clergy should be permitted to live as they did in the East or in Spain, 'where priests have wives'. The ban on priestly marriage did not derive from Christ and had brought forth more bad fruit than good (Denzler, op. cit., I, p. 177f.). The document was not approved.

At the same time, many priests continued to ignore the ban. Although Spain was governed by the same canon law as any other Western country, marriage among priests appears to have been an established practice there. Francesco de Borgia (1510–72), third General of the Society of Jesus and a great-grandsom of Pope Alexander VI, spent his boyhood at the bishop's palace in Zaragoza, where his grandparents, Archbishop Don Alonso of Aragon and the noblewoman Anna Urrea, cohabited quite openly and officially. The Basque priest Pedro Lopez, brother of Ignatius of Loyola, who founded the Jesuit order, left four children when he died in 1529, nor was his an exceptional case.

Where the German priesthood was concerned, Canon Karl von Bodmann of Mainz stated in 1525 that there had been 'an almost incredible growth of unchastity . . . since the new gospel, so called, was proclaimed [by Luther]'. Luther, an Augustinian friar, had addressed himself directly to the issue of celibacy, and the effect of his attacks on it and monastic vows was so great that a pro-marriage movement took possession of the entire clergy and extended its influence to monks and nuns. Apart from Melanchthon (d. 1560), all the earliest reformers were priests. The celebrated humanist and cleric Erasmus of Rotterdam (d. 1536), second son of a priest and a physician's daughter, also supported 'the transformation of concubines into wives' ('De conscribendis episcopis', 47).

In 1542, when the papal nuncio Giovanni di Morone drew Archbishop Albrecht of Brandenburg's attention to the urgent necessity for celibacy, Albrecht replied: 'I know that all my priests are concubinarians, but how can I prevent it? If I forbid them their concubines they either want wives or become Lutherans' (cf. Morone's letter to Cardinal Farnese in 'Monumenta Vaticana', ed. by H. Laemmer, 1861, p. 412). It did equally little good for Pope Paul IV (d. 1559) to commission the artist Daniele de Volterra to overpaint clothes on the naked bodies in Michelangelo's gigantic 'Last Judgment'. In 1561, Papal Nuncio Commendone reported to Rome from the court of the Duke of Cleves that the latter's territories contained 'barely five priests that do not live in open concubinage' (A. Franzen, 'Zölibat und Priesterehe', p. 82). Augustine Baumgartner, Duke Albrecht of Bavaria's delegate to the Council of Trent in 1562, reported that the most recent visitations (tours of inspection) in Bavaria had found 'scarcely three or four out of a hundred priests who did not live in open concubinage or had not already married in secret or quite openly'. Baumgartner emphasised in his sensational address to the council that most of the Protestant German provinces would have remained loyal to Rome had Rome showed itself accommodating in the matter of celibacy, which he described as secondary ('Concilium Tridentinum', Görresgesellschaft, 1901–, VIII, p. 620f.).

But the Council of Trent, which still forms the essential basis of Catholic doctrine to this day, proved less than accommodating. 'If anyone denies that it is better and more godly to abide in virginity or celibacy than to marry,' it declared bluntly, 'he shall be excommunicated.' There were three possible assessments: either that marriage was superior to celibacy in the sight of God, or that marriage and celibacy were of equal merit, or that celibacy was superior to marriage. Of these the celibatarian fathers of the council chose the last. This was understandable, given that they were jealous of their own superior status and anxious to entrench it in dogma. What rendered their celibatarian arrogance intolerable was the ukase that any married man bold enough to suggest that marriage and celibacy were equal in the sight of God should be excommunicated.

In 1564, when the Council of Trent had ended, Emperor Ferdinand wrote to several cardinals stressing that, had priests been granted the right to marry, the vast majority of those who were defecting to the 'sectarians' (Lutherans) would remain in the Catholic Church (Denzler, op. cit., II, p. 225). This made no difference, however. Celibatarian zealots were shocked, for instance, by the situation prevailing in the diocese of Constance. Writing to the suffragan bishop of Constance in 1576, Nuncio Bartholomæus complained that concubinage was regarded there as neither shameful nor vicious. Priests did not scruple to serve at the altar with impure hearts and hands sullied by fornication, there to touch the Sacred Body of Christ in the presence of the angels. He, Bartolomæus, could not dwell on such impiety without bursting into tears (ibid., p. 242).

Fines were often imposed for contraventions of the rule of celibacy. The bishop of Constance, Hugo von Landenberg, was said by his Protestant opponents to make as much as six thousand gulden for his diocese out of the fifteen hundred-odd children fathered annually by its priests ('Flugschriften aus den ersten Jahren der Reformation', IV, 7, Schottenloher, 1911, p. 305f.). Thus the ban on married priests played a significant part in the spread of the Reformation. Many Catholic priests turned Protestant to save money, e.g. Samuel Frick of Maienfeld, who had, before becoming a Lutheran, paid his episcopal dues punctually in respect of seven children from 1515 to 1521 (O. Vasella, 'Reform und Reformation in der Schweiz', p. 51). For him as for many others, this change of denomination was financially advantageous. The visitators could infer whether a priest was Lutheran or Catholic from whether he described the woman residing in his house as an *uxor* (wife) or a *famula* (maidservant). These two terms became keys to confessional differentiation. All that sometimes distinguished one priest from another in this process of denominational formation and self-identification was whether he declared his wife to be a cleaning-woman or his cleaning-woman to be a wife: in the first instance he was a Catholic, in the second a Lutheran. The Catholic vice-curate of Heerdt devised an ecumenical formula: in 1569 he bluntly informed the visitators that he could not run his wretched little farm without the assistance of his *famula* and his four children (A. Franzen, 'Visitationsprotokolle', p. 109f.).

Even after the Reformation, however, there were many Catholic priests who regarded themselves as married. Bishop Philipp of Worms wrote to the dean of Wimpen in 1598 that, apart from the dean himself, 'all religious persons are afflicted with the disgraceful and vexatious vice of-concubinage'. A visitation (1624–5) having revealed that most of the clergy at Osnabrück were living in concubinage, brutal and drastic measures were taken against them. The Synod of Osnabrück declared in 1651: 'We shall . . . visit the homes of suspects by day and night and have the vile creatures publicly branded by the executioners; and, should the authorities be lax or neglectful, they shall be punished by us' (Decretal 26; cf. Deschner, op. cit., p. 162). Likewise in the seventeenth century, Archbishop Ferdinand of Bavaria had priests' wives thrown into prison or deported (Franzen, 'Zölibat und Priesterehe', p. 97). Bishop Gottfried von Aschhausen of Bamberg requested the civil authorities to 'force their way into priests' houses, fetch out the concubines, publicly flog them, and place them in custody' (Deschner, op. cit., p. 164).

In England, which had broken with Rome as a result of Henry VIII's divorce, the turmoil occasioned by Luther's reformist views on the marriage of priests and religious is exemplified by the Augustinian nuns of Lacock. Founded in the thirteenth century and one of the last convents to be dissolved by Henry VIII, Lacock was sold to William Sherrington, a courtier whose descendants still own it today. The Augustinian nuns were sent home to their families, but Henry, still deeply rooted in the Catholic tradition and hostile to the newfangled Lutheran ideas from Germany, insisted that none of them be permitted to marry. Henry's ban was lifted when England became more firmly Protestant under his son Edward VI, and many of the nuns got married. Not long afterwards the throne passed to Mary, Henry's fanatically Catholic daughter by his first marriage to Catherine of Aragon. The nuns were thereupon informed that they had committed a mortal sin by marrying and ordered to resume their habits forthwith. That, however, was as much as they could do, because not even Queen Mary was powerful enough to evict William Sherrington from the handsome building that had cost him so much. When Elizabeth, Henry's third child, came to the throne, she ruled that the nuns were legally married. We know of at least one who succeeded in rejoining her husband and resuming the married life that had been interrupted by the Counter-Reformation (Bamber Gascoigne, 'The Christians', 7, pp. 172–3).

Celibacy suffered setbacks during the Enlightenment and the French Revolution, which proclaimed in 1791 that no man should be prevented from marrying. Thousands of French priests took wives, among them Bishop Talleyrand. The revival of celibacy in France was attributable to Napoleon and his concordat with Pius VII in 1801. The nineteenth century, with its dogmas of the immaculate conception (1854) and papal infallibility (1870), was an age of celibatarian as well as papalistic and Mariological supremacy. During the twentieth century the Fascists helped to buttress the ecclesiastical ideal of celibacy in Italy by means of the Lateran Pact and the concordat between the Vatican and the Italian government.

Celibatarians in our own century continue to be ruled by the notion that the body is something undesirable from which the devotee of God must be liberated. As Pius XI emphasised in his encyclical letter 'The Catholic Priesthood' (1936): 'Since God is spirit, it seems proper that everyone who devotes and consecrates himself to His service should also, in a certain manner, free himself from his body.' Modestly, he went on: 'If someone holds an office that is, in a certain respect, superior even to that of the purest spirits that stand before the Lord, is it not proper that he himself should live as far as possible like a pure spirit?' In aspiring to live like pure spirits, the upholders of celibacy have exempted themselves from their first and most important task, which is to live as men among men.

On 25 October 1969, Pope Paul VI addressed the following prayer to Mary in the Basilica Maria Maggiore: 'Teach us what we already know and humbly and devoutly profess: to be pure as you are; to be chaste, that is to say, faithful to the immense and exalted duty that is our celibacy; today, when celibacy is being debated by so many and has ceased to be understood by some.' This, however, was an appeal to the St Mary of the Roman, Western Church alone, who supports pure, chaste celibatarians in their running battle against an impure, unchaste, married priesthood. A few degrees of longitude farther east, where married priests have existed from ancient times, Mary cannot be enlisted for such doctrinal purposes.

Questionnaires circulated among West German candidates for the priesthood in 1974 revealed that, even today, celibacy is widely opposed and, thus, practised or tolerated with reluctance. 'Fifty-two per cent of candidates think it essential for the vow of celibacy to be abolished in the future and left to the decision of the individual. This step was deemed worthy of consideration by another twenty-seven per cent, unnecessary by eleven per cent, and unjustifiable by only nine per cent' ('Geist und Leben', Yr 49, 1976, No. 1, p. 65). Similar findings were made in the case of priests, or at least of the younger ones among them: 'Where celibacy is concerned, ordinands take much the same view as younger priests' (ibid.).

It is understandable, therefore, that many priests are turning their back on celibacy. Estimates for West Germany run as high as six thousand ('Christenrechte in der Kirche', 13th Circular, 1987, p. 61), for Italy eight thousand, for France likewise eight thousand, and for the United States seventeen thousand, male and female members of religious orders not included (Ursula Goldmann-Posch, 'Unheilige Ehen. Gespräche mit Priesterfrauen', p. 12). 'The Confederation of Catholic Priests and Their Wives', founded at Bad Nauheim in 1984, quoted a worldwide figure of eighty thousand, or some twenty per cent of the entire Catholic clergy. 'During the pontificate of Pope Paul VI (1963–78) some thirty thousand priests all over the world were laicised, that is to say, removed from office and thus released from the vow of celibacy. Since John Paul II's accession the Vatican has pronounced almost no laicisations. There is talk in Rome of a "Laicisation backlog" ... Meanwhile – according to unofficial figures – over ten thousand applications are on ice' (ibid., p. 13). Those wishing to renounce celibacy for marriage would undoubtedly be even more numerous if they were not confronted by a professional and financial void after laicisation.

If the number of married priests is substantial, it would seem obvious that they are considerably outnumbered by those who have sexual relations with women outside marriage. This is clearly acknowledged by priests among themselves. A poll recently conducted in the arch-diocese of Cologne elicited that seventy-six per cent of the fifteen hundred priests questioned believed that many priests would cohabit with a woman regardless of the consequences (ibid., p. 15).

Celibacy has thus become a fiction, a dying patient whom no amount of artificial respiration by the Vatican will succeed in saving. Papal attempts to justify celibacy are questionable in the extreme, one of the most threadbare being contained in John Paul II's letter to 'All the Bishops and Priests of the Church' on Holy Thursday, 1979: 'Those who call for the secularization of priestly life and applaud its various manifestations will undoubtedly abandon us when we succumb to temptation. We shall then cease to be necessary and popular.' If the purpose of celibacy is to make priests 'necessary and popular', it is time to declare the system bankrupt.

EIGHT

Celibatarian Fear
of Women

Jesus was women's friend – the first of their very few friends in the Church. He caused a stir by consorting with women and including 'many' of them (Luke 8: 3) in his circle – a then unprecedented form of behaviour regarded as most unseemly in a rabbi or Jewish doctor of law. Far from being confined to twelve males, his disciples also comprised numerous females, among them persons as prominent in society as Joanna, who was married to one of Herod's senior officials. These women, who would today be called 'emancipated' or even 'women's libbers', rejected the role traditionally allotted to their sex and actively supported Jesus with 'their substance' (Luke: 3) – in other words, lent him financial assistance.

In Jesus's day, any woman who conversed with a man in the street could be summarily divorced by her husband without his having to repay her 'wedding portion'. It was equally scandalous for a rabbi's pupil (disciple), let alone the rabbi himself, to converse with a woman in the street. Jesus's female disciples did not just listen passively – indeed, they were the first to proclaim his resurrection. St Luke (24: 9) tells us that they 'returned from the sepulchre, and told all these things unto the eleven, and to all the rest.' That this was more than a word in the ear can be inferred from the use of the Greek word *apangellein* for 'told', which has an official flavour. Even Jesus's own disciples were struck by his unconstrained way with women. He asked a Samaritan woman to give him a drink from a well and conversed with her, even though the Jews and the Samaritans were on bad terms. 'And upon this came his disciples, and marvelled that he talked with the woman: yet no man said, What seekest thou? or, Why talkest thou with her?' (John, 4: 27).

102

Jesus's successors failed to emulate his relaxed approach to women and the respect he showed them. After his death, senior dignitaries of the Church developed a strange mixture of inhibition and fear, suspicion and arrogance in their relations with the opposite sex. Lyrical testimony to his pious detachment from women can be found in the second Pseudo-Clementine letter ('Ad virgines'), which probably originated in the third century but was until very recently ascribed to Pope Clement I (91–100) and thus exerted a considerable influence on the training of priests: 'We conduct ourselves, with God's help, thus: we dwell not with virgins and have naught in common with them. We neither eat nor drink with virgins, nor do we sleep where a virgin sleeps. Neither do women bathe our feet, nor do they anoint us. Nor, under any circumstances, do we sleep where sleeps a virgin consecrated to God – indeed, we do not so much as pass the night there' (ch. 1). And where Pseudo-Clement *does* pass the night 'there may no female person abide, neither maid nor married woman, neither old nor consecrated to God, neither Christian nor heathen maidservant; but men alone may abide with men' (ch. 2). The really curious feature of these pseudo-papal admonitions is their author's unmistakable desire to surpass Jesus himself in chastity. His allusions to the scene with the sinner who bathed Jesus's feet with her tears, kissed and anointed them, are all too transparent: Pseudo-Clement, in his celibatarian purity, would never have tolerated such a thing. His own criterion and example of chastity were a reproach to Jesus, who not only ate, drank and conversed with women but did not object to sleeping in a house in which they slept too.

Celibatarians have never managed to cultivate an unconstrained relationship with women. Their status and way of life are too dependent on the great divide between themselves and marriage and femininity for them not to regard women as a negation of, and a threat to, their celibatarian existence. Women have sometimes seemed to them a personification of the Devil's snares and source of supreme danger. Chrysostom made this very plain: 'There are indeed many circumstances that cause our spiritual conscience to falter, foremost among them the company of women. The priest-in-charge must not, in his concern for the male sex, neglect the female, which requires greater care on account of its ready inclination to sin. On such occasions the Evil One can find many ways of secretly stealing in. For the female eye affects and troubles our soul, and indeed, not the eye of the wanton alone, but that of the chaste woman also' ('De sacerdotio', VI, 8). Clearly, since not even celibacy could mutate men into sexless creatures, 'the female eye' remained an ever present danger.

Augustine exerted a crucial influence on the celibatarian relationship to women. This saint did more to shape the Christian ideal of piety than any man before or after him, so his negative attitude to women proved exceptionally disastrous. We can scarcely conceive of two men more dissimilar in their conduct than Jesus and Augustine. Possidius, Augustine's long-time friend and companion, noted that 'No woman ever set foot inside his house. He never conversed with a woman save in the presence of a third person and outside his parlour. Not even for his own elder sister and his nieces, nuns all three, would he make an exception' ('Vita', 26). Behaviour of that kind is suggestive of mental disorder.

Women were a moral danger that increased the more strictly the ecclesiastical authorities insisted on compulsory celibacy among priests. Gynaecophobia of the Augustinian variety could be dismissed as an individual eccentricity for as long as it did not affect canon law, but it did have repercussions immensely prejudicial to many women. The Synod of Elvira forbade priests to tolerate the presence of their own daughters at home unless they were virgins who had pledged themselves to chastity. Countless other synods condemned the presence in clerics' homes of women unrelated to them, e.g. the Fifth Synod of Orléans in 549 (no female outsiders on the premises, 'and even female relatives must not be in the house at an unseemly hour' [Hefele, 'Konziliengeschichte', III, p. 31]); Tours in 567 (a priest might have 'only mother, sister, daughter' in his home, but 'no nun, no widow, no maidservant'); Mâcon in 581 ('only grandmother, mother, sister, or niece may, if need be, dwell with them'); Toledo in 633 ('No woman may dwell with the clergy save mother, sister, daughter, or aunt'); and Rome in 743 ('No women other than their own mothers or next of kin'). The Third Synod of Toledo (589) decreed that all clergy with unrelated and suspect women in their homes should be punished, and that the women themselves should be sold into slavery by the bishop. Similarly, a provincial synod held at Seville (c. 590) instructed the secular magistrates to sell any woman found in a priest's home. The Fourth Synod of Toledo (633) reiterated its predecessor's edict: if clerics had intercourse with female outsiders, the latter were to be sold and the former fined. The Synod of Augsburg (952) resolved that 'suspect' women in clerics' houses should be scourged. The Synods of Sens (1269) and Bourges

(1286) and the German National Council at Würzburg (1287) forbade the clergy to employ female cooks.

However, suspicion attached not only to 'strange' or unrelated women in clerics' homes but to close relatives as well: Pope Gregory (d. 604) urged bishops not to share their homes even with their mothers or sisters. The Synod of Nantes (658) referred to iniquitous relationships between priests and their mothers or other kinswomen: 'The priest may not even have his mother, sister, or aunt in his home, terrible cases of incest having occurred.' The reformist Synod of Metz (888) also debarred mothers and sisters from sharing clerics' homes, and the Synod of Mainz declared in the same year: 'Clerics may not have any female persons in their homes, since some have transgressed even with their own sisters.' These rulings convey some idea of the unhappiness inflicted on so many people by compulsory celibacy.

Other rulings were equally consistent with the Church's idea of woman as the eternal temptress. The Synod of Paris (846) decreed that no woman might enter premises occupied by a priest. Abbot Regino of Prüm, acting at the behest of Archbishop Ratbod of Treves, decreed in his instructions for the supervision of priests (906) that heed must be paid to whether a priest had 'a small chamber' near his church or whether there were 'suspicious little doors' in the neighbourhood (v. Deschner, 'Das Kreuz mit der Kirche', p. 160). The Synod of Coyaca (1050), convened by Ferdinand I of Castile and León, ordained that no women were to live in the immediate vicinity of a church. The same synod demanded that women in clerics' homes should wear black.

Augustine's saintly example has had saintly imitators in more modern times as well. La Varende, the biographer of Giovanni Bosco, who died in 1888 and was canonised in 1934, records that he was 'so chaste that he only allowed his mother to wait on him'. On that basis, many a son has equal claims to sanctity. In 1895, when he was a boy of fourteen, Pope John XXIII entered the following, thoroughly Augustinian resolution in his spiritual diary: '[I must] never converse familiarly or play or jest ... with women, whatever may be their state of life, their age or relationship ...' (Pope John XXIII, 'Journal of a Soul', p. 7). In 1897 he wrote: 'With women of whatever station in life, even if they are related to me or are holy women, I will be particularly cautious,

105

avoiding their familiarity, company or conversation, especially if they are young. Nor will I ever fix my eyes on their face, mindful of what the Holy Spirit teaches us: "Do not look intently at a virgin, lest you stumble and incur penalties for her"' (ibid., p. 16). This translation has been doctored: the original Italian has 'fleeing like the Devil' instead of 'avoiding'. Another equally gynaecophobic entry dated 1947, when the future pope was papal nuncio in Paris, has simply been omitted. Needless to say, the pope entirely misconstrued the above passage from Ecclesiasticus (9: 5), which merely urges the reader to refrain from seducing a girl so as not to have to marry her and pay the father an indemnity.

Celibatarians still regard women as a danger to be heeded when training young men for the priesthood. Their methods are apparent from a West German television programme broadcast in 1966 and a subsequent book bearing the same title (Leo Waltermann [ed.], 'Klerus zwischen Wissenschaft und Seelsorge'). The numerous priests and theology students interviewed had to remain anonymous, unfortunately, because the Catholic Church does not encourage free speech. (The bullying of compliant ordinands into awestruck obedience to their masters would make a separate chapter in itself.) Anonymous or not, one or two of the interviewees dared to state, for instance, that seminarians had been 'exhorted not to speak to the nuns and maids on the premises' (p. 83). A curate alluded to 'the ban on saying good day to the maids who cleaned the corridors' (p. 146). A parish priest wrote: 'Where problems of celibacy were concerned, we were in fact left almost to our own devices and advised that the best mode of procedure, generally speaking, was to avoid women altogether' (p. 158). Another curate: 'As for the priestly way of life, the "celibacy" topic was taboo. When the director was asked if he wouldn't, just for once, use the in-house classes to say something about it instead of addressing us on the usual subjects (rubrics, house rules, manners, translating Latin hymns from the breviary), his sole response was: "What is there to be said? You're not allowed to marry, and that's that." Later on he did say something after all: "Be wary of women . . ." and "You can burn your fingers even on consecrated candles"' (p. 167).

Awareness of their own spiritual superiority helps celibatarians to maintain a proper distance from the opposite sex. If they ever deign to compliment a woman, their compliments take the form of stilted phrases whose absurdity can be even more dismaying than their wonted, everyday disdain. Indeed, where clerical arrogance is concerned, the celibatarians' contempt for women is surpassed only by their esteem. To cite a pat on the back I once received in a letter (dated 11 May 1964) from a former bishop of Essen: 'I'm delighted that a woman and a mother like yourself can also be so spiritually active.'

NINE

Celibatarian Repression
of Women

A biblical passage much beloved by churchmen (I Cor. 14: 24) states
that women should 'keep silence' in church. Although the Bible is the
word of God, the word of man sometimes intrudes, and this is clearly a
case in point. While not attempting to soften St Paul's injunction, I
would merely pose one counter-question: how do those who insist on
feminine silence account for the fact that in the same epistle (11: 5) Paul
alludes to women preaching publicly in church, and that he does so as
if speaking of something so commonplace that it requires no further
explanation? Innumerable attempts have been made to explain his
demand for silence (it was inserted later by someone else or refers
simply to 'interruptions', because men, too, are enjoined to silence a
few verses earlier [14: 28 and 30], and so on and so forth). Whatever
construction one places on the remark, it is not as straightforwardly or
unreservedly hostile to women as many clerics choose to think.

This is not to deny that, unlike Jesus, women's friend, Paul and other
New Testament writers sometimes voice 'male chauvinist' sentiments. I
Timothy (2: 12), for instance, categorically states: 'But I suffer not a
woman to teach.' If I Corinthians (14: 24) is not enough, therefore, the
epistles to Timothy can be cited, whether or not they were written by
Paul. There it is in biblical black and white – or is it? The same passage
from I Timothy occurs in close proximity to a demand that women
should not adorn themselves 'with broided hair, or gold, or pearls'
(2: 9). This is taken less literally today – at least, it is not standard
practice for female churchgoers to surrender their earrings and brooches
for safekeeping in the sacristy or submit their plaits – if any – for
inspections.

The truth is, many people use the Bible like a supermarket and pick out whatever meets their current needs. In the case of another much-loved verse – 'Wives, submit yourselves unto your own husbands' (Eph., 5: 22) – there is a regular tendency to omit Paul's main injunction – 'Submitting yourselves one to another' (5: 21) – which implies that men should also submit to their wives. This would leave men and women quits if it were not for a further demand, a few verses below, that women should be subject to their husbands 'in everything' (5: 24). It would not, therefore, be overstating the case to concede that the New Testament does lay more stress on woman's subordination to man than man's subordination to woman. This inequality is not only regrettable but at odds with woman's status in the time of Jesus, for the non-Christian woman was in many ways better off. It was only as Christianity took hold that women lost the functions still accorded them in Paul's epistles.

Women were initially active in propagating the Gospel. Paul states (I Cor. 11: 5) that they preached in church like men. The word used here, 'prophesy', is better translated as 'preach' because it signifies 'forth-tell' rather than 'foretell' and was an act of formal proclamation. Women like Phebe were deaconesses (Rom. 16: 1f.), and Paul refers to himself as a deacon or 'minister' (Col. 1: 25), one of whose duties (according to Col. 1: 28) was to teach. Priscilla is called Paul's 'helper in Jesus Christ' (Rom. 16: 3), a designation he always associates with official authority. Official service within the Christian community is described by I Corinthians 16: 16 as a form of 'labour', Romans 16: 12 alludes to three women who 'labour in the Lord', and I Thessalonians 5: 12 describes those who labour in this way as being 'over you [i.e. "supervisors"] in the Lord.'

Paul states that a woman named Junia was 'of note among the apostles' (Rom. 16: 7). Although she has since undergone a sex change and been transmogrified into a man, the early Church knew better. Jerome and Chrysostom, for example, took it for granted that Junia was a woman. Chrysostom writes: 'How enlightened and capable a woman she must have been, to be esteemed worthy of the title apostle, nay more, to be pre-eminent among the apostles' ('In epistolam ad Romanos homilia', 31, 12). Until the late Middle Ages, not a single interpreter of Romans 16: 7 construed Junia as a man's name (v. B. Brooten in E. Moltmann-Wendel [ed.], 'Frauenbefreiung. Biblische und

theologische Argumente', pp. 148–51). Since then, it has been appropri-
ated by men in the course of women's persistent repression by the
Church. The history of Christianity is also the history of women's
progressive silencing and incapacitation. If this development has been
checked in the Christian West, it is in spite of the Church, not thanks to
it and certainly not within it.

The Church's denigration of women is rooted in the idea that they
are somehow impure and inconsistent with sanctity. In the clerical view,
women were second-class men. Clement of Alexandria (d. before 215)
said of woman that 'the very awareness of her own nature must arouse
a sense of shame' ('Paidagogos', II, 33, 2). Although he did not explain
the reason for her natural shame, he enlightened her on how she should
dress: 'The woman should be completely veiled save when at home. By
covering her face she will tempt no one to sin, for it is the will of the
Word that it befits her to be covered at prayer' (ibid., III, 79, 4). The
rule that women should be veiled applied primarily to the ecclesiastical
domain. The Apostolic Constitutions (c. 380) also laid it down (II, 57)
that women could communicate only when veiled, and the veiling of
women in church was likewise demanded by Pope Nicholas I in his
celebrated letter to the Bulgars in 866. In the sixth century, it was even
insisted that women cover their hands: 'A woman may not receive the
Eucharist with bare hands' (Mansi, 'Sacr. conc. collectio', 9, 915).
Clerical injunctions to women to cover themselves up, which were
frequent at that time, constituted only one of many repressive measures
against the female sex.

But the covering-up rule was not confined to the ecclesiastical domain.
Chrysostom, invoking St Paul (who was not, in fact, referring to the
same subject at all), declared that a woman 'should be veiled, not only
while praying but at all times' (Homily 26 on I Cor. 11: 5). 'Paul says
not that she must be covered, but veiled, that is to say, most carefully
enshrouded' (ibid. on 11: 6). Chrysostom was not only exaggerating
but mistranslating. Paul did not enjoin women to wear veils. He was
alluding to a specific *hairstyle* affected by devout Jewish women and
Pharisees in particular. 'With her head uncovered' was tantamount to
saying 'with her hair loose' – the mark of a dissolute life. 'Covering the
head' meant simply 'doing one's hair', but Chrysostom was not alone
in misconstruing Paul here. In some countries, women may even today
be compelled to borrow a hat or a veil before entering a church.

The heading 'On the Veiling of Women', a later addition found in many translations of I Corinthians 11, is equally erroneous. The passage refers to women's coiffure. The respectable Jewish woman of Jesus's day began by plaiting her hair and arranging the plaits atop a woollen cloth worn low over the eyes. Then came a headband and another small cloth over the plaits to hold them iin place. Finally, the whole edifice was reinforced with a hair-net. The wife of the celebrated rabbi Akiba (d. 135) is reported to have sold her plaits to finance her husband's studies. This indicates that many women purchased a coiffure appropriate to their social status if not endowed by nature with sufficient hair of their own (v. H. L. Strack and P. Billerbeck, 'Kommentar zum Neuen Testament aus Talmud und Midrasch', III, p. 427f.). The great sinner who dried Jesus's feet with her hair was a woman whose loose hair betokened a loose way of life. By contrast, the Talmud mentions that a woman whose seven sons were high priests never went around, even at home, with her hair loose (ibid., p. 430). If a woman could not dress her hair respectably, Paul argued, she might as well complete her disgrace by having her head shorn completely (I Cor. 11: 6). At all events, he was referring to hair, not to veils or hats, and he was not the last to confuse fashions in dress with questions of respectability and morality.

Even if Paul was not speaking of veils or hats, it must nonetheless be conceded that his insistence on tidy hair in women implied a wish to make them conform to patriarchal custom. He did not, however, go as far as his repressive celibatarian exegetists. It is noteworthy that he enjoined women to cover themselves (dress their hair properly) while praying and *preaching in public*. Characteristically enough, Chrysostom omits this reference to preaching altogether. The process whereby women were muzzled and concealed as far as possible from the public gaze was already in full swing. The female preacher vanished from the ecclesiastical stage. From the Church's point of view, the most meritorious woman became she who was least often mentioned, seen, and heard. Paul's ruling on hairstyles was transformed into a celibatarian cloak of invisibility in which women could be completely enveloped. Of all the New Testament's topical precepts, the Church has been most at pains to preserve and add to those that relate to woman's inferior status. Where others are concerned, e.g. the ban on usury, it adopts a more broad-minded attitude. Papal banks have long been accustomed to charging interest.

Like Chrysostom, Ambrose urged women to walk the streets veiled:

'Let the women veil her head, that she see her chastity and modesty assured, even in public. Her countenance must not readily present itself to a young man's gaze, wherefore she must be covered with the nuptial veil' ('De poenitentia', I. 16). The Apostolic Constitutions likewise prescribed that women be veiled in public.

The Church took still other steps to lower women's status. The Synod of Elvira (early fourth century) decreed in Canon 81 that women should neither write nor receive letters in their own name. The Synod of Gangra (also fourth century) forbade women to cut their hair, a prohibition aimed at the female followers of Eustathius of Sebaste (d.c. 380), who had founded a rigorously ascetic sect. 'In I Corinthians (11: 10) the Apostle Paul considers women's long hair, which is given them as a natural veil, to be a token of their subjection to man. Since many [female] Eustathians were throwing off the yoke and leaving their husbands, as we learn from the Synod of Gangra, they also discarded that token of subjection, their long hair' (Hefele, 'Konziliengeschichte', I, p. 760).

Celibatarian regimentation of women extended to their private lives as well. The Apostolic Constitutions adjured them not to wash too often: 'Furthermore, she [woman] shall not wash herself with undue frequency, neither at midday, nor, as far as possible, daily. As the proper time for a bath, however, let the tenth hour be assigned her' (I, 9). Clement of Alexandria addressed himself to the subject of sport for women. Having recommended athletics for young men – 'Men should either engage in wrestling stripped or play ball' ('Paidagogos', III, 50, 1) – he goes on: 'Even women should be permitted some form of physical exercise, not on the wrestling-mat or the running track, but in spinning and weaving and, if need arise, supervising the cooking. Moreover, they are to fetch whatever we need from the larder with their own hand' (ibid., 49, 2f.).

Chrysostom (d. 407) heaved a pious sigh over women in general – 'The whole sex is frail and frivolous' (Homily 9 on I Tim., 2: 15) – but had an answer to their problem: 'What, then? Is there no hope for them? Indeed there is! What form does it take? Salvation through children' (ibid.). Ambrose (d. 397), on the other hand, considered children and their attendant responsibilities, as well as their manifest evidence that the mother had known carnal pleasure, to be definite grounds for rejecting motherhood and recommending virginity instead: 'However much a noble woman may pride herself on a numerous brood

112

of children, her burdens increase in proportion to their number. However much she may count the consolations her children bring her, she may also count her tribulations. She becomes a mother, but tribulations are not long in coming: before ever she can press her child to her heart, she must cry out in her birth-pangs ... The daughters of this world are married and marry; the daughter of the kingdom of heaven abstains from all carnal pleasure' ('De virginibus', I, 6).

Thanks to theologians of this type, women were ousted from the ecclesiastical domain at an early stage. It is not surprising that they were forbidden to hold ecclesiastical office. This was laid down by the Apostolic Constitutions, the most extensive canonical and liturgical compilation of the fourth century, which claimed to have been written by the Apostles and wielded great influence on that account. (It was largely incorporated in the Decretum Gratiani [c. 1140], of which more will be said in due course, and has thus retained its importance to this day.)

> We do not permit women to exercise the office of teacher within the Church; they are only to pray and listen to the teachers. For our teacher and Lord Jesus Himself sent us only the Twelve to instruct the people and the heathen, but never women, although there was no lack of the same. For there were with us the mother of the Lord, and her sister, and Mary Magdalene, and Mary the mother of James, and Martha and Mary the sisters of Lazarus, and Salome, and sundry others. Thus, had it been proper for women, He would Himself have appointed them. But, if a man be the head of a woman, it is unfitting that the rest of the body rule the head.
>
> ('Apostolic Constitutions', III, 6)

Women had to keep as silent in church as their pastors ordained – so silent that they were only permitted to move their lips. 'Maidens shall silently pray or silently read the Psalms, moving their lips alone so that no one hears; "for I suffer not a woman to speak in church". Women shall do likewise. When they pray, their lips shall move, but no one may hear their voice.' Thus Cyril of Jerusalem (d. 386; 'Introductory Catechesis', 14).

Mary did not baptise Jesus. This, so the Apostolic Constitutions claimed, proved that women were unqualified to perform baptisms or other priestly functions. 'If we have previously not permitted women to

113

preach, how should anyone unnaturally accord them priestly office? To make priestesses of women is an error of heathen godlessness, not a commandment of Christ. [Heathen priests were evidently less hostile to women than their Christian counterparts.] But if women, too, were permitted to baptise, the Lord would surely have been baptised by His own mother, and not by John' ('Apostolic Constitutions', III, 9). Tertullian (d.c. 220) was equally insistent that women should not be allowed to baptise or teach. While emphasising that baptism could be performed 'by all', he strictly excluded women: 'Let us hope that the wild presumption of women, which has dared to wish to teach, will not also arrogate the right to baptise' ('De baptismo', 17).

Women were also forbidden to officiate at the altar. The Synod of Laodicea (fourth century; Canon 44) stated that 'women may not approach the altar'. The Synod of Nîmes (394) debarred women from 'priestly office' in opposition to the Priscillianists, a Christian sect that admitted women priests. Pope Gelasius, writing to the bishops of Lucania in 494, likewise regarded ministration by women as an abuse: 'We have learned to our annoyance that even women, so it is said, are ministering at holy altars, and that all that is entrusted exclusively to the ministration of men is being performed by the sex not entitled thereto.' A similar complaint was made at the Synod of Nantes (658). In the East, too, at a Persian synod in Nisibis (485), Metropolitan Barsumas and his bishops forbade women to enter the baptistery and witness baptisms on the ground that sins of impurity and impermissible marriages had resulted from their presence. The Synod of Aachen (789) decreed that women should not set foot in the sanctuary, the synodal statutes of St Boniface (d. 754) forbade women to sing in church, and the reformist Synod of Paris (829) bemoaned the following deplorable state of affairs: 'It occurs in some provinces that women cluster about the altar, touch the sacred vessels, hand the priests their priestly robes – indeed, even dispense the body and blood of Our Lord to the people. This is disgraceful and must not occur . . . It has doubless arisen owing to the carelessness and negligence of many bishops.'

The Second Pseudo-Isidorian Decretal, a forgery (probably c. 850) attributed to Pope Soter (168–77) but entirely consistent with the repression of women preached by leaders of the Church, stated that 'It has been reported to the Apostolic See that female persons consecrated to God or nuns touch your sacred vessels and consecrated linen. That all this merits strong disapproval and reproof cannot be doubted by any who know what is proper. We therefore declare by the authority of this Holy See that you are to do away with all this and thus prevent this plague from spreading to every province.' Cited as papal authority by Gratian *c.* 1140, this forgery still wields considerable influence (v. Raming, 'Der Ausschluss der Frau vom priesterlichen Amt', p. 9). It has helped to ensure that women in general, and not just the 'plague' of nuns, have been excluded from the altar down the centuries to the present day.

The ban has been maintained in the twentieth century, too. In 1917 it was firmly entrenched in the ecclesiastical legal code (Codex Iuris Canonici, or CIC for short): 'A female person may not minister. An exception is permitted only when no male person is available and just cause is present. The female person may not, however, approach the altar under any circumstances, and may only respond from afar' (Canon 813/2). Celebration (Mass) with a nun as ministrant is permitted in a convent chapel, but: 'Were a male ministrant readily available, a venial sin would be committed. It is, however, forbidden on pain of grave sin for the female ministrant to approach the altar' (Heribert Jone, 'Katholische Moraltheologie', p. 444). Canon 906 of the revised CIC, which has been in force since 1983, is only an apparent advance in that it calls for 'the participation of a believer' in celebrating Mass and thus seems to remove the ban on women ministrants. Canon 230/1 makes it clear, however, that the office of 'acolyte' – which covers that of ministrant – may be entrusted to men alone. Besides, Pope John Paul II had already stipulated in an instruction prettily entitled 'The Inestimable Gift' (1980) that 'women are not permitted the functions of a ministrant'. And that, for the moment, is that.

From ancient times until very recently, women were forbidden to sing in church choirs. Even in our own century, Pius X re-emphasised this prohibition on the ground that women were not permitted to fulfil any liturgical function ('Motu proprio de musica sacra', 1903). Ph. Hartmann's 'Repertorium Rituum' of 1912 stated: 'Only men of known piety and probity, who show themselves worthy of that sacred office, shall be admitted to membership of a church choir. Since singers in church occupy a liturgical office, women's voices may not be employed in church singing. Thus, if it is required to employ high soprano and alto voices, boys must be enlisted' (p. 360). The tide did not turn until a few decades ago. Johannes Kley's edition of the 'Repertorium Rituum' (1940) reproduces the above passage verbatim but adds: 'though women, too, are now generally admitted' (p. 403). Pius XII cautiously sanctioned female choristers, though only 'outside the presbytery or the altar precincts' ('Instructio de musica sacra', AAS 48 [1958] 658). It is not beyond the bounds of possibility, however, that reformers like the present Pope will some day purge church choirs of female interlopers.

In the past, castrated choristers provided a means of resisting any invasion by the female sex. The 'Lexikon für Theologie und Kirche' informs us that

> The castration of boys in order to preserve their soprano or alto voices was practised in Italy, in particular, from the 16th to the 18th centuries. There, in contrast to Germany and France, the earliest castrati quickly gained admission to church choirs; under Clement VIII (1592–1605) they took the place of falsetto sopranos in the Sistine Chapel, though they failed to establish themselves as altos. They disappeared from secular music at the beginning of the 19th century, but castrati were still singing in the Sistine Chapel at the beginning of the 20th.
>
> (VI, 1961, p. 16)

If things develop in line with papal notions of the sanctity of divine service, they may even raise their voices once more.

To anyone taking an overall view of the repression and suppression of women, their denigration and disparagement, the whole of ecclesiastical history seems one long series of narrow-minded, arbitrary male impositions upon the opposite sex. This tyranny still endures. The subjection of woman to man has remained a theologian's postulate throughout, and the male-dominated Church of today continues to regard that subjection as a God-given dogma. It has never grasped that the reality of the Church is founded on the common humanity and fellowship of man *and* woman. The apartheid practised against women by the rulers of the Church is as much of an affront to justice as political apartheid. Far from improving matters, their invocation of divine authority merely imparts a blasphemous flavour to an unjust mode of conduct. Above all, though, a purely masculine Church has long ceased to be a church in the full sense, however it may style itself, because masculine arrogance has prompted it to dispense with one vital aspect of the catholicity – the universality – of which it should be a living example. It has long since exchanged its universality for arrogant sexism.

The masculine Church has reduced Christianity to a shrunken relic of its original self, a desiccated celibatarians' credo. That is why the clergy have so largely lost sight of the true nature of the Christian faith. Cardinal Hengsbach of Essen typified this at a recent service of ordination. According to the 'Westdeutsche Allgemeine Zeitung' of 24 May 1988, he described 'the current sensational demand for the abolition of the bond between celibacy and priesthood' as 'a crisis of faith'. Worse still, he declared this to be 'the true religious crisis of the present time.' In other words, to question obligatory celibacy constitutes a crisis of faith, whereas blind adherence to that obligation is true faith. If such prelatic pronouncements prove anything, it is that their authors are blind to the real exigencies of the present age. If they wished to broaden their pastoral horizons sufficiently to gain sight of true human needs and the true crisis of faith, women – if so permitted – could be of assistance to them.

TEN

The Monasticising of
the Laity

Let us now turn from the monasticising of the clergy, which, though canonically consummated in the West, has not always succeeded in practice, to the laborious and unconsummated attempt to monasticise the laity by means of 'bachelor theology' (Friedrich Heer).

Despite Augustine's concession to the Pelagians at the end of his life – that Adam and Eve may have engaged in some form of controlled, quasi-pleasureless sexual intercourse – his successors clung to the view he had held in his prime: that the Garden of Eden was innocent of sexual pleasure. Great stress was always laid on a verse from the Psalms (50, 7 or 51, 5 in the Anglican Book of Common Prayer): 'Behold, I was shapen in wickedness: and in sin hath my mother conceived me.' It was inferred from this, in conformity with Augustine's teaching, that the sexual pleasure attendant on every act of procreation formed the vehicle for original sin.

Many of Augustine's theological successors were even harsher in their condemnation of sexual pleasure. Marital intercourse for generative purposes, or in fulfilment of one's conjugal obligation, had been defined by Augustine as sinless, whereas Pope Leo the Great (d. 461) was the first to proclaim, in a Christian sermon, that *all* marital intercourse was sinful. Leo extolled Mary – it was Christmas, after all – for having conceived without sin, 'whereas conception in all other mothers on this earth is not without sin' ('Sermones', 22, 3). Fulgentius of Ruspe (d. 553), the leading theologian of his day, did not go quite as far as this celebrated pope, but adhered more closely to Augustine and his two exemptions from sinful marital intercourse. Converted to monasticism by Augustine's writings and subsequently elected a bishop, Fulgentius

118

fully shared Augustine's views. He believed, for instance, that the pleasure attendant on the procreative act sullies and infects the child with original sin, and that, consequently, unbaptised children are debarred from everlasting bliss. While taking over Augustine's doctrines unaltered, Fulgentius improved on St Paul. He not only distorted the meaning of I Cor. 7: 1 by ascribing the words to Paul himself, rather than to his Corinthian questioners, but reinforced them as follows: 'It is *very* good [*magnum bonum est*] for a man not to touch a woman' (Ep. 1, 6–9, 20.22; 'De veritate praedestinationis et gratiae', I, 10). Pleasurelessness had become the *summum bonum* of a misguided Christianity, and Fulgentius urged the faithful to strive after this superior mode of existence.

The age of the 'Fathers of the Church', who occupy a special place in theological history, ended with Pope Gregory the Great (d. 604). Gregory, too, adhered strictly to Augustine and his ideal of the paradisal marriage: God had originally created mankind in such a way that children were generated 'without the sin of carnal pleasure' and brought forth without sin like the fruits of the earth ('In VII psalmos poenitentiae' on Psalm 5 [101], 26). Now, marital intercourse was sinless only when engaged in with procreation in mind. If spouses sought pleasure, on the other hand, 'they besmirch the beauteous nature of the conjugal union with an admixture of lust'. Like Augustine, Gregory invoked Paul's authority in stating that such persons, by keeping within the bounds of marriage, received pardon. To gratify the sexual urge was sinful even in marriage, therefore, though that sin was pardonable in accordance with I Cor. 7: 6 ('Moralis in Job', 32, 29; 'Liber regulae pastoralis', 3, 27).

The married need not have concerned themselves with these monkish theological speculations on the sinfulness (or sinlessness) of marital intercourse, had not such speculations affected them in practice. Rules of continence were heavily influenced by three passages from the Old Testament. To prepare themselves for God's manifestation on Sinai, Moses insisted that the Israelites leave their wives untouched for two days (Exod. 19: 14f.). Ahimelech the priest would not give David the loaves of hallowed bread until he was assured that David had abstained from sexual intercourse for several days (I Sam. 21: 1–6). Finally, Leviticus 15: 18 states that married couples remain unclean until the evening. Although such Old Testament passages are few and far between, for Judaism is anything but a desexualiser of the married state,

Christian theologians from the fourth century onwards increasingly came to regard the proceess of desexualisation as their principal task.

Throughout the Middle Ages, immense importance was attached to questions such as when intercourse was permitted, when not, and for how long an offender had to do penance on bread and water if it occurred at the wrong time. (We shall here exclude the prohibitions on intercourse during menstruation and after childbirth because they were partly accounted for by medical misconceptions about the virulence of menstrual or puerperal blood.) Intercourse was banned on holy days, so called. These included all Sundays, all feast days (of which there were very many), the forty Lenten days before Easter, at least twenty days before Christmas, very often twenty or more days before Pentecost, and three or more days prior to Communion. Consequently, most people tended to communicate only at the time of the major festivals – Christmas, Easter and Pentecost – because they then had to fast and abstain from intercourse in any case. The temporal extent of obligatory continence varied from region to region, but it never amounted to less than five months, not counting individual lulls occasioned by menstruation and childbirth.

Although many of the faithful complained that this left them little scope for intercourse, theologians had ways of imposing their demands. Pope Gregory the Great, for example, included the following object-lesson among his many miraculous tales. It concerned a newly-wed lady of quality whom her mother-in-law had invited to attend the dedication of St Sebastian's church. 'The previous night she was overcome with carnal desire and could not abstain from intercourse with her husband. Because she feared embarrassment in the sight of men more than the dread judgment of God, she went to church despite her pangs of conscience. Just as the relics of the holy martyr were borne in, the Evil Spirit entered into the young wife and threw her to the ground in agony.' The demon was eventually exorcised by Bishop Fortunatus of Todi (Dialogi I, 10). Pope Gregory's mother-in-law anecdote was told and retold for centuries by innumerable preachers and devout writers.

Bishop Caesarius of Arles (d. 542) edified his congregations with even more deterrent examples. 'The children born to anyone who cannot remain continent before a Sunday, or before some other feast day, will be leprous or epileptic or possessed by the Devil. Lepers are born, not to discerning persons who remain chaste on feast days, but, for the most part, to peasants incapable of self-control. If beasts devoid of reason come together only at certain proper times, how much more so should human beings, who are created in the image of God?' (Peter Browe, 'Beiträge zur Sexualethik des Mittelalters', p. 48). In the course of the same sermon, Caesarius predicted that children conceived during menstruation would be afflicted with similar disabilities. 'Whenever you come to church on a feast day' he went on, 'and desire to receive the sacraments, abide in chastity for several days beforehand, so that you may approach God's altar with an easy mind. You must faithfully do this throughout Lent and until the Sunday after Easter, that the most holy festival find you chaste and pure. The good Christian not only remains chaste for several days before Communion but has intercourse with his wife only from a desire for offspring' (ibid., p. 51).

St Gregory of Tours (d. 594) was once shown a blind, crippled child by a woman who 'confessed in tears that she had conceived it on a Sunday ... I told her that it had occurred on account of her sin in violating Sunday night. Beware, you men. Let it suffice that you indulge your lust on other days and leave this day unsullied to the glory of God, else the children born to you will be crippled, or epileptic, or leprous' (ibid., p. 48). Pope Nicholas I, in his celebrated letter to Boris, Bulgaria's newly converted ruler, took care to stress that continence on Sundays was part of the joyous Christian message: 'If one must abstain from worldly labour on Sunday, how much more must one beware of carnal desire and all bodily pollution?' (n. 63). Naturally enough, his letters to the Bulgars also enjoined continence during Lent and at other times (n. 99).

The penances imposed by priests for transgressions of these rules were generally of the order of twenty to forty days of strict fasting on bread and water. Anyone who imagines that these prohibitions on intercourse during Lent, on feast days and before Communion were simply advisory, and that their infringement was not a grave sin rendering the married liable to severe penalties, is ignoring a millennium of very real tyranny and projecting the milder attitude of more modern times into the past. Sermons and treatises of the Merovingian and Carolingian periods, Gallican bishops and councils, penitentials (lists of sins and graduated penances), synods and confessors – all these were at one in enjoining continence on the married and varied only in the terms and penalties they prescribed. In 966, for instance, a synodal ordinance of Bishop Rather of Verona went to extremes: in addition to the usual days (Sundays, et cetera) it banned intercourse on Fridays as well. An

Irish collection of canons extended this ban to Wednesdays and three forty-day periods of fasting each year (ibid., p. 42).

Needless to say, no weddings could take place during periods of abstinence, 'For at this time married persons may not, after all, have intercourse with one another', the Burgundian abbot Henry of Vienna explained at the end of the fourteenth century (ibid., p. 46). Many episcopal edicts exhorted priests to instruct their congregations in these prohibitions and preach on the subject, especially during Lent. Confessors were expected to question married couples about their self-restraint, so we learn from numerous penitentials, e.g. the Decretum of Burchard of Worms (d. 1225; XIX, 5). The penitential of Abbot Regino of Prüm (d. 915) states that the bishop, when conducting a visitation, should ask his priests 'whether they have taught their flock on what days husbands must abstain from their wives'. Regino goes on to suggest the form this interrogation should take: 'Have you engaged in marital intercourse on a Sunday? If so, you must do three days' penance . . . Have you polluted yourself with your wife during Lent? If so, you must do one year's penance or give twenty-six soldi in alms. If you did it while drunk, you shall do only forty days' penance.' The priest was also to ensure that husbands did not touch their wives for twenty days before Christmas and Pentecost, on Sundays, and when pregnancy had been confirmed (Browe, op. cit. p. 47). Strict prohibitions were still in force almost everywhere as late as the twelfth century. Gratian, the father of canon law, embodied them in his concordance of 1142 and thereby guaranteed their influence for centuries to come. St Elisabeth of Schönau (d. 1165) warned married couples to practise continence or risk bringing down the wrath of God on themselves and their children ('Liber viarum Dei', 13).

A letter cited countless times since the eighth century – the 'Responsum Gregorii' or reply by Pope Gregory I to Bishop Augustine of Canterbury – not only failed to mitigate the rigour of these controls on the timing of marital intercourse but reinforced the notion that all marital intercourse was sinful. 'May a man enter the church or even communicate after marital intercourse?' Thus ran one of the questions (the tenth) to which this celebrated letter was a reply. The fact that it has recently – perhaps wrongly – been regarded as a forgery dating from 731 does not detract from the influence it continued to wield until our own century, when it was still attributed to Gregory the Great and cited again and again. 'Sexual pleasure can never be without sin', the letter stated. 'The Psalmist was born of a legitimate union, not of adultery or fornication, yet he said: "Behold, I was shapen in wickedness: and in sin hath my mother conceived me."' Augustine's complex, schizophrenic distinction between feeling and experiencing sexual pleasure (sinless) and seeking and enjoying the same (sinful) had been dropped to the detriment of married couples – if, indeed, anything worse could befall them after Augustine. The only perfect man was he 'who contrives not to burn in the midst of the fire', declared Gregory (or his forger); ergo, he advised the hypothetical Englishman to stay away from church.

Albertus Magnus (d. 1280) held that the reasoning behind Gregory's answer to this question was that the spirit is, so to speak, stifled by the flesh during coitus ('In IV Sent.', 31 a., 28 soll.). He went on to wonder why purely spiritual sins, being far more serious, did not preclude the sinner from attending church. His answer: Because such sins do not prostrate the soul to the same extent and arouse no sense of shame. Sexual intercourse, by contrast, debilitates (*enervat*) the spirit, and that is why man must abstain from the sight of sacred objects (ibid., ad 5).

But to revert to the document that inspired such profundities in Albertus Magnus, the 'Responsum Gregorii' itself. What if the man had had intercourse for procreative purposes only? 'If, however, the man has had intercourse for procreative purposes only, he may enter the church.' In other words, Saturday or Sunday procreation was permitted after all. There was only one problem: Gregory presupposed that the man had nothing but procreation in mind throughout – that he knew 'how not to burn in the midst of the fire' – and left it to him to decide if that applied in his particular case. Celibate theologians later stripped him of this right: having decided that he and all other married men were unendowed with Gregorian frigidity, they debarred any husband from communicating after marital intercourse.

The 'Responsum Gregorii' also explored the question of when a man might resume intercourse with his wife after the birth of a child. We have already seen that post-puerperal bleeding imposed the same prohibition as menstrual bleeding (Gregory wrote that 'the law of God punishes a man with death if he has intercourse with a woman during menstruation'). But Christian theologians, Gregory included, went further: 'It has, however, become an evil custom among the married that wives are no longer willing to suckle their children, but entrust them to other women for that purpose. The sole cause of this evil custom appears to be incontinence. Being unwilling to remain continent, they deprive their children of mother's milk.' The belief that sexual intercourse spoils mother's milk was a medical misconception that continued to exert a great influence on the practice of wet-nursing until very recent times (v. Elisabeth Badinter's interesting book, 'The Myth of Motherhood').

Where Sundays and feast and fast days were concerned, Scholastic theologians of the eleventh to thirteenth centuries began to shift the emphasis away from these rigid timetables and apply themselves to classifying the motives for each conjugal act. With Augustine as their guiding light, these theologians distinguished between the partner who demanded intercourse and the partner who acceded to it, defining the motives of each in each and every case. The best motive of all was procreation, but this was to be equated less with the wish to generate a child or heir than with joy at the prospect of producing a new servant of God. Another crucial determinant was the part played in intercourse by desire: whether it was tolerated with distaste, reluctance and regret; whether it was deliberately sought, exclusively sought, inordinately sought, or sought in an unnatural manner; what form the 'very first impulses' for the sexual act had taken; and what thoughts had passed through the individual partner's mind at the beginning, in the middle, and at the conclusion of intercourse. In this way, theologians provided themselves with a rich new field of activity. Being primarily concerned with motivation, many of them now regarded transgressions of the marital timetable as venial sins only.

But the belief that intercourse at certain times was reprehensible lived on for many years in episcopal edicts and sermons and in the confessional. In thirteenth-century Lausanne, five women had marital intercourse prior to the feast of the local patron saint. On entering the cathedral they were afflicted with a form of epileptic fit which did not subside until they had confessed their guilt to the entire congregation and promised to abstain from such conduct before any future high day ('Cartulaire du Chapitre de ND de Lausanne; Mémoires et documents publ. par la Soc. D'hist. de la Suisse Romande', I, 6[1851], 576).

The great preacher Berthold of Ratisbon (d. 1272) did, at least by implication, moderate the rigidity of the timetable by distinguishing between the motives of those involved. In one of his nuptial sermons he declared:

> One must remain chaste the night before mandatory feast days, likewise throughout the day that is being celebrated, until night-fall. You wives, I know full well that you obey me more faithfully

than your husbands. We often find that wives are more chaste than their husbands, who desire licence in everything and, through eating and drinking, want their way and become so unrestrained that they refuse to heed the time. Wife, do your best to dissuade him. But if he turns so devilish that he scolds you and makes to leave you for another woman, and waxes earnest and you cannot refuse him, then, wife, rather than let him go to another woman, yield with a sorrowful heart – yes, be it even on Christmas Eve or the eve of Good Friday. For you are innocent provided your heart is not in it. But all the saints whose times you have not observed will complain of you on Judgment Day.

(Franz Pfeiffer, 'Berthold von Regensburg', vol. I, p. 324)

While Berthold's sermons drew certain distinctions between the motives for intercourse, the pastoral instructions given his clergy by Bishop Gulielmus Durandus of Mende (d. 1296) forbade it absolutely at improper times. So did a decretal of the diocesan synod of Nîmes in 1284 and a Castilian guide to confession of the thirteenth century (Browe, op. cit., p. 76f.). St Bernardino of Siena, preaching at Padua in 1443, called it 'swinish irreverence' and a mortal sin for married couples not to abstain from intercourse for some days prior to Communion (ibid., p. 77f.). Thus, Bernardino differed from almost all the theologians of his day in regarding Gratian's canons on the subject as strictly binding. Married couples were just as strictly enjoined to continence before Communion, as well as on feast and fast days, by a manual for the clergy of the diocese of Salisbury dated 1506, but this was by then an exception. Although the Tridentine Catechism (1566) still generally prescribed continence at specified times, invoking the practice of the past, this was regarded only as an 'exhortation', not an obligation. Subsequent synods (Besançon 1571, Bourges 1584, and Würzburg 1584) 'exhorted' continence but did not make it mandatory.

Thomas Sanchez (d. 1610) affords us an overview of theological opinion: some authorities held it to be venially sinful to demand marital intercourse on the eve of Communion; others, though only a few, thought it sinless to communicate immediately thereafter. Sanchez himself considered it very proper not to communicate after intercourse except when the act was performed for procreative purposes. In the latter instance, carnal pollution and sexual pleasure were offset by the good of progeny. The same applied to intercourse in fulfilment of one's conjugal obligation or to avoid personal incontinence. If intercourse was engaged in for sexual pleasure's sake, however, it was venially sinful to receive Communion the following day. The spiritual sluggishness induced by intercourse was unseemly in a communicant. It could nonetheless be sinless to communicate under such circumstances if non-attendance at Communion would excite unwelcome attention (Dominikus Lindner, 'Der Usus matrimonii', p. 222).

The Jansenists, of whom more later, were considerably more stringent. Alfonso de' Liguori (d. 1787), who was less so, endorsed Thomas Sanchez's view. To the extent that intercourse 'for sexual pleasure's sake' ceased to be defined as sinful during the nineteenth century (provided, of course, that nothing was done to impede generation), the receiving of Communion thereafter was also pronounced free from sin. As late as 1923, however, the twentieth edition of 'Abhandlung über das 6. Gebot und den Ehegebrauch' ('Treatise on the 6th Commandment and Matrimonial Usage') by the eminent moral theologian Hieronymus Noldin (d. 1922) exhorted married persons not to attend Communion after venially sinful marital intercourse (this depending largely on how far their motives were tainted with sexual pleasure) unless they had some important reason for so doing.* Lindner's 'Usus matrimonii' (1929) stated that 'It is not disputed, even now, that abstention from carnal intercourse on the day of Communion is very highly recommended' (p. 224). There are many married women alive today who have, in the past, confessed to having had intercourse with their husbands on the eve of Communion.

* This admonition was omitted from the twenty-first edition of Noldin/Schmitt in 1926.

ELEVEN

Penitentials and
Penitential Tariffs

Contraception was opposed with even greater rigour after Augustine's
time.

Bishop Caesarius (d. 542) of Arles (the Gaulish Rome), a former
monk, was instructed by Pope Symmachus (d. 514) to assume responsibility for 'the matter of religion in Gaul and Spain'. Caesarius was the
initiator of thirteen synods during the sixth century, and his influence
extended to the Ostrogothic and Frankish episcopate. In a letter devoted
to moral problems and addressed to all the bishops and priests within
his sphere of influence, Caesarius urged his brethren in Christ to instruct
their flocks in the Christian virtues. After describing abortion as
homicide, he turned to contraception:

> Who would neglect to point out, in admonition, that no woman
> may imbibe any potion that will render her incapable of concep-
> tion or impair the natural vigour of her who should, pursuant to
> God's will, be fruitful? As often as she should have conceived or
> given birth, so often will she be deemed guilty of murder, and,
> should she not submit to a fitting penance, she will be condemned
> to everlasting death in Hell. If a woman desires no children, she
> shall devoutly and conscientiously agree upon the same with her
> husband, for a Christian wife is rendered infertile by chastity
> alone.
>
> (letter included in 'Sermones', 1, 12)

Caesarius was so taken with the handy slogan 'So much contraception, so many murders' that he rammed it home in another two sermons
(44, 2 and 51, 4).

So Caesarius gave women a choice between damnation after death and penitence in this life, or as the Synod of Agde (506; Canon 37) decreed under his presidency, between excommunication and penance. The latter was not what it is today. Persons in the 'penitential state' were obliged, like monks, to lead a life of complete renunciation. This could entail years of abstinence from marital intercourse, which was why the Synod of Agde warned against inflicting it too readily on the young. Caesarius himself said in his sermons that young married persons doing penance should not be enjoined to marital continence unless they had committed a very grave crime requiring expiation of that order. Pope Leo I, writing to the bishop of Narbonne in 458, also stated that certain youthful penitents should be permitted to marry and have marital intercourse ('Epistola ad Rusticum', 13). Similarly, the Councils of Arles (443) and Orléans (538) laid it down that married persons should accept long-term penances only with the consent of their spouses (Browe, 'Beiträge zur Sexualethik des Mittelalters', p. 44). In view of their extreme severity, such penances were usually accepted only by the old and the dying.

Archbishop Martin of Braga (d. 580), another former monk, put contraception on a par with infanticide and set the penance for that sin at ten years: 'If any woman has fornicated and has killed the resulting infant, or has desired to undergo an abortion and to kill what she has conceived, or to take steps against conceiving, regardless of whether she does this in adultery or in legitimate wedlock, the earlier canons decreeed that such women might receive Communion only at death; we, however, mercifully resolve that such women, or other women jointly guilty of their crimes, shall do ten years' penance' ('Capitula Martini', 77).

The regulation of lay sexuality by monkish bishops like Caesarius and Martin and popes like Gregory is reflected in its own literary genre: the penitentials, which listed various sins and prescribed the appropriate penance in each case. These show that contraception was classified, without exception, as a sin of exceptional gravity. The earliest penitentials originated in the monasteries of Ireland and were compiled by Irish abbots. (Irish monks played a major part in propagating the Gospel in Europe.) Other widely used penitentials included those compiled by Regino of Prüm (d. 915) and Burchard of Worms. The latter dates from 1010, when Worms was an important ecclesiastical centre. Seventeen imperial synods were held there between 764 and 1122.

One passage from Regino's penitential, which was later adopted by Burchard, had a vast influence on the Church's doctrine relating to contraception because it passed into canon law in the thirteenth century. Regino included it among the questions to be asked by a bishop during a visitation: 'If anyone [*Si aliquis*] to satisfy his [or her] lust or in wilful hatred does something to a man or a woman so that no children be born to him or her, or gives them to drink so that he cannot beget nor she conceive, let it be accounted homicide.' This dictum, which formed part of the Catholic Church's legal code until 1917, did much to dramatise the question of contraception.

Acts condemned as contraceptive, apart from the administering of potions, comprised various forms on non-procreative marital sex: coitus interruptus and anal and oral intercourse. The penances imposed for these three forms of intercourse were draconian. Although penalties varied from one penitential to another, it is a striking fact that anal and oral intercourse (coitus interruptus is mentioned less often) were frequently punished with greater severity than abortion, or even than wilful murder. The authors of the penitentials evidently considered certain sexual practices even more reprehensible than the killing of another human being. It is no coincidence that the Catholic Church still displays greater commitment when campaigning against sexual sins, some of them only putative, than it does in opposing crimes against human life stemming from war, genocide and capital punishment. Ernst Block was referring to the perversion of morality in the Christian West by such false value judgments when he wrote these bitter words in 1936: 'Women with bare arms may not enter a church, but naked Jews may dig their own graves.'

The Anglo-Saxon penitential of Theodore, a Greek monk who hailed from St Paul's Tarsus, became archbishop of Canterbury, and is regarded as the founder of the English diocesan system, came into being between 690 and 710. It set the penances for oral intercourse at seven or fifteen years or even life, for abortion at three periods of forty days, and for deliberate homicide (wilful murder) at seven years. The Anglo-Saxon penitential of Pseudo-Egbert (c. 800) decreed seven years' or lifelong penance for oral intercourse, ten years' for anal intercourse, seven or ten years' for abortion, and seven years' for wilful murder. The Canones Gregorii, which date from 690–710 and are attributed to Archbishop Theodore, prescribed fifteen years' penance for anal intercourse and seven years' for wilful murder, and the Anglo-Saxon penitential of Egbert, archbishop of York (d. 766), punished anal intercourse with seven years and murder with four to five years. The Frankish Hubertense penitential (c. 680–780), so called after St Hubert's, the Ardennes monastery where it came to light, demanded ten years' penance each for coitus interruptus, contraception by means of potions, and wilful murder. Considerably milder terms of penance measuring days or weeks were imposed on married couples who deviated from the sexual norm prescribed by the monks, which was that the man should mount the woman, not vice versa. The latter position was regarded as a special form of pleasure-seeking and an impediment to contraception. If it was habitually employed for contraceptive purposes, it attracted severe penalties. Egbert prescribed three years' penance, Pseudo-Theodore (ninth century) a term of one to three years (John T. Noonan, 'Contraception: A History of its Treatment by the Catholic Theologians and Canonists', p. 152f.).

From the eighth century onwards, confessors were instructed to question penitents about their contraceptive practices. The fullest example of this form of interrogation occurs in Burchard's Decretum, which was very widely known. Burchard instructed confessors to put their questions 'gently and kindly'. He had a large number of questions 'affecting women in particular' and dealing primarily with abortion and contraception. His questions for men included the following:

> Have you coupled with your wife or another woman from behind, like dogs? If so, ten days' penance on water and bread. If you have coupled with your wife during menstruation, ten days' penance on water and bread. If your wife has attended church after childbirth and before lustration, she shall do penance for as long as she should have abstained from attendance. If you have coupled with her during that time, you shall do twenty days' penance on water and bread. If you have coupled with your wife after the child has stirred in the womb or during the forty days prior to her confinement, you shall do twenty days' penance on water and bread. If you have coupled with your wife after conception was assured, you shall do ten days' penance on water and bread. If you have coupled with your wife on the Lord's day, you shall do four days' penance on water and bread. Did you pollute yourself with your wife during Lent? You must then do forty days' penance on water and bread. If it occurred while you were drunk, twenty days' penance on water and bread. You must

remain continent for twenty days before Christmas, on all Sundays, during all times of fasting prescribed by law, on all feast
days of the Apostles, and on all high days. If you have not
observed this, you shall do forty days' penance on water and
bread.

The penitentials forbade intercourse with a pregnant wife and
between sterile or elderly married persons, though penances were often
waived in the case of pregnancy and always in that of sterility. This is
remarkable in view of Augustine's vehement insistence on the exclusively generative function of intercourse. The earliest Irish penitential,
that of Finnian (sixth century), for example, prohibited intercourse
during pregnancy and between the sterile but prescribed no penance for
those who transgressed, while the Columban penitential (also Irish, late
sixth century) made no mention of the subject (ibid., p. 164f.).

It may have been the penitentials' undue leniency – or what passed
for it in papal eyes – that prompted Pope John IV to write to the Irish
bishops in 640 execrating 'the poison of the Pelagian heresy, which is
reviving amongst you' and drawing their attention to Psalm 50,7 (51,5):
'I was shapen in wickedness: and in sin hath my mother conceived me'
(letter in Bede, 'Historia ecclesiastica', 2, 19). He clearly felt that the
Irish bishops had not sufficiently alerted their flocks to the perils of
sexual pleasure. It is, in fact, noteworthy that all the penitentials,
Continental as well as Irish, were more Pelagian than Augustinian in
omitting to penalise sexual desire during the conjugal act.

Unlike the Irish, who prescribed no penance for intercourse with a
pregnant wife, the Frankish penitential of Pseudo-Theodore imposed a
penance of forty days for intercourse during the last three months of
pregnancy. The Ecclesiarum Germaniae penitential (eleventh century)
prescribed ten days on bread and water for intercourse in cognisance of
pregnancy and twenty days when it occurred after the child had first
stirred. Many penitentials confined themselves to banning intercourse
during the last three months of pregnancy. All these regulations
concerning intercourse during pregnancy were largely inspired by
concern for the unborn child. The physician Soranus of Ephesus (second
century AD) had stated that intercourse should be eschewed altogether
during the early stages of pregnancy, lest the womb, when jolted, expel
the embryo in the same way as the stomach brings up food. His near
contemporary Galen, on the other hand, held that intercourse in the
early stages was permissible in moderation.

Although the Fathers condemned intercourse with a pregnant wife largely because no further procreation could occur, and thus because no justification for marital intercourse existed, the ban was more and more often ascribed to concern for the unborn child. From the thirteenth century onwards, this reason was the only one cited. Albertus Magnus (d. 1280) wrote that sexual intercourse could cause the womb to open and the embryo to fall out, and that this danger was particularly acute during the first four months of pregnancy ('Commentary on the Sentences', 4. 31, 22). Thomas Aquinas (d. 1274) held that intercourse with a pregnant wife was a mortal sin only when a miscarriage might result (ibid., 4, 31, 2, 3), and that remained Church doctrine in centuries to come.

The penitentials also forbade intercourse during menstruation. Forty days' penance were prescribed for this offence by the Canones Gregorii and the Anglo-Saxon penitential of Bede (d. 735), thirty by Pseudo-Theodore, and only twenty by the Old Irish Penitential (c. 780). Whether their authors believed, like Isidore of Seville (d. 636), that children could not be conceived during menstruation, or whether they assumed, like Jerome, that they would be born with some physical defect, we are not told. They certainly never neglected to preach abstinence at times reserved for prayer, penance, and religious celebration.

TWELVE

Early Scholasticism (1):
Conjugal Lechery and the Marian Marriage

Augustine's sexual pessimism, intensified still further by Pope Gregory the Great (d. 604) in his response to the bishop of Canterbury ('Sexual pleasure can never be without sin'), also dominated the Scholastic period, the so-called golden age of theology that spanned the eleventh to thirteenth centuries. The man regarded as Scholasticism's supreme exponent is Thomas Aquinas (d. 1274), who still stands second only to Augustine as an authority on sexual matters, even though he utterly degraded the Christian theology of marriage and paved the way for the demonisation of marriage itself. Although Pope Innocent VIII's 'Witches' Bull' (1484) was promulgated two hundred years after Thomas's death and cannot be directly laid at his door, it owed much to his superstitious belief in sexual intercourse with devils and his demand that heretics be destroyed.

Like Augustine, the early Scholastic theologians (eleventh to early thirteenth centuries) discerned two purposes in marriage: procreation as prescribed by the Old Testament account of the Creation ('Be fruitful and multiply'), and the avoidance of fornication pursuant to I Cor. 7. Again like Augustine, the early Schoolmen believed that mankind had multiplied sufficiently in pre-Christian times to populate heaven with saints, but that now, in post-New Testament times, celibacy and virginity were the divine order of the day.

Augustine had emphasised the procreative purpose of marriage and played down its 'remedial' function, whereas the early Schoolmen laid stress on the latter. To them, the predominant purpose of marriage was the avoidance of fornication, but they still, like Augustine, accorded moral precedence to procreation. In other words, the remedial function stopped short where procreation was impaired or merely impeded. As these theologians saw it, marriage was a sort of hospital for those too weak-minded to observe the continence incumbent on them, for Augustine had shown that mankind's penalty for the Fall afflicted 'not the eye or some other part of the body, but only the sexual organs, whose proper function is generative' (Guillaume de Champeaux [d. 1121], 'Sententiae', q. 26).

Thus the early Schoolman regarded all married persons as potential fornicators whose fundamental disease – 'the disease consists in an inability to abstain from sexual intercourse' (Peter Lombard, 'IV Sent.', 26, 2) – was sexual desire, which Augustine had shown to have been absent from Paradise. The disease afflicting the married found its remedy and exculpation in marriage. That, too, had been demonstrated by Augustine with his grounds for excusing conjugal union. The remedy for lust was marital intercourse or '*copula*', which had always been available. Archbishop Stephen Langton of Canterbury (d. 1228) went so far as to demand that marital *copula* had to be tolerated even at the risk of one's life: 'Rather must the wife suffer herself to be killed than that her husband should sin.' She had therefore to do her conjugal duty, even in childbed, if she thought it 'very' probable that her husband would otherwise yield to incontinence (Michael Müller, 'Die Paradiesehe des heiligen Augustinus und ihre Auswirkungen auf die Sexualethik des 12. und 13. Jahrhunderts bis Thomas von Aquin', p. 173). Under such circumstances, the wife was obliged to have intercourse even during Lent and other periods of abstinence.

Woman in her nurse's role broke the temporal framework constructed for marital intercourse by celibate theologians who had arbitrarily restricted the right of married couples to physical union. This error was gradually superseded by another: the belief that the husband (with whom theologians were very largely preoccupied) was a mortally sick patient doomed to eternal damnation unless his nurse-wife sacrificed herself, or even put her life at risk, in order to fulfil her conjugal obligations by dosing him against incontinence *ad libitum*. In practical terms, this signified her sexual enslavement.

Though not spelled out, the masculine conception of woman as man's nurse, but not vice versa, is implicit in a rule laid down by Odo (d.c. 1165), chancellor of the University of Paris. If it was the wife who demanded intercourse on a holy day, declared Odo, the husband must not only deny her request but 'quell her impudence with fasting and beating' ('In IV Sent.', 32, 3). He did not suggest that the wife should beat her husband for the same offence.

Guillaume d'Auvergne (d. 1249), bishop of Paris, discovered proof that the medicine of marital intercourse was effective against sexual desire. 'Eschew all physical pleasure' was his married couples' maxim, for pleasure hampered spiritual development. His conversations with married couples had elicited the happy circumstance that 'young men sometimes remain cold towards their wives, even when the latter are beautiful' ('De sacramento matrimonii', 8 and 9). The same joyful discovery was made *c.* 1200 by an anonymous theologian who wrote that the practical effects of the remedy were attested by young men who declared that they were 'positively cold toward their beautiful wives and almost cold toward other women' (Müller, op. cit., p. 203). Where penitentials had sought to limit the human sex drive by imposing timetables, the early Schoolmen were more in favour of homeopathic remedies: marital intercourse became an antidote to marital intercourse.

As Albertus Magnus (d. 1280) later pointed out, some theologians objected that sexual frailty could not be cured by the gratification of sexual desire, but only by its opposite, perfect continence and strict physical self-discipline. Albertus replied that sexual desire was too deeply rooted in the innately sinful human being, and was so endemic that drastic asceticism would be injurious to a person's nature ('In IV Sent.', d. 26, a. 8). Fortunately for the survival of the human race, the monks renounced their attempt to monasticise the married and contented themselves with diminishing their libido.

When theologians crystallised the seven sacraments during the twelfth century, marriage, though included among them, was classified separately because its remedial function rendered it inferior to the rest in early-Scholastic eyes. The 'Sententiae' of Peter Lombard (d. 1164), which remained *the* theological lecturer's textbook and manual of instruction until well into the sixteenth century, recognised three kinds of sacraments: (i) those that conferred grace, such as the Eucharist and Holy Orders; (ii) those that, in addition to conferring grace, were remedies for sin, like baptism; and (iii) marriage, which was a remedy for sin but not a means of grace (IV, 2, 1). Raymond of Pennafort (d. 1275), a Spanish Dominican, held that the first five sacraments were designed for all, the sixth, Holy Orders, for the perfect, and the seventh, marriage, for the imperfect ('Raimundiana', 3, 24, 2).

Although many theologians of the High Scholastic period (thirteenth century) spoke of grace in connection with the sacrament of marriage, they did so rather like Thomas Aquinas: 'Wherever some form of authority is granted by God, there, too, will be granted assistance in its proper exercise. Since man in marriage is granted authority to use his wife for procreation, he is also granted the grace without which he cannot fittingly [*convenienter*] exercise the same' ('Summa theologica suppl.', q. 42, a. 3). What was 'fitting' in respect of marital intercourse was laid down by pleasure-hating celibatarians of whom Thomas Aquinas was one, all arguments to the contrary notwithstanding. As he himself wrote: 'lustfulness' was 'driven back into its roots' by the grace of marriage ('In IV Sent.', 26, q. 1, a. 4). Or, as his master Albertus Magnus had put it: the 'medicinal grace' of marriage had a diminishing effect on lust (ibid., 26, a. 8).

Many modern theologians claim that the transition from early Scholasticism (marriage conferred no grace but was merely a remedy for sexual desire) to High Scholasticism (the grace conferred by marriage consisted in its suppression of sexual desire) represented a great advance. This is semantic whitewash, however. Thomas Aquinas is represented as a progressive although he actually reinforced Augustine's sexual hostility with Aristotle's biological and patriarchal fallacies. No early Schoolman ever wrote more scathingly about the sacramentality of marriage than he: 'It was needful to employ a particular remedy against sexual desire by means of a sacrament, first because sexual desire vitiates not only the person but nature, and, secondly, because it paralyses reason by virtue of its inconstancy' ('Summa theologica', III, q. 65, a. 1 ad 5). That he should have classified marriage as the last and least of the sacraments 'because it possesses a minimum of spirituality' (ibid., a. 2 and 1) was a logical consequence of his views.

So the ecclesiastical programme designed to imbue married persons with grace, alias frigidity, was eventually compelled to enlist the aid of marital intercourse itself. The monasticising of the laity bore fruit, as we have heard: Christian husbands cooled towards their beautiful wives. Their frigidity in respect of beautiful outsiders was not quite as complete, but, adultery being forbidden to Christian males, coolness toward their wives was the primary consideration. Their pleasurelessness had to prove itself within wedlock, the ultimate test whose ultimate object was children. Continence was useful and necessary for their sake too. Guillaume d'Auvergne held that maximal continence produced a larger number of better-bred children because the 'ardour' of the sexual act not only infringed the greater good of continence but carried the disadvantage that 'those who must burn with desire have but few children or none at all' ('De sacramento matrimonii', 8). Children born to couples who practised restraint were 'bigger, stronger, and more commendable in every respect' (ibid., 9). The moral quintessence: the less pleasurable the sexual act, the more numerous and well-bred its human products.

The Franciscan monk Odo Rigaldus (d. 1275) had a useful tip for married couples who found it difficult to cope with the vestiges of sexual pleasure that still resisted celibatarian suppression. Sinful lust, declared Odo, can be suppressed by an even stronger sensation. A horse with an injured foot, for example, can be spurred by its rider into striding without limping. Similarly, the perfect Christian husband can forestall the onset of sexual excitement by entertaining the correct (i.e. generative) intention and so effectively subordinate it to its proper purpose by the exercise of reason that sexual intercourse remains free from sin ('In II Sent.', d. 20, q. 6). He must, of course, beware of allowing sexual excitement to occur prior to intercourse, this – according to Odo and many others – being a sinful phenomenon. The correct sequence of events is as follows: married couples must first form the intention to procreate, thereby initiating sexual excitement. All their subsequent actions will then be directed toward their proper goal by that overriding good intention. Even the preliminaries to intercourse will be free from sin if these requirements are met, whereas sexual excitement is sinful if it occurs first and is only later directed by reason toward procreation or the performance of one's conjugal duty ('In IV Sent.', d. 31).

It became fashionable for theologians to dissect sexual intercourse into numerous separate acts in order to weed out those that were sinful. Simon of Tournai (d. 1201) asserted that the conjugal act could be initiated without sin (i.e. without pleasure) but not completed without it (Disp. 25, q. 1), an idea he had adopted from his teacher Abbot Odo of Ourskamp (d. after 1171). In the view of Cardinal Robert Courson, who died as a Crusade preacher before the walls of Damietta in 1219, the sin inherent in the conjugal act was located in its middle reaches: 'If a man know his wife for the purpose of procreation or in rendering her due, the first and last parts of that act, during which he strives after God, are meritorious, whereas the middle parts, during which the whole man is ruled by the flesh and becomes all flesh, are venially sinful' ('Summa theologiae moralis', 128). There were, however, a few married men who could morally cleanse the crucial mid-section and/or the crucial culmination. To cite Guillaume d'Auxerre (d. 1231): 'If a holy man ... has intercourse with his wife and the sexual desire arising therefrom ... so far from pleasing, disgusts him, his intercourse is without sin. But that seldom happens' (Müller, op. cit., p. 185). This theological discovery so appealed to Roland of Cremona (d. 1259), a Dominican, that he reiterated it (ibid., p. 194).

Anselm of Laon (d. 1117), who bears the honorary title 'Father of Scholasticism', postulated that the intensity of a man's sexual desire determined the gravity of his sin (ibid., p. 114).

This set theologians to arguing among themselves over which was more sinful, lust felt for a beautiful woman or an ugly one. Petrus Cantor (d. 1197) held that, sin being proportionate to enjoyment, intercourse with a beautiful woman was more sinful because it was more delectable. Accordingly, he sought to render beautiful women distasteful by speaking of them in the sort of language subsequently favoured by Spanish ascetics of the sixteenth century: 'Reflect that even the fairest woman originated in an evil-smelling drop of semen; then reflect that her midriff is a receptacle for filth; and then reflect on her end, when she will become food for the worms' (ibid., p. 151).

Alanus ab Insulis (d. 1202) differed from Petrus Cantor. His response to the question of who sinned more, the lover of the beautiful woman or the ugly, was that the man who had intercourse with the former sinned less 'because he is more overcome by the sight of her beauty', and 'where the compulsion is greater, the sin is less'. Bazian (d. 1197), a distinguished canonist from Bologna, shared this view (ibid., p. 138).

A staunch advocate of the contrary view – that the woman's beauty aggravated the man's sin – was Cardinal Huguccio of Ferrara (d. 1210), a celebrated canonist and Camaldolese monk who was tutor to Pope Innocent III. In these two men, the Augustinian-Gregorian theory that all sexual pleasure is evil attained its culmination. Huguccio never tired of citing Gregory's assertion that sexual desire can never be without sin. Consequently, he took a less indulgent view of the husband who found intercourse with his wife detestable and was allegedly free from sin: even that saintly man was guilty of sin because the emission of semen is inseparable from pleasure. Only 'he that feels nothing sins not' (ibid., p. 111). Any sensation of sexual pleasure was sinful, whatever its cause or occasion. It was immaterial whether a virgin experienced it while being raped, or a husband while procreating, or a man while ejaculating in his sleep: sexual pleasure could never be devoid of sin. Methodically, Huguccio carried this abstruse Augustinian-Gregorian idea to its logical conclusion.

It should be added that moral theologians were greatly exercised by the celibatarian's very own problem: were nocturnal emissions on the part of monks and priests sinful and, if so, to what extent? Their effusions on the subject filled whole libraries. Did the fault lie with excessive indulgence in food and drink? With erotic fantasies during the day?

Huguccio firmly rejected all previous explanations. Gluttony and day-dreams, though sins in themselves, were no guide to the sinfulness of a nocturnal emission: the sole criterion was the degree of pleasure experienced. He who felt pleasure sinned venially; he who delighted in that pleasurable sensation committed a mortal sin (ibid., p. 112).

Since any feeling of sexual pleasure was a sin, Huguccio believed, like Augustine, that Jesus had not wished to be generated by marital intercourse. Augustine had based his notion of original sin on those oft-repeated words from Psalm 50 (51): 'Behold, I was shapen in wicked-ness . . .' Huguccio emphasised the same point (ibid., p. 110f.). He was so consistent in condemning sexual pleasure, however, that he collided with the pioneer of its theological denigration, Augustine himself, and with the theological consensus that no sin attached to marital inter-course for the purpose of procreation or in performance of one's conjugal duty. Huguccio held that these two forms of intercourse were free from sin, but that the pleasure inseparable from them was not. On the subject of the Creator's injunction to 'Be fruitful and multiply' he wrote: 'It may be asserted that God commands and does much that neither is, nor can be, without sin.' The Almighty had also commanded men to provide themselves with wives and children, which they could hardly do without sinning. The obligation of spouses to grant each other intercourse was an obligation, not to sin, but to perform an act impossible of accomplishment without sinning (ibid., p. 113). Theolo-gians are not easily abashed! Huguccio did concede the existence of a certain problem, but it only spurred him on and made him the prophet of a novel form of marital intercourse – one that was sinless even by his own strict standards. This was what later came to be called 'the restrained embrace', the *amplexus reservatus* or coitus reservatus (not to be confused with coitus interruptus), which continues to exercise moral theologians to this day (v. chapter 14).

Cardinal Huguccio instilled order into the motives for intercourse. Theologians gradually came to accept four principal, classical motives for marital intercourse: (i) procreation and (ii) conjugal duty (these two alone considered sinless by Augustine; (iii) fear of incontinence (considered sinless by some but regarded by most, Huguccio included, as venially sinful); and (iv) self-gratification (regarded by most, Huguccio included, as a mortal sin). Many authorites were unclear about the motivational distinction between (iii) and (iv), incontinence and the deliberate pursuit of sexual pleasure. Huguccio dispelled this obscurity. In the case of physical union motivated by incontinence, he said, the man became sexually aroused and resolved on intercourse with his wife in that order; in him, such intercourse was a venial sin. It was free from sin (since Augustine) only when the partner performed his or her conjugal duty on demand. In the case of intercourse for the purpose of self-gratification, Huguccio declared, the man himself induced sexual excitement by means of thoughts, physical contacts, or aphrodisiac substances calculated to promote more frequent intercourse. Such intercourse was a mortal sin. In the ensuing centuries, moral theologians devoted much thought to the precise definition of intercourse in pursuit of pleasure, to whether it was always a mortal sin, and to whether the third motive for intercourse (fear of incontinence) might not, after all, be free from sin.

Like many of the early Schoolmen, Huguccio was dominated by the contemporary notion that the husband was an invalid for ever in danger of lapsing into mortally sinful fornication unless the medicine of marital intercourse was made readily available to him, at any hour of the night or day, by his nurse-cum-wife. Bans on sex at holy times of year, which the penitentials had so rigorously propagated for centuries that little time was left for marital intercourse, were now regarded by Huguccio as advisory rather than mandatory. For instance, he rejected the assertion that any form of intercourse at Easter, from whatever motive, was a mortal sin. To him, mortal sin was intercourse in pursuit of pleasure, intercourse prompted by libido, and 'unnatural' intercourse at any time. Huguccio further sanctioned intercourse during pregnancy, which many penitentials had forbidden, for fear of incontinence, fornication, and adultery.

In connection with the constant availability of 'medicinal' conjugal sex, Huguccio devised the following extreme example. If a married man became pope against his wife's wishes, he would even then be bound to fulfil his marital obligations toward her. If he failed to persuade her to remain continent, she could demand his return from the college of cardinals, thereby terminating his papal career. Even in an extreme case of that kind, therefore, the risk of fornication took precedence over all other considerations and marital intercourse could not be withheld. This, incidentally, is one of the few instances where a theologian has upheld a woman's right. However, this preferential treatment was only a product of ecclesiastical discrimination. Under canon law, no woman could become pope; had the positions been reversed, Huguccio would have entitled the husband to demand the restoration of his wife.

Innocent III (d. 1216), the greatest medieval pope, was a pupil of Huguccio's. Huguccio had followed Gregory the Great in denigrating sexual desire and condemning most forms of marital intercourse as sinful. Innocent III was the consummation of this attitude. 'Who can be unaware', he wrote, 'that marital intercourse can never take place without lascivious ardour, without the filth of lust whereby the seed conceived is sullied and corrupted.' Like all pleasure-haters, he went on to cite Psalm 50, 7 (51,5): 'The parents commit an actual sin . . . the child becomes infected with original sin. Wherefore the Psalmist says: "Behold, I was conceived in the wickedness committed by my parents at my conception."' Where Augustine's compensating 'goods of marriage' were concerned, Innocent held that they absolved marital intercourse only of grave but not of venial sin ('Commentary of the Seven Penitential Psalms', 4).

A whole series of early Scholastic theologians strongly condemned the consumption of sexually stimulating foods and, more especially, any deviation from the 'normal' coital position. The latter practice, if prompted by a desire for sexual pleasure, was a mortal sin. One anonymous thirteenth-century 'summa' (the Codex latinus monacensis 22233 that cited Pliny's chaste elephant as a paragon of continence in chapter 1) stated that a wife's acquiescence in any deviation from the normal coital position was as grave a sin as murder. This view was shared by the Dominicans Roland of Cremona, chancellor of Paris university, his successor Hugo of St Cher (d. 1263), and Guillaume of

Rennes (*c.* 1250). The anonymous Summa, Roland of Cremona, and Guillaume of Rennes did sanction such deviations, at least in isolated cases, if normal intercourse was precluded by some medical condition, e.g. by excessive obesity which no amount of dieting had succeeded in curing. In such cases Roland of Cremona urged the obese 'to come together after the manner of the beasts' but 'always with spiritual sorrow'. His recommended diet for the overweight comprised manual labour, sweating, less sleep, little meat, millet bread, and vinegar to drink ('Summa de matrimonio solutio'). Such a deviation from the norm was accounted 'against nature' and, thus, numbered among the gravest sins. What contributed to its gravely sinful character, according to the Summa's anonymous author, was that it rendered conception almost impossible. We are better informed on this subject today. This makes it all the more grotesque that, even in our own century, Theodor van de Velde's 'Ideal Marriage' (1926) was placed on the Index of Prohibited Books, a work whose only deviation from the normal doctrine was its advocacy of deviations from the normal coital position.

It was, as we have seen, characteristic of the early Schoolmen to dramatise the sinfulness of sexual pleasure and the potency of the sexual urge. This overriding view of marriage as a remedy for the perils of sexual desire, this unwholesome celibatarian preoccupation with the conjugal act as a sin and a remedy for sin combined – these simultaneous execrations of sexual intercourse and exhortations to engage in it (even if it endangered the woman's life) – gave rise during the twelfth century to a sharp reaction on the part of Hugo of St Victor (d. 1141; formerly Count von Blankenburg). This German theologian and mystic recommended an extreme form of the pure, ethereal, Marian marriage, a spiritual union innocent of carnality, because he believed that the true, genuine, perfect marriage was consummated in the mind alone. He was fascinated by the relationship of Mary and Joseph, the celibatarian's sexless dream-couple, and wanted every other marriage to be modelled on it.

Like Augustine, Hugo was convinced that Mary and Joseph's was a true marriage. His inference was that, as Augustine constantly emphasised (v. Müller, op. cit., p. 32), the carnal act is not inherent in the ideal nature of marriage. According to Anselm of Laon, an older contemporary of Hugo's, Mary had agreed to marital intercourse when she married Joseph in the firm belief that he would never require her to fulfil her conjugal obligation. Hugo indignantly rejected this view of the

Marian marriage because it was, in his opinion, based on a misconception. Sexual intercourse was not an essential part of marriage, he argued, or Mary would have had to assent to it, and that was a criminal aspersion on the blessed Virgin ('De beatae Mariae virginitate').

The problems arising from the celibatarian notion of the asexual Marian or 'Josephan' marriage are still reflected in devout ecclesiastical parlance today: although Mary's marriage is not denied in principle, it is played down in practice by referring to Joseph as her 'bridegroom' because, to devout ears, bridegroom sounds 'cleaner' than husband. Hugo, for his part, regarded Joseph as the ideal husband and the Josephan marriage as the true form of matrimony. Having once dissociated true marriage from the 'evil' of sexual excitement, Hugo found some fine and lofty things to say about conjugal love – a subject seldom if ever mentioned by other theologians, whose thoughts were continuously focused on the lust-besmirched domain of marital intercourse. It was only by divorcing mind from body – just as Augustine did, once he had excluded the physical element – that Hugo contrived to discourse on conjugal love, amplifying and reinforcing the crude conception of marriage as, first and foremost, a procreative institution or a remedy for incontinence. His verdict on the latter aspect of marriage, since he considered the experiencing of sexual desire a '*malum*', or evil, was harsh: marriage restricted 'the ardour of immoderate lust' to the marital union, and its advantages 'excused' the said evil 'that it be not added to damnation'. Marriage did not, however, make the evil any less evil; it merely prevented it from being damnable.

Rather than rehabilitating carnality and sexuality and dismantling Augustine's whole system of excuses for marriage, Hugo chose to dissociate himself from the carnal consummation of marriage and construct a purely spiritual edifice. In so doing, he denigrated physical love still more. What exemplifies this greater denigration is that, unlike many of the early Schoolmen, he strictly forbade marital intercourse at holy times and equated it with 'unnatural intercourse' ('De sacramentis', 2, 11, 7.9.10).

God's chief reason for instituting marriage, according to Hugo, was neither the generation of offspring nor the purging of lust. His principal motive could be inferred from Adam's words when Eve was brought to him: 'Therefore shall a man leave his father and his mother, and shall cleave unto his wife' (Genesis 2). Adam's ensuing words defined the 'function' of marriage, which consisted in 'being one flesh', but spiritual love took precedence. Marriage was founded on a union, not of the flesh but of the heart (v. Müller, op. cit., p. 81f.). If the paramount factor or 'alliance of love' was absent the marriage would be 'invalid' even if a union of the flesh was present (ibid., p. 83). Conversely, Hugo argued, the ideal marriage would be more perfectly consummated if no intercourse ensued: the sanctity of love would be assured, and nothing would happen 'at which chastity could not but blush' (ibid., p. 79). The sexual intercourse essential to procreation and the performance of one's conjugal duty did not form part of the nature of marriage itself, only of the conjugal function subordinate thereto. Hugo pronounced a physically unconsummated marriage 'more perfect and holy' than a physically consummated one. He consequently held that two persons could still contract a valid marriage if solely desirous of spiritual love and communion, and that the desire for sexual union was not essential (ibid., p. 78). 'Rather, I believe that marriage is more truly and holily present when sealed with the bond of love alone, not in carnal concupiscence and lust . . . Is it not [worth] more when two become one in spirit than when they become one in the flesh?' (ibid., p. 81).

Hugo's relatively sensitive remarks on marriage, love, and the precedence of the heart struck an unwonted and agreeable note at a time when theologians insulted all married couples by concentrating on their sexuality alone and regarding it primarily as a dangerous spur to fornication and adultery. He did not, however, succeed in reconciling physical union with his spiritualised view of marriage. On the contrary, he became the most extreme advocate of the *consensus* theory, so called, and the fiercest opponent of the *copula* theory.

Authorities on ecclesiastical law have debated these two theories for centuries, the salient point at issue being whether a marriage is validated by sexual union, or by mutual consent to marriage, or by both. Roman law held that matrimony was founded on mutual consent and not on sexual conjunction (*consensus facit matrimonium et non concubitus*). This legal principle was adopted by Catholic marriage law, e.g. by Pope Nicholas in his letter to the newly converted Bulgars in 866. Where its application and emphasis were concerned, however, two opposing schools of thought evolved.

The question was first invested with practical significance by a case that caused a great stir in its day. Having married the daughter of one Count Regimund, an Aquitanian nobleman named Stephanus packed her off home immediately after the wedding and before consummating the union. Count Regimund duly complained to the Frankish bishops assembled at the Synod of Touzy in 860. The bishops instructed the leading theologian of the time, Hinkmar of Rheims (d. 882), to investigate the matter. Hinkmar's opinion, 'The Marriage of Stephanus and the Daughter of Count Regimund', supported the *copula* theory – sexual consummation was so essential to marriage that no marriage could be deemed valid without it – and cited a dictum attributed to Augustine: 'A wedding is not in the image of the wedding of Christ and the Church if the participants do not avail themselves of their conjugal rights – in other words, if no intercourse takes place.'

By the twelfth century the two schools of thought were locked in battle. The *consensus* theory was mainly espoused by the University of Paris, the *copula* theory by that of Bologna. Bologna's leading jurist, the monk Gratian (d. 1142), regarded intercourse or *copula* as constitutive of marriage. Hugo, realising that this would invalidate his conception of the Marian marriage (Mary would not have been married at all), held that the sole constitutive factor was mutual consent and excluded all reference to the sexual element.

This controversy was resolved by a compromise that holds good to this day. Pope Alexander III (d. 1181) largely endorsed the *consensus* theory. Thus, a marriage is valid prior to its consummation but indissoluble thereafter. This means that an unconsummated marriage may be dissolved, whereas a consummated marriage may not. Even today, Catholic canon law permits a married person who has not had intercourse after marriage to apply for a dissolution and marry again.

THIRTEEN

Early Scholasticism (2):
Abelard's 'Crime' and Punishment

At the turn of the twelfth to thirteenth centuries, as we have seen, marital intercourse was almost universally deemed sinful by theologians of whom Huguccio represented the most extreme. This view was opposed by the only married theologian, Peter Abelard (1079–1142), renowned for his ill-starred love affair with Héloïse (1101–64) and his great success as a teacher in Paris. A lone voice among a mass of antisexual theologians who kept harping on the same vexed subject, he was also one of the few to oppose the wholesale slaughter of Jews during the crusades of the twelfth century. Bernard of Clairvaux, who accused him of heresy during his lifetime, eventually prevailed upon Pope Innocent II to seal his lips for ever. Abelard died shortly thereafter.

He had already acquired an international reputation when teaching in Paris, but in 1118 his university career was cut short. At that time he was lodging with Canon Fulbert, whose sixteen-year-old niece, Héloïse, a girl as intelligent as she was beautiful, could converse with equal fluency in Latin and French and was even studying Hebrew. Abelard, not yet an ordained priest, was employed as her private tutor. He later recorded the outcome of these tutorials in a personal account of his misfortunes:

> Utterly aflame with my passion for this maiden, I sought to discover means whereby I might have daily and familiar speech with her ... I persuaded the girl's uncle ... to take me into his household ... in return for the payment of a small sum ... Now, he was a man keen in avarice, and likewise he was most desirous for his niece that her study of letters should ever go forward ... Learning held out to us the secret opportunities that our passion

craved . . . and our kisses far outnumbered our reasoned words. Our hands sought less the book than each other's bosoms; love drew our eyes together far more than the lesson drew them to the pages of our text.

(Peter Abelard, 'The Story of My Misfortunes', pp. 17–18)

When Héloïse became pregnant Abelard eloped with her and took her to his sister in Brittany, promising her indignant uncle that he would marry her provided the marriage was kept secret. Under the Gregorian Reform married men were precluded from entering the priesthood unless their wives retired to a convent. Héloïse was unwilling to take the veil but had no wish to blight her lover's academic career, which required him to take holy orders. She therefore resolved to remain his mistress. Abelard, however, persuaded her to marry him in secret. Leaving their son Astrolabe with Abelard's sister, they married in Fulbert's presence. Héloïse went back to live with her uncle while Abelard returned to his bachelor quarters, and they saw each other only rarely. Fulbert, who found this clandestine relationship damaging to his reputation, publicised the fact of their marriage. Abelard thereupon abducted Héloïse a second time and bore her off to a convent at Argenteuil, where he bade her don the habit without taking her vows. When Fulbert and his kinsmen learned of this,

> they were convinced that now I had completely played them false and had rid myself for ever of Héloïse by forcing her to become a nun. Violently incensed, they laid a plot against me, and one night, while I, all unsuspecting, was asleep in a secret room in my lodgings, they broke in with the help of one of my servants, whom they had bribed. There they had vengeance on me with a most cruel and most shameful punishment, for they cut off those parts of my body with which I had done that which was the cause of their sorrow. That done, straightway they fled, but two of them were captured and suffered the loss of their eyes and their genital organs.
>
> (Ibid., pp. 29–30)

All Paris and its clergy took Abelard's side, and his sympathetic students rallied round. Héloïse, whom he persuaded to take the veil, later became an abbess. He himself became a monk at St Denis and resumed lecturing with the encouragement of his students and his abbot.

The fate of Abelard and Héloïse has since become famed for all time as the story of two lovers sacrificed on the altar of celibacy. ·

Abelard accused his contemporaries of placing impossible constraints upon marital intercourse and declared that reason, not tradition, must be the criterion of a theory's accuracy. 'No natural pleasure of the flesh may be declared a sin,' he wrote, 'nor may one describe it as a fault if someone is delighted by pleasure, given that the latter must be deemed necessary', for 'from the first day of our creation, since life in Paradise was without sin', marital intercourse and the consumption of tasty foods were, by their very nature, associated with pleasure. Nature, said Abelard, had been so constituted by God himself (Eth. 3). Although he was naturally acquainted with the Augustinian doctrine that sexual pleasure is a consequence of and penalty for the Fall, he made no mention of it whatever. He charged his contemporaries with illogicality for sanctioning marital intercourse as a means of procreation and a duty but condemning the pleasure inseparable from it. He also disputed the traditional interpretation of I Corinthians 7: 6, which was that St Paul, by 'excusing' marital intercourse, had implicitly branded it a sin. Paul, said Abelard, had left married couples free to have intercourse or not as they chose. Moreover, the oft-cited words from Psalm 50 (51) – 'I was shapen in wickedness' – did not imply that a child was sullied by its parents' sexual desire; they merely related to the original sin inherent in every human being.

It was consistent with his attempt to rehabilitate sexual pleasure that Abelard should have supported the immaculate conception, in other words, the doctrine that Mary herself had been conceived without original sin. His opponent Bernard of Clairvaux (d. 1153), who suffered from Augustinian sexual pessimism, fiercely contested this and accused him of heresy. Since it was assumed that Mary had been generated by normal sexual intercourse – the legendary names of her parents were Ioacim (Joachim) and Anna (Anne) – neither Augustine nor his follow-ers could acquit her of original sin. Bernard, for example, stressed that sexual desire (*libido*) was inherent in marital intercourse, that sexual desire was sinful, and that the Holy Ghost could not be present where sin prevailed. It was thus impossible for Mary's soul to have been the recipient of sanctifying grace at the moment of her conception (Ep. 174,1.5.6.7.9). Just as sexual pleasure and sin were regarded as inseparable, so were sexual pleasure and the transmission of original sin. Abelard, the defender of sexual pleasure, was the first to deny this false connection.

Sensational as his hypotheses sounded, Abelard was in many respects a traditionalist – as, for instance, when he stated that the ideal motive for marital intercourse was a desire for children, and that holy women such as St Anne might have dispensed with it altogether had some other means of procreation been available (Eth. 3). Even he regarded celibacy and continence as more perfect and meritorious in the sight of God than the married state.

Augustine's condemnation of sexual pleasure was too deeply entrenched to be dislodged by Abelard's arguments in favour of its acceptance as a natural phenomenon. On the contrary, Augustinian antisexualism retained its influence after Abelard's time and culminated, as we saw, in Huguccio, whose bizarre suggestion for a sin-free form of marital intercourse will be examined in the following chapter.

FOURTEEN

The Restrained Embrace:
A Formula for Sinless Marital Intercourse

The method of marital intercourse favoured by Cardinal Huguccio (d. 1210) was designed for the husband alone. Although it precluded procreation and was later, as we shall see, declared to be a form of contraception on that account, it should not be confused with coitus interruptus, which Huguccio, like all orthodox Catholics up to the present day, considered a mortal sin. Huguccio's theological problem was this: how could intercourse, in which the husband was duty-bound to engage at his wife's request, be converted into a sinless activity on his part even though ejaculation was inseparable from pleasure and thus, according to Huguccio ('only he that feels nothing commits no sin'), a sin – albeit not a grave one.

His solution was as follows: 'I can so render my wife her due and wait in such a manner that she assuages her desire. Indeed, often on such occasions a woman is wont to anticipate her husband, and, when the wife's desire for the carnal work is assuaged, I can, if I wish, withdraw, free from all sin, without assuaging my own desire or emitting my seed of propagation' ('Summa', 2, 13; cf. John T. Noonan in 'Contraception: A History of its Treatment by the Catholic Theologians and Canonists', pp. 296–7). In other words, unlike the mortally sinful addict of coitus interruptus, the husband had to concentrate on retaining his semen – a somewhat effortful but worthwhile proceeding. In performing such a conjugal act, the husband who aspired to sanctity remained sinless because he was pleasureless. He withdrew his penis from the vagina without permitting any subsequent ejaculation. The orgasm experienced by the wife whose incontinence had prompted her to demand intercourse was venially sinful, for Augustine had taught that, where the request for intercourse was concerned, only the partner who acceded to a demand for procreation was sinless. Huguccio, who surpassed even Augustine in his hostility to sexual pleasure, considered this 'restrained embrace' superior to Augustine's sinless intercourse for posterity's or duty's sake. In Huguccio's opinion, only the restrained embrace was truly sinless because it involved no pleasurable sensation. The extent to which a man can feel pleasure even without ejaculating, thereby negating the whole procedure, was a question he left unexplored.

People have wondered how a monk like Huguccio could have hit upon such a method. He himself mentioned that it was 'often' employed. Noonan surmises that it was an Albigensian method of contraception commonly practised in Northern Italy (Noonan, op. cit., p. 366). It is also referred to in the troubadours' literature of courtly love. First introduced into theology by Huguccio as a means of excluding sexual enjoyment from marital intercourse, it was later to become a bone of contention because of its contraceptive side effect.

The ensuing theological controversy might be entitled 'The tabooing of male semen, and how married couples have been tyrannised thereby.' The concept of the restrained embrace and the centuries-long theological dispute associated with it are so abstruse that it is hard to decide which monkish theologians are guilty of the greater absurdity, those who recommend it or those who forbid it. Those who forbid it suspect that too much pleasure results or may result from it, whereas those who recommend it do so to deprive the act of as much pleasure as possible. Hostility to sexual enjoyment is the basic motive common to both schools of thought.

Although no Catholic theologians have ever defined coitus interruptus as other than a grave sin, many of them continue to maintain a favourable attitude toward the *amplexus reservatus* or restrained embrace. The question remains a topical one, and interest in the practice was revived in 1960, when Cardinal Suenens recommended it as a contraceptive method for use by married couples with valid reasons for wishing to avoid a pregnancy ('A Crucial Problem', p. 81f.).

Nothing more was heard of Huguccio's suggestion until over a century later, when Archbishop Petrus de Palude (d. 1342) condemned coitus interruptus on the part of husbands who wanted no more children because they could not afford to feed them. He did, however sanction *amplexus reservatus* in certain circumstances: 'If, however, the husband withdraws before the act is complete and does not permit his semen to discharge itself, he clearly commits no mortal sin unless the wife be thereby incited to an emission of semen' ('Commentary on the Sentences', 4, 31, 3, 2). By an 'emission of semen' the archbishop meant, in the wife's case, an orgasm. If that occurred during a restrained embrace, it was a mortal sin.

The term 'female semen' derived from Galen (second century), the Greek who was personal physician to Emperor Marcus Aurelius. Galen described female semen as colder and moister than the male variety but considered it essential to procreation, unlike Aristotle, who held that male semen alone was generative. From Albertus Magnus and Thomas Aquinas onwards, most theologians subscribed to Aristotle's biology. In so far as they mentioned 'female semen' at all – whatever they meant by the term – they were in no doubt that its emission was an orgasmic process analogous to ejaculation in the male. To Huguccio, the female orgasm was an integral part of his system. He classified intercourse by means of *amplexus reservatus* as a male obligation fulfilled without any pleasurable, alias sinful, sensations on the husband's part. Archbishop Palude insisted that the wife should have no orgasm either, because this form of intercourse was not classified as contraceptive.

St Antoninus (d. 1459), a Dominican friar who became archbishop of Florence, introduced the restrained embrace to an even wider audience. His 'Summa theologica moralis' (3, 120) restated Archbishop Palude's exposition word for word, as did two fifteenth-century manuals for confessors: the 'Summa of Cases of Conscience' by the Franciscan Trovamala (d. after 1494), who listed the subject under the heading '*Debitum*' (obligation); and 'Moral Leprosy: The Genital Abuse of the Married' by a German Dominican named Nider (d. 1439). During the period 1450–1750 the restrained embrace was more and more often cited by theologians as a permissible method of contraception.

Dissenting voices were also heard, however. The first was that of the Dominican Sylvester da Prierio (d. 1523), who made a name for himself by rebutting Luther's theses against the sale of indulgences. Prierio denounced Palude's opinion as 'nonsensical in the extreme' ('Summa de debito conjugali'). Others agreed with him, insisting that any non-generative sexual act merited condemnation. They included the Dominican inquisitor Bartholomæus Fundo (d. 1545), who considered the method a mortal sin, the Italian Dominican Ignatius Conradi (d. 1606), and the Spanish Jesuit Henriquez (d. 1608).

Archbishop Palude's contention that the restrained embrace was a permissible contraceptive act, and that it did not become a mortal sin unless it induced an orgasm in the wife, was endorsed by Cardinal Cajetan (d. 1534), another of Luther's opponents, and by the Jesuit Thomas Sanchez (d. 1610). Sanchez held that the method could justifiably be sanctioned if a couple were too poor to feed their numerous children ('De sancto matrimonii sacramento', 9, 19).

Alfonso de' Liguori (d. 1787) characterised the restrained embrace as a mortal sin if it induced an orgasm ('an emission of semen') in the wife, but otherwise as a venial sin. It was also defined as a venial sin by the German Jesuit Paul Laymann (d. 1635), Emperor Ferdinand II's confessor, in his standard work on moral theology, and by Charles-René Billuart (d. 1757). Another moral theologian, Antonio Diana (d. 1663), whom Pascal attacked on account of his 'laxity', stated that the method was 'commonly' employed.

Theologians pursued their absurd dispute over the restrained embrace throughout the nineteenth century and into the twentieth. Augustinus Lehmkuhl (d. 1918) considered the method permissible but 'seldom expedient' because it excited sexual desire rather than assuaged it. Others condemned it on the assumption that most married couples were really practising coitus interruptus. In our own century, Bishop de Smet of Bruges recommended *amplexus reservatus* as a 'lesser evil' for married couples who would otherwise employ contraceptive devices. Arthur Vermeersch (d. 1936) held that most people who practised it were committing a sin because they could not avoid the danger of coitus interruptus, though he was prepared to pardon the occasional (unintentional) ejaculation. Two books by the Catholic layman Paul Chanson, published in 1948 by permission of the archdiocese of Paris, were withdrawn from sale in 1950 on instructions from the Holy Office. Chanson had recommended the restrained embrace as an act of self-control – 'of the humanisation of the flesh'. The said act could last between ten and thirty minutes, he wrote, and was designed to enhance conjugal love.

In 1951, the Dominican H. M. Hering launched the fiercest attack ever directed against this method. He denounced the whole practice as 'immoral' because – unlike kissing, for example – it involved those sexual organs whose function was defined by Canon 1081/2 of the CIC as the generation of offspring. It was, therefore, 'the gravest of sins' and 'one of the unnatural vices'. Chanson, said Hering, had forgotten the primary purpose of marriage (procreation), and the whole thing amounted in many cases to coitus interruptus because the couples concerned could not control themselves. Chanson had further ignored a number of articles of faith, e.g. 'the doctrine of original sin and its consequences, notably carnal desire' ('De amplexu reservato' in 'Angelicum').

In 1952 the Jesuits' leading moralist, Franz Hürth, entered the lists against Hering and claimed that the restrained embrace was not, after all, an unnatural practice. A compromise ensued on 30 June 1952, when the Holy Office issued a monitum to the effect that priests must not speak of the restrained embrace as if it were immune from criticism.

More recent moral theologians sanction the reserved embrace and differ only in their degree of approval. Bernhard Häring neither recommends *copula sicca* ('dry' copulation) nor does he condemn it provided husband and wife can control themselves and preserve their 'respect for the Creator and for each other'. 'What is positive in this is the firm determination to remain true to life even though no conception is planned' ('The Law of Christ', III, p. 373). Coitus interruptus he naturally condemns out of hand. Josef Fuchs concurs with his fellow Jesuit Franz Hürth in viewing the restrained embrace with favour. Cardinal Suenens, whom we already met above, is a prominent advocate of the method and recommends it in cases where there are valid grounds for avoiding pregnancy. Noonan (op. cit., pp. 336–7, 338, 447–8, 449–50) provides a good picture of the whole controversy. It is symptomatic of the disastrous predicament in which Catholic moral theologians find themselves that their supreme objective should be to prevent the emission of semen and force married couples into a strait-jacket designed by celibatarians who represent their hostility to sexual pleasure as 'respect for the Creator'.

Some of them now appear to have dropped their admonitions against the female orgasm, though this, in the view of many theologians, remained the deciding factor for centuries. As we have seen, they equated the female orgasm with an emission of 'female semen', a term still employed by the moral theologian Heribert Jone in 1930 and by Hering as recently as 1951 (op. cit., p. 323). Since theologians' biological knowledge now approximates somewhat more closely to the biological facts of life (the human ovum was discovered in 1827), one or two of them have renounced their belief in the existence of female semen and swept the female orgasm under the carpet. By so doing, however, they have focused the whole 'restrained embrace' debate even more sharply on the man and his semen.

All now depends on whether or not the man practises coitus interruptus. With the abandonment of the idea of female semen and the orgasm thought to be associated with it, male semen has become a special object of pastoral concern. Taboo and not to be wasted, it cannot be allowed to flow free. Eternal salvation depends on the fluid that must never see the light of day, the fluid whose only proper place is in the vagina, but which cannot always lodge there because circumstances sometimes justify its exclusion. If unwanted there, however, it is unwanted anywhere; if unbidden there it is forbidden everywhere.

Such absurdities are the product of a misguided sexual ethic still loath to abandon the dictatorship it has presumed to enforce on the matrimonial bedroom for almost two thousand years. It is amazing what an abundance of men have spiritually reproduced themselves throughout history – men who, though quite unqualified to pronounce on their pet subject, have consistently laid claim to supreme competence, enveloped themselves in a divine aura, and devoted much of their lives to the pursuit of utter nonsense. This pseudo-theological specimen cabinet would be a rich source of amusement if one did not know that the figures on display there had, in their day, been responsible for countless marital tragedies.

FIFTEEN

The Thirteenth Century: Theology's Golden Age, Woman's Darkest Hour

Many modern authorities seek to represent the great theologians of the heyday of Scholasticism, notably Albertus Magnus and his pupil Thomas Aquinas, as turning points in the Augustinian tradition of hostility to sexual pleasure. This change of direction is supposed to have resulted from the incorporation of Aristotelian biology in the Church's doctrinal edifice. Since Aristotle had defined the pleasure accruing from a good action as good and natural, sexual hostility allegedly diminished in consequence. None of this is true.

The only benefit Adam and Eve derived from Aristotle was that Albertus and Thomas held that sexual desire in Paradise was both greater and smaller than it is now – smaller because in those happy days it was wholly controlled by reason. Augustine had conceded as much to Julian the Pelagian at the end of his life, but this fact had become obscured during the early medieval and early Scholastic periods. In other respects, the absorption of Aristotelianism by theology wrought nothing but havoc. Its abstruse biology bred an even greater contempt for womankind and engendered even greater sexual hostility because Albertus and (more especially) Thomas contrived to turn Aristotle's pronouncements on the ecstatic and stupefying nature of the orgasm into additional, negative, contributions to Augustinian sexual pessimism. Moreover, the only effect of Aristotle's definition of sexual intercourse as 'a natural act' common to both man and beast – which might have diminished the suspicion attaching to sexual pleasure – was to relegate sex in general to the animal or, more properly, the bestial domain. 'In intercourse man becomes like unto the beast (*bestialis efficitur*)' Thomas declared ('Summa theologica', I, q. 98, a. 2).

Although he went further than his mentor in classifying marital sex as a bestial activity, his dry systematics contain none of the malicious slurs on women to which Albertus was so prone.

Albertus Magnus had a supreme contempt for the opposite sex. 'Woman is less suited to morality [than man]', he wrote.

> For woman contains more fluid than man, and it is characteristic of fluid to absorb readily and retain poorly. Fluid is easily moved, so women are inconstant and inquisitive. When a woman has intercourse with one man she would fain lie beneath another at the same time. Woman is a stranger to fidelity. Believe me, if you put your faith in her you will be disappointed. Believe an experienced teacher. Prudent husbands, therefore, apprise their wives of their plans and doings least of all. Woman is an imperfect man and possesses, compared to him, a defective and deficient nature. She is therefore insecure in herself. That which she herself cannot receive, she endeavours to obtain by means of mendacity and devilish tricks. In short, therefore, one must beware of every woman as one would of a poisonous serpent and the horned devil. If I were at liberty to tell what I know of women, the whole world would stand amazed ... Woman is not more intelligent than man, properly speaking, but more cunning. Intelligence has a good ring, cunning an evil one. Thus, woman is cleverer, that is to say, more cunning, than man in evil and perverse dealings. Woman's emotion impels her toward all that is evil, just as man's intelligence prompts him to all that is good.
>
> ('Quaestiones super de animalibus', XV, q. 11)

Remarks of this nature disclose the extent to which celibacy warped and corrupted even its most eminent advocates. Any slur on women was all right with them as long as it helped to promote the monasticising of society. Albertus afforded still further insights into his gleanings from the confessional: 'I have learned while hearing confessions at Cologne that subtle suitors seduce women by discreetly fondling them. The more reluctant the women appear, the more they truly desire such attentions and are minded to yield to them. In order to seem chaste, however, they feign disapproval' (ibid., XIII, q. 18). The sainted theologian was, in fact, sanctifying an age-old masculine theory: the more a woman resists, the more amenable she is. Albertus Magnus deserves to be dubbed the patron saint of rapists.

It may be noted in passing that Albertus played a not unimportant part in the history of Christian anti-Semitism. A ruthless suppressor and annihilator of Jewish scholarship, he was a senior member of the committee of inquiry that met at Paris in 1248 to investigate the burning of two hundred and forty wagonloads of Talmudic literature six years earlier. Albertus personally endorsed the committee's seal of approval on this disastrous act of vandalism. This resulted in more bonfires, a ban on Talmudic studies, and the destruction of major centres of Jewish scholarship.

Pope Innocent IV had appointed the committee in 1247, in response to complaints from the Jewish community. Writing to King ('Saint') Louis IX of France on 9 May 1244, he stated that one reason for the Talmud burnings of 1242 had been 'fictions relating to the Most Blessed Virgin', by which he meant the Jews' denial of the Virgin Birth. We are well informed about Louis IX, in whose reign the Talmud burnings took place. Sieur Jean de Joinville, his friend and fellow Crusader (he lost his enthusiasm for campaigning and remained behind at his castle during Louis's second Crusade), is regarded as a trustworthy chronicler and accurate royal biographer. According to Joinville, Louis IX decreed that no layman should debate the Virgin Birth with a Jew: if he heard one slander the Christian faith he should simply drive his sword into the man's body 'as far as it would go'. In this connection, Joinville described the fate of a Jew who was severely beaten at Cluny Abbey because he could not bring himself to profess the Virgin Birth.

Albertus Magnus, Louis's contemporary, was another who glorified Mary at the expense of all other women. Eve, by contrast, had bequeathed her sex a threefold 'woe'. Apart from the tribulations of pregnancy and childbirth, her legacy included lustful temptation, the depravity attendant on the sexual act, and inordinate pleasure in conception ('In Lucam', 1, 28).

The claim set out at the start of this chapter that Albertus pioneered a less inhibited attitude to sexual pleasure is, as I have said, quite untrue. He (and Thomas) remained absolutely faithful to the Augustinian tradition and incorporated Aristotle's approval of pleasure in their Augustinian system only when it did not conflict with Augustine's hostility to the same. In other words, Albertus and Thomas both emphasised that sexual pleasure was good only in so far as it contributed to the survival of the human race. Albertus himself believed, like Aristotle, that Nature had made intercourse pleasurable so that it was desired for that end ('In Sententias IV', 26, 2 and 31, 21, n. 3). Thus, sexual pleasure was good only as a means to an end. To seek it for its own sake continued to be a sin.

None of the theologians of the High Scholastic period yielded an inch in this respect. On the contrary, they took advantage of Aristotle's slightly less inhibited view of sex to emphasise still further that the generative function of marriage was its fundamental and natural purpose: sexual pleasure was simply a means to that end – a guarantee that procreation would occur. Anyone who had intercourse for pleasure's sake was making an end of the means, and that, being at odds with the divinely ordained scheme of things, was a sin. Indeed, to have intercourse 'for pleasure's sake alone' was a mortal sin entailing eternal damnation.

Thus, none of this represented an advance on early Scholasticism. Albertus and Thomas merely eschewed the language of the Responsum Gregorii ('Pleasure can never be without sin'), in accordance with which all sexual pleasure deriving from marital intercourse had been defined as a venial sin, at best, from the fifth century to the twelfth. They adhered more closely to Augustine, who had affirmed the sinlessness of intercourse for the purpose of procreation and as a duty performed at the other party's request. Although neither Albertus nor Thomas regarded sexual pleasure in these two cases as a sin, Albertus shared Augustine's view that it was 'an evil', 'a punishment', 'filthy', 'polluting', 'nasty', 'shameful', 'unwholesome', 'spiritually debasing', 'a humbling of the spirit by the flesh', 'vile', 'disgraceful', 'demeaning', 'common to the beasts', 'brutish', 'corrupt', 'depraved', 'infected', and 'infective [with original sin]' (v. Leopold Brandl, 'Die Sexualethik des heiligen Albertus Magnus', pp. 45, 61, 73, 79, 80, 82–3, 95–6, 216).

It was consistent with such a cascade of aspersions on sexual pleasure that Albertus (in company with Gratian, the father of canon law) should have urged newly-weds to remain chaste for thirty nights after their nuptials, just in case they decided to renounce matrimony for a monastery or convent ('In IV Sent.', d. 27, a. 8). Monkish theologians did not abandon all hope of converting married couples to celibacy on their wedding-night itself – indeed, even on their honeymoon. If it was too late for them to enter a religious order, they could still strive for perfection within marriage: the husband who performed his conjugal duty 'reluctantly' was more perfect (ibid., d. 32, a. 3) but not completely so, for only celibatarians like Albertus himself could be that. Albertus, too, considered it unseemly to engage in marital intercourse on feast, fast, or processional days (ibid., d. 32, a. 10). The married were entitled to communicate only if prior intercourse had occurred for morally unobjectionable reasons, i.e. for posterity's or duty's sake, though this usually applied to the consenting party alone. If the party demanding intercourse had been motivated, not by a desire to procreate, but by a certain measure of sexual desire, Albertus held that the confessor should advise him or her against receiving Communion (ibid., d. 32, a. 13 ad q. 1). Confession was of the utmost importance, as we can see, because it enabled a confessor to analyse the motives of his married penitents and draw subtle moral distinctions of this kind.

Albertus stressed the great difference between demanding one's conjugal due and granting it when he stated that spouses who consented to intercourse did not approve of it but deplored their partner's sexual desire. They intended, not to stimulate their partner's libido, but to heal his or her sickness. The two of them co-operated, of course, but their moral attitude differed entirely. 'The requesting spouse is prompted by sexual desire, the consenting spouse by the virtue of conjugal fidelity. Thus the demand is sinful, the performance of the duty meritorious' (ibid., 32, 9; v. also Michael Müller, 'Die Lehre des heiligen Augustinus von der Paradiesehe und ihre Auswirkungen auf die Sexualethik des 12. und 13. Jahrhunderts bis Thomas von Aquin', p. 254).

There are sins and sins, of course. Albertus cited the pleasure-haters' standard dictum, which Jerome, as we have seen, introduced into the celibatarian repertoire: 'He that loves his wife to excess commits a mortal sin.' The husband who loved his wife but was not inordinately passionate committed a venial sin and merited apostolic 'forgiveness'. Like Augustine before him, Albertus inferred this from I Corinthians 7: 6 ('In IV Sent.', 31, 5).

Albertus based his supervision and regulation of marital intercourse not only on theological arguments but, more especially, on 'scientific' considerations. Undue indulgence in the conjugal act resulted in premature senility and death ('De animalibus', 1. 9 tr. I, 2 and 1. 15 tr. 2, 6). Excessive intercourse 'thinned' the brain and rendered the eyes weak and sunken. 'I was told by one Master Clement of Bohemia,' wrote Albertus, 'how a certain monk, whose hair had already turned grey, betook himself to a beautiful lady like a man ravenous with hunger. Six and three score times he desired her until the knock came for matins, but by morning he lay ill abed and died the same day. And, because he was of noble birth, his body was opened. And it was discovered that his brain had quite emptied, so that all that remained of it was no bigger than a pomegranate, and his eyes were ruined in just the same manner' ('Quaestiones super de animalibus', XV, q. 14). Frequent intercourse also induced premature baldness by desiccating and cooling the body (ibid., XIX, q. 7–9). Albertus had further observed that dogs ran after people who copulated frequently. His explanation: 'Dogs are fond of strong odours and run after corpses, and the body of a person who has frequent intercourse approximates to the condition of a corpse owing to its abundance of putrid semen' (ibid., V, q. 11–14).

Where semen was concerned, Albertus believed that women, too, excreted it during intercourse – in fact he dealt with the subject at considerable length. As we have seen the woman's emission of semen was generally associated with an orgasm, though the latter sometimes derived from a 'titillating vital spirit' ('De animalibus', XV, 2, 11). Female semen was whitish in colour. Black women produced more semen because they were more passionate, but dark-haired women produced most of all. Thin women produced more semen than fat ones. In conformity with Aristotelian biology, Albertus assailed those who credited female semen with generative powers. A woman's semen was watery and thin and 'not suited to procreation' ('Quaestiones super de animalibus', XV, q. 19). In his view, therefore, the term 'female semen', which as we saw in the last chapter derived from the physician Galen (second century), was incorrect ('De animalibus', IX, 2, 3). Male semen resembled the artist or master craftsman responsible for imparting shape, female semen was the thing shaped (ibid., III, 2, 8). The shaping process undertaken by male semen, which always strove to produce a perfect male form, could be frustrated by unfavourable circumstances, in which case the outcome was a woman.

This brings us back to Aristotle's disparagement of womanhood, which Albertus Magnus fashioned into a celibatarian constituent of theology. 'Having been threatened in the ancient world by Gnostic dualism, woman then, in the thirteenth century, sustained her greatest injury from the wholesale acceptance of Aristotelian biology' (Müller, 'Grundlagen der katholischen Sexualethik', p. 62).

SIXTEEN

Thomas Aquinas, the Church's Misguided 'Guiding Light'

Although Thomas Aquinas (d. 1274) did no more, in essence, than systematise the views of the High Scholastics as a whole, and although he said no more, in relation to the acceptance of Aristotelian biology, than his master Albertus Magnus had set forth at greater length but less methodically, his sexual ethic merits careful examination because its influence persists to this day. Thomas and Augustine are still *the* authorities on Catholic sexual morality. In his standard work, 'Die Lehre des heiligen Augustinus von der Paradiesehe und ihre Auswirkungen auf die Sexualethik des 12. and 13. Jahrhunderts bis Thomas von Aquin', Michael Müller finds it 'surprising' that, where the substance of individual questions is concerned, Thomas's doctrine was 'for the most part, merely a reiteration of the usual Scholastic views of the stricter kind, underpinned by elements of Aristotelian doctrine' (p. 255).

Discounting the fact that there is nothing 'surprising' about this, Müller's description of the greatest Catholic theologian's oeuvre is accurate. Only someone who believes that the Catholic Church's denigration and disparagement of women became substantially modified between Augustine in the fourth and fifth centuries and Thomas in the thirteenth century, or that Thomas's predominant influence effected a change in the interval between his century and our own, could be 'surprised' to find that everything had remained essentially unaltered. 'Religious perfection entails perpetual continence', wrote Thomas. 'Hence the condemnation of Jovinian, who thought marriage the equal of celibacy' ('Summa theologica', II/II, q. 186, a. 4). He several times repeated the computation Jerome had made eight centuries before, to wit, that the following categories are rewarded in heaven thus: celibatarians one hundred per cent, widows and widowers sixty, and the married thirty (ibid., q. 152, a. 5 ad 2). Then as now, any attempt to put marriage on a par with celibacy is still regarded as a debasement of the latter to the (inferior) status of the former; in other words, as a slur on virginity in general and the Virgin Mary in particular.

There has been absolutely no change, either, in woman's status vis-à-vis the male-dominated Church. Augustine wrote that all mankind's misfortunes began with Eve, the immediate cause of Adam's expulsion from Paradise, and until the turn of the present century the Old Testament story of the Creation and Fall was papally regarded as a semi-documentary account. Why did the Devil accost Eve rather than Adam? He addressed himself first to 'the frailer part of that first human society', Augustine replied, because he believed 'that man is less gullible and can be more easily deluded into following a bad example [Eve's] than into making a mistake himself'. There were mitigating circumstances in Adam's case. 'The man yielded to his wife under the compulsion of their close union without considering her words to be true ... Eve accepted the Serpent's words as true, whereas Adam refused to be separated from his partner, even in a union of sin' ('De civitate Dei', 14, 11). In other words, love of woman dragged man down to perdition.

The nun Hildegard of Bingen (d. 1179) took over Augustine's explanation and put it into even plainer language: 'The Devil ... saw that Adam was inflamed with so passionate a love for Eve that he would do whatever she told him' (Scivias 1, visio 2). This was all of a piece with the traditional condemnation of womanhood, celibatarian theology's eternal foe, and women themselves were only too often inclined to regard their femininity as a species of divinely ordained leprosy.

Theologians of the thirteenth century, notably Albertus and Thomas, used Aristotle to reinforce their traditional, Augustinian disdain for the female sex. Aristotle opened monastic eyes to the most fundamental cause of woman's inferiority: she owed her existence to a misdirection and aberration in her process of development. Woman, in fact, was an 'imperfect' or 'incomplete' man. Although Aristotle's biological discovery could not have meshed better with the Augustinian fancies of the male-dominated Church, it was not adopted without a struggle. Guillaume d'Auvergne (d. 1249) declared in 'De sacramento matrimonii' that, if woman were defined as an imperfect man, man could be defined as a perfect woman, and that smacked suspiciously of the 'sodomitic heresy' (male homosexuality). However, churchmen's fear of the Greek esteem for homosexuality that went with Aristotle's contempt for women was outweighed by their desire to find, at long last, a plausible explanation for woman's inferiority to man. On this point, the theologian-patriarchs of Christendom were prepared to take tuition from the philosopher-patriarchs of heathendom. Having banished women to the kitchen and nursery and monopolised all other forms of activity, in so far as these interested them, men (both Christian and heathen) hit upon the idea that the male was 'active' and the female 'passive'. It was the fact of male activity, wrote Albertus Magnus, that endowed man with greater merit. Augustine's dictum, 'The active is more meritorious than the passive', was therefore 'correct' ('Summa theologica', ps. 2, tr. 13, q. 82, m. 2, obj. 1; cf. Michael Müller, 'Grundlagen der katholischen Sexualethik', p. 62).

According to Aristotle, male activity and female passivity extended to the generative act: men 'beget' or 'engender' offspring while women merely 'receive' or 'conceive' them. This terminology persists despite K. E. von Baer's discovery of the human ovum in 1827, which proved that woman has a half share in the reproductive process. The idea that male sperm is the only active element became so entrenched, thanks to Thomas Aquinas, that the ecclesiastical hierarchy ignored the discovery of the ovum as soon as it threatened to have theological repercussions, for instance on the birth of Jesus. Until the discovery of the ovum in 1827 it was possible to say that Mary had conceived Jesus 'of the Holy Ghost'; this can no longer be said without denying the ovum's existence. To accept it, on the other hand, is to deny the sole agency of God and limit the Holy Ghost's participation to fifty per cent (v. U. Ranke-Heinemann, 'Widerworte', p. 283f.)

Aristotle did not invent the idea that man is the sole generative agent. This accorded with man's existing conception of himself. Aeschylus (b. 525 BC), the progenitor of modern tragic drama, regarded man as the sole generator, so Orestes committed a less serious crime by murdering his mother Clytemnestra than he would have had he slain his father. 'The mother is no parent of that which is called her child,' says Apollo, 'but only nurse of the new-planted seed that grows. The parent is he who mounts.' He then cites Pallas Athene, who sprang from the head of her father, Zeus. 'There can be a father without any mother. There she stands, the living witness, daughter of Olympian Zeus, she who was never fostered in the dark of the womb.' And Athene, her father's daughter, proclaims: 'There is no mother anywhere who gave me birth ... So, in a case where the wife has killed her husband, lord of the house, her death shall not mean most to me' ('Oresteia', Part 3, 658f.).

The disdainful notion of woman as a sort of flower-pot for the nurturing of male seed was developed by Aristotle into a theory that has endured for over two thousand years. He, Albertus and Thomas subscribed to the principle that 'anything active produces something similar to itself'. Properly, therefore, all children should be male because the active element in male semen tends to produce something equally perfect, namely, another man. Women, being imperfect men, owe their existence to unfavourable circumstances. Aristotle called woman '*arren peperomenon*', a 'mutilated male' ('De animalium generatione', 2, 3), which Albertus and Thomas translated as '*mas occasionatus*'. Albertus stated that '*occasio* signifies a defect at variance with nature's intention' ('De animalibus', 1, 250), and Thomas regarded it as 'a thing that is not intended but stems from some defect' ('In II Sent.', 20, 2, 1, 1; 'De veritate', 5, 9 ad 9).

So every woman is born in the wake of a failure – indeed, woman *is* a failure. Among the untoward circumstances that prevent a man from generating something as perfect as himself Thomas included humid south winds and frequent downpours, which produced human beings with a greater water content ('Summa theologica', I, q. 92, a. 1). He also knew what these troublesome meteorological conditions could lead to, beyond determining sex that is: 'Because women contain more water, they are more readily led astray by sexual desire' (ibid., II/II, q. 49, a. 4). Albertus, too, made the winds partly responsible for the development of a female instead of a male child: 'The north wind augments strength, the south wind diminishes it ... The north wind conduces to the generation of the male and the south wind to that of the female because the north wind, being pure, purges and cleanses the air and vapours and stimulates natural energy. The south wind, however, is moist and fraught with rain' ('Quaestiones super de animalibus', XVIII, q. 1). Thomas took a similar view ('Summa theologica', I, q. 99, a. 2 ad 2).

In other words, woman is a freak product of environmental pollution. To quote Thomas's philosophically abstract rather than ecologically descriptive language, woman does not correspond to 'Nature's primary aim', which is directed toward perfection (man); she accords with 'the secondary aim of nature, like decay, deformity and decrepitude'

('Summa theologica suppl.', q. 52, a. 1 ad 2). Woman is therefore a substitute produced by nature when it fails in its primary, masculine aim: she is a stunted male suffering from arrested development. At the same time, this human failure is part of the divine plan – not a primary part, of course – because 'woman is destined for procreation' ('Summa theologica', I, q. 92, a. 1). In Thomas's monkish view, that was the sum total of her usefulness.

Thomas cited Augustine without naming him: the sole function of the female help-mate whom God had created for Adam was procreative, because a man would have availed him more in every other sphere of activity. Albertus said much the same ('In II Sent.', 20, 1; 'In IV Sententias', 26, 6). Both these male theologians developed Augustine's theory that wives were of no importance to their husbands' spiritual life. On the contrary, wrote Thomas, echoing Augustine, contact with his wife debased a husband's soul and brought his body under her sway, 'a servitude more bitter than any other' ('In I Cor.'). 'Nothing so debases a man's spirit as the caresses of a woman and the physical contacts without which a husband cannot possess his wife' ('Summa theologica', II/II, q. 151, a. 3 ad 2).

Women possessed less physical and spiritual strength, men 'more consummate intelligence' and 'greater virtue' ('Summa contra gentiles', III, 123). Because of their 'defective intelligence', a disability 'also manifest in children and imbeciles', women were not permitted to witness wills ('Summa theologica', II/II, q. 70, a. 3.; canon law forbade women to bear witness in testamentary disputes and criminal proceedings, though not in other cases). Children, for their part, were urged to heed their father's superior qualities: 'The father is more to be loved than the mother because he is the active generative element, whereas the mother is the passive' (ibid., q. 26, a. 10).

There were differences even in the conjugal act: 'The husband has the nobler share in the conjugal act, so it is natural that he should have less need than his wife to blush when demanding his conjugal due' ('Summa theologica suppl.' q. 64, a. 5 ad 2). The conjugal act 'always has something shameful in it and causes embarrassment' (ibid., q. 49, a. 4 ad 4). Women were more sexually incontinent than men, Thomas insisted, citing Aristotle ('Summa theologica', II/II, q. 56, a. 1) – a circumstance later regarded by the 'Malleus Maleficarum' (1487) as the reason why female witches outnumbered male (I, q. 6).

As deficient beings, women were competent to bear children – with whom they themselves were somehow on a par – but not to educate them. Only the spiritually superior father could attend to their spiritual education. Thomas largely justified the indissolubility of marriage by asserting that the mother 'far from suffices' for the education of offspring. The father was more important to his children's education than the mother. He was better equipped to 'instruct' them because of his 'more consummate intelligence' and better able to 'curb them' because of his 'greater virtue' ('Contra gentiles', III, 122).

But Thomas justified the indissolubility of marriage on other grounds as well. The wife had need of her husband 'not only for procreation and the education of children' but as her own 'master' (*gubernator*, a word originally meaning 'helmsman'); for the man, Thomas reiterated, was endowed with 'more consummate intelligence' and greater 'strength' or 'virtue', whichever. Many men suppose themselves to possess more virtue (*virtus*) because of their greater physical strength (*virtus* again). Thus the Latin word *virtus* may be rendered as virtue, or strength, or plain manliness. Even the Romans, in their day, derived the concept of virtue from that of masculine strength. There is much evidence to suggest that the first aristocrats to emerge in human society and gain ascendancy over their fellow creatures – men over women, churchmen over female members of the Church – were those through whom the stronger made themselves masters of the weaker and thereby acquired renown and prestige. Thus strength and masculine, warlike valour (*virtus* yet again) became synonymous with virtue in the modern sense.

Be that as it may, Thomas held that woman was 'subordinate to her husband in his capacity as her master' because he possessed 'more consummate intelligence' and – what else: the 'strength' required to curb her, or the 'virtue' required to instruct her? He probably meant both. At all events, a woman enjoyed the same advantages as her children, who were 'instructed and curbed' by her more intelligent and virtuous spouse (ibid., III, 123; 122). Her own value to him was purely procreative, as we already know, because another man would have been a greater help in every other respect.

It was because women were 'in a state of subjection', said Thomas, that they could not be ordained ('Summa theologica suppl.', q. 39, a. 1). To him, the fact of their subjection to men was the fundamental disability that debarred them from holding ecclesiastical office, though he contradicted himself when speaking of women who were *not* subject to men: 'in taking the vow of chastity or widowhood and thus becoming brides of Christ, they are raised to the rank of man [*promoventur in dignitatem virilem*], whereby they are released from subjection to man and directly bound to Christ' ('In I Cor.', 11, 2). Quite why *those* women could not become priests, Thomas did not say, but the reason may have lain less with them than with the opposite sex. Centuries earlier, Jerome had given vent to the absurd notion that a woman ceased to be a woman and could be termed a man 'if she is desirous of serving Christ more than the world' ('Commentary on Ephesians', III, 5).

A small digression is in order here. Demeaning though the Church's treatment of women has been, the worst charge of all – that it doubted whether women had souls and questioned their very humanity – must be dismissed as absolutely unfounded. It is often said and written that this subject was debated at the Second Synod of Mâcon (585). The truth is rather different. Gregory of Tours, who attended the synod in person, records that a bishop mooted 'whether woman may be termed "*homo*"' (the Latin for 'man' as well as 'human being'). The bishop's point was a philological one, therefore, even though it was prompted by the superior value attached to themselves by the males of the species. According to Gregory, the other bishops referred the questioner to the story of the Creation, in which God had made 'man' (*homo* in the sense of human being) both male and female. They also pointed out that Jesus was called 'the Son of Man' (*filius hominis*), although he was really 'the Son of the Virgin', in other words, the son of a woman. That settled the question: *homo* could signify a human being of either sex and therefore covered woman as well as man (Gregory of Tours, 'Historia Francorum', 8, 20).

Thomas felt assured of Aristotle's posthumous support, not only for his belittlement of women, but for his hostility to sexual pleasure. Aristotle's assertion that sexual desire hampers thought ('Nicomachean Ethics', 7, 12) was grist to his mill and reinforced his Augustinian sexual pessimism. He borrowed Aristotle's Homeric quotation to the effect that Aphrodite 'doth cozen the wits of even the most sagacious man' and stressed that 'sexual desire completely suppresses thought' ('Summa theologica', II/II, q. 55, a. 8 ad 1). Among Thomas's other pronouncements on the same subject, to which he continually reverted, were that sexual desire 'entirely inhibits the exercise of reason', 'suppresses reason', and 'absorbs the mind'.

We now find it hard to comprehend the fanatical aversion with which

Thomas Aquinas in particular, and Augustinian theologians in general, opposed the sexual act on the grounds that it 'clouded' or even 'dissolved' the mind. Thomas claimed that frequent sexual intercourse led to 'mental debility' (*mentem enervat*; 'In IV Sent.', 33), so his reasons were far from primarily theological. Only a modern reader convinced that frequent intercourse dulls the intellect and causes the brain cells to disintegrate could share his primitive biological fears, for that is more or less what Thomas appears to have meant by '*enervare*'. In describing celibacy, that 'finest of virtues' ('Summa theologica', II/II, q. 52, a. 5), he states that it confers immunity from the 'mental impairment' (*corruptio rationis*) to which those who engage in sex are subject ('In IV Sent.', 33, 3, 1 soll. and 4). Clearly, celibatarians like Thomas not only laid claim to more of God's grace (one hundred per cent as opposed to the married person's thirty) but were convinced that their unimpaired minds endowed them with more intelligence. One can only regret that they did not put a figure on their IQ as well as their salvation quotient, equally interesting though this would have been.

The connection between sex and original sin and the debasement of the mind by sexual desire had been Augustine's prime considerations when evolving his doctrine of the 'goods' that excuse marriage. Thomas took over this doctrine. Like Augustine, he defined pleasure in the conjugal act, not as absolutely and necessarily sinful, but as a penal consequence of the Fall – hence the need for marital saving graces, chief among which was procreation. Entirely in line with Augustine, he declared that 'No reasonable man should incur a loss unless it be balanced by something of equal or greater value.' Marriage was an estate in which losses were incurred: reason, as Aristotle had said, was absorbed by lust, and Paul had taught that it was subject to 'exigencies of the flesh'. On that account, the decision to marry could be regarded as proper only when its disadvantages were offset by 'a corresponding compensation that renders the conjugal bond honourable: and that is effected by the goods that excuse matrimony and make it estimable'. Thomas cited eating and drinking for purposes of comparison: being unassociated with desire so fierce as to absorb the power of reason, they needed no corresponding compensation. Unlike eating and drinking, 'the sexual energy that transmits original sin is infected and corrupted' ('Summa theologica suppl.', q. 49, a. 1 ad 1). Thomas regarded 'the resistance of the flesh to the spirit, which manifests itself particularly in the organs of generation, as a greater punishment than hunger and thirst, since the latter are purely physical whereas the former are spiritual as well' ('De malo', 15, 2 ad 8). Even Josef Fuchs, the Jesuit authority on Thomas Aquinas, finds his view of this matter 'somewhat one-sided' ('Die Sexualethik des heiligen Thomas von Aquin', p. 40).

If original sin is transmitted by sexual desire, this might be taken to mean that someone who feels nothing transmits nothing, and that the children of frigid parents are devoid of original sin. But no, the theologians had thought of that too. Thomas: 'Even if, by the power of God, it is granted to someone to feel no unbridled pleasure in the generative act, he would transmit original sin to the child notwithstanding.' Why? Because the sexual pleasure that transmits original sin is not actual (experienced at the moment of generation) but habitual (inherent in the human condition), and that is common to all humankind ('Summa theologica', I/II, q. 82, a. 4 ad 3). So the frigid are out of luck too. They are latently lustful, so to speak; they have a *tendency* toward mind-absorbing lust, and that is enough. Not even their God-given exemption from actual, stupefying pleasure in the generative act can prevent the transmission of original sin.

No married couple can escape the theologians' toils. That Mary's parents represented a sole exception to this rule was not laid down until 1854, in the Dogma of the Immaculate Conception. According to Thomas, freedom from original sin applied only to Jesus, not to his mother. Since every conjugal act entailed the 'corruption' and 'defilement' (*pollutio*) of the womb, Mary had conceived Jesus without engaging in marital intercourse 'for reasons of purity and non-defilement' ('In Matt. I' [19:247]). Thomas held that Jesus alone was pure, i.e. conceived without sexual contamination and uninfected with original sin by the parental act of procreation. 'What Thomas understood by this sexual "impurity",' writes Josef Fuchs (op. cit., p. 52), 'cannot be precisely ascertained.' Thomas Aquinas being a prince among theologians, theologians tend to put a favourable gloss on his every statement. When this proves impossible, they plead an inability to understand him rather than admit, straight out, that he was talking nonsense and had fallen prey to the nonsense talked by another great theologian named Augustine.

Here is a brief list of the sainted Thomas's saintly characterisations of marital intercourse, which Josef Fuchs finds surprising (ibid., p. 50), but which can only surprise those who fail to see that the whole of the Catholic sexual ethic has gone astray from the first: 'filth' (*immunditia*), 'a stain' (*macula*), 'foulness' (*foeditas*), 'vileness' (*turpitudo*), 'disgrace' (*ignominia*). According to Thomas, the clergy preserved their 'bodily purity' by virtue of their celibacy. Thomas was part of a long tradition, Fuchs adds in mitigation, 'so he could not easily expound a more liberal doctrine' (ibid., p. 51). No one is under an obligation to parrot nonsense. Reinforced by Thomas himself, the tradition has since grown still longer. The same old nonsense continues to be parroted, and the 'more liberal doctrine' lies buried beneath an even greater weight of tradition.

St Thomas, the Doctor Angelicus or angelic teacher, had some more circumlocutions for marital sex, e.g. 'degeneracy' (*deformitas*), 'a disease' (*morbus*), 'a corruption of the inviolate' (*corruptio integritatis*) ('Summa theologica', I, q. 98, a. 2), and an object of 'disgust' (*repugnantia*). According to him, the ordained priest was averse to matrimony 'on account of the conjugal act' because the latter 'hindered spiritual acts' and was a bar to 'greater esteem' ('Summa theologica suppl.', q. 53, a. 3 ad 1). He devoted more time than other medieval theologians to expounding and interpreting Pope Gregory I's doctrine of the 'eight daughters of incontinence'. One deplorable result of incontinence was 'the effemination of the human heart' ('Summa theologica', II/II, q. 83, a. 5 ad 2). The men of heathen antiquity had promoted *virtus*, meaning manly vigour, into their word for 'virtue'. Christian celibatarians, and Thomas in particular, downgraded womanhood into a synonym for disgrace. Celibatarian sexual hostility is hostility toward women. 'Thomas was fond of repeating what Paul said in I Cor. 7:1: "It is good for a man not to touch a woman"' (Fuchs, op. cit., p. 261).

Paul quoted this Gnostic maxim in order to refute it. Much havoc has been wrought in the past two thousand years by its attribution to the apostle himself. Paul's alleged statement became the mainstay of celibacy, and Thomas repeated the long-established tariff according to which virgins received one hundred per cent of their heavenly reward, widows sixty, and the married only thirty. For this purpose, celibate males were classified as virgins ('Summa theologica', II/II, q. 152, a. 5 ad 2; I/II, q. 70, a. 3 ad 2; 'Summa theologica suppl.', q. 96, a. 4).

Like Augustine and all traditionalists, Thomas considered 'a marriage without carnal intercourse' to be 'holier' ('In IV Sent.', 26, 2, 4). It is evident, from the attention devoted to vows of marital continence by Thomas and theologians in general, that monkish married couples were not uncommon. Both Gratian and Peter Lombard dealt with such marriages and the question of what chaste spouses had to do, were permitted to do, might not do any longer, et cetera. Their model in every case was the marriage of Mary and Joseph.

Although husbands were at the bottom or thirty-per-cent end of the celestial wage scale, their wives formed an even lower-paid group. This is implied by Peter Browe, a Jesuit authority on the Christian Middle Ages: 'Married women were never permitted to communicate often; they were not thought sufficiently pure and worthy. Only if their husbands were dead or if both spouses had vowed to remain continent could they truly begin to strive for perfection and, if possible, to communicate with greater frequency' (Browe, 'Die häufige Kommunion im Mittelalter', 1938, p. 120).

But not all married persons attained this monkish ideal of bereavement or total abstinence. If perfection eluded them, they could at least refrain from lapsing into sin. For this purpose Augustine and Thomas made two forms of marital intercourse available to them: (i) intercourse with procreation in mind, and (ii) intercourse dutifully engaged in by one spouse at the other's request. The latter form Thomas described as 'intended to banish danger' ('Summa theologica suppl.', q. 64, a. 2 ad 1; ad 4), meaning that it served to 'prevent fornication [on the other spouse's part]' (ibid., q. 48, a. 2). All other motives for intercourse, however good and noble (e.g. love, to which Thomas made no reference at all), could only result in an act that was either sinful or at least venially so (ibid., q. 49, a. 5).

A few of the early Schoolmen had held that intercourse in avoidance of one's own unchastity was sinless. A manual for confessors dating from the middle of the thirteenth century and attributed to Cardinal Hugo of St Cher (d. 1263) prescribed that penitents should be questioned as follows: 'Have you known your wife only for the sake of delight? Because you ought to know her only for the sake of generating, or avoiding fornication, or returning the debt' (John T. Noonan, 'Contraception: A History of its Treatment by the Catholic Theologians and Canonists', p. 272). Thomas, in strict adherence to Augustine, condemned such laxity: 'If anyone intends to prevent fornication in himself by means of marital intercourse ... it is a venial sin, for marriage is not instituted to that end.' Intercourse could, on the other hand, be sinlessly engaged in to prevent fornication on the part of one's spouse, this being a way of performing one's conjugal duty ('Summa theologica suppl.', q. 49, a. 5 ad 2).

172

Theologians have expatiated for centuries on the danger of fornication on the part of oneself and one's spouse and its avoidance through marital intercourse, or on the danger of fornication on the part of one's spouse but not of oneself (personal unchastity is better avoided, according to Thomas, by means of fasting and prayer). No one reading their effusions can fail to regard this view of the conjugal act as an affront to all married persons. It implies that, once having produced the maximal or optimal number of children, a parent cannot have non-generative intercourse without sin unless a refusal to do his or her conjugal duty might drive the other partner to commit adultery. The celibatarian imputation that married couples are in constant danger of committing adultery, and that intercourse should be permitted them as a concession, is insufferable nonsense.

The Second Vatican Council, erroneously described as an advance in the field of sexual morality, also stated that 'when circumstances arise in which the family, for a time at least, cannot be added to . . . marital fidelity may be jeopardised.' Regardless of this, however, no 'immoral solutions' (i.e. contraception and abortion) may be resorted to. The risk of infidelity was the first thing that occurred to the council when discussing the subject of contraception. The only other risk its members could see was that 'the resolution of mind to increase the family' might be endangered ('Gaudium et Spes: Pastoral Constitution on the Church in the World of Today', 51).

To take these 'risks' in reverse order: the second one that arises when parents can have no more children, as the Church sees it, is that they may not *wish* to have any more; the first is that they may commit adultery. Celibate theologians are so obsessed with the 'danger' of adultery that they fail to discern the very real danger that married couples may turn their backs on the celibatarian, monkish Church because they have tired of its absurd and incompetent supervision and wish to have intercourse, not in avoidance of any 'risks', but for reasons that clearly surpass the celibatarian imagination. The Second Vatican Council's advice to married couples to practise 'the virtue of marital chastity' instead of 'embarking on ways which the Church's teaching authority, in expounding the divine law, condemns' (ibid.) amounts to so gross an interference in their personal concerns that they are no longer prepared to tolerate it.

* * *

But to revert to Thomas. He numbered any deviation from the normal coital position among the unnatural vices classified by Augustinian traditionalists as worse than intercourse between mother and son. That he should have condemned marital intercourse of this kind as an unnatural sin was not altogether in keeping with his scheme of things, because all the other unnatural vices listed by him precluded procreation, which a simple deviation from the normal position did not. Even he sanctioned deviation in exceptional cases, as, for instance, when medical factors such as obesity prevented a married couple from having intercourse in any other manner ('In IV Sent.', 31). The other unnatural and, thus, mortally sinful vices – vices even worse than incest, rape and adultery – were, according to Thomas, onanism (in the sense of masturbation), bestiality (copulation with animals), homosexuality, anal or oral intercourse, and coitus interruptus ('Summa theologica', II/ II, q. 54, a. 11). Thomas included deviation from the normal position among the gravest, procreation-impeding sins because he believed that it rendered conception difficult if not impossible. His master, Albertus Magnus, had taught that semen could not readily penetrate the uterus of a woman lying on her side, and that, if she bestrode her husband, her matrix turned 'upside down' and voided its contents ('De animalibus', 10, 2).

However one chooses to resolve the theological controversy over why Thomas classified positional deviation as an unnatural, i.e. procreation-impeding act, he and all his theological successors numbered it among 'the gravest sins of unchastity' if practised for sexual pleasure's sake. Although the theory that it hinders procreation has since been recognised as biologically false, theologians continue, even in our own century, to condemn the quest for sexual pleasure by such means. In this connection we shall later have occasion to discuss 'Ideal Marriage' by Theodor van de Velde, whose condemnable sin it was to wish to introduce some variety into the uniform, model sex life prescribed by the Church.

Early medieval penitentials and medieval theologians dealt in detail with 'unnatural' coital positions. Albertus Magnus strove to point up the only 'natural' position with the aid of physiological, anatomical arguments: 'Whether the man should lie beneath or above, whether he should stand or lie or sit, whether union should take place from behind or in front … such disgraceful questions should never properly be discussed if the peculiar things one hears in the confessional nowadays did not require it [in other words, if celibatarian priests did not take advantage of the confessional to meddle in other people's business]' ('In IV Sent.', 31).

To Thomas, marital intercourse meant the deliberate emission and absorption of semen with generative intent. Procreation was the sole purpose of the sexual act ('Summa contra gentiles', 3, 122) and the sole function of the sexual organs ('De malo', 15, 1c). But Thomas's prescribed and purposive emission of semen had to follow a certain pattern, and the sexual act was moral only if it conformed thereto. The expressions 'proper manner' ('Summa theologica', II/II, q. 153, a. 2) and 'order' (ibid., q. 125, a. 2) recur constantly in his writings. It was the procedure best suited to the purpose of procreation that had to be followed. Any deviation from the ejaculative formula laid down by the Church was *contra naturam* or unnatural: 'The manner in which intercourse takes place is prescribed by nature' ('In IV Sent.', 31). The act had to follow the proper pattern, even when the wife was infertile and could not conceive. To deviate from the 'natural' procedure was unnatural and gravely sinful under all circumstances.

The effects of Thomas's prescribed procedure for the purposive emission of semen, which he advanced on the authority of God and nature, can still be observed today. In 1987 the Vatican Congregatio pro Doctrina Fidei forbade 'homologous insemination': 'Homologous artificial insemination within marriage cannot be permitted.' There is, however, one exception: if the husband's semen is collected in a condom during marital intercourse, the said condom must be punctured to preserve the semblance of a natural generative act and preclude illicit contraception. In other words, marital intercourse must take place as if it will result in generation and the condom must be punctured as if conception in this manner is possible (cf. 'Publik-Forum', 29 May 1987, p. 8). An unproductive conjugal act performed as if it were productive is the only roundabout means whereby a couple can legitimately be assisted to have children. The 'natural' form of marital intercourse, so called, has become the overriding consideration. It remains so even when procreation – its original, Church-prescribed purpose – cannot occur, and when the husband's semen could be obtained with equal ease or less difficulty by means of masturbation. Masturbation, however, is still classified as one of the most sinful and unnatural forms of non-generative sexual activity, even when procreation is its very purpose. The means (regulation procedure) has become more important than the end (procreation). In the field of moral theology, what is 'natural' is determined by ancient traditions jealously guarded by old men remote from married life.

That generative intercourse in the Church-prescribed manner should take place only between husband and wife was another of Thomas's natural laws. He had discovered – like Aristotle and Konrad Lorenz – that among certain creatures, e.g. birds, the male and female remain together after mating and rear their young jointly 'because the female would not be sufficient to rear them alone'. This proved that the indissolubility of marriage was preordained by nature, for the human mother resembled the female bird (the position with dogs was somewhat different, Thomas conceded) in being incapable of rearing her children alone, especially as their upbringing lasted 'a long time' ('Summa contra gentiles', 3, 122). If only on that account, heterologous or extramarital insemination cannot be countenanced by the Catholic Church and is rejected point-blank because it conflicts with the regulation form of generative intercourse.

'In accordance with nature', Thomas wrote, 'the estimable habits of animals recur among men, and in a more consummate form' ('Summa theologica suppl.', q. 54, a. 3 ad 3). Ergo, any novel method of generation must first have been foreshadowed in the animal kingdom. 'Thomas continually reverts to the animal kingdom' (Fuchs, op. cit., p. 115). 'Comparisons between the sex lives of human beings and animals are . . . enlisted as a method far more often by him than by other theologians' (ibid., p. 277). Thomas believed in mandatory compliance with nature's instructions to all living creatures, and those could best be inferred from the behaviour of animals. The most important message he derived from the animal kingdom is still binding upon the Catholic Church, even today. Animals mate for reproductive reasons alone (so theologians believe, at any rate): from this we can infer the purpose of the human sexual act. Animals use no contraceptives: from this we can infer that contraceptive devices are unnatural. Such are the articles of faith to which Thomas's pseudo-theological brand of behavioural science gave rise.

SEVENTEEN

The Growing Campaign against Contraception ('Unnatural Intercourse') and its Enduring Effects on Canon Law

Medieval Europe derived its scientific knowledge of contraception from the Arabs. The first two medical schools were founded at Salerno in the eleventh century and Montpellier in the twelfth. At these centres, Mohammedan textbooks were the medium through which European students of medicine became acquainted with Graeco-Roman information on the subject and with the Arabs' more recent findings. The best-known work was Avicenna's (ibn Sina's) 'Canon of Medicine' compiled at Damascus in the eleventh century and translated into Latin at Toledo in the twelfth. This remained the most important standard medical work available to European physicians until the middle of the seventeenth century.

Avicenna's pharmacopoeia enumerated the contraceptive properties of various plants, e.g. 'Oil of cedar spoils semen and prevents impregnation if the penis be anointed with it prior to intercourse' (2, 2, 163). Aristotle had previously drawn attention to oil of cedar in his 'Historia animalium'. Avicenna also listed the ancient prescriptions of Hippocrates, Soranus of Ephesus, and Pliny, together with sundry new ones. Like Soranus, he recommended contraception particularly in cases where pregnancy would endanger the mother's life.

Avicenna was the main source of Albertus Magnus's medical knowledge. It was, for instance, from him that Albertus inherited the belief that a woman's matrix becomes inverted if she lies uppermost during intercourse 'so that its contents flow out again'. Albertus described this cause of infertility in 'De animalibus', where it appears under the heading 'That medicine can treat sterility'. In listing all that must be done to avoid sterility, he also presented a detailed account of what the Arabs and the writers of antiquity knew about ways of inducing it. As soon as he stopped expounding Avicenna like a scientist and started writing like a theologian, however, he concurred with all his fellow Schoolmen (eleventh to thirteenth centuries) in borrowing from Augustine's 'Aliquando' text and referring to artificial methods of contraception as 'poisons of infertility'.

Not every theological writer dealt with contraceptive and abortifacient medicines as fully as Albertus. Bishop Vincent of Beauvais (d.c. 1264), a Dominican who compiled the first sizeable medieval encyclopedia, wrote of rue that it 'inhibits and represses evil desires and diminishes and entirely desiccates semen' ('Speculum naturale', 10, 138). He said the same of lettuce. Only in the case of one such remedy for carnal desire did he mention that it was also a contraceptive. St Hildegard of Bingen (d. 1179), abbess of Ruppertsberg and author of a work on naturopathy, offered no hints on contraception or abortion; instead, faithful to the Catholic ideal of piety, she recommended plants that would 'extinguish lust in a man or woman, as, for example, the wild lettuce' ('Subtilitatum', I, 92). To this day, almost the only form of 'contraception' sanctioned by the Catholic Church is a nunnish suppression of the libido.

Since most ancient prescriptions are now known to be ineffective, those who took them would not have suffered either way from a certain inconsistency on the part of the physician Magnino of Milan (c. 1300), a graduate of the Salerno school. His book, 'A Healthy Regimen', commended those 'estimable' persons 'desirous of continency' and advised them to swallow decoctions of many plants which Avicenna had described as aphrodisiacs. Another of Magnino's recommendations: eating a bee 'makes a woman sterile but eases childbirth' (2, 7). Magnino dedicated his work to the bishop of Arezzo. Medicine and theology were both taken on trust in those days.

From the eleventh century onwards the Church's campaign against contraception entered a new phase. In the first place, its hostility to contraceptive practices was exacerbated by the controversy with the Cathars (a name derived from *catharos*, meaning 'pure'), a heretical sect opposed to all procreation. Secondly, the Schoolmen initiated an Augustinian revival by making theology an object of scientific endeavour. Augustine's opponents in the fourth century had been his erstwhile kindred spirits, the Gnostic Manichaeans, who condemned procreation

as devilish. Now, early in the eleventh century, a new tide of antipro-
creative sentiment flowed across Western Europe. It was made up of
many separate groups and ideologies – Bogomils, troubadours, Cathars,
Albigensians – but all were at one in their rejection of procreation. This
is not the place to explore the complex question of how far, if at all,
these groups cohered and whether, for example, the troubadours'
glorification of love and non-generative sexual pleasure was a reaction
against the impoverishment of human relations by Christian sexual
doctrine. (Many minnesingers countered the one-sided theological
emphasis on procreation by denying the existence of love within
marriage.) What is certain is that Augustine's campaign against Manichaean contraception was echoed, if anything more strongly, by the
medieval campaign against contraception among the Cathars in
particular.

Three texts were destined to play a pre-eminent part in this campaign,
two by Augustine ('Aliquando' and 'Adulterii malum') and the text
know as 'Si aliquis'. 'Aliquando' and 'Adulterii malum' were first
brought to prominence by Bishop Ivo of Chartres (d. 1116), whose
work has been called 'a milestone in the formation of the canonical
approach to contraception' (John T. Noonan, 'Contraception: A History of its Treatment by the Catholic Theologians and Canonists',
p. 173). A supporter of the Gregorian Reform, Ivo was dissatisfied with
the Decretum of Burchard of Worms and preferred to give precedence
in his collection of authorities to a forgotten text in which Augustine
had written of 'poisons of infertility' and referred to any wife who
employed them as 'her husband's whore'. This text, already cited in the
chapter on Augustine, has since Ivo's day been known by its opening
word, *Aliquando*, meaning 'sometimes'. Ivo's code also incorporated
three Augustinian texts on 'unnatural intercourse in marriage' from
which it emerged that coitus interruptus, for example, was a more
heinous sin than fornication and adultery (Decretum 9, 119.128.106) –
more heinous even than intercourse with one's own mother, this being
'natural' in that it did not rule out procreation. These three Augustinian
texts were later combined under the name 'Adulterii malum'. Ivo's
object in anthologising Augustine was to seek documentary support for
his stern condemnation of all contraceptive methods.

'Aliquando' and 'Adulterii malum' acquired an influence that was to
endure for centuries because of their inclusion in two standard works
of even greater importance than Ivo's. The first, which originated in

1142, was regarded as a major component of the Western Church's basic canon law until 1917, when the CIC or ecclesiastical legal code was introduced. This was the unofficial but universally accepted code compiled in Bologna by the monk Gratian and entitled 'Concordantia discordantium canonum' ('Concordance of Discordant Canons'). Popularly known as the 'Decretum Gratiani', it remained the daily fare of ecclesiastical jurists for centuries, and every student of canon law was acquainted, thanks to Gratian, with the 'Aliquando' text under the heading 'They that procure poisons of infertility are fornicators, not spouses' (Decretum 2, 32, 2, 7).

Gratian compiled a 'scale of fornication' based on Ivo's quotations from Augustine, thus: 'The evil of adultery [*Adulterii malum*] surpasses fornication, but is surpassed by incest; for it is worse to sleep with one's mother than with another man's wife. But the worst of all these things is what is done contrary to nature, as when a man wishes to use a member of his wife not conceded for this.' Also included under the heading of 'unnatural intercourse' were coitus interruptus and any form of contraception. Indeed, this pitch of unnaturalness was taken a stage further: 'It is more disgraceful if a married woman suffers this to be done to herself than to another woman' (Decretum 2, 32, 7, 11). Although Augustine had, in this immediate connection, concentrated more on anal and oral intercourse, Gratian's 'concordance of discordant canons' criminalised contraceptive marital intercourse to a legally unprecedented degree: it was the absolute *ne plus ultra* of impurity, and not even intercourse with one's own mother or contraceptive intercourse with a prostitute could compare with it.

Another theological compilation came into being around the middle of the twelfth century. This was 'Libri Sententiarum IV' by Peter Lombard (d. 1164), bishop of Paris and a highly respected teacher of theology. As we saw in chapter 12 Peter Lombard's 'Sentences' continued to be the standard textbook for lecturers on theology – Luther among them – until the sixteenth century. What Gratian, 'the father of canon law', was to ecclesiastical jurisprudence, Peter Lombard was to the science of theology and remained so until his textbook was superseded in the sixteenth century by Thomas Aquinas's 'Summa theologica', which retains its authority to this day.

Peter Lombard often took his cue from Gratian. He, too, assailed contraception with the aid of Augustine's 'Aliquando' text. Beneath the heading 'They that procure poisons of infertility are fornicators, not spouses' he wrote: 'She is her husband's whore, he an adulterer with his own wife' ('Sentences', 4, 31, 4). He also adopted Gratian's 'scale of fornication', in which intercourse 'contrary to nature' (contraception), especially with one's own wife, represented the height – or depths – of iniquity.

Both Gratian and Peter Lombard based themselves on Augustine. Peter Lombard drew attention to the Augustinian nexus between original sin and marital intercourse: 'The cause of original sin is a pollution which [the child] incurs from the ardour of its parents and their lustful desire'. The transmission of original sin, in its turn, contaminated the limbs with the 'lethal concupiscence without which carnal intercourse cannot occur'. Thus 'coitus is reprehensible and evil unless it be excused by the goods of marriage' (ibid., 2, 31, 6; 4, 26, 2). So Gratian and Peter Lombard, while basing themselves on Augustine, carried his doctrines a stage further: their compilations not only included the 'Responsum Gregorii', with its fateful assertion that sexual pleasure can never be sinless, but laid special stress on contraception.

The practical effect of their strict ban on contraception is illustrated by the following case. A woman had sustained an umbilical hernia in childbirth, and the physicians declared that she would not survive another confinement. Certain people suggested 'that the woman should procure a sterilising poison and thus enable herself to continue to do her conjugal duty in the certainty that she would not get herself with child'. This was disputed by Petrus Cantor (d. 1197), who ruled, in accordance with the strictly anticontraceptive text 'Aliquando', that the woman must under no circumstances procure any 'sterilising poisons' ('Summa de sacramentis 350: quaestiones et miscellanea').

It is clear that faith in contraceptive potions was far from universal in those days – an attitude that remained unchanged until the advent of the Pill, which moral theologians now call an 'infertility drug'. This being so, the Church had less pastoral recourse to 'Aliquando' than to the second classic Augustinian text, the 'scale of fornication', which classified contraception in marriage as the most iniquitous of all 'unnatural' sexual vices. The relevant forms of contraception were those described by the best-selling German moral theologian Bernard Häring as 'destructive of the natural integrity of the conjugal act' ('The Law of Christ', p. 355). Foremost among these was coitus interruptus, which, as we saw, surpassed intercourse with one's own mother in iniquity. In contemporary theological parlance, coitus interruptus was generally expressed by 'seminating outside the proper vessel' (or 'organ' [instrumentum], as Thomas preferred to call it). Theologians of the thirteenth, fourteenth and fifteenth centuries devoted more attention to 'sins against nature' than to 'poisons of sterility'. Nuptial sermons concerned themselves with the former, and priests were instructed to ask about them in the confessional.

St Catherine of Siena (d. 1380), herself the twenty-fifth of twenty-five children, illustrates the extent to which reprobation of contraceptive marital intercourse had infiltrated the world of ideas. Her visions of Hell included a group of lost souls who had 'sinned in the estate of matrimony'. Her confessor and biographer, Raymond of Capua, who later became general of the Dominican Order, asked her 'why that sin, which was not more serious than others, was so severely punished'. Her response: 'Because they do not have as much conscience about it, and consequently not as much contrition, as they have about other sins; they also offend more regularly and often in this sin than in others' (Noonan, op. cit., p. 227). Even in those days, therefore, married couples obviously failed to see sin where theologians and their pious parrots, male and female, chose to discern it in them. St Catherine was entirely in the tradition of Gratian, Peter Lombard, and Thomas Aquinas, who classed contraception as a 'sin against nature' and, thus, as the worst form of fornication.

The celebrated preacher Bernardino of Siena (d. 1444), whose aim in life was to promote the veneration of the Virgin and St Joseph, clearly shared the belief that married persons needed alerting to the sins they failed to see, which were only apparent to the eagle-eyed gaze of the unmarried clergy: 'The married wallow in wretched ignorance like a pig in its trough full of filth' ('De religione christiana', 17, ante 1). 'You shall see that you have committed many sins in this estate of matrimony which you have neither confessed nor known that it was a sin or sins . . . It is depraved for a man to have intercourse with his mother, but far worse if he has unnatural intercourse with his wife' ('Sermones seraphici', 19, 1). 'It is better for a woman to have intercourse in a natural manner with her own father than against nature with her own husband' ('De religione christiana', 17, 1, 1). Bernardino had some statistics at his fingertips: 'Of every thousand marriages, nine hundred and ninety-nine are, I believe, of the Devil.' Why? Because of 'sins against nature', and these, according to Bernardino, comprised every emission of semen 'whensoever and howsoever one cannot generate' ('Sermones seraphici',

19, 1). 'Every time you came together in such a manner that you could not conceive and generate children, it was a sin' ('Le prediche volgari', Milan, 1836, p. 433).

When preaching before the French court, Jean Gerson (d. 1429) went so far as to invoke a decree issued by the Christian emperor Valentinian in 390, which punished homosexuality with death by fire (Codex Theodosianus, 9, 7, 6). Gerson put any form of marital intercourse that hindered conception on a par with homosexuality and condemned 'the ingenious indecencies' of married sinners. Such acts 'are often deserving of the stake and are worse than if committed with wives not one's own. May a person copulate at all and preclude the fruit of matrimony? That, I say, is often a sin deserving of the fire . . . Every imaginable way that impedes offspring in the conjunction of man and woman is improper and to be reprobated' ('Sermon against Lechery', Second Sunday in Advent, 'Collected Works', III, Antwerp, 1706, p. 916).

The Dominican Savonarola (1452–98), who drove the Medici out of Florence, proclaimed Christ king and burned the city's worldly trappings (only to be burned himself later on), instructed confessors as follows: 'You shall inquire after this sin . . . whether it was in the vessel, in an improper vessel, or outside the vessel' (Penitential, sin against the Sixth Commandment). He was referring to: (i) pessaries, (ii) anal/oral intercourse, and (iii) coitus interruptus.

The sacrament of penance afforded the primary means of alerting people to their conjugal sins, on which they could be separately interrogated in the confessional. Early medieval penitentials and the Decretum Burcardi (compiled by Burchard, d. 1025), which enjoyed general acceptance until well into the twelfth century, were quite explicit in the questions they put. The only problem was, many people gleaned undesirable hints on sex from their interrogations in the confessional. From the end of the twelfth century onward, therefore, the questions asked became somewhat less explicit. The penitential of Bartholomew of Exeter (d. 1184) warned confessors against giving detailed descriptions of conjugal sins against nature, 'for we have heard that men and women have been prompted to unfamiliar sins by circumstantial accounts of crimes with which they were previously unacquainted' ('Penitential', c. 38). It is clear that interrogations in the confessional sometimes fulfilled a function now reserved for pornography. Most of the laity were as sexually ignorant as most confessors were well informed. Quite how the latter derived their detailed knowledge, one can only speculate.

The penitential of Alanus ab Insulis (d. 1201) likewise counselled discretion. In cases where a penitent confessed to illicit intercourse, the priest was to ask whether this had involved fornication, adultery, incest, or a sin against nature. These inquiries were important because sins against nature were the gravest of all, but the priest was not 'to go into undue detail' lest he gave the penitent occasion for further lapses from grace ('Penitential', PL 210: 286–8). Similar advice was given by Robert of Flamborough, a penitentiary of the abbey of St Victor in Paris, whose penitential dates from shortly after 1208.

In 1215 the Fourth Lateran Council enjoined all Christians to confess and communicate at least once a year, with the result that many guides for confessors originated in the thirteenth century. The author of one of these, Cardinal Hostiensis, explained the procedure very clearly under the heading: 'What Questions Can or Should Be Asked by One Hearing Confessions?' When these related to lechery, wrote Hostiensis, the priest was to define sins against nature as follows: 'You have sinned against nature if you have known your wife otherwise than nature demands.' He was not, however, to detail the various ways in which an act could be contrary to nature. Instead, he might 'cautiously' question the penitent as follows: 'You know full well which way is natural. Have you ever polluted yourself in any other way? If he says no, do not question him further. If he says yes, you may perhaps ask him: while asleep or awake? If he says awake, you may ask: with a woman? If he says with a woman, you may ask: outside the vessel or within it, and how?' (Summa 5, 'Penances and Remissions', 49). In a similar work generally attributed to Cardinal Hugo of St Cher (d. 1263), confessors were instructed – under the heading 'Adultery' – to question penitents thus: 'Or have you sinned against nature with your own wife? If the sinner asks: What does that mean, against nature?, then may the priest say: The Lord has permitted one way alone, to which all men must keep. If, therefore, you have done [it] otherwise than in that one way, you have committed a mortal sin.'

Although priests were urged to be discreet, their questions in the confessional sometimes dismayed the more ingenuous penitents, especially the womenfolk, or whetted their curiosity. This emerges from a remark made by Bernardino of Siena: 'Foolish wives quite often go to their husbands and, in order to appear respectable, say: "The priest questioned me about this filth and wanted to know what I do with you." And the gullible husband regularly loses his temper with the priest.' Some priests tended to hold back on that account, but he, Bernardino, preferred to be vigilant rather than play 'the dumb dog'. He therefore insisted that confessors should couch their questions in plain language ('Sermones seraphici', 19, 1). One consequence of St Bernardino's plain language must have been that many wives stayed away from divine service when he was preaching, because he reproached their husbands for leaving them at home 'so that they do not learn these necessary truths' ('De religione christiana', 17, ante 1). Evidently, some married couples regarded their sexual relations as less unnatural and outrageous than Bernardino's homilies on the subject and the questions asked them in the confessional.

Severe penances were prescribed for contraception and coitus interruptus, one major penalty being the withdrawal of conjugal rights. The innocent spouse, usually the wife, was made responsible for inflicting this punishment on her guilty husband. For her, the denial of sexual intercourse counted as a moral obligation whose non-fulfilment rendered her as guilty as her partner. Alexander of Hales's thirteenth-century Summa stated that the wife 'may on no account yield to her husband in the matter of a sin against nature, and if she consents she commits a mortal sin' ('Summa theologica', II/II, 3, 5, 1, 3). Jean Gerson insisted that, if one spouse desired some 'improper' form of marital intercourse, the other should resist 'unto death' ('Collected Works', III, p. 916), and Bernardino of Siena proclaimed to his congregations that, where sins against nature were concerned, 'you wives should die rather than consent' ('Sermones seraphici', 19, 1; similarly in 'Le prediche volgari', p. 435). All three – Alexander, Gerson, and Bernardino – expressly included coitus interruptus in their list of unnatural sins (Noonan, op. cit., p. 262).

The third classical text to condemn contraception was even more extreme, if possible, than 'Aliquando' and 'Adulterii malum'. It appeared in a third major compilation of Scholastic texts commissioned by Pope Gregory IX (d. 1241) from his chaplain, the Dominican Raymond of Pennafort. Like the Decretum Gratiani, this collection of papal decretals formed the basis and/or contents of the Church's legal code, the CIC of 1917, and included the text already cited in connection with penitentials: 'If anyone [Si aliquis] practises witchcraft or administers sterilising poisons, that person is a homicide.' Compiled by papal command and invested with papal authority, a universally binding legal code had defined contraception as murder: condemnation of the practice could go no further.

Though typical of the rhetoric of Jerome and Chrysostom, those eloquent fourth- and fifth-century Fathers, and largely responsible for the outlawing of contraception by the Catholic Church, 'Si aliquis' was a foreign body in canon law from the first. This was because canon law assumed that the foetus became animate by degrees, so abortion was not penalised as murder until the process of ensoulment was complete. Gratian and Peter Lombard restricted the term murder to the abortion of an animate foetus. A letter from Pope Innocent III (d. 1216) likewise indicates that, strictly speaking, contraception was not regarded as murder and abortion did not become so until gestation had been in progress for some time (eighty days or thereabouts). This letter referred to a Carthusian monk who had persuaded his mistress to abort herself. The pope ruled that he was innocent of murder provided the embryo had not been 'quickened', meaning 'ensouled' in accordance with Aristotelian biology. Innocent's ruling would have been endorsed not only by Augustine but also – when he was expressing himself canonically rather than rhetorically – by Jerome.

Thomas Aquinas, that master of precise differentiation, wrote in regard to 'Si aliquis' that the use of poisons of sterility was a grave sin 'and against nature, since not even animals prevent their young from coming into being, but not as grave as murder, since conception might not have occurred for other reasons'. The term murder could be applied only to the abortion of an already-formed foetus ('In IV Sent.', 31.2, exp. text). It was despite this inconsistency, therefore, that the papal decretals defined contraception as murder and, thus, the most heinous of sins. In describing the ingestion of sterilising poisons as 'a sin against nature' Thomas was, incidentally, departing from conventional parlance. 'Sin against nature' was a term generally restricted to forms of intercourse that did not convey semen into the proper 'vessel' (the vagina), and murder was applied to the ingestion of sterilising poisons.

Even today, canon law draws a distinction between these two categories: the taking of the Pill on the one hand and coitus interruptus and condom-protected intercourse on the other. Canon 1061 of the new CIC, which has been in force since 1983, states: 'A valid marriage between baptised persons, when not consummated, is termed "contracted" [*ratum*] only. It is "contracted and consummated" when the spouses have, in a humane manner, together consummated the conjugal act, which is of itself appropriate to the generation of offspring, to which matrimony is of its nature appointed, and through which the spouses become one flesh.' As we have already seen, this compromise between the *consensus* and *copula* theories means that a 'contracted' marriage may be dissolved, enabling the partners to remarry. A 'contracted and consummated' marriage, by contrast, is indissoluble, so neither partner may remarry during the other's lifetime. Canon law now draws the following distinction: marital intercourse after the Pill has been taken counts as consummation, so the Pill-marriage is indissoluble; coitus interruptus, on the other hand, does not count as consummation under canon law, so a marriage in which intercourse has been limited thereto may be dissolved.

Condom-protected intercourse presents canon law with special problems. The present bone of contention between ecclesiastical jurists is this: is semination *into* the vagina the deciding factor, or is semination *within* the vagina sufficient to consummate a marriage? These celibatarian deliberations matter little to the persons concerned because, even if ecclesiastical jurists ruled that only ejaculation *into* the vagina can consummate a marriage and render it indissoluble, no condom-users could get their marriages dissolved in any case. Rome has hitherto rejected all such applications on the grounds that the condom affords no absolute guarantee of protection, so 'a drop [of semen] may have penetrated the vagina'. It seems that the indissolubility of marriage is sometimes a matter for the rubber goods industry.

As we have seen, Thomas Aquinas was primarily responsible for the paramount importance attached to male semen. That holes in a condom can be advantageous to other married couples we already learned when discussing homologous insemination, which would be impermissible without them. For condom-users, the canon law controversy over the potential puncture may not result in a dissoluble marriage, but it certainly presents an insoluble problem.

A marriage is also held to be unconsummated by *amplexus reservatus*, the restrained or 'dry' embrace in which the penis is withdrawn from the vagina without ejaculating. This, too, illustrates the importance of male semen, and is still regarded by many theologians as a permissible contraceptive method. The restrained embrace differs from the use of a condom in presenting theologians with a straightforward, clear-cut problem, because no semen is discharged either *into* or *within* the vagina. Unfortunately, not all the dilemmas afflicting Catholic theology are as easy to resolve.

Marital intercourse using a diaphragm, a device inserted in the vagina so as to block the entrance to the womb, *does* count as consummation. Again, it is the injection of male sperm into the vagina that is the deciding factor; the woman's part in procreation matters less. We shall re-encounter this form of sexual discrimination when examining the question of impotence.

To revert to Thomas's attitude to 'Si aliquis'. Although he rejected its definition of contraception as murder and restricted that term to the abortion of an animate foetus, it was he who fostered and reinforced the official, canonical idea that contraception is quasi-murderous. If the popes of our own century have criminalised contraception, this is largely attributable to the theories of Thomas Aquinas.

Thomas held that every sexual act must be a conjugal act and every conjugal act an act of generation. He regarded any transgression of the sexual commandments as an offence against life because male semen contained the makings of a whole human being – or, more precisely, of a whole man, since women were merely a product of defective development ('De malo', 15, a. 2). Any irregular emission of semen was to the detriment of nature, whose welfare consisted in the preservation of the species. 'Thus the sin whereby the generation of human nature is impeded stands second [only] to the sin of murder, whereby human nature already in existence is destroyed' ('Summa contra gentiles', III, 122). So contraception, though not identical with murder, is very nearly so. Like Aristotle, Thomas regarded male seed as 'something divine' ('De malo', 15, 2). 'One act of copulation may result in the begetting of a man, wherefore inordinate copulation, being detrimental to the welfare of the child-to-be, is a mortal sin' ('Summa theologica', II/II, q. 154, a. 2 ad 6).

While Thomas rejected 'Si aliquis', others went further than that canon and applied the definition murder, not only to contraception with the aid of poisonous medicines, but also to coitus interruptus. Petrus Cantor and, more especially, Bernardino of Siena, the most celebrated preacher of his day, advocated that the term 'murder' be applied to contraception, by which Petrus Cantor meant primarily coitus interruptus, the Old Testament sin of Onan, 'who spilled his seed on the ground' ('The Sodomitic Vice' in 'Verbum abbreviatum', 138). In the fifteenth sermon of his cycle on 'The Eternal Gospel', which he devoted to 'the frightful sin against nature', Bernardino quoted some words which he wrongly ascribed to Augustine: 'Those afflicted with this vice are murderers of men, not by the sword, but in fact.' Indeed, he added, 'Not only are they murderers of men, but they must ... truly be described as murderers of their own children.' The said sin was committed by both men and women 'and most commonly of all by those who are in the holy estate of matrimony' (15, 2, 1; Noonan, op. cit., p. 236f.).

Although contraception's absurd and incredible 'elevation' to the rank of murder by 'Si aliquis' was intended only as a guide to the imposition of penances, it affected secular legislation as well. Many people suffered terribly in consequence. 'Si aliquis' found penal expression in the 'Bamberger Strafrecht' of 1507 and Charles V's 'Peinliche Gerichtsordnung' of 1532, Article 133 of which prescribed the death penalty for contraception and the abortion of an animate foetus, this to take the form of decapitation for men and drowning for women. Penalties for the abortion of a child that was 'not yet alive [i.e. prior to ensoulment]' were less severe.

But there were still other victims of ecclesiastical folly. Innocent III, uncle of Gregory IX, the 'Si aliquis' pope, had in 1215 summoned the Fourth Lateran Council to wage war on the Cathars and assured all Catholics who took part in this Crusade against heresy of the same privileges as Crusaders in the Holy Land, thereby initiating a reign of terror that was to afflict the Cathars for centuries. In fighting for the life of the unborn, the campaigners against contraception had become murderers devoid of pity for the living. The penalty for heretics who opposed the true faith was death at the stake.

The bonfires kindled at that time were only a modest beginning, however. In 1326, after sex-demonising theologians had whipped up a mood of mass hysteria with their chimerical notions of intercourse between witches and devils, Pope John XXII pronounced witchcraft and heresy equally condemnable, and the authors of the 'Malleus Maleficarum' ('The Hammer of the Magicians') (1487) advocated that 'witch-midwives' be made subject to the 'Si aliquis' canon and put to death. In Germany, many women and very many midwives were reduced to ashes in the ensuing witch- and heretic-hunts.

EIGHTEEN

Incest

Bad as it was, unnatural (e.g. contraceptive) intercourse did have its advantages, from the aspect of ecclesiastical law, where the complicated subject of impediments to marriage was concerned. Though not immediately apparent, the connection can soon be discerned. A man was forbidden to marry not only his sister-in-law, for instance, but other women whose affinity to him was more remote. If a man had had intercourse with a woman before marriage, his brothers were debarred from marrying her by the impediment of affinity arising from illicit intercourse. In this context, importance attached to whether or not the said intercourse had been contraceptive. Pope Urban II (d. 1099) was once asked to rule on the following question: assuming that a man had had unnatural intercourse with a certain woman, did that constitute an affinity sufficient to debar one of his brothers from marrying her? Urban replied in the negative: improper semination was not a form of intercourse that would constitute an impediment to marriage arising from affinity. Thus, one of his brothers would be at liberty to marry the said woman.

From another angle, however, this advantage was a disadvantage, because a man could no longer divorce his brother's former mistress on the grounds of affinity arising from illicit intercourse, whereas a husband's careful investigation of his own or his wife's past had often been rewarded with a decree of nullity. Marriage within the prohibited degrees of affinity was incest, and the simplest way to obtain a divorce in the Middle Ages was to delve into the past or explore the ramifications of one's own or one's spouse's family tree. The most celebrated divorcee in ecclesiastical history, Henry VIII, illustrates this point.

Impediments to marriage could stem from (i) consanguinity, (ii) affinity, (iii) affinity rising from illicit intercourse, (iv) betrothal, and (v) spiritual affinity (with godparents and sponsors and their families). Invented by celibatarians and carried to grotesque extremes in order to monasticise the laity by making marriage as difficult as possible (Pope Innocent III [d. 1216] 'relaxed' the ban on marriage between seventh cousins, but only by three degrees), this whole edifice of impediments became a means of ridding oneself of an unwanted spouse.

In the Old Testament, Numbers and Deuteronomy prohibit relatively few marriages between kinsfolk and relations by marriage. A man was debarred from marrying his mother, sister, granddaughter, aunt, step-mother, mother-in-law, daughter-in-law, stepdaughter, step-grand-daughter, stepmother's daughter by a previous marriage, father's brother's wife, or brother's wife. If his brother's widow was left childless, on the other hand, he was duty-bound to help her have issue by means of a leviratical marriage. Even today, marriage between kindred is not only *not* prohibited but positively encouraged among the Jews: 'Let a man take no wife until his sister's daughter be full-grown; only if she please him not may he look about him for another' (H.L. Strack and P. Billerbeck, 'Kommentar zum Neuen Testament aus Talmud und Midrasch', II, p. 380). Marriages between the children of brothers and sisters – first cousins, in other words – were common: Isaac married Rebecca, Jacob married Leah and Rachel.

John the Baptist was beheaded because he had rebuked Herod Antipas for marrying Herodias, the wife of his brother Philip: 'It is not lawful for thee to have thy brother's wife' (Mark 6: 18). In so doing he was citing the Old Testament law set forth in Leviticus 28: 16 and 20: 21. He condemned Herod's marriage to the wife of a *living* brother, but not because he advocated the indissolubility of marriage and opposed the remarriage of divorced persons, as the Christian Church was later to do. He was merely repeating the Old Testament law that sanctioned divorce, and even polygamy, but prohibited marriage to the wife of a living brother. He did not mention that it was a man's duty to marry (or father children on) his brother's widow. Pope Gregory the Great (d. 604) was wrong to invoke John the Baptist in his letter to England and make him a martyr of the Christian ban on marriages between in-laws.

Unlike the Jews, who were relatively moderate in this respect, Christians evolved a greater abundance of quibbling impediments to marriage than any other religion has ever managed to devise, even in theory, their only possible motive being the Catholic hostility to sex and pleasure in general. (Cf. on what follows G.H. Joyce, 'Christian Marriage: The Prohibited Degrees of Kindred and Affinity', p. 507f.)

In 314 the Council of Neocæsarea ruled that a woman who married two brothers in succession should be excommunicated for five years. The Synod of Elvira (early fourth century) prescribed that, if a man married the sister of his deceased wife, she should be excommunicated for a similar term. She could not be admitted to the sacrament of penance unless dangerously ill, and then only if she promised to renounce the relationship. The Old Testament had said nothing of the kind. It prohibited marriage to the wife of a surviving brother, not to the sister of a deceased wife. St Ambrose, too, was mistaken when he forbade a man to marry his niece on the grounds that Leviticus prohibited marriages between the children of brothers and sisters, so marriages between uncles and nieces were covered by that ban (Letter to Paternus, 397). Neither statement was true. To give him his due, Augustine conceded that the Old Testament took a different view of the matter. Although marriages between the children of brothers and sisters had been permitted in those days, he wrote, the practice was now forbidden as improper because 'a person to whom one owes respect for reasons of kinship is not to be approached with impure desire, even for the sake of procreation' ('De civitate Dei', 15, 16).

By the sixth century, the ban on marriage because of incest extended to third cousins. Although Gregory the Great made some small concessions in regard to more remote degrees of consanguinity when writing to the newly converted English, he strictly forbade marriage between first cousins. 'Experience has taught us,' he declared, 'that such marriages are infertile.'

Only in very recent times has it become fashionable for hereditary defects to be cited in support of the ban on 'incestuous' marriages by theologians such as Fritz Tillmann, whose 'Handbuch der katholischen Sittenlehre' ('Manual of Catholic Moral Doctrine') appeared during the Nazi era, and Bernhard Häring, author of 'Das Gesetz Christi' ('The Law of Christ'). The health of children depends not on their parents' degree of consanguinity, of course, but on their genetic make-up. Gregory the Great forbade the English to marry their brothers' widows: 'On that account was St John the Baptist beheaded.' As to whether those who had contracted such marriages prior to the arrival of

Christian missionaries should separate, the pope had glad tidings to impart: 'Since, so we are told, there are many among the English people who lived in such condemnable marriages at the time when they were still heathens, they must, if they accept the faith, be enjoined to abstinence. Let them fear the dread judgment of God, lest, for carnal pleasure's sake, they incur eternal pain and torment.' They were not, however, expected to put away their wives from the bad old heathen days. The newly converted Letts fared worse in the thirteenth century, but more of them later.

During the eighth and ninth centuries, synods such as those of Verberie (756) and Compiègne (757) demanded that married couples related to within the sixth degree should part and take other spouses. In 800 Pope Leo III urged the bishops of Bavaria to prohibit marriages between persons whose consanguinity could be traced back to the seventh generation because the Lord had 'rested from all his work' on the seventh day (Wetzer/Welte, 'Kirchenlexikon', XII, p. 847). Although it was almost impossible to prove that a betrothed couple were not related in the seventh degree, the subsequent discovery of such consanguinity rendered their union invalid. A council held at Cologne in 922 reduced this restriction to the fifth degree.

The Synod of Compiègne (757) was the first to pronounce on the question of affinity arising from illicit intercourse: if a woman married the brother of a man with whom she had previously had immoral relations, her marriage was invalid. An analogous case from the eighth century was that of Count Stephanus, dealt with in detail in chapter 12. Stephanus, who had sent his young bride back to her father, Count Regimund, after their wedding but before their wedding-night, argued that he had previously slept with a lady related to her, thus incurring the impediment of affinity arising from illicit intercourse. With the help of the theologian Hinkmar, he persuaded the Frankish bishops to concede that such an affinity formed a sufficient impediment to his marriage.

Emperor Henry III (d. 1056) transgressed the laws of the Church by marrying Agnes, the daughter of William of Aquitaine, because they were the great-grandchildren of two stepsisters, Albreda and Mathilde, and deemed to be related in the fourth degree. Together with marriage among the priesthood, 'incestuous' marriages were one of the chief targets of Gregory VII's eleventh-century reform. St Peter Damian (d. 1072) went so far as to insist that the holy canons forbade marriage between kinsfolk while any memory of their kinship endured, and in 1066–7 Pope Alexander II prohibited a marriage on grounds of incest because the prospective bride was related in the fourth degree to a woman who had formerly been her prospective bridegroom's mistress.

It had become difficult to find a spouse at all. No married couple could be certain that their union would not be denounced as incestuous before the ecclesiastical courts by some jealous and ill-intentioned person who had discovered that they were distantly related. If their children were suddenly declared illegitimate, it affected their legal status and rights of inheritance. Certain concessions were made in response to the understandable uneasiness this caused. Pope Alexander III (d. 1181) decreed that, if a fourth-degree marriage had lasted for eighteen to twenty years, it should not be challenged, and Pope Lucius III (d. 1185) permitted the archbishop of Spalato to leave a fifth-degree marriage in being.

In 1215 Pope Innocent III reduced the prohibited degrees of consanguinity and affinity from the seventh to the fourth. Far from putting an end to the imposition of special regulations, however, this measure left considerable scope for papal decisions in particular instances, as the following case illustrates. A woman who had applied to have her marriage annulled because she was related to her husband in the fourth degree was informed by Innocent III that the fourth-degree prohibition was humanly, not divinely ordained, and that her marriage could be tolerated by papal dispensation. She did not, therefore, succeed in getting rid of her husband. On another occasion, the bishop of Riga asked Innocent III how he was to treat the newly converted Letts, whose custom it had been to marry their brothers' widows. Unless they were permitted to keep their wives, he said, many of them would refuse baptism. The pope (citing the leviratical law of the Old Testament) ruled that, if a woman had children from her first marriage, her second marriage must be dissolved if she or her second husband wished to be baptised. If her first marriage had been childless, her second marriage might, by way of exception, remain in being. However, no man would be allowed to marry his sister-in-law after baptism. The practical effects of this ruling were as follows: a woman with children by her first marriage could not become a Christian unless she renounced her present husband, who had formerly been her brother-in-law. He, if he wished to become a Christian, had to put away his wife and former sister-in-law whatever her own age or that of her children. Innocent III made no mention of what was to happen to any children they had in common. It may have suited many a man's book to turn his wife out, so Christianity owed some of its converts – in Latvia at least – to marital strife.

Dispensations were sometimes granted. Many of those who wanted annulments rather than dispensations, like the woman who petitioned Innocent III, were granted dispensations regardless, whereas many who did want dispensations failed to obtain them. Cardinal Turrecremata (d. 1468), an eminent ecclesiastical jurist, informed Pope Eugene IV that it was not within his power to grant the dauphin, later Louis XI of France, a dispensation to marry the sister of his deceased wife. This impediment was not formally abolished until 1983, though it had long been the custom to grant dispensations contrary to Turrecremata's ruling.

The first dispensation in respect of a deceased wife's sister was granted in 1500 by Pope Alexander VI to King Manoel of Portugal, who wished to marry Maria of Aragon, the sister of his late wife Isabella. In 1503, Catherine of Aragon, the sister of Maria and Isabella, was granted a dispensation to marry her deceased husband's brother, Henry VIII of England. This dispensation was destined to become the occasion of England's break with Rome. The Council of Trent later ruled that dispensations in the second degree should, for the sake of the public good, be restricted to persons of royal birth (Sess. 24, c. 5, De reform. matr.).

Henry VIII made fruitless attempts to get his marriage to Catherine of Aragon annulled. Pope Julius II having granted him a dispensation to marry his brother Arthur's widow, Henry could hardly expect Pope Clement VII to revoke it, so he eventually took matters into his own hands. Expert opinions drafted by his own ecclesiastical jurists confirmed what he proposed to establish, which was that Julius had not been entitled to grant such a dispensation in the first place and had broken a divine prohibition. Henry had received personal proof of this: in his opinion, a series of miscarriages and the birth of a lone daughter (later 'Bloody' Mary I) were attributable to the threat implicit in Leviticus 20: 21 – 'And if a man shall take his brother's wife, it is an unclean thing: he hath uncovered his brother's nakedness; they shall die childless.' The convocations of Canterbury and York ruled in Henry's favour by 244 votes to nineteen and forty-nine votes to two respectively. He also gained the approval of the Protestants, who held that the prohibited degrees in Leviticus were as binding as the Ten Command-ments, so no pope was empowered to waive them.

In the case of his second wife, Anne Boleyn, Henry got their daughter Elizabeth declared a bastard with the aid of the impediment of affinity arising from illicit intercourse. (He had since become head of the English Church and no longer consulted Rome.) Anne herself he got rid of by having her beheaded. Before marrying her, he had had intercourse with her elder sister Mary – regular or 'natural' intercourse, so an impedi-ment did exist otherwise than in the case on which Urban II had pronounced. In the view of his ecclesiastical jurists, therefore, he had never been validly married to Anne Boleyn at all. Elizabeth was an illegitimate child and, thus, deprived of any claim to the throne until times changed and she inherited it after all.

Despite a widespread desire to see the prohibited degrees of consan-guinity and affinity reduced, the Council of Trent (1545–63) abided by the fourth degree. No relaxation occurred until 1917, when marriage was prohibited only within the third degree of consanguinity. From 1917 onwards, therefore, it became possible to marry the child of a second cousin – roughly the position that had prevailed in the fifth century. A further reduction was introduced in 1983. Prior to that year a girl required a dispensation to marry a cousin of her father's; since then that impediment has ceased to obtain.

The impediment of spiritual affinity, too, was finally and completely abolished in 1983. In 530 Emperor Justinian had prohibited marriage between godchild and godparent. Marriage between a godparent and the parent of a godchild was forbidden by Trullanum II in 692 (Canon 53) and the Synod of Rome in 721. Pope Nicholas I (d. 867) further forbade marriage between the offspring of godparents and godchildren. The Frankish Synod of Verberie (756) demanded that married couples separate if the husband had entered into spiritual affinity with his wife by standing sponsor at the confirmation of her godchild. Women anxious to divorce their husbands began to take advantage of this device, which created an 'incestuous' relationship between them, so the Synod of Châlons (813) decreed that no divorce should occur in such cases, but that the guilty party should be condemned to lifelong penance.

The following references to 'spiritual affinity' in Wetzer/Welte's encyclopedia (1901) may serve to show how thoroughly the ecclesiasti-cal authorities explored and regulated the whole field. Thomas Aquinas applied himself to spiritual affinity in such painstaking detail that we can only marvel at the nicety with which he expounded such arrant nonsense and sought to substantiate it (Summa theologica suppl., q. 56, a. 4 and 5). Here is Wetzer/Welte's historical survey of the said nonsense:

> Impediments to marriage attained their widest extent thereafter [from the ninth century onwards]. On account of *paternitas spiritualis*, marriage was prohibited above all between the baptised and the baptiser and between the godchild or confirmand and his or her godparent, but also between the spouse of the baptiser or godparent and the godchild or confirmand should the baptiser or godparent be married and have consummated that marriage (*paternitas indirecta*) ... Because of *compaternitas* or *commaternitas spiritualis*, marriage was prohibited between the baptiser and the godchild on the one hand and the natural parents of the child on the other. An impediment also existed between the spouse of the baptiser or godparent, should the marriage have been consummated, and the parents of the godchild (*compaternitas indirecta*) ... Finally, on account of *fraternitas spiritualis*, marriage was prohibited between the godchild or confirmand and the children of the godparent or baptiser.
>
> (XII, p. 851)

Alfonso de' Liguori (d. 1787) devoted page after page to where and when a godparent had to touch a godchild in order to create an impediment to marriage between whom and whom, and to which spouse might no longer demand marital intercourse of his or her spouse or grant it only at his or her request because he or she, by touching a godchild during baptism, whether common to them both or not, had suddenly established a spiritual affinity with his or her partner and was henceforth living in incest because he or she had, or had not, deliberately or with evil intent stood sponsor to the said child ('Theologia moralis', 6, p. 148f.). Incredible as it may seem, Alfonso's exposition of the subject was relatively simple, the Council of Trent having discarded many previous impediments to marriage based on spiritual affinity.

Luther, it should be added, had dismissed the impediment of spiritual affinity in 1520: 'In the same way, the nonsense about compaternity, commaternity, confraternity, consorority, and confiliality ought to be completely blotted out ... See how Christian liberty has been suppressed by the blindness of human superstition' ('Early Reformation

Writings of Martin Luther', pp. 299–300). It was not in fact until 1983, or five hundred years after his birth, that the impediment of spiritual affinity was removed from Catholic canon law.

In 1522, in his sermon on married life, Luther accused the Catholic Church of abusing its authority. The ordinances contained in the Old Testament should not be extended, he said. They referred to named persons, not to degrees of consanguinity. Calvin, who disputed this, held that the Old Testament laws should be analogously augmented. If a woman could not marry two brothers in succession, for example, neither could a man marry his wife's sister. Anything that exceeded such parallels Calvin denounced as devilish deceit on the part of the popes. The Council of Trent attacked the two reformers' views and excommunicated all who claimed that 'only those degrees of consanguinity and affinity named in Leviticus can prevent a marriage from being contracted or, if it has already occurred, annul the contract, and that the Church cannot exempt certain persons of those degrees from impediment or prescribe that degrees other than those can prohibit and sunder a marriage.'

The Eastern Church saved itself a great deal of trouble by never acknowledging the impediment of affinity arising from illicit intercourse, which first emerged in the West during the eighth century. In other respects, its laws relating to consanguinity and affinity were not appreciably different from those of Rome. When Patriarch Marcus of Alexandria pointed out to Theodore of Balsamon (d. after 1195), the celebrated canonist and patriarch of Constantinople, that the Christian community of Alexandria was so intermarried that such unions had become hard to avoid, Theodore retorted that this did not excuse the committing of sins.

Josef Fuchs, the authority on Thomas Aquinas, gives him a special accolade for his detailed substantiation of the ban on incest. 'Many a traditional doctrine, which other theologians simply passed on, was not only retained by him but submitted to entirely new and independent examination. Compare, for instance, his exhaustive substantiation of the ban on incest with the unquestioning transmission of tradition by other theologians: not even Guillaume d'Auxerre, for example, so thoroughly independent in other respects, provides any internal substantiation' (Fuchs, 'Die Sexualethik des heiligen Thomas von Aquin', p. 277f.) When substantiation is absurd, its absence is less absurd than its presence. Thomas's accolade is identical with the charge that must be levelled at him, namely, that he substantiated where there was nothing to substantiate, accepted nonsense uncritically, and promptly proceeded to justify it.

Thomas found it peculiarly easy to justify the exaggerated ban on incest because it accorded, so to speak, with his repression of marriage. One of the arguments he borrowed from Augustine was 'the augmentation of friendship' (meaning friendship arising from consanguinity and affinity). According to him, it enhanced the friendly ties between human beings if marriage was restricted to unrelated persons. Another argument he claimed to have found, this time in Aristotle (though Aristotle would have been amazed at the far-flung extent of the impediments to marriage for which he is supposed to have furnished reasons), ran as follows: if sexual love was added to love of kindred, there was a risk of excessive passion. 'Since it is natural that a man should have affection for a woman of his kindred, if to this be added the love deriving from sexual intercourse, his love would be too passionate, and would become a very great incentive to lust; and this militates against chastity' ('Summa theologica', II/II q. 154, a. 9).

Thomas explained the incongruity between Mosaic law and Christian in respect of degrees of consanguinity by asserting that more degrees of kinship had been prohibited by 'the new law of the spirit and of love', and that it was necessary for men to be 'drawn away from the carnal and devote themselves to spiritual things' – in other words, for the laity to be monasticised. Consequently, Thomas found it 'reasonable' that the ban on marriage should have encompassed the seventh degree of consanguinity and affinity – reasonable because of the difficulty of tracing one's ancestry back beyond the seventh generation, and also because 'it accords with the sevenfold grace of the Holy Spirit'. In latter years, Thomas went on, a reduction to the fourth degree had occurred (a reference to its reduction by Innocent III at the Fourth Lateran Council in 1215). Thomas found four degrees 'fitting' because the prevalence of sexual desire and neglect was such that non-compliance with the many prohibited degrees of kindred had proved 'a pitfall of damnation for many'.

Seven degrees or four – Thomas justified both and would doubtless have discovered reasonable and God-given arguments in favour of a ban on the fourteenth degree, if necessary, arraying them all beneath the monastic banner of 'more friendship and less passion'.

NINETEEN

Witchcraft-Induced Impotence, Demonic Intercourse, Witches, Changelings

Thomas Aquinas is important to sexual ethics, not because he introduced a change of direction in moral theology, but – on the contrary – because he was a great conformist who crystallised the more conservative doctrines of his time and defended them against liberalisation. His gravest mistake, and the one that was to have the most disastrous consequences, given his great personal authority, was to assail those who doubted that devils were peculiarly active in the sexual domain – that they could, for example, induce impotence by magical means. In his view, these rational sceptics – and some there were, even in the superstition-ridden thirteenth century – were at odds with the Catholic faith. 'The Catholic faith teaches us,' he declared, 'that demons are of consequence; that they can not only harm people but inhibit sexual intercourse.' The targets of his wrath were 'some who have said that such bewitchment does not occur and is merely a product of unbelief. Such people take the view that demons are only a delusion, in other words, that people imagine them and then, in terror, take harm therefrom' ('Quaestiones quodlibet X', q. 9, a. 10).

Even here, Thomas was not the originator of a superstition but its most influential custodian. The idea of witchcraft-induced impotence can be found as early as 860 in a letter written by Archbishop Hinkmar of Rheims, and Burchard of Worms (d. 1025) had advised confessors to question penitents as follows: 'Have you done that which wanton women do? If they perceive that their lover desires to contract a legitimate marriage, they mortify his desire so that he can have no intercourse with his wife. If you have acted thus, you must do forty days' penance on water and bread.' The same superstition had been incorporated in their canonical compilations by Ivo of Chartres in the eleventh century and Gratian in the twelfth, and by Peter Lombard (also twelfth century) in his 'Sentences'.

It was not, however, until the thirteenth century, Thomas's 'golden age of theology', that the belief gained strength to an unimaginable extent, though contrary opinions were voiced even then. Peter Browe, the Jesuit authority on the medieval Church, writes: 'It seems, however, that the Devil's power over the male procreative urge was disputed by a few theologians and laymen; certainly, very many textbooks express the recurrent objection that these were merely attempts to explain effects whose causes, being unknown, were attributed to demons and their instruments; but it [the objection] was rebutted by Thomas Aquinas, among others . . . as latitudinarian and un-Catholic' ('Beiträge zur Sexualethik des Mittelalters', p. 124). Thomas's mentor Albertus had already taken issue with such un-Catholic free-thinkers. 'No one should doubt,' he declared, 'that there are many [!] who have been bewitched by the power of demons' ('In IV Sententias', d. 34, a. 8).

St Bonaventure (d. 1274), the great Franciscan theologian, had an explanation of why the Devil inhibited men's marital intercourse, in particular, but did not prevent them from eating and drinking: 'It is because the sexual act has become corrupted and, to a certain extent, fetid [on account of original sin], and because most men are too lustful in that respect, that the Devil has so much power and licence over it. This can be proved by an example and by scriptural authority, for it is related that a devil named Asmodeus killed seven men in bed, but not at table' (ibid., d. 34, a. 2, q. 2). Bonaventure is here alluding to the Old Testament Book of Tobit, which, as we saw in chapter 1, was falsified for his own antisexual purposes by its translator, St Jerome, but is still regarded by Catholic theologians as biblical evidence of the pure and God-given procreative purpose of the conjugal act (e.g. by Bernhard Häring in 'The Law of Christ', p. 371f.). It was further regarded until well into the eighteenth century as proof that the Devil, though unable to kill a man in his marriage-bed, could afflict him with impotence. The Book of Tobit describes how young Tobias marries his kinswoman Sarah, who has already been the bride of seven men whom the demon Asmodeus slew on their wedding-night. The archangel Raphael gives Tobias the following advice (Jerome's): 'The Devil has power over those married persons who shut God out and give themselves over to their lust like horses and mules, which have no understanding. But do

201

you abstain from her three days long and pray with her during that time
. . . When the third night is past, take the virgin unto you in fear of the
Lord, more for love of posterity than for lust.' Three days and nights
later, Tobias says: 'And now, O Lord, thou knowest that I take not this
my sister for lust, but only for love of posterity' (Tobit 6: 14–22 and
8: 9). The original text of the Book of Tobit (second century BC) stated
that Tobias had intercourse with his bride the very first night, whereas
the archangel's admonition and Tobias' own virtuous words were
concocted by Jerome the ascetic.

From the beginning of the thirteenth century onwards, sorceresses
'who bewitch married persons so that they cannot engage in conjugal
union' were condemned by countless synods including those of Salisbury
(1217), Rouen (*c.* 1235), Fritzlar (1243), Valencia (1255), Clermont
(1268), Grado (1296), Bayeux (1300), Lucca (1308), Mainz (1310),
Utrecht (1310), Würzburg (1329), Ferrara (1332), and Basle (1434)
(v. Browe, op. cit., p. 127).

In 1484 two German Dominicans, Jacob Sprenger (professor of
theology at Cologne) and Heinrich Institoris (co-author with Sprenger
of the 'Malleus Maleficarum'), were appointed inquisitors by Innocent
VIII in his notorious 'Hexenbulle' or 'Witches' Bull'. The pope had
heard that numerous persons of both sexes were practising witchcraft
in the bishoprics of Mainz, Cologne, Trier and Salzburg, 'whereby they
have prevented men from generating and women from conceiving, and
rendered the conjugal act impossible'. In their 'Malleus Maleficarum' of
1487, Institoris and Sprenger cited the 'Si aliquis' canon, which defined
contraception as murder, in support of their demand for the death
penalty for witchcraft calculated to induce impotence and sterility
(I, q. 8). They believed, incidentally, that God himself meted out sum-
mary justice to those who practised another form of contraception: 'For
no sin has God more often punished many with sudden death' than for
vices that militated 'against the nature of procreation', e.g. 'coitus
outside the proper vessel' (I, q. 4). Even in the absence of witchcraft,
contraception was deemed a capital offence by the authors of the
'Malleus Maleficarum'.

The belief in witchcraft-induced impotence and the growth of mass
hysteria on the subject were deliberately fostered by higher authority.
Just as Thomas had condemned free-thinkers as unbelievers if they
questioned the possibility of such impotence and the Devil's role in the
sexual act, so Innocent's Witches' Bull was aimed primarily at those

who, 'irrespective of what ranks, offices, honours, entitlements, patents of nobility, prerogatives or privileges they may possess', did, 'whether religious or lay, claim to know more than their due' and 'impede, resist, or rebel against' the trials conducted by the pope's appointed inquisitors, whom he referred to as his 'beloved sons'. The penalties imposed on these know-it-alls, who were clearly numerous in contemporary Germany, were to be 'increased in severity'.

The 'Malleus Maleficarum', too, made sceptics its principal target. It began by questioning 'whether the assertion that witches exist is so truly Catholic that the stubborn defence of the contrary opinion must be deemed thoroughly heretical'. The answer, needless to say, was yes, and the chief authority for such Catholic doctrine was Thomas Aquinas. 'Although this error [the denial that there are witches who "can inhibit generative power or the enjoyment of love"] is rejected as plainly false by all other scholars, it is still more vehemently contested by St Thomas because he condemns it as a heresy by saying that this error stemmed from the root of unbelief; and, since unbelief in a Christian is called heresy, these persons are justly suspected of the same' (I, q. 8).

More trials for witchcraft were held in Germany than in any other country, opposition to them having been jointly broken by the Witches' Bull (1484) and the 'Malleus Maleficarum'. Although such trials had been rare there prior to the Witches' Bull, they multiplied so hugely thereafter that in 1630, almost a century and a half later, the Jesuit Friedrich von Spee risked death at the stake by opposing them in his 'Cautio criminalis', which stated that 'pyres are smoking everywhere, particularly in Germany' (q. 2). Spee attributed the fact that such trials were commoner in Germany than in any other country in the world to 'Jacob Sprenger and Heinrich Institoris, who were dispatched to Germany by the Apostolic See'. 'I begin to fear,' he went on, 'nay, the fearful thought has often occurred to me ere now, that the whole host of witches was introduced into Germany by the aforementioned inquisitors [themselves], with their most ingenious and subtly apportioned tortures' (q. 23). Spee was here alluding to the most horrible of the practices introduced by the 'Malleus Maleficarum'. 'Apportioned tortures' meant the endlessly protracted inflicting of pain whereby inquisitors extorted all the confessions and denunciations they needed.

* * *

The 'Malleus Maleficarum' devoted careful consideration to 'why the Devil is invested by God with greater sorcerous power over coitus than over other human activities'. This question, to which its criminal and sexually pathological authors reverted over and over again (I, qq. 3, 6, 8, 9, 10; II, q. 1; q. 1 c. 6), they answered with another reference to Thomas Aquinas: 'For he says that since the first corruption by sin, through which man became the Devil's slave, entered into us by way of the coital act, God granted the Devil more sorcerous power over that act than any other' (I, q. 6). The authors of the 'Malleus Maleficarum' were quite justified in invoking Thomas here. As Josef Fuchs wrote in 1949: 'With reference to sexual energy's role in the transmission of original sin, Thomas pronounced the sexual domain, too, to be a special province of the Devil' (Fuchs, 'Die Sexualethik des Heiligen Thomas von Aquin', p. 60). Thomas, in his turn, cited Pope Gregory I (d. 604) in support of his belief that the Devil was more of a tempter in the realm of sex than elsewhere ('De malo', 15, 2 o. 6). The leitmotif of the 'Malleus Maleficarum' consisted of a recurrent question, 'Why should the Devil be permitted to practise sorcery in respect of the sexual act in particular, and not of man's other activities?', and the inevitable response: 'Because of the frightfulness of the coital act, and because original sin is transmitted to all men thereby' (I, q. 3; q. 10).

Another question that particularly exercised the two authors was why 'witch-midwives surpass all other witches in their abominations' (III, q. 34). Drawing on their experience as inquisitors, they told how 'contrite witches have often confessed to us and others that no one does the Catholic faith more harm than midwives' (I, q. 11). At Cologne, where the city's midwives were almost exterminated between 1627 and 1630, they accounted for one in three of all the women executed. It was the Cologne trials that prompted Spee, who had acompanied many witches to the stake, to write several chapters of his 'Cautio criminalis'.

Heinsohn and Steiger's 'Die Vernichtung der Weisen Frauen' ('The Destruction of the Wise Women', p. 131) states that Spee 'saw numerous witches at work', but this is absurd. The words to which they refer are a rhetorical question on Spee's part: 'What could today seem more nonsensical than to believe that the number of true witches is dwindling? And yet . . . the truth had no greater enemy than prejudice' (q. 9). To describe the prejudice Spee cites as Spee's own opinion is nonsensical in itself. Only a few pages later, he wrote: 'So I must admit that I have, in divers places, accompanied to their deaths many witches of whose innocence I am even now no more in doubt than I was at pains, sometimes excessively so, to discover the truth . . . but I could nowhere find aught save innocence' (q. 11).

The main charge levelled at 'witch-midwives' by Institoris and Sprenger was that they killed unbaptised children – 'for the Devil knows that such children are precluded from entering the Kingdom of Heaven by the penalty of damnation or original sin' (II, q. 1 c. 13). The idea of a connection between the Devil and dead babies was a consequence of Augustine's ludicrous doctrine that God condemns unbaptised infants to hell. The 'Malleus Maleficarum' adduced no evidence in support of its charge that midwives were guilty of killing the new-born. Its second charge was that they 'prevented conception in the womb by various means' (II, q. 1 c. 5). It is as obvious that midwives were a source of contraceptive advice, or what passed for it in those days, as it is that they were not responsible for every case of sterility. The absurd traditional doctrine that contraception equals murder, which Institoris and Sprenger adopted by invoking 'Si aliquis', was their second major reason for 'incinerating' midwives, to quote the grisly term they regularly employed in the course of their extermination campaign.

The High Middle Ages knew of fifty or sixty ways in which demons could inhibit the conjugal act. Of these the 'Malleus Maleficarum' listed a whole series, e.g. 'active enfeeblement of the member that serves to fertilise' (I, q. 8). To buttress their contention that chastity, in the sense of frigidity, protected one against the demons' habit of 'conjuring away male members' (II, q. 1 c. 7), the two authors busily quoted the Book of Tobit in Jerome's fraudulent translation: 'Over them that are devoted to lust hath the Devil gained ascendancy' (I, qq. 8, 9, 15; II, q. 1 c. 7, q. 1 c. 11, q. 2 c. 2, q. 2 c. 5).

A sorcerous practice regarded with especial dread was 'lace-tying', which the French called *'nouer l'aiguillette'*. This entailed tying a knot or turning a key in a lock while a wedding was in progress. The effects varied in duration according to the spell recited during this procedure by the male or female witch, and conjugal intercourse remained impossible until the spell was broken. Francis Bacon, Baron Verulam, Lord Keeper of the Great Seal and Lord Chancellor (d. 1626), referred to lace-tying as a phenomenon commonly found in Saintes and Gascony ('Sylva sylvarum seu historia naturalis', n. 888).

But rational voices, too, were heard. The practice of lace-tying receives thorough discussion in the essays of Montaigne (d. 1592), who dealt with *'le nouement d'aiguillette'* in a chapter entitled 'The Power of Imagination', 'for people speak of nothing else'. He recounted how he had helped a friend, the Duc de Gurson, to overcome his fear of witchcraft-induced impotence on the occasion of his marriage. Montaigne's sympathetic advice to bridegrooms obsessed with fears of impotence was to be lenient and patient with their own powers of imagination. He considered them more likely to succeed than those who were stubbornly bent on self-conquest.

Unlike this humane sceptic, the Church superstitiously condemned sorcerers and witches. A Lombardic provincial synod convened in 1579 by St Carlo Borromeo levelled threats of dire punishment at those who inhibited marital intercourse by means of witchcraft, as did the Synods of Ermeland (1610) and Liège (1618), and the Synod of Namur (1639) renewed an earlier edict against such practices 'because we know that marriages are daily thrown into disarray by witchcraft' (Browe, op. cit., p. 128f.). The Synod of Cologne (1662), too, addressed itself to impotence induced by witchcraft. The Bavarian Jesuit Kaspar Schott (d. 1667), a long-time professor of physics at Palermo, declared: 'No other form of witchcraft is today more widespread or more feared; in some places bride and bridegroom no longer dare to wed openly in church before a priest and witnesses, but do so at home the previous day and then, the following day, go to church' (ibid., p. 129). Many young couples got married behind closed doors or at night and consummated the marriage before daybreak lest sorcerers or witches set eyes on them (ibid.). Several Italian and French provincial synods, e.g. those of Naples (1576), Rheims (1583) and Bourges (1584), forbade superstitious weddings of this kind. As an antidote, the Synod of Rheims prescribed what the Book of Tobit, alias Jerome, had recommended: that couples should 'consummate marriage for love of posterity, and not for lust'. The belief in witchcraft-induced impotence continued to afflict married couples with anxiety psychoses until well into the eighteenth century (Alfonso de' Liguori [d. 1787] discussed the phenomenon at length and was firmly convinced of its existence).

Legal consequences flowed from the theologians' defence of demonic impotence against the sceptics. Hinkmar of Rheims had favoured divorce and remarriage in cases where no consummation could take place because of witchcraft. Rome originally declined to recognise such divorces and demanded that spouses should live together like brother and sister. Once Hinkmar's opinion had been embodied in Gratian's Decretum and Peter Lombard's 'Sentences' in the twelfth century, however, almost all theologians held that impotence induced by witchcraft was an impediment to marriage. Pope Innocent III ruled in 1207 that Philip II (Philip Augustus) of France could divorce Ingeborg of Denmark for that reason if he failed in a renewed attempt to consummate the marriage with the aid of therapeutic activities such as prayer, alms-giving, and attendance at Mass. The marriage of John of Tirol to Margaret of Carinthia was dissolved on similar ground in 1349. Even today, so-called relative impotence (impotence only in regard to one's spouse) is considered an impediment to marriage if chronic and irremediable. A marriage can be declared null on that account (Canon 1084, CIC 1983), and both parties may remarry. Problems of impotence are no longer attributed to demons and witchcraft, however, but viewed from the medical or psychological standpoint.

Pope Innocent VIII declared at the beginning of his Witches' Bull that witches of both sexes, apart from inducing impotence by sorcerous means, were practising another abomination, to wit, intercourse with devils: 'We have lately learned, not without great sorrow, that in certain parts of Southern Germany, and likewise in the provinces, cities, districts, townships and bishoprics of Mainz, Cologne, Trier and Salzburg, a great number of persons of both sexes, heedless of their own salvation and deserting the Catholic faith, are engaging in fornication with devils in the guise of men or women . . .'

The pope's further remarks were based on the theological notion that sexual intercourse was governed by a standard coital position with which devils, too, complied. Male devils lay on top, female devils beneath, so the pope referred to those devils who fornicated with witches, female or male, as 'incubi' ('on-lying') and 'succubi' ('under-lying') respectively. The chief source for the Witches' Bull and the 'Malleus Maleficarum', of which the latter regarded itself as a commentary on the former, was Thomas Aquinas's idea of demonic intercourse with 'on-lying' or 'under-lying' devils. The baneful 'Malleus Maleficarum' quoted more liberally from Thomas than from any other authority. He had, after all, clearly described the process of sexual intercourse with devils and the begetting of devils' children. He had also evolved a semen-transmission theory: one and the same devil could procure male semen by copulating with a man in female guise (as a succubus) and then, after assuming male form, transfer that semen to a woman (as an incubus). The devils' children begotten in this way – they were often recognisable by their exceptional stature – were thus human children, properly speaking, because they had been generated by human semen ('Summa theologica', I, q. 51, a. 3 ad 6). Thomas had supplied no details of how semen obtained from a male witch remained fresh and generative until transferred to a female witch, but the 'Malleus Maleficarum' plugged such gaps: devils possessed a contrivance for keeping semen fresh and warm until it was transferred (I, q. 3).

That Thomas Aquinas, the greatest Catholic theologian, was responsible for systematising the theory of demonic intercourse is stressed by Sigmund von Riezler in his history of the Bavarian witchcraft trials:

> His successors based themselves on his authority. Whenever one examines the sources cited for this view, one finds that only those of Thomas are unequivocally doctrinal in character. The 'Angelic Doctor', the celebrated saint and scholar of the Dominican Order, must therefore be accounted the man who did most to entrench this lunacy. It was for this reason, as the authors of the 'Malleus Maleficarum' record, that their colleague the Inquisitor of Como had forty-one women burned at the stake in a single year in the county of Bormio or Wormserbad, while many others escaped a similar fate only by fleeing across the frontier to Tirol.
>
> ('Geschichte der Hexenprozesse in Bayern', p. 42f.)

The joint authors of the 'Malleus Maleficarum' applied themselves to the question of why intercourse between men and succubi was rarer than that between women and incubi – in other words, why there were more female witches than male (II, q. 2 c. 1). This gave the pair an opportunity to develop their image of womanhood in concert with all the theological denigrators of women of whom Catholic tradition possesses such a superabundance. They took care to include the Aristotelian theory of women's greater water content, to which Albertus and Thomas had ascribed their alleged inconstancy and unreliability, and which had since become such a theological commonplace that the authors dispensed with an explicit quotation (I, q. 6), nor did they fail to cite Chrysostom (d. 407) on Matthew 19: 'It is not good to marry. What else is woman but the foe of friendship, an inescapable punishment, a necessary evil, a natural temptation, a desirable misfortune, a domestic danger, a delectable detriment, a deficiency of nature, painted in handsome colours?' (I, q. 6). They based their contention that 'wickedness' was commoner among women than men on 'experience'. Woman were in any case 'deficient in all forms of strength, spiritual as well as physical . . . for where intelligence is concerned, or the apprehension of things spiritual, they seem to be of a kind dissimilar to men, [a circumstance] to which authorities, a reason, and divers examples from the Scriptures refer'.

Authorities can be always found. Sprenger and Institoris enlisted the gynaecophobic effusions of Terence and Lactantius. They also struck it rich in the Bible, notably in Proverbs: 'As a jewel of gold in a swine's snout, so is a fair woman which is without discretion.' That left the 'reason': 'The reason is one drawn from nature: she [woman] is more carnally inclined than man, as is evident from [her] many carnal obscenities.'

Sprenger and Institoris even cited some scurrilous references to a woman's tears. 'For Cato says: "If a woman weeps, she assuredly has some cunning deceit in mind." It is also said: "When a woman weeps, she means to deceive a man"' (I, q. 6). On the other hand, failure to weep was evidence of guilt and witchcraft. The physiological fact that a person is incapable of shedding tears under torture was interpreted by the two inquisitors to the detriment of their female victims and earned the poor creatures an extra dose of pain. 'Experience has taught,' they wrote, 'that the more they were adjured the less able they were to weep . . . They may perhaps be capable of weeping before their guards, in the judge's absence and remote from the place and time of torture. If one inquires into the reason whereby witches are prevented from weeping, it may be said: because in penitents the grace of tears is numbered among their excellent gifts.' If a witch did weep, however, the two sadists knew what to make of it: 'But what if even a witch were to weep through the Devil's cunning and with God's permission, since tears, plotting and deceptions are accounted female characteristics? It may be answered that God moves in a mysterious way . . .' And so on and so forth (III, q. 15).

The inferiority of woman (*femina*) was apparent from her very name: 'The word *femina* derives from *fe* and *minus*. *Fe* signifies *fides*, or faith, and *minus* signifies less, so *femina* signifies she who has less faith. Because woman always has and keeps less faith on account of her naturally credulous disposition, the most blessed Virgin may never have wavered in her faith in consequence of grace and by nature, whereas all men did so waver at the time of Christ's passion' (I, q. 6). Like the vast majority of Christianity's great denigrators of woman, the authors of the 'Malleus Maleficarum' – especially Institoris, who earned much commendation by popularising the rosary – were fervent venerators of the Virgin Mary.

But the two inquisitors had still other charges to bring against women: 'If we seek, we find that almost all the kingdoms of the earth have been destroyed by women, the first of them, which was a fortunate kingdom, being Troy . . .' They believed that 'if women's iniquities did not exist, not to speak of witches, the world would be spared countless perils.' This, too, occurred to them on the subject of women: 'Let us hear of yet another characteristic: the voice. For just as woman is mendacious by nature, so she is in speech. For she goads and delights at one and the same time, wherefore also is her voice likened to the song of the sirens, who, by means of their sweet melody, entice passers-by and then slay them. They slay them because they empty their purses, rob them of strength, and compel them to despise God . . . Proverbs 5: "Her mouth" – that is, her speech – "is smoother than oil: but her end is bitter as wormwood"' (I, q. 6).

However, woman was predestined for demonic intercourse by her hair as well as her voice: 'It is also remarked by Gulielmus that incubi [devils in the shape of men] seem more greatly to disturb women and girls with handsome hair . . . because they desire to inflame men by means of their hair or are accustomed to doing so. Or because they boast thereof in a vain manner; or because the goodness of heaven permits this so that women are deterred from inflaming men by means of that wherewith the demons wished to see men inflamed' (II, q. 2 c. 1). Whatever the truth, a handsome head of hair was somehow associated with proximity to the Evil One.

The inquisitors' response to the question of why female witches outnumbered male culminated in the following assertion: 'To conclude: all happens from carnal desire, which in them is insatiable . . . That is why they have to do with demons, to assuage their lust. Still more could be said on the subject, but to the discerning it has been made clear enough . . . Logically, therefore, the heresy to be named is that of female witches, not male . . . Praise be to the Highest, who has till now so well preserved the male gender from such infamy. Having desired to be born and to suffer for us in that gender, he has also, on that account, granted it such preference' (I, q. 6).

After this detailed exposition of the nature of woman we can well understand why the two authors felt a special affinity with Thomas Aquinas, of whom they recorded the following:

> We likewise read that such a blessing was bestowed on St Thomas, the Doctor of our Order [Dominican], who, having been imprisoned by his kinsfolk for entering the said Order, was carnally tempted that he should be seduced by a whore whom his kinsfolk had sent to him in gorgeous raiment and jewels. As soon as the Doctor saw her he ran to the real fire, seized a firebrand, and drove the temptress to fiery lust from the prison. Thereafter, having at once gone down on his knees to pray for the gift of chastity, he fell asleep. There then appeared unto him two angels, who told him: 'Behold, we gird you by God's will with the girdle of chastity, which can be loosed by no subsequent temptation; and that which is not attained by human virtue, by merit, is bestowed by God as a gift.' So he felt the girding, that is to say, the touch of the girdle, and awoke with a cry. And he felt himself to be endowed with such chastity that he thenceforth shrank from all voluptuousness, so that he could not even converse with women without constraint, but was possessed of perfect chastity.

As the authors of the 'Malleus Maleficarum' saw it, Thomas had been fortunate enough to belong to 'the three kinds of men' who alone could feel 'safe from witches' and confident that they would not be 'bewitched or seduced and enticed into witchcraft in the eighteen ways described below, which will be dealt with in turn.' (II, q. 1).

Alfonso de' Liguori also devoted close attention to demonic intercourse in a chapter entitled 'How the Confessor Shall Deal with Those Troubled by the Devil'. Citing Thomas, he described how devils' children were generated by intercourse between devils and women, and pointed out that the child of such a union was not truly a devil's child but the child of the man from whom the devil had previously obtained semen.

Alfonso's advice to confessors ran thus:

> If, therefore, someone comes who has been assailed by the Evil One, the confessor shall zealously ensure that he is well-provided with weapons for his dire struggle . . . He shall exhort him as far

as possible to eschew sensual pleasure . . . he shall further inquire of the penitent if he has ever invoked the Evil One or formed an alliance with the same . . . He shall ask him in what form the Devil appears to him, whether in male or female or bestial guise, for then, if sexual intercourse with the Devil has taken place, that would compound the sin against chastity and against religion with those of fornication, sodomy, incest, adultery, or sacrilege . . . He shall also inquire at what place and at what time this intercourse occurred . . . Let him seek to urge the penitent to make a full confession, for lost persons of this kind readily let slip their sins while confessing.

('Istruzione e pratica per li confessori', VII, pp. 110–13)

As late as 1906, the moral theologian F.A. Göpfert likewise offered instructions to confessors on how to deal with penitents who confessed to demonic intercourse (v. chapter 29 of this book).

The concept of demonic intercourse had terrible repercussions, not only on witches but on numerous 'devils'' children as well. Walter Bachmann's 'Das unselige Erbe des Christentums: Die Wechselbälge – Zur Geschichte der Heilpädagogik' ('The Baneful Legacy of Christianity: Changelings – On the History of Therapeutic Training') records that many handicapped children continued to suffer from its effects in the nineteenth century. The 'Malleus Maleficarum' referred to these 'substituted' children thus: 'There is yet another frightful sanction of God upon mankind, in that demons sometimes deprive women of their own sons and children and foist others upon them. And these children are generally termed *campsores* or, in the vernacular, changelings . . . Certain of them are always thin and cry' (II, q. 2 c. 8). Luther advised that changelings be drowned because 'such changelings are only a lump of flesh, there being no soul within' (Bachmann, op. cit., pp. 183, 191, 195).

The first German to oppose witch hunts and the inhumane treatment of the mentally and physically handicapped was the Calvinist physician Johann Weyer (d. 1588). His book 'Von den Blendwerken der Dämonen, von Zauberei und Hexerei' ('On Demonic Delusions, Sorcery, and Witchcraft'), published in 1563, was promptly placed on the Index of

Prohibited Books. Weyer was personal physician to Duke Johann Wilhelm of Jülich and Cleves. He was eventually accused of having unbalanced the duke's mind by witchcraft and compelled to flee from Düsseldorf. His voice went unheard.

M.G. Voigt's 'Naturwissenschaftliche Untersuchung über die untergeschobenen Kinder' ('Scientific Inquiry into Substituted Children'), Wittenberg, 1667, stated among other things that 'the function of these children is to extol the Devil', that 'substituted children possess no rational soul', and that 'substituted children are not human' (Bachmann, op. cit., pp. 38, 45). Johann Melchior Goeze, a senior Lutheran pastor from Hamburg noted for his controversy with the critic and dramatist Gotthold Lessing, declared that it was irreligious and presumptuous to try to teach deaf-mutes to speak. Augustine himself had laid it down that deaf-mutes were debarred from the Catholic faith by citing Paul's assertion that 'faith cometh by hearing' ('Contra Julianum', 3, 10).

Abbé Charles Michel de l'Épée (d. 1789) is regarded as the 'deaf-mute's saviour'. Writing of him in the first volume of their work on therapeutic training (Leipzig, 1861), Georgens and Deinhardt stated that 'The abbé, a devout and compassionate man who several times gave proof of his independence of mind, was ... so profoundly moved and affected by his acquaintanceship with two deaf-mute sisters, well-mannered and well-educated persons whom a priest had endeavoured to instruct by means of pictures ... that he formed a wish to help unfortunates of this kind'. In so doing 'he had to contend with the fiercest opposition, with derision and persecution; but, steadfastly continuing on his way, he was, in the evening of his days, assured of universal approbation and esteem', and, 'something he valued more than fame, knew that the future of his children, the deaf-mutes of his institute, was secure' (Bachmann, op. cit., p. 233).

Bachmann's caustic summation on the subject of changelings: 'It is doubtful if the handicapped have ever, in any other cultural domain in human history, been more wronged and despised or treated with greater intolerance and inhumanity, than in Christendom' (ibid., p. 442).

TWENTY

The Council of Trent and
Pope Sixtus the Fanatical

During the seven centuries since Catholic theology attained its zenith in Thomas Aquinas (d. 1274), theologians have resolved (after fierce debate) only two marital 'problems'. Augustine had ruled that only marital intercourse for procreative purposes or as a duty performed at one's partner's request was free from sin. The sinlessness of intercourse in avoidance of personal fornication was sometimes affirmed *c.* 1300 but disputed by Thomas, who followed the Augustinian line and classified it as a venial sin. The fourth motivational category, marital intercourse for pleasure's sake, was generally regarded *c.* 1300 as venially sinful at best and mortally sinful under certain circumstances. To summarise the position in the words of the moral theologian Heinrich Klomps:

> From the aspect of moral theology, the outcome of these subjec-
> tive existential deliberations consists in the theory of excuse and
> the theory of indulgence. The former states that Christian spouses
> are wholly excused if their ethical aspirations are focused on
> procreation . . . or on the performance of their conjugal duty . . .
> in which case the goods of progeny and fidelity offset the negative
> effects of lustfulness and sexual desire. According to the theory of
> indulgence, however, the saving graces of marriage intervene in
> such a way as to mitigate guilt if the consummation of marriage
> is motivated by a wish to preserve the chastity of one's own
> person or by a wish to satisfy sexual desire.
>
> (Klomps, 'Ehemoral und Jansenismus', p. 209)

This attempt to cram conjugal love into a corset – to make it subject to a scale of values ranging from procreation to lust via the avoidance

214

of fornication in one's partner and oneself – is not only unrealistic but staggering in its absurdity. All that has been achieved in the seven centuries since Thomas's time is that Intercourse No. 3 and Intercourse No. 4 are also regarded as free from sin. It should, however, be borne in mind in the case of Intercourse No. 4, the most enduring bone of contention, that 'intercourse for pleasure's sake *alone*' may not, pursuant to a ruling given by Pope Innocent XI in 1679, be regarded as sinless. As things now stand, therefore, the product of centuries of thought amounts to this: marital intercourse is free from sin if undertaken 'for pleasure's sake' but not 'for pleasure's sake *alone*'.

Denis (d. 1471), a Dutch Carthusian from Roermond, dedicated a book in Latin on 'The Praiseworthy Life of the Married' to his 'learned' and 'much beloved' married friends. Among the questions it examined was whether married couples could legitimately love each other 'with sensual delight'. Denis considered this permissible but pointed out, to be on the safe side, that St Bridget of Sweden (d. 1373) had spoken in her 'Revelations' of a man who had been damned for having loved his wife too passionately. Husbands with pretty wives and wives with attractive husbands, said Denis, should be suitably careful (John T. Noonan, 'Contraception: A History of its Treatment by the Catholic Theologians and Canonists', p. 305).

In the fifteenth and sixteenth centuries we encounter a trio of theologians who, clearly unimpressed by St Bridget's deterrent vision, attained the stage reached in the twentieth century. They did not go beyond it, however, for they too, while exonerating intercourse in avoidance of fornication (No. 3) and for pleasure's sake (No. 4), regarded contraception by means of coitus interruptus or medicaments as a mortal sin.

The first of the three was Martin Le Maistre (d. 1481), Rector Magnificus of the University of Paris and a celebrated teacher. Le Maistre contested the prevailing theological view that intercourse in avoidance of personal fornication (No. 3) was a venial sin and that intercourse for pleasure's sake (No. 4) could even be a mortal one. Dissociating himself from the standard Augustinian model of a four-stage scale based on degrees of pleasure, he sought to abolish the Augustinian differentiation of motives for the conjugal act and legitimise marital intercourse without reservation. He described the view that marital intercourse for pleasure's sake could be a mortal sin as 'far more of a threat to human morality' than his own attitude. The latter he based on his own common sense: 'Plain reason tells me that it is permissible to seek sexual union for pleasure's sake.' Then, speaking of his theological opponents: 'I wonder to how many dangers they expose the consciences of over-conscientious husbands, for there is many a one whose wife becomes pregnant immediately after sexual conjunction, and now, after that has occurred, they put every man in peril of mortal sin who desires his conjugal due unless it is certain that he does so only in avoidance of fornication.'

Le Maistre contrasted this with his own, unprecedented view: 'I say that someone can wish to enjoy pleasure, first, from sheer delight in that pleasure, and, secondly, in order to escape the tedium of life and the anguish of melancholy that arise from lack of sensual pleasure. Marital intercourse, which seeks to lighten the gloom engendered by an absence of sexual enjoyment, is no sin.' As for the two authorities continually cited by his opponents, Augustine and Aristotle, Le Maistre held that Augustine was only against 'unbridled' and 'unnatural' intercourse. He sought to gloss over Thomas Aquinas's eternal recourse to Aristotle in support of his contention that marital intercourse impaired reason and must be offset by 'the goods that excuse matrimony': even if that were so, which Le Maistre found implausible, this loss of reason would at once be offset by the beneficial effects of marital intercourse. Further-more, Aristotle had sanctioned the enjoyment of sexual pleasure when it conduced to 'the health and well-being of body and soul'.

It even occurred to Le Maistre's critical mind to wonder why coitus interruptus should be thought unnatural 'when the thing is not unnatu-ral, the organ is not unnatural, and the coital act is not unnatural'. In answering this question, however, he promptly reverted to the Church-approved line: semen was not discharged 'into the organ destined by nature for its reception', and that was 'a very grave sin against nature'. This statement he supported by citing the Old Testament story of Onan. Indeed, in his opinion coitus interruptus and the use of contraceptive medicines came into the category of murder.

So not even Le Maistre sought to pursue his common-sense questions in the face of so many wrong but time-honoured answers. He exempli-fies the dilemma that still confronts the popes and Catholic theologians of today, five centuries later, because they uphold the alleged unnatural-ness of contraception for no reason other than that it has always been upheld. Anything of long standing must be right in their eyes, but no lapse of time, however long, can transform a delusion into an eternal truth.

The motive of which Le Maistre suspected married couples anxious to avoid having children turned up again, unchanged and in premier position, in Pope Pius XI's encyclical 'Casti connubii' (1930). Le Maistre knew of only one motive for contraception: it was practised in marriage by those 'who lead a loose life, in order to derive greater pleasure from the sexual act'. 'Casti connubii' states: 'Some justify this criminal abuse on the ground that they are weary of children and wish to gratify their desires without their consequent burden.'

The same encyclical illustrates the 'strides' made by theological thought in the five hundred years since Le Maistre's day by naming a second category of contraception-practising, criminally licentious married persons: those who 'say that they cannot . . . remain continent'. So, in addition to those who seek sexual gratification, there are others who cannot do without it. Before going on, like Le Maistre, to speak of Onan, the bedroom bugbear whom 'God killed', 'Casti connubii' sets the record straight: 'But no reason, however grave, may be put forward by which anything intrinsically against nature may become conformable to nature and morally good. Since, therefore, the conjugal act is destined primarily by nature for the begetting of children . . .' And so on and so forth. Celibatarians and monks have, once and for all, sanctioned the conjugal act for procreative purposes alone, so procreation may not be precluded under any circumstances (on Le Maistre v. Noonan, pp. 342–3, 349–50, 359f.).

Le Maistre was ahead of his time. His liberal views were perpetuated at the University of Paris by John Major (d. 1550), a Scot reputed to be the most erudite theologian of his generation. His pupil, the Scottish reformer John Knox, wrote of him that he was regarded as 'an oracle' in matters of religion. Major held that intercourse in avoidance of personal fornication (No. 3) and intercourse for pleasure's sake (No. 4) were both free from sin. He censured the early Scholastic cardinal and ecclesiastical jurist Huguccio (d. 1210) for having accepted the famous dictum from the 'Responsum Gregorii' – 'Pleasure can never be without sin' – and, consequently, for having regarded all marital intercourse as sinful: 'Behold, this otherwise so reasonable man is prepared, on account of those few words, to place a noose about the neck of all men. I would rather, if no answer occurred to me, disregard ten authorities of Gregory's standing than make such assertions. I would say: he asserts that, by all means, but he does not prove it. And, when something conflicts with probability, it requires bold examination. Whatever may be said, it is surely hard to prove that a husband sins if he goes to his wife for pleasure's sake' ('In IV Sententias', d. 31, q. un. concl. 7).

Major was equally unimpressed by the chaste elephant which so many theologians held up as an example to married couples. 'If it is pointed out, for instance, that the elephant shuns its gravid mate, or that other beasts refrain from mating after fertilisation, and if it is inferred therefrom that a wife may not desire marital intercourse during pregnancy or at the age of sterility, one cannot but reply that the inference is false, for different living creatures have different capacities and aspirations . . . Whether a sensation of pleasure is great or small signifies nothing whatever' (ibid., d. 31, un. fol. 204).

Major's pupil Jacques Almain (d. 1515), who was called 'the keenest debater' (*disputator acutissimus*) at Paris university and died when only thirty-five, shared Le Maistre's and Major's views. 'To say that everyone seeking intercourse in order to be pleased commits sin seems hard' (Noonan, op. cit., p. 311). 'To wish to be without passion would denote hebetude' (Klomps, op. cit., p. 57).

With the passing of these three theologians, reasonable views such as theirs ceased to be voiced by official moral theologians for centuries – or, if they were advanced at all, were speedily silenced. Nothing similar was heard from the reformers of the sixteenth century, still less from the Jansenists of the seventeenth century or from Thomas Sanchez (d. 1610), one of the 'lax Jesuits' criticised by them, nor yet from Alfonso de' Liguori (d. 1787), whose influence dominated the eighteenth and nineteenth centuries.

The fact was that no Catholic university could permit the kind of free speech favoured by Le Maistre, Major and Almain after the Council of Trent (1545–63). The Roman Catechism, commissioned by the Council and published for the use of priests in 1566, still carries great authority to this day. Its sole reference to the conjugal act – not to marriage as a whole, on which even the Roman Catechism had more to say, e.g. the injunction from Ephesians: 'Husbands, love your wives' (Catechism, 8, 2, 16) – consisted in the following ukase:

> The faithful shall chiefly be instructed in two matters: (1) not to have intercourse for the sake of pleasure or lust, but within the

bounds set by the Lord. For it is proper to be mindful of the Apostle's admonition: 'Let those that have wives be as if they had none', and, further, of the words of St Jerome: 'The wise man shall love his wife within reason, not with passion. Let him master the stirrings of lust and refrain from being rashly impelled to intercourse. Nothing is more shameful than to love one's wife like an adulteress'; and (2) from time to time to abstain from intercourse for prayer.

In other words, if a husband is troubled by (1), the ban on sex for pleasure's sake, he can resort to (2) and abstain therefrom – 'above all, for three days at least before receiving the Holy Eucharist but more often during the solemn forty days of Lent, as it was correctly and holily written by our Fathers'. These two points having been clarified (no others are listed under the heading 'What Shall be Taught of Conjugal Obligations'), those who adhere to this two-point programme are promised an increment in divine favour and assured that they will 'attain everlasting life by the grace of God' (2, 8, 33). St Bridget's vision of the man who was damned for loving his wife with excessive ardour is menacingly echoed by the Roman Catechism, especially as it makes a point of enlisting that bogeyman of the nuptial couch, Tobias, and cites St Jerome's 'additional dialogue', according to which Tobias's seven short-lived predecessors in Sarah's bed failed to survive because they had 'indulged in lust' (2, 8, 13).

It should, however, be noted that the Roman Catechism's motives for the conjugal act do not lay an Augustinian stress on procreative intention. More important than the constant thought of children during marital intercourse, it seems, is the constant avoidance of any thought of pleasure. On the other hand, Augustine's basic scheme is retained because Augustine was a pleasure-hater, not a child-lover. His opponent Julian of Eclanum called him 'a persecutor of the new-born' for having damned unbaptised infants. Augustine was more concerned that people should practise celibacy than that they should produce children. The Roman Catechism, too, opens its eighth main section, 'On the Sacrament of Matrimony', by stating that it would really be desirable for all Christians to remain unmarried – 'that all might strive for the virtue of continence, for nothing more blessed in this life can befall the faithful than that their spirit, distracted by no worldly concern and with every carnal desire stilled and subdued, should abide solely in the zeal of devotion and the contemplation of celestial things'.

Despite these echoes of Augustine, the Roman Catechism was, in its own way, a long-overdue departure from the four Augustinian motives for intercourse and a pointer in the direction of the twentieth century: procreation need not be the motive for all marital intercourse, but it must never be precluded. The Roman Catechism equated contraception with murder: 'It is, therefore, a most grave crime for those joined in matrimony to use medicines [*medicamenta*] to impede conception or to abort birth; this infamous conspiracy to murder must be extirpated' (2, 7, 13).

That the Council of Trent heralded a tightening of the rules governing marriage is evidenced by a second Roman decree which, though not in force for long, was even stricter than the Roman Catechism. This briefly suspended the rule that regained its validity and retained it until the nineteenth century: that the abortion of a male foetus was exempt from punishment up to forty days and of a female foetus up to eighty days after conception. Since there was no way of determining the sex of a foetus, this meant in practical terms that abortion was sanctioned up to eighty days. In 1588 the fanatical Pope Sixtus V invalidated this rule by publishing a bull entitled 'Effraenatam'. The 'Si aliquis' canon (which stood sponsor to the Roman Catechism's equating of contraception with murder) had hitherto been confined to the realm of confession and penance, though the authors of the 'Malleus Maleficarum' (1487) had demanded the death penalty for contraception, in the sense of witch-craft-induced impotence and sterilisation, and for the administering of contraceptive potions. 'Effraenatam' strove to translate 'Si aliquis' into criminal law. Sixtus V threatened those who administered or knowingly ingested contraceptive substances ('accursed medicaments') with excommunication and the death penalty, likewise those who performed abortions from the moment of conception onwards. 'Effraenatam' was promptly rescinded (1591) after Sixtus V's death by Gregory XIV, who succeeded his short-lived successor Urban VII, so abortion was once more punishable by excommunication after the eightieth day.

Sixtus had made it his aim to reform the Church and, in particular, to root out sexual sins. He threatened adulterers with death by hanging and ordered the execution of a woman who had prostituted her daughter. Ludwig von Pastor observes in his history of the popes that 'it cannot be denied that Sixtus V went too far' but does not allow this to mar his favourable opinion of the said pontiff: 'Historians of the most diverse views agree that Sixtus V was one of the greatest of the many important popes produced by the age of Catholic reformation and restoration . . . Posterity has . . . unjustly denied this pope the title "the Great"' ('Geschichte der Päpste', X, p. 6f.).

Pastor describes the case of the hanged procuress as follows: 'The execution of a Roman woman who had sold her daughter's honour, which took place early in June 1586, also met with general disapproval. This sentence was all the more harshly enforced because the daughter, decked out in the jewellery given her by her paramour, was compelled to attend the execution and stand for an hour beneath the gallows from which her mother's corpse hung. A contemporary account of the occurrence argues, in defence of this measure, that procuring was so widespread in Rome that girls were less well protected with their own mothers than with strangers' (ibid., p. 70). 'In the same month Sixtus V had a priest and a boy burned at the stake for sodomy, although both had freely confessed their guilt' (ibid., p. 71). 'The death penalty was imposed not only for incest and crimes against the beginnings of life but also for the dissemination of oral and written calumnies' (ibid., p. 69). We already saw in chapter 19 what the Church understood by incest.

> The execution in August 1586 of a Roman noblewoman and two accomplices was widely deplored. Sixtus V was so little moved by this that, at the beginning of October, he commanded Cardinal Santori to draft a bull proclaiming adultery a capital offence. Attempts were made to dissuade the pope by pointing out that the Reformers would exploit such a document for their own ends, as evidence of moral depravity at the Curia, but to no avail. The bull, which was published on 3 November 1586, prescribed that adulterers and adulteresses, together with parents who prostituted their daughters, should be sentenced to death, and that married couples who divorced on their own authority should be similarly punished at the judges' discretion . . . The accused were so numerous that this decree could not be fully enforced.
>
> (Ibid., p. 71f.)

In 1587 the same terrible pope promulgated a decree that was to have tragic repercussions on many people. This ordained that no man might marry who could not produce real semen, meaning semen emanating from the testes – a ruling not rescinded until 1977. On 28 June 1587, Sixtus V wrote to the apostolic nuncio of Spain and bishop of Navarra concerning the fitness to marry of those who lacked both testes but could copulate and produce a semenlike fluid 'in no way suited to generation and matrimony'. Such men could not excrete veritable semen (*verum semen*), wrote Sixtus. They were eunuchs and *spadones* (a Latin term for eunuch), yet they had mingled with women with 'filthy lustfulness' and 'impure embraces' and had even presumed to contract marriages – indeed, they 'stubbornly' asserted this right. That the wives knew of their husbands' 'defect' made the crime even more heinous in the pope's eyes.

Sixtus instructed the nuncio to see to it that such couples were parted and their marriages declared null. He found it intolerable that they should sleep in the same bed and devote themselves to 'carnal and libidinous acts' instead of living together in continence. Thus, men devoid of the ability to generate (*potentia generandi*) were forbidden to marry and declared unfit to do so. Sixtus V based his ruling on the fact that Augustine and Thomas Aquinas had defined procreation as the true and primary purpose of marriage. He continued to tolerate sterility or infertility from unknown causes but declared sterility whose cause *was* known (no testes) to be an impediment to marriage. The absence of testes was, after all, readily ascertainable.

The causes of sterility in women were harder to determine – in fact some biblical women had given birth in old age. This uncertainty gave rise to some odd and muddled ecclesiastical judgments. It was, for example, ruled on 3 February 1887, 3 July 1890, 31 July 1895, 2 April 1909 and 12 October 1916 that women should not be forbidden to marry even though their internal organs of generation were entirely missing, e.g. because these had been surgically removed. The ruling that a wholly 'excised woman' (*mulier excisa*) could marry was based on doubts 'whether the operation . . . had really precluded all possibility of conception' (v. Klaus Lüdicke, 'Familienplanung und Ehewille', p. 175). According to a judgment dated 3 February 1916, on the other hand, a marriage was declared null on account of impotence because there was no connection between the wife's vagina and her post-vaginal organs (ibid., p. 83). In that instance sterility was deemed manifest and beyond dispute. In general, however, judgments concerning women, as opposed to men, required only that they possess the ability to copulate (*potentia coeundi*). Until 1977, ecclesiastical jurists required more, biologically speaking, of men than women. One wonders, therefore, whether this was not a hangover from Aristotelian biology, which held that the man was the sole generative agent, an idea shaken in 1827 by the discovery of the human ovum but still not eradicated, so it seems, from conservative minds.

Thus, where the man was concerned, the legal view was that the ability to copulate was insufficient by itself and must be allied with the ability to produce 'veritable semen'. The Holy Office had, it is true, ruled on 16 February 1935, in response to an inquiry from Aachen as to whether a man compulsorily sterilised by complete and irreversible vasectomy should be permitted to marry, that the marriage should not be prohibited because the operation had been an unjust and coercive measure undertaken by the state. On 22 January 1944, however, the Rota Romana (court of appeal) expressly dissociated itself from this decision, citing a speech delivered by Pius XII on 3 October 1941. The man from Aachen, who had been compulsorily sterilised by Hitler, did not meet Sixtus V's requirements of 1587: he was no more capable of producing 'veritable semen' than the lecherous eunuchs and *spadones* condemned by 'Effraenatam'.

Since 1977, men like the man from Aachen have no longer required this ability. The impotence decretal of Sacra Congregatio pro Doctrina Fidei, whose object was to end this long dispute, opens with the following words: 'The Sacra Congregatio pro Doctrina Fidei *has always taken the view* [my italics] that those who have undergone a vasectomy or are in similar circumstances should not be prevented from contracting marriages.' To claim that something has *always* been so is a salient characteristic of the Catholic Church, and one in which it persists even when the real historical truth is altogether different. A glance at the Church's new legal code, the revised Codex Iuris Canonici of 1983, discloses that its judgments have far from always taken the same line. It no longer states, like the CIC of 1917, that impotence renders a marriage invalid but restricts such invalidity to the inability to copulate by tacking the little word '*coeundi*' on to the original '*impotentia*'. Canon 1068 of the CIC of 1917 ran: 'Chronic impotence (*impotentia*) antecedent to marriage, whether on the part of the husband or of the wife . . . renders the marriage invalid.' Canon 1084 of the CIC of 1983 runs: 'Chronic coital incapacity (*impotentia coeundi*) antecedent to marriage, whether on the part of the husband or of the wife . . . renders the marriage invalid.'

That there has been a genuine shift here can be gauged from the outrage expressed in 1976, a year before the publication of the impotence decretal, by the eminent Italian canonist Pio Fedele. Referring to the fact that no 'veritable semen' would in future be required of the husband, he wrote: 'So it was not worthwhile to fatigue the mind and endure fasting and vigils if the endless and perilous voyage through so many reefs was to end in the decision which the said committee has, albeit by a majority, so unexpectedly reached.' Fedele went on to deplore the fact that this decision would betoken an abandonment of the Second Vatican Council and 'Humanae vitae' (the 'Pill encyclical'). 'In what respect do these findings ... genuinely reflect the idea that marriage and conjugal love are, by their nature, instituted for the generation of offspring?' (Ibid., p. 247f.)

Anyone as remote from the real nature of human sexuality as the Catholic Church's celibatarian ruling class, and anyone who insists on the generative purpose of marriage purely because he considers sexual pleasure suspect, creates insuperable pseudo-problems for himself. Although the majority of the Church's deskbound Roman masters take comfort in the belief that the 1977 decision was merely a reiteration of its predecessors, some have been utterly dismayed and bewildered by its slight shift in the direction of common sense.

Overdue by almost four centuries, the impotence decretal of 1977 rescinded Pope Sixtus V's baneful decision concerning eunuchs. All Pio Fedele's lamentations notwithstanding, however, it does not represent much of an advance. This is apparent from a report that appeared in most German newspapers on 3 December 1982. The 'Westdeutsche Allgemeine Zeitung' described the case thus: 'Two handicapped youngsters were refused permission to take their marriage vows in a Catholic church in Munich. According to the couple, a twenty-five-year-old man suffering from muscular dystrophy and his almost-blind girlfriend, the priest would not marry them without proof of their ability to have children. The bride, who is the same age, is a Protestant, so they then got married in a Protestant church. The archiepiscopal authorities in Munich stated on Thursday that, under Catholic marriage law, generative incapacity is a natural impediment to marriage from which the Church can grant no exemptions.' On 9 December 1982, under the headline 'Munich's Junge Union condemns "Penis Test"', the same newspaper reported that 'Munich's Junge Union regards a Catholic priest's refusal to wed a handicapped couple in church as a violation of the humanitarian commandment and human dignity. As already reported, the priest based his decision on the husband's "generative incapacity". In an open letter to the archiepiscopal authorities the Junge Union described this "penis test" as a supreme instance of the Catholic Church's "unrealistic and reactionary" attitude in sexual matters.'

Even if we assume that the young couple, and not the archiepiscopal authorities at Munich, were mistaken in citing *generative* incapacity as the priest's reason for refusing to marry them, since the authorities would have known that *coital* incapacity was now the decisive impediment to marriage, Catholic marriage law remains as intolerable to many a paraplegic as it was to the couple in question. The argument that only coital, not generative, capacity has been required since 1977 is of no help to a man whose inability to have an erection renders him incapable of coitus but far from incapable, under certain circumstances, of fathering a child. By stipulating the precise and universally applicable form to be taken by the conjugal act, the Church reduces a paraplegic and his partner to nonage because the Catholic sexual ethic restricts physical intimacies to marriage. This interference with everyone's right to marry is not only intolerable but a further demonstration that the celibatarian ecclesiastical authorities would be better advised not to meddle in such matters.

Before its canon law amendment in 1977, Sixtus V's ban on marriage by castrates had for centuries been the cause of many personal tragedies. In the Greek Church, castrati were widely employed as choristers from the twelfth century onwards. Their first appearance in the Western Church probably occurred in Spain during the sixteenth century, and it was they who provided the occasion for Sixtus V's fateful bull of 1587. Other countries had emulated Spain. Francesco Soto, a Spanish castrato, was admitted to the Sistine choir in 1562, and Girolamo Rossini (d. 1644), the first Italian castrato to sing in the same choir, joined it in 1579. Documentary evidence indicates that the Gonzagas' court ensemble at Mantua included castrati in 1563. Women had been forbidden to sing in churches since the fourth century at latest. In 1588 Sixtus V promoted an increase in castration, which he regarded as an impediment to marriage, by being the first to forbid women to appear on stage at public theatres and opera houses in Rome and the States of the Church. This pontifical ban on actresses and female singers was soon adopted by other Italian and non-Italian states. Reiterated by Pope Innocent XI (d. 1689), it remained in force throughout the seventeenth and eighteenth centuries. Goethe heard castrati sing at Rome and approved of them, but the French Revolution put an end to Sixtus V's muzzling of the female sex, and by 1798 women were back on the Roman stage.

In 1936 Peter Browe, a Jesuit, accused the popes of having been 'the first to enlist or tolerate castrati in their choirs at the end of the 16th century, when they were still unknown in theatres or in other Italian churches.' Having forbidden actresses and female singers to appear on stage in the papal states, 'they must have been out of touch with life not to have discovered that castrati were taking their place'. Any defence of the popes was therefore 'devious' ('Zur Geschichte der Entmannung', p. 102).

In 1748, when asked by his bishops whether their synods should issue a decretal against castrate choristers, Pope Benedict XIV firmly rejected the idea on the grounds that churches deprived of castrati would remain empty. 'This view . . . which was dominated by a fear of empty churches, naturally fostered castrate singing and delayed its suppression, and it also helped to ensure that no provincial or diocesan synod of the 18th or 19th century imposed a ban on the same. Moreover, it encouraged castration itself and impeded its abolition' (ibid., p. 115f.).

The Sicilian Jesuit Tommaso Tamburini (d. 1675) was a great advocate of castration because it ensured that 'God's praises are the more sweetly heard'. Alfonso de' Liguori described the view that to preserve the voice by means of such mutilation was forbidden as 'more probable' than the contrary opinion espoused by Tamburini and many other theologians, whom he listed. He did, however, point out that theologians could cite the Church's toleration of this practice ('Theologia moralis', IV, n. 374). The last castrato to have sung at St Peter's died in 1924.

Many castrati led the life of 'stars' and were highly paid. They were also lionised by women but forbidden by the Church to marry. Bartolomeo de Sorlisi, who had married Dorotea Lichtwer in secret and fought for years to be allowed to live with her, died of a broken heart when he failed. The castrato Finazzi was luckier. He fell in love with a Protestant who did not feel bound by the Church's marriage laws and made him a good wife.

Sixtus V, whom Pastor describes as having been unjustly denied the title 'Great' by posterity, terrorised many men until 1977 because of his insistence that their semen be 'veritable' semen and not 'a fluid somewhat similar to semen'. Sixtus not only forbade such emitters of non-seminal fluid to marry but demanded that, if they were presumptuous enough to do so, they should be parted from their wives. Male semen had become the alpha and omega of marriage – indeed, almost a sacrament in itself – and any man incapable of producing such papally approved fluid was debarred from matrimony. Since 1977 this prohibition has applied only to those whose excreted fluid, whether seminal or not, cannot find its way along the regulation route prescribed by the Church.

Sixtus V's outrageous letter – valid until 1977 – concerning the 'lust' (*tentigo*) of the eunuchs 'most commonly' found in Spain, who were to be parted from their wives on account of their 'filthy embraces', since these were 'a scandal' amounting to 'spiritual damnation', indicated that the Council of Trent had finally superseded the rather more liberal line adopted *c.*1500 at the University of Paris.

On 4 February 1611, the Holy Office ruled at Rome that 'nothing trivial' existed in the realm of sex. On 24 April of the following year Claudio Aquaviva, the general of the Jesuits, instructed all members of his order neither to teach nor to advise that sins of impurity could be trivial. This meant that all wilful indulgence in sexual pleasure outside marriage was a grave sin. Aquaviva threatened transgressors with excommunication and removal from any teaching posts they might hold. Unlike minor cases of theft, for example, any stirring of sexual desire between couples holding hands while courting constituted a mortal sin if intentional – the desire, that is, not the sin. It remains a mortal sin to this day.

TWENTY-ONE

Luther and His Influence on the Catholic Sexual Ethic

A harsher note was struck after the Council of Trent, as we have seen. At the same time, the Lutheran controversy gave rise to a certain anti-Augustinianism, mainly among the Jesuits, and, thus, to a marginally more liberal view of sexual morality. These two trends, which developed during the second half of the sixteenth century, ultimately led to a fierce confrontation between true-blue Augustinian Jansenism on the one hand and, on the other, what the Jansenists referred to as 'Jesuit moral laxity'. Alfonso de' Liguori (d. 1787), whose moral theology still retains authority, effected a certain compromise between the two: stricter than that of the 'lax Jesuits' of the sixteenth and seventeenth centuries, his approach was less hidebound than that of the prudish Jansenists.

Where Luther is concerned, Catholic theologians are fond of pointing out that, as a former Augustinian friar (an 'Augustinian Hermit'), he far from washed his hands of the Augustinian sexual ethic. On the contrary, they say: his exaggerated emphasis on human impairment by original sin, the sexual urge included, was less progressive than reactionary in this respect. As Hartmann Grisar, Jesuit author of the standard work on Luther, observed in 1911: 'It is tragic enough that Luther, of all people . . . despite his allegedly exalted view of marital intercourse . . . should nonetheless have defined the conjugal act as a grave sin on account of concupiscence. His Wartburg tract "De votis monasticis" stated: "It [the conjugal act] is a sin according to Psalm 50,7 [51,5], in no way different from adultery and fornication in so far as sensual passion and ugly lust are concerned. God does not hold this against the married, however, and for no reason other than his compassion, it being impossible for us to avoid the same despite our duty to dispense with it'.

It is true: Luther reiterated the whole antisexual rigmarole, for the most part in the highly coloured antisexual language of the early Schoolmen, but he jettisoned it nonetheless. Grisar himself hints as much when he goes on, rather sourly, to speak of Luther's 'intrinsically impossible' theory according to which God is 'capable of overlooking a sin that is actually present'. Despite his Augustinian origins and his insistence on original sin, Luther brought an appreciable advance in sexual morality. By ironing out the Catholic theologians' laborious differentiation between venial and mortal sins, his doctrine of justification, 'Faith alone saves', paved the way for a more liberal trend. The differentiation between mortal and venial sins disappeared from Protestant parlance, the concept of the individual mortal sinner receded, and that of the universal sinner – which embraces us all, sinners and righteous alike – took its place.

Whatever one's views on the Lutheran doctrine of justification, it was a boon to sexual morality, for Catholic theologians had engendered a sense of sin where no sin existed. It cut away the jungle of motives and compensating 'goods' and saving graces that had rendered carnal pleasure acceptable, tolerable, forgivable, pardonable, permissible, or unpardonable, depending on circumstances. An edifice founded on sexual chimeras regarding alleged affronts to human dignity was toppled, at least temporarily, by Luther's 'Faith alone saves'. The prudery of Puritanism was an unwholesome offshoot of reformed Protestantism.

Luther's pioneering feat in this field – publicly demonstrated by his marriage to a former nun – consisted in his abolition of the unnatural subordination of marriage to celibacy. His sermon on marriage in 1531 declared: 'Under the Papacy marriage has been held in low esteem and all praise heaped on the unmarried state, into which almost all have been coerced.'

The Catholic reaction to Luther's Augustinian emphasis on original sin and the need for redemption – which he promptly offset by an even greater emphasis on divine forgiveness and mercy – was a certain anti-Augustinianism which had a slightly moderating effect on the Catholic sexual ethic. The decline of Augustinian pessimism among Catholic theologians of the late sixteenth century was connected with the debates that raged between them and the reformers on the subject of original sin. Although it did not render the great sexual pessimist suspect in their eyes, the importance attached to Augustine by Protestantism did provoke some criticism of his ideas. Cardinal Roberto Bellarmino (d. 1621), the most influential Jesuit theologian of his time, stated that Augustine's belief in the transmission of original sin by sexual pleasure could not be taken literally because he had never been absolutely certain of his facts. Bellarmino himself offered no solution to the problem but limited himself to the exoneration of sexual pleasure ('Controversiarum de amissione gratiae et statu peccati libri sex', IV, 12). The effect of the Lutheran controversy on Bellarmino and, more especially, on the many Jesuits influenced by him during the seventeenth century, was to breed a cautiously optimistic attitude to human nature and, thus, to human sexual propensities. They based their approach on Thomas Aquinas (d. 1274), who had followed Aristotle in defining sexual pleasure as a natural sensation. Having superseded the 'Sententiae' of Peter Lombard (d. 1164) in the sixteenth century, Thomas's 'Summa theologica' became the Catholics' most authoritative theological textbook and remains so to this day.

One moderately progressive Jesuit to venture a few steps further than Augustine was the Spaniard Thomas Sanchez of Cordoba (d. 1610), who became the pre-eminent authority on marital questions. Of his minor advances on Augustine, one was the fact that he regarded marital intercourse No. 3 (in avoidance of personal fornication) as sinless, though only if other legitimate means such as fasting, vigils and good works had proved of no avail ('De sancto matrimonii sacramento', lib. 9, dist. 9). In making this first advance on Augustine he had been preceded by three Dominicans, Cardinal Cajetan (d. 1534) and Silvestro da Prierio (d. 1523), both of whom were prominent opponents of Luther, and Dominicus Soto (d. 1560), court theologian to Emperor Charles V.

There is a common-sense, modern ring to Sanchez's statement that there were no real grounds for assigning a married couple's motives for intercourse to one particular motivational category. It was not sinful 'for spouses to desire conjunction simply because they are spouses' (ibid., lib. 9, dist. 8). That one should be agreeably impressed by such simple truths is an indication of the extent to which celibatarians had inhibited marital intercourse by confining it in four compartments. But Sanchez promptly qualified his progressive and rational approach by not regarding marital intercourse No. 4 (for pleasure's sake) as sinless. He dissociated himself from Major and Almain, whose extreme views on the subject were almost the only ones he cited, and endorsed the majority opinion that intercourse for pleasure's sake was a venial sin (ibid., lib. 9, dist. 11, n. 2).

In another of his progressive statements, he explored the question of whether married persons might legitimately 'embrace, kiss, and engage in such other physical contacts as are customary among spouses, to evidence their love of one another' even when there was a danger of ejaculation. 'In how many teachers', he wrote, 'have I read the assertion that, in those threatened by the danger of *pollutio* [self-defilement], this constitutes a mortal sin.' He enumerated the said authorities and strove to refute them. He himself believed that an act which could lead to unintentional ejaculation was not always evil, and that 'an urgent reason' could justify the risk. In a husband, one such urgent reason was the desire 'to manifest and reinforce mutual love . . . It would be very harsh, and love would be much impaired thereby, were spouses to abstain from such contacts.' Sanchez therefore defended sexual contacts between spouses outside the context of marital intercourse even though 'the danger exists' that semen would be wasted and fail to play the part assigned to it by all Catholic moral theologians: in the standardised conjugal act that makes no attempt to impede generation (ibid., lib. 9, 45, 33–7; cf. John T. Noonan, 'Contraception: A History of its Treatment by the Catholic Theologians and Canonists', p. 325f.).

Sanchez's progressive approach is in clear contrast to the reactionary attitude of our own century as exemplified by Bernhard Häring, who wrote in 1967 that, if pregnancy was to be avoided because it presented a threat to the mother's life, 'the expression of love must in my opinion be kept within the bounds of pure affection, which can in itself be rendered *without the risk of gratification* [my italics]' ('The Law of Christ', III, p. 357). In this view Häring followed Alfonso de' Liguori, the founder of his order. Little enough was permitted to unmarried, betrothed or married couples by Sanchez in the sixteenth century, but they were permitted even less by Alfonso in the eighteenth, and the effects of his warnings about 'the risk of gratification', alias ejaculation, alias sexual pleasure, have lingered on into the twentieth. (Examples of Alfonso's still authoritative view, as expounded by Häring, may be found in his 'Theologia moralis', III, n. 416; VI, n. 854; and VI, n. 934.) Even Sanchez hastened to point out that married couples must not, of course, intend their caresses to bring about an emission of semen, whereas Alfonso and Häring deny them all physical contact if there is any 'risk of gratification'.

Sanchez, too, called coitus interruptus a mortal sin against nature ('De sancto matrimonii sacramento', 9, 20, 1). On the other hand, he adopted a progressive attitude to the question of whether a victim of rape might legitimately rid herself of semen. This he answered in the affirmative, defining the rapist's semen as an unjust assailant and its removal as an act of self-defence (ibid., 2, 22, 17) provided no fertilisation had yet taken place. Some hundred and fifty years later Sanchez's view was disputed by Alfonso de' Liguori, who insisted that semen could never be removed 'without inflicting an injustice on nature or mankind, whose propagation [by means of rape, be it noted!] would be impaired'. Besides, the semen was now in 'peaceful' possession, i.e. conducting itself peaceably. Alfonso held that, although the rapist's victim could legitimately defend herself while being raped by him, even in such a way as to cause him to emit semen outside the 'vessel' designed to receive it, she could no longer do so once the rape was over ('Theologia moralis', VI, n. 954). The rapist's semen had thus attained the status of a quasi-person entitled to the protection due to any law-abiding citizen.

A number of seventeenth-century theologians, many of them Spaniards like Sanchez, differed from him in holding that even marital intercourse No. 4 (for pleasure) could be sinless. They included the Augustinian friar Ponce de Leon (d. 1629), the Jesuit Gaspar Hurtado (d. 1647), Martin Perez (d. 1660), and Juan Sanchez (d. 1624), an astute secular and well-known 'laxist' whose work on the sacraments quoted Major and Almain by the page and enthusiastically credited them with 'fine words . . . golden words' (Heinrich Klomps, 'Ehemoral und Jansenismus', p. 71). This implied that all four of the motives for marital intercourse devised by celibatarians were free from sin, which is more or less the stage we have reached today. Less importance is attached to the motives for the conjugal act, procreative intention first and foremost, than to the avoidance of anything that conflicts with the procedure laid down by nature for marital intercourse, because that would be contrary to nature and gravely sinful. In plain language, this means a ban on contraception. Married couples need no longer bear procreation constantly in mind; they must merely refrain from rendering it impossible.

According to Heinrich Klomps, this initiated 'an entirely new line of argument in the history of conjugal morality . . . Morality of intention was superseded by morality of action, and the concept of the *natura actus* [the nature of the conjugal act] acquired central importance' (ibid., p. 72f.). And this, in turn, meant that 'the back and forth of the laborious debate on the doctrine of motivation was placed on an entirely new footing' (ibid., p. 72). Married couples need no longer ensure that they have intercourse *à la* Augustine for motives 1 and 2 because sin begins at 3. They will always be in the right as long as they eschew contraception and do not deviate from a standard pattern of intercourse allegedly sanctified by nature but really prescribed by celibatarian priests: as long, in fact, as they do 'nothing against nature', as the popes of our own century never weary of impressing upon their weary married listeners.

On closer examination, however, their circumstances remain essentially unchanged. No longer subject to Augustine's old four-point system, they have been dragooned into a new one-point programme. One restrictive norm has been superseded by another. In a system as muddled as the Augustinian sexual ethic, every forward step leads to a new dead-end from which the married can escape only by throwing off the monkish, celibatarian yoke – by obeying the dictates of reason and conscience.

On 2 March 1679, the Magisterium intervened in the controversy over pleasure in the conjugal act: Pope Innocent XI condemned the proposition, advanced by Juan Sanchez and others, that marital intercourse for pleasure alone was entirely free from sin. The pope's was only one of many dissenting voices, and not even the most vigorous. Jansenist condemnation of the development of Jesuit 'laxism', Thomas Sanchez's views included, was far more vehement. Eager to replace Augustine on his pedestal intact and undiminished, the Jansenists took exception to the word 'alone' in the papal condemnation. Pleasure *per se*, whether alone or not, was abhorrent to them, and they readily foresaw how the Jesuits would exploit that little word: they would argue – as the Spanish Jesuit Didacus de la Fuente Hurtado (d. 1686) promptly did – that the papal ban did not apply to intercourse for pleasure's sake, only to intercourse for pleasure's sake *alone*.

Hardly anyone was satisfied with this condemnation. Dyed-in-the-wool pleasure-haters disliked the word 'alone' as much as their laxer or lax opponents found it objectionable that marital intercourse for pleasure should have been condemned at all. However, the pope's use of the word 'alone' provided celibatarians with a tasty new theological morsel to chew on for two centuries to come: what differentiates intercourse 'for pleasure's sake' from intercourse 'for pleasure's sake alone'?

TWENTY-TWO

The Jansenists and Jesuit Moral Laxity

Jansenism took its name from the Belgian bishop Cornelis Jansen (d. 1638; on what follows v. Heinrich Klomps, 'Ehemoral und Jansenismus', p. 97f.). Jansen's chief work, 'Augustinus', sought to reassert the authority of Augustine's strict marital ethic over all its more recent dilutions and counter 'the most excellent advocates of pleasure'. He attributed the low moral standards of his day, which he described as '*saeculum corruptissimum*', 'a most corrupt age', to the 'more recent theology' that had turned away from Augustine and the Fathers of the Church. Thomas Aquinas he numbered among the orthodox theologians who had kept faith with the Augustinian tradition. The motive for marital intercourse must be exclusively generative, not pleasure-seeking in any way. 'Carnal conjunction is brutish [*bestialis*] if sought, not on the child's account, but under the compulsion of sensual desire.' Marital intercourse with pregnant, infertile or post-menopausal women was thus prohibited. Intercourse in avoidance of personal fornication, let alone for pleasure's sake, was 'Pelagian,' and 'laxist'. Like Augustine, Jansen held that the performance of one's conjugal duty was the only legitimate motive apart from procreation. Pleasure-free intercourse was the ideal, and even the blurring of generative intention by the expectation of pleasure was culpable. Having made a lifelong study of Augustine's works, many of which he had read twenty or thirty times, he was appalled that more recent theologians should have distorted a doctrine which he himself had done his utmost to understand.

The outcome of his labours: 'That, truly, is the ideal form of Christian marital conduct, which resists the sexual desire to have conjunction with a wife who is menstruating, pregnant, wholly infertile, or precluded by her age from bearing children. Furthermore, I say that nothing whatsoever may be done for sexual pleasure's sake. Indeed, if the progeny on whose account the married have intercourse could be conceived in some other manner, without experiencing pleasure, they would be duty-bound to abstain from conjugal union.' Jansen regarded intercourse during pregnancy as immoral and tainted with sin, not because it might harm the foetus (though that was an aggravating factor), but because no further generation was possible. Unanimous on this point, all Jansenists invoked Augustine, Ambrose, Jerome, Clemens Alexandrinus, and the rest (op. cit., pp. 184, 186f.).

Jansen continually reverted to I Corinthians (7: 6), in which St Paul – according to Augustine's misinterpretation – had described non-generative marital intercourse as requiring forgiveness, in other words, sinful. According to Jansen, sexual desire was a penalty imposed on us by the sin of Adam and Eve and could be morally overcome only by accepting it as such. To cite Klomps's verdict on the Jansenist theologians: '*Delectatio carnalis* (carnal pleasure) must thus be seen as an infringement of human dignity. Had the possibility of artificial insemination existed at the time, our authors would, in conformity with their ideas, have been bound to lay it down as the norm' (ibid., p. 203).

At a time when other theologians were trying to throw off the motivational constraints governing each and every conjugal act, the Jansenists reapplied them in full measure. No moral theologian could deny that Jansen's interpretation of the Augustinian marital ethic was perfectly in accord with its author's original doctrine. Although Pope Innocent X condemned five propositions in Jansen's 'Augustinus' as heretical in 1653, these related to dogmatic questions of grace and predestination, not to conjugal morality. The book's marital ethic was so fully in keeping with Augustine that the Church never condemned it, neither then nor subsequently. The Catholic Church has never accepted, still less openly admitted, that it was led astray by its greatest Doctor in a matter of practical and daily concern to most people, or that countless consciences have been – and are still being – unjustly burdened as a result. Pope Innocent XI issued a condemnation in 1679, but not of the Jansenist marital ethic: spurred on by the Jansenists themselves, he condemned the proposition that marital intercourse for pleasure's sake alone was no sin. The targets of his rebuke were not the unduly strict but those whom the unduly strict considered unduly 'lax'.

Great influence was wielded, even in our own century, by 'De la fréquente communion' (1643), a work by the eminent Jansenist Antoine Arnauld (popularly known as 'le grand Arnauld'). This book, which was prompted by a dispute between two noblewomen over how often they should communicate, laid down strict conditions for the receiving of Communion and instructed the married to abstain from intercourse both before and after. It also inveighed against the 'lax Jesuits' who urged people to communicate frequently. The book's inhibiting effect on communicants persisted until Pius X issued his Communion Decretal in 1905.

Even more instrumental in the spread of Jansenism were the celebrated 'Lettres provinciales' of Blaise Pascal (d. 1662). Jansenism was a complex structure, but its universal feature was an aversion to the Jesuits. If many still regard them in a dubious light to this day, it was Pascal who brought this about. Jansen's 'Augustinus' had revived not only Augustine's marital ethic but, more especially, his doctrine of grace. Pascal's 'letters to a friend in the country' – the 'friend' was fictitious – concerned themselves with this Augustinian-Jansenist doctrine and accused the Jesuits of misapprehending the nature of grace and morality. He made little mention of sexual and conjugal morality, however. Recalling a conversation with a Jesuit priest who had expounded the views of Jesuit theologians on questions relating to the married and betrothed, Pascal wrote: 'He then told me the strangest things imaginable. Although I could fill several letters with them, I shall not even quote them here because you show my letters to all and sundry, and I have no wish that someone should read them purely for amusement's sake' (Letter 9). Thomas Sanchez, the Jesuits' expert on questions of sexual and conjugal morality, whom Pascal mentioned in Letters 5, 7, 8 and 9 with reference to other aspects of morality, must have been one of those whom he declined to cite. Sanchez's deviation from the strict Augustinian sexual ethic, though minimal, was too much for Pascal.

Pascal wrote the above letters in support of his friend Antoine Arnauld, who was about to be expelled from the Sorbonne. In Letters 15 and 16, for instance, he praises Arnauld's book on frequent Communion and its strict demands on communicants, opining that the Jesuits' laxer requirements would 'profane the Sacrament' (letter 16).

When Pascal died at the age of thirty-nine he was found to be wearing a coarse shirt studded with little iron hooks – his way of punishing himself for the smallest misdemeanour. The brilliantly ironical tone of the letters in which he contrived to make his Jesuit opponents look ridiculous is such as to obscure the fact that, in questions of conjugal morality, the 'lax Jesuits' tended to be closer to the truth than he himself. On the other hand, Pascal was right to criticise the development of Catholic moral theology since the sixteenth century and pillory its interminable quibbles and case histories, which went far beyond Augustine and Thomas Aquinas, often with ludicrous results. He wittily demolished these in his 'Lettres provinciales' but preferred to draw a decent veil over the subject of sexual morality, correctly sensing that an obsession with detail in that particular field was improper, whether one considered the theologians who suffered from it too lax (as he himself did) or too strict (by modern standards). The further development of Catholic moral theology in the eighteenth and nineteenth centuries, with its assiduous concentration on sexual matters, was to prove him only too right.

Pascal succeeded in persuading many people that the Jesuits were unreliable in matters relating to moral theology. The result of this, although he himself discreetly avoided the subject, was that many believers were more impressed by the Jansenists, with their rigorous demands on the married, than by the 'lax' Jesuits. It was due in no small measure to Pascal that Jansenism made so great an impact, and that it continued to wield a decisive influence until well into the nineteenth century, especially in France, Belgium, and the English-speaking Catholic world.

Laurentius Neesen (d. 1679), Jansenist regent of the seminary at Mechlin in Belgium, presumed to draw the following analogy: just as the state did not expressly approve of brothels but reluctantly sanctioned them in avoidance of a greater evil, so the married should not inwardly approve of sexual pleasure but merely tolerate and acquiesce in it on the legitimate grounds of procreation and conjugal duty, for only thus could corrupt human nature become a means to a good end, namely, the generation of offspring (Klomps, op. cit., p. 182f.)

Ludwig Habert (d. 1718), one of the most influential French Jansenist theologians of the seventeenth century and adviser to several French bishops, believed that mankind had already been destroyed once by the Flood because of sins committed in marriage. This Flood had been occasioned by 'the pollution, defilement and profanation of [what else?] the marriage-bed'. The married were infused with Tobias' attitude ('conjunction for love of posterity alone, not for pleasure's sake') by the grace of the sacrament of matrimony. This was of vital importance because it preserved mankind 'from another Flood' (ibid., p. 160) and rendered husbands and wives capable, not of loving one another 'like heathens in the sickness of lust', but of putting 'the evil of lust' to proper use (ibid., p. 158). The Jansenists continually enlisted the example of Tobias in Jerome's Old Testament translation as a kind of nuptial Dracula designed to put the fear of God into Christian newly-weds, who had for fifteen hundred years been unnerved by its account of the demons that had carried off Sarah's seven lustful bridegrooms on their wedding-night.

The Jansenists' hostility to sexual pleasure naturally gave rise to Augustinian inferences in regard to Marian doctrine. These were typified by Gulielmus Estius (d. 1613), a Belgian who taught at Douai and was one of Jansenism's pioneers: because of the 'filthiness' of the carnal urge, Jesus wished to be born of a virgin, not generated by the conjugal act (ibid., p. 78). Franciscus Sylvius (d. 1649), who succeeded to Estius's chair at Douai, explained how Marian purity could be emulated by normal married persons. They had to exclude all inward approval of the excitement arising from the generative act just as a cripple approved of walking but not of his limp (ibid., p. 80). Although the word 'filth' is no longer applied to marital intercourse, thanks not least to the 'lax' Jesuits, it is still 'filth' from which the Church's present celibatarian authorities seek to preserve Mary by dissociating her from normal marriage and married women in respect of conception and childbirth.

TWENTY-THREE

Contraception between 1500 and 1750

Whereas contraception and women's infertile periods had been objects of scientific study in antiquity and the Middle Ages, witch hunts and the belief in demons engendered the view that these were a province of the Devil. The question of contraception became suspect and dangerous, above all in the aftermath of the 'Witches' Bull' (1484) and the 'Malleus Maleficarum' (1487), which led to such a dramatic increase in the number of burnings at the stake, especially of so-called 'witch-mid-wives'. Fomented by popes and theologians, superstition obstructed all scientific progress in this field. The 'Witches' Bull', with its denunciation of the sorcerous arts 'that prevent men from generating and women from conceiving', and the 'incineration' of witches in ensuing centuries, notably in Germany, did not furnish the soil in which an unprejudiced study of the subject could flourish.

Thus, only two contraceptive methods were open to Christian spouses. The first and most Catholic was abstinence, which required the co-operation of both partners. Not even the Anglican priest Jonathan Swift (d. 1745) could come up with any better suggestion for birth control than that which he advanced in 'Gulliver's Travels'. The perfectly rational inhabitants of his land of the Houyhnhnms, or wise horses, acted in such a way as to 'prevent the country from being overburdened by numbers'. Members of the Houyhnhnm upper class desisted from marital intercourse as soon as they had produced one child of each sex, but inferior Houyhnhnms were allowed to produce three children so that there were enough servants to go round. Referring to this contraceptive method, Noonan states: 'No major theologian denied that continence, to avoid too numerous progeny, was lawful'

('Contraception: A History of its Treatment by the Catholic Theologians and Canonists', p. 336). Lawful here means permissible. The married were thus permitted something, at least, and it is to be presumed that no 'minor theologian' disputed this.

Noonan's statement symptomises the predicament of married couples wholly subject to clericocratic nursemaiding: their every action, if not prohibited, requires the approval of moral theologians. Marital continence by mutual consent was a Christian virtue recommended very early on, and medieval writers prescribed a number of aids to its attainment, e.g. the 'chaste-lamb' tree mentioned by Pliny (d. 79) in his 'Historia naturalis'. Francis of Sales (d. 1622) wrote of this in his 'Introduction to the Devout Life' ('Philothea'), which was widely read until recent times, that 'whosoever makes his bed on the leaves of the *agnus castus* [chaste-lamb] tree becomes chaste and modest himself' (3, 13).

If husband and wife were at odds on the subject of continence, the situation became complicated. It was at first denied that a wife might legitimately deny her husband his conjugal due because of dire poverty. Le Maistre (d. 1481) held that a woman who refused intercourse 'can be compelled to grant it by a judge' ('Quaestiones morales', II, fol. 49r.), and it was not until the sixteenth century that one or two theologians ruled otherwise. Dominicus Soto (d. 1560), for example, declared that to refuse intercourse was not a mortal sin 'when they are constrained by dire poverty and cannot on that account feed so many offspring'. This was not only an innovation but a great concession on the part of Charles V's court theologian.

Thomas Sanchez (d. 1610) endorsed Soto's opinion, and Paul Laymann (d. 1635), a German Jesuit whose work on moral theology remained the standard textbook used by German teachers of theology, most of whom were Jesuits, for a hundred and fifty years, ruled that the denial of intercourse was permissible in cases of 'extreme poverty' ('De sancto matrimonii sancramento', 5, 10, 31, 16).

However, all those who so generously waived the wife's conjugal obligation in cases of great poverty agreed that it was a mortal sin for her to deny her husband intercourse if he lapsed into incontinence, i.e. committed adultery. There could scarcely be a more blatant indication that marital intercourse was thought to have no connection with love, since a husband's threat to commit adultery was hardly calculated to endear him to his wife.

Alfonso de' Liguori (d. 1787), who was destined to be the most authoritative moral theologian of the nineteenth and twentieth centuries (he was canonised in 1839 and promoted a Doctor of the Church in 1871), differed from many of his predecessors in asserting that to withhold a husband's conjugal due in cases of great poverty was *not* permissible, precisely because it might lead to fornication. In other words, a husband's potential infidelity is accounted a sin on the part of his harassed wife if she refuses intercourse, however destitute the couple may be. To refuse a faithful, benevolent and loving husband for a far less cogent reason was no sin, according to Alfonso, provided he did not insist ('Theologia moralis', VI, n. 940 and 941). That is to say, the wife who refuses to have intercourse with a potentially adulterous husband because he cannot support a larger family is guilty of a grave sin, whereas the wife who refuses a faithful husband for no particular reason is guilty only of a minor sin. Where marital intercourse is concerned, prior consideration for the adulterer has been one of the basic motives underlying the Church's marital ethic up to and including the Second Vatican Council. Intercourse in avoidance of fornication and adultery receives the greatest attention and takes precedence over grave potential harm to the mother. Catholic marital morality is largely a master-race ethic and a merciless sexual exploitation of the female sex.

To date, no objective thought has been devoted to the concept of intercourse for love's sake (a non-runner in the theologians' four-horse classic), nor to the possibility that contraception may sometimes betoken consideration. In celibatarian eyes, marital intercourse exists solely for the avoidance of fornication, the generation of offspring, or the avoidance of fornication coupled with an acceptance that children may result. Despite their occasional fine words, theologians have not budged an inch. Had they devoted as much thought, starting with Augustine, to love between married couples as to the risk of fornication and infidelity, primarily on the husband's part, they would have constructed a different moral edifice far more humane than the present brutal system. As things stand, the interests of married Christians have suffered at the hands of their exclusively unmarried arbiters.

The second expedient to which Christian spouses could resort, other than abstinence by mutual consent, was of course the 'restrained embrace'. All other forms of contraception, notably coitus interruptus and the taking of 'potions' (medicines), were mortal sins. Coitus interruptus was condemned as a grave sin, for instance by Cardinal

Cajetan (d. 1534). Francis of Sales stated that 'Onan's act was detestable before God' and criticised 'certain modern teachers of heresies who held that it was Onan's evil intention, and not his act, that displeased God' (Francis of Sales, 'Philothea', 3, 39). (Onan was not concerned to practise contraception as such, but unwilling to beget children on behalf of his dead brother.) In writing of the modern innovators who advocated coitus interruptus as a contraceptive method, Francis of Sales was not referring to the Reformers, who clung to the Augustinian doctrine of marriage and were quite unprogressive in this respect.

Where coitus interruptus is concerned, theologians have always been interested in one particular point, namely, the wife's attitude. If she knows that her husband intends to practise coitus interruptus, should she, as St Bernardino (d. 1444) believed, resist him unto death? Alfonso de' Liguori, like Le Maistre and Thomas Sanchez before him, took the following view: the wife was not only permitted but obliged to grant intercourse if she expected a refusal to have evil consequences. This did not formally render her an accomplice in sin – indeed, she might even request intercourse herself if she would otherwise lapse into incontinence ('Theologia moralis', VI, n. 947). We here re-encounter the Church's solicitude for potential adulterers and its disregard for the views of those who decline to regard marital intercourse as a substitute for adultery. Alfonso's mouthpiece in our own century, the German moral theologian and Redemptorist Bernhard Häring, likewise condones a wife's co-operation in coitus interruptus for the sake of 'preservation from adultery', though he makes no mention of her being permitted to request such intercourse ('The Law of Christ', III, p. 375f.).

Häring was mistaken, incidentally, in extolling the founder of his order as follows in 1982: 'Those who regard Alfonso as an archconservative will above all be surprised that he should apply this principle in an area that is particularly controversial today, namely coitus interruptus: "Marital intercourse may legitimately be interrupted provided there is a commensurate reason" ("Theologia moralis", lib. VI, n. 947). The rigorists considered this sinful under any circumstances' ('Moral für Erlösten' in 'Theologie der Gegenwart', I, 1982, p. 2).

In the above quote, Alfonso is not sanctioning coitus interruptus, but merely debating whether an innocent wife committed a grave sin by having intercourse with her gravely sinful husband. Nor did he by any means sanction coitus interruptus as a contraceptive method in another passage ('Theologia moralis', lib. VI, c. 2, n. 882) cited by Häring in

'Theologie der Gegenwart', IV, 1986, p. 214. On the contrary, he expressly stated that it was excused 'neither by the threat of poverty nor by danger in childbirth' and that it was 'an offence against the prime purpose of marriage'. He simply questioned whether a spouse was obliged to persevere with intercourse if its continuation endangered health, or spelled death at the hands of an enemy, or was impeded by some outside agency. No theologian, even of the darkest hue, has ever insisted that husband and wife are obliged to let themselves be killed by an enemy, risk a heart attack, ignore an interruption, or tolerate the intervention of a third party rather than discontinue marital intercourse. To discontinue it for contraceptive purposes, however, was nonetheless a mortal sin in Alfonso's eyes, and so it remains to this day. The Catholic theologian who 'decriminalises' coitus interruptus with Rome's approval has yet to be begotten.

Alfonso's fellow Redemptorist Häring has cautiously striven to turn him into a progressive exonerator of coitus interruptus and will doubtless continue to do so until the Magisterium puts a stop to his endeavours. Alfonso did *not* sanction coitus interruptus. It is, however, noteworthy that he did not, like St Bernardino of Siena among others, demand that a wife should die rather than assent to intercourse if she thought it probable that her husband would deliberately ejaculate outside the vagina. As we shall see, Alfonso's verdict on this form of contraception was surpassed in rigour during the nineteenth and twentieth centuries, e.g. by the Roman rulings on 1822, 1823, and 1916.

Contraception by means of medicines ('potions') was, as we have already seen, governed by the ancient 'Si aliquis' canon. Equated with murder by the Council of Trent's 'Roman Catechism' and declared a capital offence by Sixtus V in 1588, it was branded as 'quasi-homicide' and a mortal sin by the Jesuit Laymann ('Theologia moralis', 3, 3, 3, 2). Laymann asked: 'May a woman take a medicine to prevent contraception if she learns from her physician or suspects from her own prior experience that the birth of a child may occasion her death?' No, he replied, contraception militates against the principal purpose of marriage. His reasoning: 'Were it in some cases permitted to such women to prevent conception, this would be wonderfully abused and human generation would incur great loss.' He promptly cites the other contraceptive method, coitus interruptus: 'For a similar reason, the Doctors of

Divinity unanimously state that it is in no case lawful to procure the emission of semen' (ibid., 5, 10, 3, 1).

Though not shared by all theologians, the view that contraception is equivalent to murder was reinforced in 1677 by the discovery of motile spermatic filaments in male seminal fluid. This discovery lent visual expression, as it were, to the 'potential human being' whom Thomas Aquinas had believed male semen to contain. During the seventeenth and eighteenth centuries man was often likened to a sower who scatters his seed in a furrow and deposits a minuscule human being in the woman's uterus. Contraception thus approximated even more closely to murder than it had in terms of 'Si aliquis'. It was not until the middle of the eighteenth century that Alfonso de' Liguori's influence brought about a change of view and contraception ceased to be considered a homicidal act. 'A tradition as old as Regino of Prüm and Burchard, indeed as ancient as St Jerome, had fallen into disuse. With St Alphonsus the homicide approach ended its theological life' (Noonan, op. cit., pp. 364–5).

The condom was invented in the middle of the seventeenth century, but it was too expensive and unreliable to be of major importance and was generally reserved for extramarital affairs. The Marquise de Sévigné doubtless had this unreliability in mind when she wrote in 1671 to her daughter, the Comtesse de Grignan, that condoms inhibited desire and were no more contraceptive than a spider's web. At all events, the seventeenth-century condom was not an outstanding success.

Priests had two main means of acquainting their flocks with the ban on contraception: the pulpit and the confessional. Their sermons on the subject were less outspoken than St Bernardino. It seems that only a few priests favourable to Jansenism failed to practise Pascal's discreet restraint in this respect, e.g. Philippe Boucher, who early in the eighteenth century preached against 'the execrable crime of Onan' (coitus interruptus), sodomy (anal intercourse), and the use of contraceptive potions, and insisted that poverty was no legitimate reason for a harassed wife 'to refuse the marital debt' (ibid., p. 373). In general, preachers adhered to the instructions given in the Tridentine Roman Catechism. The section headed 'What Shall be Taught of Conjugal Obligations' stated: 'Here shall priests speak in such a manner that no word escapes their lips that might seem unworthy to the ears of the faithful, or affront devout souls, or give rise to laughter' (II, 33). As to how a priest should handle the Sixth Commandment (Thou shalt not commit adultery): 'But let the priest, in treating of this subject, be discreet and wise and refer to the matter in veiled language' (3, 7, 1). 'Many other and divers forms of fornication and lust may remain unmentioned, whereof the priest must admonish each in secret as the circumstances of time and persons require' (3, 7, 5). Explicit references were to be made only to contraception by means of medicines, 'for that must be accounted a godless assault by murderers' (2, 8, 13).

Confessors' questions about contraception were less inhibited prior to the Council of Trent. Thereafter the Roman 'Rituale', the authoritative code of practice governing the administration of the sacraments, gave confessors only one hint on how to question penitents about sexual matters. It warned them to refrain from putting 'incautious questions' to the young of either sex 'about things of which they knew nothing', lest they 'take offence and learn to sin therefrom'. Carlo Borromeo (d. 1584) enjoined confessors to 'extreme caution' where sins of lust were concerned ('Instructiones de recta administratione sacramenti poenitentiae', 12), and Alfonso de' Liguori instructed them as follows: 'The confessor is not in general obliged, nor does it behove him, to inquire into married persons' sins in respect of the marital debt, except that he may, perhaps, with the utmost modesty, ask married women whether they have rendered that debt by inquiring, for example, if they have obeyed their husband in everything. About other matters let him keep silent unless asked' ('Praxis confessarii ad bene excipiendas confessiones', II, 41).

This prudent reticence regarding contraception in marriage was not maintained for long. In the nineteenth and twentieth centuries, questions on the subject were to become the principal theme explored by confessors when dealing with married penitents. Alfonso's reference to a wife's duty of total obedience to her husband accorded with the continuing depreciation of womanhood by the Catholic Church.

Although Alfonso wisely instructed his confessors not to question married penitents on contraception, his recommended procedure for interrogating children and unmarried persons in the confessional was brazenly officious. The Tridentine injunction to couch such questions in 'veiled language' prompted him to favour a murky obscurity that made matters even worse. His instructions to priests hearing children's confessions ran as follows:

> Children must be treated with the utmost love and gentleness. He [the confessor] shall cause them to recite all the sins they can remember. They may then be asked the following questions . . . Whether they have committed a nasty sin. The confessor must, however, question them very discreetly on this subject. Let him begin at a distance in general terms, [asking] first whether they have used bad words, whether they have jested with other boys or girls, and whether they have done so in secret. After that, he shall ask whether they have performed disreputable acts. Even when the children say 'no', it is often expedient to ask them leading questions, for example: 'And now tell me, how often have you done this? Five times, ten times?' They shall then be asked with whom they sleep and whether they have played with their fingers in bed . . .
>
> (Ibid., VII, 90)

TWENTY-FOUR

John Paul II and the Joys of Abstinence

By proclaiming in 1679 that 'marital intercourse for mere pleasure' was not free from sin, Pope Innocent XI ensured that students of theology busied themselves with the subject of sexual morality for centuries to come. Whereas the Jansenists altogether rejected pleasure as a motive for the conjugal act and were thus in accord with Augustine and the Roman Catechism of 1566, more moderate theologians sought to permit at least a modicum of pleasure and debated the difference between marital intercourse for pleasure's sake and marital intercourse for pleasure's sake alone, since the pope's decretal had covered the latter only.

The solution of Alfonso de' Liguori (d. 1787) was laborious in the extreme. He held that intercourse for mere pleasure was generally considered to be venially sinful, not sinless (it was mortally sinful under certain circumstances only), because the pleasure destined by nature as an aid to generation had been made the purpose of the conjugal act. It was not a sin, on the other hand, if spouses were primarily intent on generation and made moderate use of its concomitant pleasure to prompt themselves to the conjugal act ('Theologia moralis', VI, 912). Pleasure might thus be sought, but not primarily and exclusively. Theologians of the nineteenth century, e.g. the Jesuit Antonio Ballerini (d. 1881), reduced this problem to a shortened formula: intercourse for mere pleasure is an act that *excludes* the other, moral, functions of matrimony. This signifies their exclusion from the motives for marital intercourse, not the exclusion of progeny by contraceptive means, for that would be a mortal, not a venial sin.

Thus, although Augustine and the Roman Catechism held that

marriage should never be consummated for pleasure's sake, the question that had exercised moral theologians since the seventeenth century – can marital intercourse be legitimately motivated by a little sexual pleasure? – had at last been answered in the affirmative.

Even in our own century, however, higher authority was to make plain its attitude towards any writer bold enough to suggest that the conjugal act may be rendered more pleasurable by ringing the changes and deviating from the standard coital position. When the German bishops, almost to a man, declared that Hitler was 'a bastion against Bolshevism and the epidemic of obscene literature', they were thinking not least of one particular 'obscenity', which had run through fifty-one impressions by 1930. Placed on the Church's Index of Prohibited Books and confiscated by the Nazi regime, it came under fire from Pope Pius XI in his encyclical 'Casti connubii'. The book in question was 'Ideal Marriage' by Theodor Hendrik van de Velde, a Dutch gynaecologist and former director of the women's clinic at Haarlem. Pius XI (who concluded a concordat with Hitler four months after the Nazis came to power) re-entitled it 'Depraved Marriage', thereby creating an entirely new marital category and helping to assure the book of an even wider readership. It suffered a second major blow in 1967, thirty years after the author's death. Having been robbed of substance by previous cuts, it underwent some confusing editorial amplifications.

For many married couples – or devotees of conjugal depravity, as Pius XI might have styled them – van de Velde became a kind of Galileo of the marriage-bed, especially in the Christian West, where sexual pleasure is suspect and the culture of the sex act underdeveloped in consequence. He removed the taboo from marital intercourse and promoted it from the inarticulately animal to the personal plane by writing about it, albeit mainly in Latin terms because 'these are more "medical" and less likely to be offensive' ('Ideal Marriage', p. 46).

Van de Velde wanted to introduce some variety into the conjugal bedroom. Since he was ultimately concerned with conjugal fidelity and love, and since he shared the traditional Catholic approach to divorce, contraception, and coitus interruptus, he felt convinced that 'on the whole, its [Catholic moral theology's] conclusions harmonise with mine' (ibid., p. 282). He was sorely mistaken. The Catholic sexual ethic prohibits such books on the intimate relations between husband and wife, which celibatarian watch-dogs think it an essential function of the Church to supervise and regulate.

Hieronymus Noldin (d. 1922), the leading moral theologian of his day, was not quite as hostile to pleasure as Augustine, but his approval of it was only specious. 'The Creator', he wrote in 1911, 'has infused human nature with sexual pleasure and the desire for it so as to entice people into something that is filthy in itself and burdensome in its consequences' ('De sexto praecepto et de usu matrimonii', p. 9).

To theologians of that kind, van de Velde was utterly beyond the pale. He tolerated the filthy business of sex not solely for the purpose of having burdensome children but discerned meaning and purpose in the filthy business itself. Small wonder that the Roman Magisterium tried with all its might to smash him. The encyclical 'Casti connubii' (1930) was directed mainly against married persons who 'are weary of children and wish to gratify their desires without their consequent burden', but it also aimed a crushing and quite unmerited blow at van de Velde – unmerited because of his wholly traditional belief that 'pregnancy, to a woman of normal instincts, is enormously desirable, for it means Motherhood' (van de Velde, op. cit., p. 235). His crime was to focus attention on sexual pleasure *per se* and attempt to rescue it from its shadowy existence as a means to the end of procreation, the sole approved focus of the Christian marital ethic. By preaching this 'idolatry of the flesh', this 'base slavery of the passions' and these 'godless ideas', he was helping to bring about 'the dishonour of man's dignity' ('Casti connubii', III).

Van de Velde transformed the confessors' poison cupboard into a pharmacopoeia for the married. What others had condemned for almost two thousand years as a recipe for everlasting death, even in tiny doses, he prescribed quite freely in the belief that perversion was an attitude of mind, not a physical position. The waves that once broke over van de Velde have now subsided. Since his book was published the Church has devoted greater attention to its ban on contraception, which it continues to uphold with all its old sexual pessimism, stubbornly and incorrigibly ignoring the real doubts and sufferings of mankind.

Bernard Häring fires a parting broadside of his own at van de Velde's book in 'The Law of Christ'. He condemns it for its 'revolting detailed instructions'. In lieu of these, he offers a universal formula: his section on 'Love Technique' recommends that married couples practise 'a common orientation' toward God (Häring, op. cit., p. 363).

Häring informs his readers how much pleasure is permissible. Writing of 'Marital Union for Pleasure Alone', he declares: 'If the act, however, still retains its basic character as service to life [i.e. if no contraception is practised] . . . it is "only" a venial sin, for the fault is ultimately a defect of integral motivation, and as an individual act is not mortal sin' (ibid., p. 371). The quotation marks around Häring's 'only' are presumably an indication that the matter is not to be taken lightly. And indeed, he goes on: 'But our judgment would be far more severe if there were questions of a general attitude rather than of an individual or isolated act. An attitude of mind which is governed by indulgence of venereal pleasure as the sole motivation for marital union divorces the sheer sexual instinct from authentic marital love and the reverential spirit of service to life. Such an approach to marital relations is one of the most dangerous sources of impurity. It is totally and utterly unchaste.' Häring makes his meaning even plainer: 'The spirit and disposition of Tobias must govern marital conduct in its entirety, even though it need not directly affect each particular act: "And now, Lord, thou knowest that not for fleshly lust do I take my sister to wife, but only for the love of posterity . . ."' (ibid., p. 372). So no one engaging in marital intercourse must lose sight of its procreative function, though a little pleasure may also be intended. 'In such instances the craving for gratification is rather the occasion, strictly speaking, than the ultimate motive of the action' and 'is good' (ibid.).

Pope John Paul II has also acknowledged that married people desire a little sexual pleasure in 'Familiaris consortio' (1981), in which he sanctions periodic abstinence as a method of birth control. The Augustinian insistence on procreation as the most important motive for every conjugal act has thus been dropped, and the Pope's concession to pleasure is manifestly at odds with Augustine's condemnation of the rhythm technique as a 'procurer's method'. Nevertheless, John Paul II is still steering a truly Augustinian course. Children as the motive for every conjugal act may have been dropped, but not hostility to sexual pleasure, and, since Augustine abhorred pleasure more than he favoured children, Catholic tradition has been upheld. Procreation may be avoided in a pleasureless way: by abstinence. (One suspects that, in harping so incessantly on procreation as the primary purpose of marriage, celibatarians are concerned less with children in general than with their own little pet obsession, which is that the married should as far as possible abstain from sex.)

In spite of his conflict of method with Augustine, therefore, John Paul II has reasserted the true and underlying thrust of the Augustinian sexual ethic, i.e. hostility to pleasure. Children are not his primary concern either – they will sometimes be precluded by contraception one way or another, Catholically or non-Catholically. He, too, is primarily at pains to curtail sexual pleasure. The Church is striving here to save whatever remains to be saved. Luckily, the rhythm method is still very complicated and the period of abstinence quite extensive. With great satisfaction, John Paul II cites Paul VI's 'Pill encyclical' of 1968: 'To dominate instinct by means of one's reason and free will undoubtedly requires ascetical practices, so that the affective manifestations of conjugal life may observe the correct order, in particular with regard to the observance of periodic continence' ('Familiaris consortio', 33). How fortunate that scientists are in no immediate danger of narrowing down the fertile period to a single day, or even to a few precisely calculable hours, for what a blow that would be to the observance of the 'correct' order' governing manifestations of conjugal love and spells of asceticism! Still quoting from his predecessor's encyclical, John Paul II goes on:

> Yet this discipline which is proper to the purity of married couples, far from harming conjugal love, rather confers on it a higher human value. It demands continual effort, yet, thanks to its beneficent influence, husband and wife fully develop their personalities, being enriched with spiritual values. Such a discipline bestows upon family life fruits of serenity and peace, and facilitates the solution of other problems; it favours consideration for one's partner, helps both parties to drive out selfishness, the enemy of true love, and deepens their sense of responsibility. By its means, parents acquire the capacity of having a deeper and more efficacious influence in the education of their offspring.
>
> (ibid.)

In short, continence is a spiritual panacea. It confers all that could possibly be desired upon fathers, mothers and children (and doubtless, indirectly at least, upon grandfathers and grandmothers as well). It is the means whereby all problems – marital, educational, and existential – can be resolved.

In view of the miraculous effects of periodic abstinence, John Paul II has given the theologians of the future a problem to solve. As we saw in chapter 6 he has extended 'a pressing invitation to theologians, asking them to unite their efforts in order to collaborate with the hierarchical

Magisterium' and 'study further *the difference, both anthropological and moral* [italics sic], between contraception and recourse to the rhythm of the cycle' (ibid., 31 and 32). Since Augustine denied that there was any difference whatever from the aspect of moral theology, their task is not only difficult but impossible, strictly speaking, for no moral difference can be found where none exists. There is, in fact, a difference, but it is papal rather than theological: the rhythm method enables the Pope to keep married couples under the yoke of abstinence for several days, whereas other methods would not.

Far from giving up the struggle, moral theologians, too, will discover a difference in due course. John Paul II himself has hinted at an answer to his conundrum: 'It is a difference far wider and deeper than is usually thought, one that ultimately involves two irreconcilable conceptions of the human person and human sexuality.' The theologians would not have hit on the answer themselves, but at least they now know where to look. 'The choice of the natural rhythms entails accepting the cycle of the person, that is, the woman, and thereby accepting dialogue, reciprocal respect, shared responsibility and self-control' (ibid., 32). Were self-control not the Pope's sole and overriding concern, no one could fail to approve of his solicitude for 'the person, that is, the woman'. Similarly, no one would think a married couple's mutual dialogue and respect anything but good, were not the fly in papal ointment that periodic continence is implicitly defined as a means to a morally superior phase of marital life and a prerequisite of all these good things.

This papal hymn to marital continence comes under the heading 'Serving Life'. The words seem rather at odds with the theme of contraception, but the Pope is here referring to another, more exalted form of 'service to life', roughly definable as follows: by abstaining from intercourse, married couples approximate – for a few days at least – to the virginal state and entitle themselves – albeit only periodically – to enter a superior phase of existence. Their 'service to life' now consists in abstaining rather than procreating. The Pope has here modified and redefined the idea of contraception. He regards periodic continence as a form of spiritual exercise for the married. His chapter entitled 'Serving Life' simply declines to acknowledge that they may use intermittent continence to avoid fertile periods, in other words, as a contraceptive method. That is why he no longer refers to periodic continence as 'contraception' – the word does not occur in this context – but as 'birth control'. In his view, that makes everything all right: births (or rather, their avoidance) remain the focus of attention.

Among those who have responded to the Pope's 'pressing invitation' is Cardinal Ratzinger. After the Synod of Bishops at Rome in 1980 he sent all the priests, deacons and pastoral clergy in the archdiocese of Munich-Freising a twenty-seven-page letter in which he paid exhaustive tribute to the synod's findings on the subject of 'Marriage and the Family'. Referring to 'Humanae vitae' (the Pill encyclical), he wrote: 'Precisely on this basis, from [womanly] experience alone, we receive a cogent picture of what theological argument has hitherto failed to make us perceive: that the choice between natural methods and contraception is not a morally insignificant matter of different means to the same end, but that they are separated by an anthropological gulf which is, for that very reason, a moral gulf as well. But how, in a very few lines, am I to indicate this when access thereto is simply obstructed by the universal attitude of mind?' Yes, indeed, it will take more than a few lines to dispel the ignorance of the married. Theologians will have to toil for generations to overcome their purblind inability or unwillingness to perceive the said difference and bring enlightenment to those who are, without exception, groping in the dark. Fortunately, the cardinal points the way to a deeper perception of these elusive ideas: 'That the Pill has robbed woman of her own temporal method and, thus, of her own way of existence, and that it has rendered her – as the world of science would have it – "usable" at all times, has been recently and cogently demonstrated by Christa Meves, who draws attention to the meaning and beauty of continence in this context, a subject of which our sick civilisation scarcely dares to speak. All this and much else has, as we know, bred a "Pill-weary" attitude which we should regard as an opportunity for renewed reflection.'

If Cardinal Ratzinger sees the Pill as a female affliction, we should in fairness cite a male affliction described by Christa Meves in a diocesan newspaper article (1976) entitled 'Has Christian [i.e. Catholic] marriage any future?':

> Because of women's increased life expectancy – their average age at death in the last century was only thirty-five, and many of them, debilitated by frequent childbirth, died in childbed itself – the number of couples who live together for thirty, fifty, or even sixty years has also increased. This longevity entails an additional

test for the husband in particular. The death of a man's wife, often at an early age, at one time enabled him to contract a new and legitimate marriage with another, usually younger, woman, whereas he is now compelled to make do with a wife who often ages faster than himself.

So everyone has a cross to bear: woman has been robbed of freedom by the Pill and rendered 'usable', man is robbed of freedom by his wife's advancing age. The Pill has contributed to this male affliction because fewer women are so debilitated by frequent childbirth that they die in the process, thereby vacating the marriage-bed in favour of younger successors. Fortunately, however, these afflictions can be remedied by papally prescribed continence. Christa Meves goes on: 'May not the Pope's instructions to women possess practical justification after all? Do they not protect women from once more becoming fair game for male sexuality? Do they not, by enjoining a husband to chastity and consideration for his wife, give him greater scope for an essential, spiritual counterweight to his physical urges?'

So only the Pope, with his gospel of continence, shields wives from the piratical impulses of their sexually unbridled husbands. A wife who takes the Pill whets her husband's carnal desires to such an extent that she is utterly at his mercy. Her sole protection is the Pope, who forbids her the Pill for her own sake, to preserve her from a hunted beast's existence. The Pope's curb on sex is justified by the carnal appetites of husbands – he merely defends wives and helps them to refuse the Pill because to take it would put them at the mercy of their sexually predatory partners. The Pope is woman's guardian angel and the Vatican a kind of home for battered wives. And, lo and behold, a miracle promptly occurs: whereas a wife who takes the Pill transforms her husband into a lecher, the wife who does not take the Pill causes him to behave in a chaste, continent manner. If we are to believe Christa Meves, the Pope must nurse a kind of Jekyll-and-Hyde conception of the Pill: husbands become beasts or saints depending on whether or not their wives take it.

Disregarding these miraculous metamorphoses, however, something else should be borne in mind. All glorifiers of marital continence, from John Paul II to Christa Meves, fail to see that it is not merely the unbridled sensualist who degrades his (or her) partner into a mere sex object, but it can be an even viler form of degradation to make one's partner the victim of sexual abstinence. This is not to argue pro the Pill and contra the rhythm method (Christa Meves: 'There is a new hypophyseal tumour that occurs only in women who take the "pill" for a long period') or pro the condom and contra coitus interruptus, or vice versa. It is simply to state that all these questions should be addressed, not by popes and theologians, but by medical science and the married themselves, whose sense of responsibility and consideration for their partners are paramount.

'Familiaris consortio' condemns 'the grave affront to human dignity' that results when governments 'seek in any way to limit the freedom of couples to decide about children'. John Paul II neglects to add that many Catholic couples regard papal curbs on their freedom in this respect as an equally grave 'affront to human dignity'. Moreover, they consider it hypocritical for the Church to preach freedom for couples to *oppose* contraception while restricting their freedom to *favour* it. The truth is, of course, that the Church advocates no kind of freedom at all for the married; it merely seeks to impose its own moral dictatorship regardless of their welfare – a dictatorship based on antisexual, celibatarian disdain for marriage and an obsession with virginity.

TWENTY-FIVE

The Nineteenth and Twentieth Centuries: The Age of Birth Control

Not even the Enlightenment and the French Revolution came out in favour of contraception, and in 1798, when the young Anglican priest Thomas Malthus published his ideas on overpopulation, pointing out that population growth tended to outstrip food production, he warned against 'violations of the marriage-bed and improper arts to conceal the consequences of irregular connections', which 'clearly come under the head of vice'. Although he urged his readers to practise 'moral restraint' rather than contraception, however, it was his 'Essay on the Principle of Population' that first injected the idea of birth control into the consciousness of the nineteenth and twentieth centuries.

In Europe coitus interruptus was the commonest method of birth control and remained so even after the vulcanisation of rubber in 1843 made condoms more readily available. The French Jesuit and most widely read moral theologian of the nineteenth century, Jean-Pierre Gury (d. 1866), wrote in 1850: 'In our own day, the abominable plague of onanism [coitus interruptus] has spread far and wide' ('Compendium theologiae moralis', II). He held that 'a woman sins gravely if she even indirectly or tacitly entices her husband into an abuse of marriage [contraceptive intercourse] by complaining of the number of their children and the exertions of bearing or rearing them, or declares that she will die the next time she gives birth' (ibid.).

If a wife was forbidden to urge her husband to practise coitus interruptus for fear of death, was she bound to resist him when he practised it on his own initiative? To this question, which had been submitted by the vicar of Chambéry, Rome replied on 15 November 1816, that a wife might co-operate in intercourse if her refusal was likely to be gravely prejudicial. Indeed, a wife might even request intercourse herself if she would otherwise lapse into incontinence. (Note, once again, the Church's concern for the potential adulterer and its neglect of those who do not desire marital intercourse as a substitute for adultery.) This Roman ruling was a virtual echo of Alfonso de' Liguori (d. 1787).

On 23 April 1822, Rome stated in response to another inquiry that a wife might 'passively submit' if threatened with death, blows, or other grave acts of cruelty. Similar rulings were given on 1 February 1823, and 3 April 1916. The prevailing tone had hardened, therefore: neither Alfonso nor the letter to the vicar of Chambéry had spoken of mortal danger, and the suggestion that a wife might under certain circumstances request intercourse herself had been dropped.

Rome first ruled on the matter of condom-protected intercourse in 1853. The question ran: 'May a wife passively submit to such intercourse?' The answer: No. In other words, she might if in danger of her life submit to coitus interruptus, but not, it seemed, to intercourse with a condom. The response in our own century, the era of the contraception and the Pill encyclicals, has been ever harsher and less equivocal. On 3 June 1916, Rome's ruling on an inquiry about the use of condoms was that a wife must resist such intercourse 'as she would a rapist'.

The following response from Rome indicates that the Catholic Church's campaign against contraception was not yet in full swing by the middle of the nineteenth century. In 1842 Bishop Bouvier had asked Rome how 'nearly all the younger married couples' in his French diocese were to be handled in the confessional because they limited the size of their families by practising coitus interruptus. Rome replied that the confessor should say nothing about such matters unless directly questioned, this being the advice of St Alfonso de' Liguori, 'a learned man most skilled in such matters' (John T. Noonan, 'Contraception: A History of its Treatment by the Catholic Theologians and Canonists', p. 401). Gury likewise cited Alfonso in support of his belief that a priest should eschew the subject of coitus interruptus in the confessional.

The Catholic Church's rabid, confessional-based campaign against contraception did not begin in earnest until the last quarter of the nineteenth century. It was triggered on the one hand by growing public interest in birth control and the mass dissemination of contraceptive devices, and, on the other hand, by the Franco-Prussian War. These factors were viewed in the light of a revival of Thomism, which tolerated the sex act purely as a conjugal duty performed for generative purposes. In a public address delivered at Beauvais on Bastille Day, 1872, Cardinal Kaspar Mermillod of Switzerland declared: 'You have rejected God, and God has struck you. You have, by hideous calculation, made tombs instead of filling cradles with children; therefore you have wanted for soldiers' (ibid., p. 414). In 1886 Rome ruled for the first time that confessors were duty-bound, if they had 'a well-founded suspicion', to question penitents on the subject of contraception.

It was in our own century that Rome removed the last restraint on the confessor's duty to interrogate, namely, the need for 'well-founded suspicion'. In 1901 an unnamed French priest addressed an inquiry to the Vatican. While hearing the confession of a man pseudonymously referred to as Titius, whom he described as 'wealthy, respectable, well-educated, and a good Christian', he had questioned him about contraception. Titius had replied that he practised coitus interruptus so as not to impair his family's financial status by fathering too many children – he already had a son and a daughter – and to spare his wife the strain of recurrent pregnancies. When the priest condemned this practice and refused to grant him absolution, Titius retorted that another confessor, a teacher of moral theology at a seminary, had sanctioned his conduct provided its purpose was to assuage his desire, not to cause an emission of semen. Titius had then left the confessional and put it about that the priest was an uneducated ignoramus. Rome's reply, dated 13 November 1901, approved the priest's course of action and affirmed the impossibility of granting absolution to a penitent unwilling to desist from his admitted onanism (coitus interruptus).

Belgian theologians, who were foremost among those who opposed the confessors' system of 'tolerant *mutisme*' at the turn of the century, insisted that even the mothers of newly-wed girls should be asked if they had advised them to 'be prudent'. Belgium's leading moral theologian, Arthur Vermeersch, sounded the loudest call to arms. If threatened with condom-protected intercourse, a wife was duty-bound to resist until physically overpowered or until she had sacrificed some good 'equivalent to life'. She was further obliged to resist her husband as she would a rapist and must be willing to accept the consequences, namely, 'domestic unhappinesses, abandonments, divorces'. Vermeersch demanded to know why it should be 'astonishing that conjugal chastity, like all the Christian virtues, claims its martyrs' (ibid., p. 432). This injunction to wives regarding condom-protected intercourse was embodied in the Roman ruling of 3 June 1916.

In 1909 Vermeersch encouraged Cardinal Mercier, the primate of Belgium, to publish a pastoral letter on 'The Duties of Married Life'. The Belgian bishops followed this up on 2 June 1909, by sending their priests and confessors 'Instructions against Onanism'. The 'very evil sin of Onan' was being practised in town and country by Belgium's rich and poor alike. Confronted by 'this common danger', they, the bishops, would be neglecting their duty if they failed to speak out against this unnatural vice, this outrageous sin. People must be exhorted to have greater faith in Providence, which would ensure that no one starved to death. The campaign against this evil must be waged with special vigour in the confessional, for a confessor's silence might be construed as approbation (ibid., p. 420).

In 1913 the bishops' conference at Fulda followed the Belgian primate's example. Contraception was 'a consequence of affluence . . . It is gravely sinful to wish to prevent an increase in the number of one's children, so that marriage is abused for pleasure alone and its principal purposes knowingly and wilfully thwarted. That is a very, very grave sin, however and by whatever means it may occur.' It was the duty of married couples 'to secure the continuing existence of Church and state' (ibid., p. 421).

The battle against contraception was not, of course, suspended even during the First World War. In 1915, Professor A. J. Rosenberg of the episcopal faculty of philosophy and theology at Paderborn declared in 'Theologie und Glaube' that 'modern wars are wars in which the masses acquire far greater significance. Thus, wilful limitation of the size of families [in France] meant that parity of national strength with Germany was renounced . . . Thousands of parents are mourning the loss of an only son . . . Discipline is essential . . . The war has put the problem of deliberate child-avoidance in a new light.' The macabre idea of holding over parents who practised contraception the threat that their existing children would die young had already been approved by the Belgian bishops in their instruction to confessors dated 1909. It was echoed during the Second World War in 'Quaestiones de castitate et luxuria' (Bruges, 1944) by the Belgian Dominican and moral theologian Benedikt Merkelbach (d. 1942).

Not quite as macabre, but macabre enough, was an article by Father H.A. Krose in the reputable Jesuit periodical 'Stimmen der Zeit' (1915):

In the course of the lively literary debate occasioned by the ominous decline in the German birth-rate, attention has repeatedly been drawn to the imperilling of the Empire's world-power status . . . It is frighteningly apparent, from the dark days we are now being forced to undergo, just how well founded that warning was. How could the German Empire withstand the onslaught of powerful adversaries on every side, had not those very age-groups capable of military service been rendered so numerous by a high birth-rate in the decades immediately ensuing on the Empire's foundation? Our adversaries are eternally amazed by the inexhaustible human reservoir that enables the German Empire . . . not only to fill the gaps torn by war, but constantly to augment its manpower.

The campaign against contraception was pursued with undiminished vigour after the First World War, still in the same chauvinistic and militaristic spirit. In 1919 the French bishops proclaimed: 'It is a grave sin against nature and against the will of God to deprive marriage of its ultimate purpose with selfish and wanton deliberation. The theories and practices that teach or promote the restriction of birth are as baneful as they are criminal. The danger to which they expose our country has been forcibly impressed on us by the war. May this object-lesson not be in vain. The gaps made by death must be filled if we wish France to belong to the French and to be strong enough to defend herself and prosper' (ibid., p. 422).

The end of the First World War provided the occasion for a pastoral letter from the Austrian bishops too, who declared that the 'profanation of marriage' was 'the greatest moral scourge of our day', and the American bishops expressed themselves in similar vein (ibid.).

The wars of 1870–1 and 1914–18 brought a corresponding increase in the vehemence with which churchmen stressed the ban on contraception. Even today, the Catholic Church guards notional children against contraception more jealously than it protects live adolescents from damnation or death on the battlefield. This it does because of its intolerable delusion that humanity's true crimes are committed in the matrimonial bedroom, not in theatres of war or beside mass graves. Catholic moral theologians have often spoken of just wars, never of justified contraception. This is not only logical but consistent, given their belief that conception must be guaranteed at least partly to meet the requirements of the battlefield. Contraception is unjustified because it hinders the waging of just wars – because under-strength age-groups are a military handicap. It might also be said that a relationship exists between the campaign against contraception and rearmament. Military preparedness must begin in the bedroom. Children being essential to the waging of war, waging war and contraception are incompatible. Human beings denied birth cannot become weapons of war, so contraception is a form of unilateral disarmament. It is more than merely coincidental that the clamour against contraception should have attained such a pitch in our own century, with its arms races and world wars.

The ban on contraception has a long, pleasure-hating pedigree. There is, however, a difference between the present pope's policy and Alfonso de' Liguori's advice to confessors as transmitted by Rome to Bishop Bouvier in 1842, which was to remain silent or restrict oneself to answering questions expressly asked by penitents. John Paul II bombards everyone with the subject uninvited, whether or not the occasion seems appropriate, though he must in fairness be acquitted of realising that the accent he imparts to Christian morality goes hand in hand with a policy of strength and military superiority.

When the worldwide debate on contraception was at its height, and after the Anglican Church had renounced its existing condemnation of the practice at the Lambeth Conference on 15 August 1930, Pope Pius XI issued an encyclical on the subject. Drafted in collaboration with Arthur Vermeersch and published on 31 December 1930, 'Casti connubii' was the forerunner of Paul VI's 'Humanae vitae' (1968) and John Paul II's 'Familiaris consortio' (1981). Ever since its publication, popes have regarded it as one of their principal duties to harp on the evils of contraception. 'Casti connubii' echoed the militant French bishops after the First World War in referring to the 'criminal abuse' of those who practised contraception and defined their motives: they 'wish to gratify their desires without their consequent burden.' It also stated that there was 'no reason, however grave' that could justify contraception and cited the deterrent example of Onan, whom God had slain for engaging in it. 'In virtue of Our supreme authority', Pius XI admonished confessors not to leave the faithful in any doubt about 'this most grave law of God' nor to confirm them in their errors by preserving a 'guilty silence'.

'Casti connubii' finally put paid to the quiet days of 1842, when only those who asked were given answers. The shrewd discretion practised by confessors on Alfonso de' Liguori's advice had become 'guilty silence'. The uninvited papal response has since been plain to all: the generation of human beings must not be prevented on any account. It is equally plain to all that human beings may legitimately be killed under certain circumstances, to wit, in war. Those in doubt as to who may legitimately be killed should seek guidance from a declaration made by the Indian bishops at Bangalore in 1957. They solemnly warned the faithful against three things: communism, immoral films, and contraception.

Admittedly, 'Casti connubii' never states, nor does it mean to state, that contraception is an impediment to military preparedness. A pope cannot employ nationalistic arguments – sexual pessimism is quite sufficient for his purposes – but that makes the following questions doubly urgent. Why doesn't the Catholic Church accord the same protection to living, breathing human beings as it bestows on their potential, notional offspring? Why doesn't it prohibit war as emphatically as it does contraception? Why should Catholic moralists sometimes embellish war with the epithet 'just' but never apply it to contraception? Has something gone awry in the Christian scale of values? War, under certain circumstances, yes; contraception, for whatever reason, never. But a decision in favour of children must connote a decision against war; it will otherwise be a decision in favour of children *for* war. Those who carry their concern for notional children to the lengths of forbidding contraception under any circumstances, 'however grave the reason', should carry their concern for living children to the lengths of preaching a total ban on war. The motto of the bishops and cardinals cited above – war, ergo children – would then, at long last, be superseded by the truly Christian motto: children yes, war never.

'Casti connubii' made only a passing reference to the rhythm method. Such intercourse was permitted 'provided that the internal structure of the act, and, thus, its subordination to the primary purpose [children], remain unimpaired'. In 1930 the rhythm method still claimed nothing like the papal attention that was to be bestowed on it in 1981 by John Paul II in 'Familiaris consortio', that Knaus-Ogino hymn to abstinence. Discovered in 1924 by Kyusaku Ogino, a Japanese, and in 1929 by Hermann Knaus, an Austrian, it did not become known worldwide until the early thirties. Pius XI was here referring more to the Pouchet method, which took its name from the Frenchman Archimède Pouchet. According to this, conception occurred only during menstruation and within one to twelve days thereafter. It was still believed in 1920 that a woman was infertile during the third week after menstruation, and as late at 1929 Dominikus Lindner's 'Der Usus matrimonii' stated that 'conception is likelier than ever at this time [during menstruation]' (p. 219). A similar assertion was made by the moral theologian Heribert Jone in 1930 ('Katholische Moraltheologie', p. 617). Thanks to this method, which had earned Pouchet the French Royal Academy of Sciences prize for experimental physiology in 1845, women who wanted no children conceived them and women who tried to conceive them with the aid of Pouchet's computations failed to do so. Pius XI thus had little reason to contest the 'right' of married couples to employ a contraceptive method of which the 'Nouvelle Revue Théologique' had written in 1900: 'Who has not heard penitents who faithfully observed these times, yet failed to prevent fecundation?'

At the beginning of the 1930s, when the Knaus-Ogino method became known and couples invoked Pius XI's approval of selected times for intercourse, some theologians objected that he had sanctioned an unreliable method rather than a reliable one. Arthur Vermeersch was foremost in complaining of 'the heresy of the empty cradle'. As for his fellow Belgian, the Jesuit Ignatius Salsmans, he claimed that the pope had been referring only to post-menopausal intercourse when he sanctioned the use of infertile periods, and that 'Oginoism' was little better than onanism (in the sense of coitus interruptus). In this he was, of course, correct and thoroughly Augustinian, though he drew the wrong conclusions by forbidding couples to employ either method. Bishops, too, warned against the rhythm method, e.g. Cardinal van Roey, the provincial of Mechlin. They declared in 1937 that to take advantage of infertile periods conjured up dangers such as increasing selfishness and the diminishment of conjugal love (ibid., p. 444).

John Paul II strikes quite a different note. 'Familiaris consortio' states that 'the choice of natural rhythms' means 'living personal love with its requirement of fidelity' and that 'in this context the couple comes to experience how conjugal communion is enriched with those values of tenderness and affection which constitute the inner soul of human sexuality' (32).

Faced with such contradictory pronouncements on one and the same method, which was held to impoverish conjugal love in 1937 and enrich it in 1981, one can only conclude that bishops and popes have amply and mutually demonstrated their incompetence, and that the proven ignorance of both camps should encourage them to keep quiet if they attach any importance to their credibility with married couples.

Other choice examples of theological imbecility include Bishop Rosset's assertion in 1895 that the only children of parents who practise contraception are 'spoiled, selfish, and effete', whereas those born to continent parents are not (Noonan, op. cit., p. 520), or that coitus interruptus causes nervous disorders and pelvic complaints in the woman (ibid., p. 521). Häring asserts the same ('The Law of Christ', III, p. 358). When theological arguments fail, medical fallacies can always be enlisted.

The Church was still busily engaged in sorting, labelling, condemning and – where applicable – tolerating coitus interruptus, condom-wearing and calendar-watching, when its leaders were overtaken in the middle of our own century by a new misfortune: the Pill. For Pope Pius XII, no pill could have been more bitter. On 12 September 1958, he declared that 'direct and impermissible sterilisation is induced if ovulation is prevented in order to preserve the organism from the consequences of a pregnancy which it cannot consummate.' This pronouncement was an outstanding spiritual feat, but not so much because Pius XII had condemned the Pill. His predecessor Pius XI having condemned all forms of contraceptive sterilisation in 'Casti connubii', the Pill had likewise to be banned.

This much was obvious and predictable, papally speaking, because no pope can be expected to dissent from his predecessors' opinions. The infallibility of preceding popes inhibits independent thought in succeeding popes. Because the Pill had yet to be invented, Pius XI was unable to furnish Pius XII with a specific reason for condemning it. Pius XII had therefore to be creative, but his reasoning turned logic upside down; to assert the superiority of nature's intention over nature's capacity to carry it out was tantamount to demanding that impotent nature be raped on nature's behalf – which in this case amounted to raping the woman herself. The pope's meaning was this: that nature's generative intention must on no account be thwarted even when nature cannot accomplish that intention and the woman dies in pregnancy. In saying such a thing, he was advocating a brutal and extremist ethic. No one who gives the biological laws of nature precedence over mutual consideration between husband and wife, making those laws the supreme moral criterion and guideline, ought to argue that nature intends a thing even when its accomplishment is impossible, and that nature's will must be obeyed at the expense of human life. If nature is biologically overtaxed, contraception should, on the contrary, be regarded as wholly natural. What really underlies such papal rulings, which seek to posit the impossible and denaturalise nature, is nothing more nor less than the Church's old, time-honoured hostility to pleasure.

That the dictates of 'nature' are not wholly or solely obeyed, even in Rome, may be inferred from the fact that not even princes of the Church go about naked, and that their dress is certainly less 'natural' than that of ordinary mortals. Nature, properly understood, doubtless embraces both forms of common sense: the kind that prompts people to don clothes when the cold becomes too much for 'the organism', and the kind that wards off the consequences of a pregnancy that can never come to term. In another sphere, where its hostility to pleasure was less immediately concerned, the Church has since shown more understanding. In 1853 some English theologians accused Queen Victoria's personal physician of having drugged his royal patient with chloroform during childbirth. This they regarded as an offence against Genesis 3: 16: 'In sorrow thou shalt bring forth children.'

In addition to the inviolable natural laws that prohibit the Pill, Paul VI cited another argument against this form of contraception in his Pill encyclical of 1968: 'Responsible men can become more deeply convinced of the truth of the doctrine laid down by the Church on this issue if they reflect on the consequences of methods and plans for the artificial restriction of increases in the birth-rate. Let them first consider how easily this course of action can lead to the way being wide open to marital infidelity and a general lowering of moral standards' ('Humanae vitae', 17). Adultery is something of a pet idea among popes and moral theologians, who frequently enlist it as an argument in favour of X or Y or both. One gains the impression, however, that their constant harping on adultery stems more from a wish to deter and intimidate than from the actual circumstances of married couples.

A third anti-contraceptive argument adduced by Paul VI was that 'a man who grows accustomed to the use of contraceptive methods may forget the reverence due to a woman' (ibid.). Given the Church's prevailing tendency to construe human rights as men's rights and human dignity as that of men in general and celibate clerical 'dignitaries' in particular, it should refrain from pronouncing on women's dignity and pinning its own lack of respect for them on their husbands. Churchmen had no need to wait for the Pill before reverencing women less than themselves. Where this papal campaign to enhance women's dignity is concerned, the Pill is merely a new excuse to asceticise and eunuchise, monasticise and celibatise marriage in general. Celibatarians find it quite incomprehensible that a husband can not only love his wife physically but revere her spiritually. Luckily, however, conjugal love and respect are unaffected by whether contraception is undertaken in a papally approved or an 'artificial' manner.

Paul VI's Pill encyclical states that contraception is as damnable (*pariter damnandum est*) as abortion (ibid., 14). This not only overdramatises the former but, without meaning to, trivialises the latter. The logical inference: if contraception is as sinful as abortion, abortion is no more sinful than contraception.

Augustine would have thought it an outrageous heresy to state, as John Paul II does in 'Familiaris consortio', his follow-up to Paul VI's 'Humanae vitae', that all salvation – everlasting spiritual salvation as well as earthly conjugal happiness – depends largely on the proper way to avoid having children. Modern couples merely shrug at this because the celibatarians have destroyed their own credibility. The Pill is a threat not to women's prestige, as the Church teaches, but to its own dwindling reputation, which it will lose altogether if it continues to presume to supervise the intimate relations between husband and wife. It is time the Church ceased to usurp the conjugal act for its own celibatarian purposes, just as it is time for the married to claim it for themselves alone, remove conjugal love from the voyeuristic domain of a clerical vice squad, and refuse to take orders from those whose competency in such matters is nil.

The Church does not, in fact, fear any diminution in the respect paid to women, as it pretends when campaigning against the Pill. All it fears is the loss of its own prestige and power and a concomitant loss of income. As the conservative 'Offertenzeitung für die katholische Geistlichkeit Deutschlands' stated in October 1977:

> 'The Pill' will undoubtedly stunt the growth of the Church in the next ten or twenty years, with all the consequent effects on recruitment to the priesthood and religious orders and on church-tax revenues. No new churches will be required ... The results will precisely ... accord with [our] warnings about the propagation of 'the Pill', namely: an ominous decline in the birth-rate, the demoralisation of society, the sexualisation of public life, overt

propaganda on behalf of pornography and nudism ... public contempt for chastity leading to *a decline in the social standing of the priesthood and religious* [my italics] ... all in all, spiritual environmental pollution on an unprecedented scale.

So Catholics are forbidden to take the Pill not only because it encourages pornography and nudism, reduces the Church's income and curtails its building programme, but, in particular, because it lowers the social status of the clergy.

TWENTY-SIX

Abortion

Until quite recently, women giving birth in Catholic hospitals could be deprived of urgent medical assistance and their lives placed in jeopardy if the hospital authorities adhered to official Catholic doctrine, which holds that it is more important to baptise a moribund child than to let it die unbaptised and save its mother's life. They are still at risk where the official line continues to hold sway, for this macabre chapter is far from closed.

As far as Germany is concerned, the danger has somewhat diminished since 7 May 1976, when the German bishops resolved to 'respect' (but not endorse) 'conscientious medical decisions in hopeless situations where a choice must be made between losing the lives of both the mother and the unborn child and losing one life only'. In plain language: if mother and child were both dying, the bishops would acquiesce in the doctor's decision to save the life of the former by sacrificing that of the latter. In even plainer language: the doctor was permitted to save the mother by aborting her only if she *and* the child would otherwise die, *not* if it was a simple choice between the mother and the child. This, however, was merely a concession to doctors who deviated from true Catholic doctrine.

Commenting on the bishops' ruling on 31 May 1978, the Jesuit periodical 'Orientierung' wrote: 'Respect does not necessarily connote approval, and no one, on the basis of this grave declaration, which betokens respect for conscientious personal decisions taken in hopeless situations, should underestimate the courage, self-sacrifice and heroism of those women who die rather than betray their consciences.' In other

269

words, the only good mother in such cases is a dead mother, for only the mother prepared to die with her foetus can be said to have a clear conscience. Bernhard Häring, the Catholic moral theologian, wrote in 1985: 'I shall not here deal in detail with the termination of pregnancy, whose sole (objective) purpose and sole (subjective) intention consist in saving the mother's life when there is no further chance of saving the life of the foetus. We must beware in such (very exceptional) cases of breeding guilt complexes, which often lead, as we all know, to extremely disturbed human relationships and to a distorted image of God' ('Theologie der Gegenwart', 1985, 4, p. 219). So a woman is entitled to live on without guilt complexes and disturbed human relationships if her life has been saved by the abortion of a foetus which was past saving in any case.

The decision is not hers, however. The German bishops consulted no expectant mothers. Their letter was addressed to doctors and acknowledged *their* right to be guided by conscience. The women concerned were merely transferred from one sphere of alien jurisdiction to another. The gods in black had ceded their right of life-or-death decision to the gods in white or green.

Many people believe that the Church now sanctions abortion if the mother's life is in danger. They are quite wrong, as Cardinal Höffner made clear in a letter to me dated 5 August 1986: 'In answer to your inquiry, I confirm that the statement you cite from "Recommendations to doctors and medical staff in hospitals since the amendment of Paragraph 218 of the Penal Code of 7 May 1976", remains valid as before and is also adhered to by myself. Should a different impression have arisen under the conditions prevailing during a recorded television interview, I can only regret this.' (Broadcast on 29 June 1986, the interview in question had seemed to imply that the Church sanctioned abortion on medical grounds if a mother's life was in danger.) The cardinal went on to repeat the gist of the German bishops' circular: that the choice was 'between the loss of both lives, if nature were permitted to take its course, or the loss of one life only'. He concluded: 'I should, however, like to point out in this connection that the statement . . . recalled by you relates to "conscientious medical decisions", and that it thus refrains from passing any moral judgment on this borderline situation.' That is: the German bishops did not endorse the doctors' decision in favour of one life rather than two deaths, they merely 'respected' it.

Thanks to them, we have now reached the stage in Germany where only one life must be sacrificed instead of two provided the obstetrician's conscience so decides. The Church's official doctrine, which remains unrevoked and in force, takes a different view, and many other countries have yet to sidestep the Vatican's rulings. Furthermore, the German bishops' declaration is nowhere near as favourable to the mother as it has been painted. They leave it to the doctor's absolute discretion which of the two lives he may legitimately save, given that both would otherwise be past saving. According to their declaration, he can rest assured of the same episcopal respect if he decides to save the child's life and kill the mother. Fortunately for expectant mothers, they have since been spared the dire consequences of such an appalling episcopal ethic by doctors' consciences and advances in medicine. It should be added, for completeness' sake, that the German bishops refuse to sanction abortion on ethical, social, or any other grounds. This they made abundantly clear in 1976.

We shall not here concern ourselves with the medical aspects of abortion, only with what theologians have officially ruled in regard to women. Although many of them point out that the incidence of extreme cases such as those decided by Rome has been drastically reduced by advances in medical science, this does not mean that the science of theology has made similar strides. Progress in medicine has merely made it easier to survive the science of theology – not that this will breathe new life into the many women whom theologians have killed over the centuries. Today's life-saving medical exercise of conscience would not have accorded with 'the most steadfast will of Our Most Sacred Lord', i.e. Jesus, as interpreted by the Vatican on 1 August 1886. These were the words it employed when confirming a decision handed down on 28 May 1884. Cardinal Caverot of Lyon had questioned whether it was legitimate to perform a craniotomy (cutting or crushing the foetal head to facilitate delivery) when mother and child would both die in default of such an operation, but when the mother alone could be saved by it. Rome's negative response of 1884 was extended on 14 August 1889 to cover 'any surgical operation that directly kills the foetus or the pregnant mother'. On 24 July 1895, a physician asked Rome if, in view of the above rulings, he was entitled to 'save the mother from certain and imminent death' by artificially delivering a not yet viable foetus using methods and operations that did not kill the foetus but endeavoured to deliver it alive, whereafter, being immature, it expired. The response was another negative, and this decision was repeated in 1898. In condemning abortion on medical grounds in 1930, the encyclical 'Casti connubii' declared: 'What could ever be a sufficient reason for excusing in any way the direct murder of the innocent? . . . Those show themselves unworthy of the noble medical profession who encompass the death of one or the other, through a pretence at practising medicine or through motives of misguided pity.'

Pius XII stressed the same point in an address to the Italian Association of Catholic Midwives on 29 October 1951 (AAS 43 [1951], pp. 784–94). Once again, be it noted, the choice was not between mother and child but between the death of both and the survival of the mother. Correct in itself, though undermined by the Church in respect of war and capital punishment, the 'Thou shalt not kill' principle has here been reduced to absurdity. It is a classic case of observing the letter of the law rather than its spirit. Even in the second half of the present century, theologians never tire of applauding this Roman sentence of death upon so many women. Here, for example, is Mausbach-Tischleder's 'Katholische Moraltheologie' in 1938: 'The argument that sparing the child usually results in the loss of *two lives*, whereas sacrificing it results in the loss of only *one*, makes most impression . . . The violent destruction of an innocent life is never permitted; it cannot be sanctioned under any circumstances without misleading people into taking other disastrous and life-destroying steps' (III, p. 125).

Referring to the papal decisions handed down between 1884 and 1951 inclusive, the moral theologian Bernhard Häring writes: 'And yet there was objection in some medical quarters to the Church's repudiation of the *vital indication* [abortion defined as one performed "if the life of the mother is in direct immediate danger of a serious nature"]. Nevertheless a truly realistic appraisal reveals that the Church's attitude furnished medical science with a salutary admonition to develop medical practice more perfectly, so that today, even in the most critical cases, both the mother's life and that of the infant can be safeguarded. There are but few exceptions' ('The Law of Christ', p. 208). In other words, although these salutary papal pronouncements may have killed a large number of women in the period 1884–1951, they inspired the medical profession to make more progress than it would otherwise have striven to accomplish. If the popes had been more squeamish and less implacable, medical science might still be back in the Middle Ages. Thanks to them, it has now reached a stage at which not many more dead mothers (only a 'few exceptions') are required to stimulate its scientific endeavours. Whether doctors appreciate the popes' admonitions or not, however, Häring concludes by summarising the position clearly: 'No matter what the final verdict of medical science may be, the Church holds fast, inexorably fast, to the principle that it can never be allowed – no matter what the circumstances – to destroy by direct action an innocent child in the mother's womb. Compare Pius XII's address on 29 October 1951' (ibid., p. 209).

The year of the pope's address to midwives, 1951, saw the publication of 'The Cardinal', a bestselling novel by Henry Morton Robinson (b. 1898). It describes how an American priest of Irish extraction rises to become the ecclesiastical dignitary of the title. The cardinal's brother-in-law, a doctor, refuses to perform a craniotomy on a 'big-headed baby' when it is already too late for a Caesarian, with the result that mother and child both die. The bereaved husband institutes legal proceedings, but the cardinal strengthens his brother-in-law in the Catholic faith. The doctor – a true martyr – loses his post at the hospital because he refuses to comply with the authorities' insistence that all members of staff sign an undertaking to perform 'what's known as a "therapeutic abortion"' when, as, and if the situation demands'. The Catholic hospitals are naturally in agreement with the cardinal. A later part of the book describes how a mother's life is sacrificed on the altar of the mother-or-child principle. While brooding on his brother-in-law's decision not to perform a craniotomy, the cardinal prays: 'When my test comes . . . grant, Lord, that I shall not murmur against the rigours of Thy love.' His prayer is answered when Mona, his favourite sister, becomes pregnant and goes into labour. 'Unless you give me permission to destroy the foetus,' says Dr Parks, 'nothing can save your sister.' In the course of this two-man debate on a woman's fate, the cardinal 'grips his chair' and, invoking the assistance of Jesus, Mary and Joseph, decides that his sister must die. She herself is never consulted, though the child – in this case – is saved (H.M. Robinson, 'The Cardinal', pp. 91f., 299). Even today, a cardinal faced with a similar dilemma would be duty-bound to sentence his sister to death.

The Catholic ban on abortion was never more absolute than it has been in the century since 1884. The German bishops' statement of 7 May 1976 represented a minor retreat, but we should not rejoice too soon at this concession, for the debate on abortion often takes two steps backward to every one forward. Medical progress alone will finally deliver women, once and for all, from the ethic that demands dead mothers. The harsh ecclesiastical decisions of 1884, 1886, 1889, 1895, 1930, and 1951, which are still officially valid, were preceded by ecclesiastical advances which reformist – or retrograde – currents of opinion cancelled out. In 1872, for example, when consulted about the permissibility of a craniotomy in a case where the mother and child would otherwise die, Rome evasively recommended that guidance on this point be sought in writers ancient and modern (ASS 7, 1872, p. 516f.).

Moral theologian Magnus Jocham of Freising wrote in 1854: 'Generally speaking, the mother's life is more likely to be saved by the death of her child than the child by the death of its mother. In such cases the mother should be advised to save her own life by sacrificing that of her child. When the same prospect of survival and the same danger exist on both sides, however, the mother must decide. Her advisers must always pronounce in favour of saving the mother's life if at all possible' ('Moraltheologie', vol. III, 1854, p. 478). Similarly Franz Xaver Linsenmann of Tübingen in 1878: 'In cases where doubt exists or may exist, that is to say, where the birth of a living child cannot occur without drastic intervention on the surgeon's part, nature itself inescapably dooms two human lives to death if medical intervention is impossible. If the physician, by dint of his skill, saves one of the two lives by sacrificing the other, he cannot be blamed for the death of that other; failure to perform his technical operation would, on the contrary, result in the loss of yet another life' ('Lehrbuch der Moraltheologie', 1878, p. 492). From 1884 onwards, views like these were negated by the official rulings listed above, which laid it down that not even the loss of both lives could justify saving the mother's life by means of an abortion.

The more rigorous rulings on abortion coincided with a change in the theory as to when an embryo became 'animate', meaning infused with a soul. From the end of the nineteenth century onwards, it was increasingly believed that the embryo became animate at the very moment of conception ('simultaneous animation'), so opposition to abortion in the earlier stages of pregnancy, let alone the later, became more intense. Till then, as we have seen, the prevailing theological doctrine had been that of 'successive animation', according to which the male embryo became 'ensouled' on about the fortieth day of gestation and the female on about the eightieth. This was why canon law had hitherto distinguished between the *fetus animatus* and the *fetus inanimatus*. Only the abortion of an animate foetus was punishable by excommunication, and, since it was impossible to ascertain the sex of a foetus, that penalty had not been applied to abortion until after the eightieth day. Although the bull 'Effraenatam' (1588) had threatened abortionists with excommunication, and even with execution, from the moment of conception onwards, this ruling was revoked by Gregory XIV in 1591, a year after the death of its fanatical author, Pope Sixtus V.

From the end of the nineteenth century, canon law drew closer to Sixtus V's ideas and excommunication was reapplied to abortion in the earliest stages of pregnancy. Pius IX had abandoned the distinction between *fetus animatus* and *fetus inanimatus* in 1869, and the CICs of 1917 and 1983 refer merely to 'the foetus'.

Embryonic 'animation' has always been a controversial subject. Basil the Great and Gregory of Nyssa (both fourth century) followed the Stoa in declaring that the human embryo became animate at the moment of conception because soul and semen were introduced into the uterus simultaneously. Albertus Magnus (thirteenth century), too, opposed the theory of successive animation, though his pupil Thomas Aquinas supported it. The tide turned more strongly in favour of simultaneous animation during the seventeenth century, influenced by the physician Thomas Fienus's assertion in 1620 that the human soul became infused on the third day of gestation, not the fortieth. In 1658 the Franciscan monk Hieronymus Florentinius demanded that every embryo be baptised if mortal danger threatened, no matter how soon after conception, because it possessed a soul, and in 1661 Paul Zacchias, personal physician to Pope Innocent X, opined that the soul became infused at the moment of conception. Such was the predominant view in medical circles at the beginning of the eighteenth century. The theologian Thomas Roncaglio spoke out in favour of simultaneous animation in 1736. Alfonso de' Liguori (d. 1787), while espousing Thomas Aquinas's theory of male embryonic animation on the fortieth day and female on the eightieth, remarked that this was 'very uncertain' ('Theologia moralis', III, p. 394).

Although the theory of simultaneous animation gained the upper hand towards the end of the nineteenth century and led to a change in ecclesiastical law, the most eminent Catholic theologian of our own century, Karl Rahner, has tended in the direction of successive animation without, however, specifying its exact timing: 'One cannot infer from the Church's dogmatic definitions that it would be against the faith to assume that the transition to spirit-person occurs only in the embryo's course of development. No theologian will claim to be able to prove that the termination of a pregnancy is in every case the murder of a human being' ('Dokumente der Paulusgesellschaft', vol. 2, 1962, p. 391f.). In an article entitled 'Zum Problem der genetischen Manipulation' ('Schriften zur Theologie', vol. 8, 1967, p. 286f.) Rahner alludes to the implications this holds for experiments with human embryonic material: 'It is surely conceivable that, given serious and definite doubts about the truly human nature of experimental material, there are grounds *for* an experiment which, if submitted to rational consideration, outweigh a human being's uncertain right to an existence subject to doubt' (ibid., p. 301).

The question of simultaneous or successive animation – that is to say, the question of when a human being becomes a human being – has affected the way in which abortion is judged. Thomas Sanchez (d. 1610), for centuries the leading authority on matrimonial matters, held that, if an expectant mother's life was in danger, it was permissible to abort an inanimate foetus up to around eighty days after conception ('De sancto matrimonii sacramento', lib. 9, disp. 20, n. 9). It is not, however, true, as some have claimed, that he sanctioned abortion on ethical and social grounds. His sole concession to the raped girl who feared for her life if found to be pregnant was to advise her to seek a husband quickly. If still uncertain of her pregnancy, she might legitimately conceal it from him. He would then assume that the rapist's child, if any, was his own. In Sanchez's view, the injury to the deceived husband was outweighed by the girl's mortal danger (ibid., n. 11).

If mortal danger threatened an expectant mother after the eightieth day, for instance during childbirth itself, she might on no account be saved by directly killing the foetus, even if that was her only chance of survival (ibid., n. 7). It was permissible for her to employ medicines and remedies directly conducive to her recovery and only indirectly conducive to the abortion of the animate foetus (ibid., n. 14). However, Sanchez followed this up with a ruling that was to prove lethal to many mothers – a ruling which, substantially reinforced by Alfonso de' Liguori nearly two centuries later, retains its dread influence to this day. Sanchez stated that a dying mother who sought to save herself by taking a medicine indirectly conducive to abortion *did* commit a grave sin if it was certain or very probable that the child would have survived her *and could have been baptised*. In this instance she was obliged to put her child's spiritual salvation before her own physical preservation. Sanchez pointed out that a priest about to baptise a dying child was not permitted to flee from an enemy if there was a risk that the child would die unbaptised. Just as a priest had to sacrifice his life in order to baptise a dying child, so a mother had, under certain circumstances, to sacrifice herself in the interests of her child's baptism (ibid., n. 17).

Based on the Augustinian theory that unbaptised infants are damned to all eternity, this idea was carried to extremes by Alfonso, whose authority, as we know, prevailed throughout the nineteenth century and largely holds sway in the twentieth. Alfonso held, contrary to Sanchez, that, if there was even the faintest hope of a child's surviving its mother just long enough to be baptised, she might take no medicine, even in the last resort, because it might put her child 'in peril of everlasting death'. A mother might take a medicine essential to her survival only if the unborn child would in any case die prior to baptism. In other words, she could legitimately take such a medicine only if she *and* the baby would both die without it ('Theologia moralis', III, n. 194). Mausbach-Tischleder's authoritative work on moral theology stated in 1938: 'It is, on the other hand, permissible . . . to employ remedies and operations which are directed not against pregnancy but against the simultaneous existence of a fatal disease in the mother, but which also *per accidens* conduce to abortion, the proviso being that the child's chances of baptism are not impaired thereby' (II, p. 123).

In connection with the priority of infant baptism over maternal survival, Alfonso debated 'whether the mother is obliged to suffer her body to be cut open so that the child may be baptised'. Happily, he began by declaring, with the support of Thomas Aquinas, that the requirements of baptism did not justify killing the mother. Indeed, he was compassionate enough to state that not even a moribund woman might be cut open to extract her child for baptism, nor was a mother obliged to consent to such an operation if it would probably cause her death. She was obliged to suffer the surgeon to cut her open without her consent if there was a probability that the child could be baptised and if the operation would not spell her *certain* death. If the probabilities were evenly balanced, she had to give her child's spiritual life precedence over her own earthly survival. In other words, a mother had to risk death at the surgeon's hands if her child had a fair chance of baptism and, thus, of everlasting life. If, on the other hand, surgery would assuredly kill her but not guarantee the child of baptism, she was not obliged to suffer certain death ('Theologia moralis', III, 194).

After engaging in this theological butchery, Alfonso addressed himself to another profoundly Christian question. If a pregnant woman had been condemned to death and her execution was deferred for the child's sake until after her confinement, should the executioner be forestalled by cutting her open if there was a danger that the child would die inside her body prior to birth? Alfonso replied in the affirmative and cited a number of theologians who shared his view. Unless this was done, the stay of execution ordered for the child's benefit would otherwise redound to its detriment. Since the woman would in any case have been cut open to save the child *after* execution, it could legitimately be removed *before* execution, thereby bringing the execution forward, because the mother's death had been postponed for the child's sake alone (ibid., VI, 106).

Augustine's cruel God, who persecuted and damned newborn babies not fortunate enough to have been baptised before death, persecuted and tortured their mothers as well. He continues to do so in our own century, though his cruelty has been somewhat blunted by the discovery of anaesthetics. Writing of the Caesarian section, an operation not as dangerous, admittedly, as it was in the days of Alfonso de' Liguori, Franz Göpfert says: 'Thus the prospect of being able validly to baptise the child justifies the danger which the operation holds for the mother ... It could under certain circumstances, with regard to the child's everlasting salvation, be held to be a maternal obligation' ('Moraltheologie', vol. 2).

Bernhard Häring, too, holds that a mother must make certain sacrifices to assure her child of baptism: 'If there is no other way to save the child, *above all no way to assure its baptism* [my italics], the mother is obliged to submit to an operation of this kind' ('The Law of Christ', III, p. 211). Having listed 'such operations' (Caesarian section, symphysiotomy), Häring states that they are 'primarily concerned with saving the life of the infant' and 'involve certain hazards for the mother'. According to him, however, saving the infant consists '*above all*' in assuring it of baptism, so its death thereafter is not ruled out. Reassuringly, he impresses on his female readers that 'a mother may today submit to this operation [Caesarian section] without any special hazard two or even three times' (ibid.). Ergo, a mother may not have to sacrifice her life until a fourth baptism is in prospect. As Häring says: 'It is false to rate ... the mother's spiritual health and maternal instincts below mere bodily safety' (ibid., p. 209). In other words, a physically dead but spiritually healthy and instinctively maternal mother is worth at least as much as one who, though physically alive, is deficient in spiritual health.

A mother's death can thus be the essential price of her child's baptism, for a child deprived of baptism is also deprived of eternal salvation. Although Catholics may not lay hands on 'the innocent child in the womb', even to save their own lives, the said child is not as innocent in the eyes of the Almighty God as one might suppose. He himself has found it guilty of an offence so heinous that he punishes it to all eternity by refusing to give it house-room, thereby sentencing it to everlasting death. If the child is to be wrested from the clutches of God the executioner and placed in the arms of God the loving father, it must be baptised. Sometimes, however, God's price for preserving the child from everlasting death is the earthly death of its mother.

Alfonso de' Liguori, founder of Bernhard Häring's order, declared a Doctor of the Church in 1871 and patron saint of confessors in 1950, is the oft-cited authority on all such matters and has stood sponsor to many an infant baptised beside its mother's corpse. Whereas Thomas Sanchez had held that an inanimate foetus less than eighty days old could be aborted if the mother's life was in danger, Alfonso disputed this and insisted that abortion should be punished from the moment of conception on. Whereas Sanchez had regarded the foetus as 'part of the mother's viscera' until the eightieth day, Alfonso described this eighty-day deferment as a 'possible' theory but rejected it himself ('Theologia moralis', III, 394). It was Alfonso who inspired the mother-sacrifice ideology that has held sway from 1884 to the present day – the ideology that was somewhat diluted in 1976 by the German bishops (not by Rome), though they did no more, even then, than affirm their 'respect for medical decisions'. Decisions are still being taken *about* women, but not *with* them, still less *by* them, and the bishops' concession applies only to cases in which both mother *and* child would otherwise die.

The last quarter of our century has thus witnessed, at least in Germany, a lessening of the dire consequences stemming from Sanchez's demand, made still more rigorous by Alfonso, that infant baptism take precedence over a mother's earthly survival. All that has prevented and still prevents many pregnant women from flying into a panic is their uncertainty about the Catholic Church's attitude to mothers in the matter of infant baptism, the rules concerning which have yet to be rescinded worldwide. Moral theologians have long debated how far a confessor should apprise expectant mothers of their duty to sacrifice their earthly existence for the sake of their child's eternal life, or to facilitate the baptism of a dying child by consenting to be cut open. They have generally voted against enlightening such mothers because, being in mortal danger, they might refuse to do their duty and die in a state of mortal sin. That theologians can sometimes be merciful enough to suppress their merciless principles is one humane aspect of an inhumane ethic.

But they are not always so agreeably discreet, as Georges Simenon, the celebrated Belgian crime writer, points out in his memoirs. When his wife Denise was in the last stages of pregnancy, they went to look at a women's clinic in Arizona that had been recommended to them as the best available. They left in a hurry, deterred by the sight of a 'black-bordered' notice hanging in the reception room. 'It informed expectant mothers that, by order of the head physician and the mother superior, in case of serious complications, the life of the child would be considered ahead of that of the mother.' Simenon writes: 'That gave us a chill, and we tiptoed out' ('Intimate Memoirs', p. 266). Their son Jean was later born in a less staunchly Catholic hospital.

TWENTY-SEVEN

Masturbation

Every epoch has its own obsessions, and one of the crazes to which the Age of Enlightenment succumbed might be termed 'onanomania'. Onan, the biblical character who incurred Jehovah's wrath and was struck dead (Genesis 38), has lent his name to onanism, a term originally synonymous with coitus interruptus but, as we saw in chapter 6, mistakenly extended (early in the eighteenth century) to masturbation, alias self-abuse. The Christian sexual ethic outlawed this practice and classed it as one of the most unnatural, i.e. heinous, sins in the sexual domain. Any emission of semen for non-generative purposes was an offence against nature. Indeed, masturbation in the view of Thomas Aquinas ('Summa theologica', II/II, q. 154, a. 11 and 12) was a vice more damnable than intercourse between mother and son.

Many people find sickness in this world a more intimidating prospect than hell-fire in the next, so the long-standing medical obsession with masturbation was a bonanza for Catholic moral theologians because it furnished them, as transmitters of God's will, with additional evidence and legitimacy. The Catholic Church has exploited medical misapprehensions on the subject in countless tracts and pamphlets aimed primarily at the morally endangered young, and anyone who derives his theology from Catholic moral theologians will be convinced, even today, that masturbation wastes the spinal marrow, softens or desiccates the brain, and can generally impair the constitution.

Bernhard Häring states that masturbation 'may wreak havoc on health, and especially on the nervous system', though he concedes that it does not necessarily produce these effects 'unless the habit takes deep hold of the individual', so intimidated sinners have recently been granted at least a glimmer of hope ('The Law of Christ', III, p. 302).

281

Masturbation was considered detrimental to health even in the ancient world (v. A. and W. Leibbrand, 'Formen des Eros: Kultur- und Geistesgeschichte der Liebe'). The progenitor of onanophobia, especially in regard to wasting of the spinal marrow, was the Greek physician Hippocrates (d. 375 BC), though he was less concerned with masturbation itself than with the physical debility he attributed to loss of semen, this being common to both masturbation and sexual intercourse. Galen (d. AD 199), whom we met in chapter 1 – another Greek who was personal physician to Emperor Marcus Aurelius – took the opposite view. He held that sexual intercourse and masturbation promoted good health and helped to preserve the body from corruptive poisons, while continence resulted in tremors, convulsions, and dementia. The Islamic philosopher Avicenna (d. 1037), taking his cue from Galen, referred to medical treatments that prescribed masturbation where sexual intercourse was impracticable. It was left to Christianity to transfer masturbation from the sphere of medical debate to that of moral condemnation and, from the seventeenth century onwards, to embroider that condemnation with such dire Hippocratic prognoses that self-abuse came to be regarded as a cause of earthly sickness as well as otherworldly punishment.

When Johann von Wesel stood trial for heresy at Mainz in 1479, the court of inquisition was concerned with morality alone and took no account of his medical counter-arguments. Wesel, priest in residence at Mainz Cathedral, had familiarised himself with the theories of Galen and Avicenna and accepted them. His writings had questioned whether continence could make monks ill and whether it was permissible, if semen had become 'putrid' and was poisoning the system, to expel it in some artificial manner, without any pleasurable sensation – indeed, whether the pleasurable sensation itself might be free from sin if the body were cleansed for purely therapeutic reasons. Johann von Wesel was commanded to disavow his writings and sentenced to confinement in a monastery.

Richard Capel, chaplain of Magdalen College, Oxford, a major centre of Protestant and Puritan doctrine, wrote in 1640 that 'self-pollution' was not only a very grave sin against nature but conducive to physical debility, conjugal incapacity, and the curtailment of life by suicidal means. These and other assertions were contained in a book entitled 'Tentations: Their Nature, Danger, Cure'.

It was a reformed Puritan physician named Bekkers who christened masturbation 'onania' or onanism. First anonymously published in London in 1710, his 'Onania or the Heinous Sin of Self-Pollution and its Frightful Consequences in Both Sexes, Considered with Spiritual and Physical Advice' stated that this vice was widespread, and that, as a physician, he felt it his bounden duty to call attention to its dire effects. These, according to Bekkers, included gastric disorders, dyspepsia, indifference to food or a voracious appetite, vomiting, nausea, wasting of the respiratory organs, coughing, hoarseness, palsy, debility of the sexual organs to the point of impotence, lack of libido, diurnal and nocturnal emissions, pains in the back, impaired sight and hearing, complete loss of physical energy, pallor, emaciation, facial cysts, loss of mental vigour, amnesia, bouts of fury, dementia, epilepsy, paralysis, fever, and, last but not least, suicide. Bekkers' publication, which evoked a spate of letters from young people requesting advice, was expanded to twice its original size and translated into almost every European language. By 1759 it was in its nineteenth English edition.

Another work entitled 'Onania', published in 1758 by Dr Simon Tissot of Lausanne, succeeded in turning the fear of masturbation into a form of mass hysteria. Tissot asserted, for example, that a masturbator's brain became so desiccated that it could be heard rattling around inside his skull. 'This treatise presented the subject in epochal guise and rendered it viable for centuries' (V.E. Pilgrim, 'Der selbstbefriedigte Mensch', p. 43). The last edition appeared in 1905. Tissot's foreword rejected all requests for information and treatment in advance on the grounds that he preferred to devote his time to those who fell sick for 'reputable' reasons.

Referring to masturbation in 'The Making of the Modern Family' (p. 101), Edward Shorter ironically remarks that:

> self-defilement was, indeed, cutting down the very flower of the [French] nation itself: the cadets in the military academies. Dr Guillaume Daignan in 1786 related this tale of a young man's road to ruin [*Tableau des variétés de la vie humaine*, Paris, 1786]: 'Joining his uncle, captain in a regiment of four battalions, he was supposed to take up the first available post. He was very well received by his numerous comrades and soon imitated all their follies, which in this profession are not always in the direction of prudence and sagacity. He had been very well raised, polite and agreeable. These qualities, which should have guaranteed him

female conquests, served only to draw him in all the more because of his intimacy with his mates. Remorse was not delayed. First, he experienced violent cramps whenever he excited himself to such acts ... which his whole mode of thinking should have made him detest, if he had not been swayed by the example of the multitude ... I encouraged him to break completely with this detestable habit, and he assured me that he wished to do so all the more because he felt not at all tempted by it. But he didn't know how to avoid the occasions. Having as yet no functions to fulfil, he could scarcely sequester himself from his comrades without appearing unusual. Upon learning that this variety of orgy took place only in the evening, I counselled him to absent himself on the pretext of a migraine headache ... The excuse worked for a time, but the damage was already done. The cramps returned frequently ... And sure enough, the lad's health turned out to be permanently ruined, a 'nervous degenerate, deprived of the sweetness of life and the charms of sociability'.

The spread of pseudo-medical onanomania in the Age of Enlightenment did not, however, extend to everyone. Count Mirabeau (d. 1791), leading light of the French Revolution, rejected such deterrent propaganda in favour of Galen's theories about the toxic effects of accumulated semen and pronounced masturbation a sensible practice. Queen Marie Antoinette, on the other hand, had ample cause to regret the prevailing mass hysteria. Before sending her to the guillotine, the revolutionary authorities sought grounds for doing so, and the records of her trial disclose how low they were prepared to stoop (v. André Castelot, 'Marie Antoinette', p. 499f.). Robespierre saw to it that the indictment, apart from charging her with treason, contained the following accusation: 'The widow Capet [i.e. Marie Antoinette], being immoral in every respect, is so perverted and so well-versed in all the vices that, heedless of her mother's estate and of the bounds imposed on her by nature, she does not shrink from indulging with her son Louis-Charles Capet, who has testified to that effect, in obscenities the very idea and name of which cause one to quake with horror.' The queen's accusers summoned her eight-year-old son (Louis XVII, titular king of France, b. 1785, d. 1795) to give evidence. Louis, who had been placed in the care of a man named Simon (whose 'educational' methods were probably responsible for the boy's early death), stated that Simon and his wife had several times caught him engaging in 'obscene and unwholesome practices' in bed. These, he further stated, had been taught him by his mother.

The testimony of a witness named Hébert was recorded thus:

> Young Capet, whose state of health was deteriorating day by day, had been taken unawares by Simon while indulging in obscene acts of self-pollution detrimental to his health. When Simon inquired who had taught him such criminal behaviour, he replied: his mother and his aunt ... These two women had often made him sleep between them in the same bed, a fact that had also transpired from young Capet's testimony before the mayor of Paris and the attorney to the Commune. It was to be assumed that this criminal form of self-indulgence had been taught the boy not for pleasure's sake but in the political hope of physically debilitating him, for it was still thought at that time that he would ascend the throne in due course, and that influence over him could be gained thereby. Thanks to the exertions and exhaustion to which he was subjected, the boy suffered a hernia and had to be bandaged. Now that he is no longer with his mother, his strength is returning.

When asked what she had to say to this testimony, Marie Antoinette replied that she did not know what the witness was talking about, and that nature forbade one even to contemplate such a charge against a mother. Many of those present agreed with her.

Medical findings continued to be adduced in support of theological precepts as the nineteenth century progressed. J. C. Debreyne, a noted moral theologian who was a Trappist monk as well as a physician, described the consequences of masturbation as follows in a celebrated article dated 1842: 'Palpitations, impaired eyesight, headaches, dizziness, tremors, painful cramps, epileptic convulsions, in many cases genuine epilepsy, general pains in the limbs or the back of the head, in the spine, in the chest, in the abdomen; severe renal debility, general symptoms of paralysis' ('Essai sur la théologie morale considérée dans ses rapports avec la physiologie et la médecine'). The medical monk's advice to those afflicted with onanism included sleeping on one's side, never on one's back, consuming cold food and beverages, sucking lumps of ice, and sluicing oneself with a solution of kitchen salt and melted snow. In the case of girls, given that the clitoris was merely an instrument of pleasure superfluous to procreation, Father Debreyne recommended its removal.

A chapter entitled 'Children under Attack by the Nineteenth Century' in V.E. Pilgrim's book 'Der selbstbefriedigte Mensch' states that:

> nineteenth-century physicians adopted the same approach to their case histories as their predecessor Tissot, who believed that a masturbator's brain became 'so extremely desiccated that one could hear it rattling inside his cranium'. The assertion that masturbation desiccates the brain sufficiently to make it rattle around inside the masturbator's skull is often encountered in the nineteenth century. Deslandes cites the case of an eighteen-year-old youth the back of whose cranium displayed some very singular changes. The youth had masturbated for several years and experienced almost incessant erections. 'This habit was enlarging the diameter of his head to such an extent that his mother found it hard to obtain a hat to fit the youngster'.

Pilgrim goes on to describe the methods employed to combat masturbation: 'In the case of boys, wires or metal clasps were threaded through the foreskin to prevent the glans from being withdrawn ["infibulation", so-called]. At night, spiked metal rings were placed around the penis . . .'

The best the century could do for women was to excise the clitoris. This operation (clitoridectomy or female circumcision), was recommended by the Austrian physician Gustav Braun in his 'Compendium der Frauenkrankheiten' (Vienna, 1863) and introduced into England by Isaac Baker-Brown, a prominent London surgeon who later became the highly respected president of the London Medical Society. Baker-Brown, who held that masturbation caused hysteria, epilepsy, and varicose veins, sought to cure it by removing the organ concerned. He performed numerous clitoridectomies on children and adults and founded a special women's hostel called The London Surgical Home. In 1866 he published forty-eight of these operations (Pilgrim, op. cit., p. 477f.).

In 1849 a physician named Demeaux addressed an urgent appeal to the French Ministry of Education. He requested *inter alia* that the dormitories of boarding-schools and colleges be equipped with special partitions separating the top third of the beds from the bottom two-thirds. This would enable the lower end of as many as a hundred beds to be kept under nightly surveillance and any suspicious movements noted, while the head end remained shrouded in darkness by the partition. Dr Demeaux further requested that trousers should have their pockets removed and that boys should undergo several unheralded physical examinations annually. The school physician, having identified the masturbators by their organic development, by their fear of self-exposure, and, above all, by their impaired state of health, would then be able to keep a special eye on them. Two of Demeaux's recommendations were rejected: the partition over the beds, because enforced immobility might do the youngsters harm; and the physical inspections, because these would destroy the sense of modesty that was the principal defence against masturbation. As for removing boys' trouser-pockets, this was already common practice ('Le conseil de l'université de France', 27 February 1849; v. Jean Paul Aaron and Roger Kempf, 'Le pénis et la démoralisation de l'occident', pp. 205f. and 239).

Onanomania was known in Russia, too. A Ruthenian physician named Kaan wrote a 'Psychopathia sexualis' of which a German translation was published at Leipzig in 1834. This work, which was dedicated to the Tsar's personal physician, described 'onania', the great sexual disease, in the style of Tissot, complete with a plethora of mental and physical disorders culminating in suicide. In 'The Life of Klim Samgin' (1925), Maxim Gorki says of his hero, who was born circa 1880: 'Klim thought of Professor Tarnowski's terrifying work on the pernicious effects of masturbation, a book which his mother had taken the precaution of slipping him some time ago.'

In 1882, Dr Demetrius Zambaco of Istanbul published a lengthy article entitled 'Masturbation and Mental Disorder in Two Little Girls', in 'L'Encéphale', a French medical journal devoted to nervous and mental diseases. The elder of the two had masturbated so incessantly that clitoridectomy was the only answer. Dr Zambaco: 'It is reasonable to concede that cauterising the clitoris with red-hot irons destroys its sensitivity – indeed, that repeated cauterisation facilitates its complete removal . . . It may readily be appreciated that, once cauterisation has deprived them of sensitivity, children become less excitable and less inclined to touch themselves.' Zambaco went on to report that he had come across several colleagues of international repute, e.g. Dr Jules Guerin of London, who had effected excellent cures by cauterising the clitoris.

Although Freud's 'Three Contributions to the Theory of Sex' (1905) helped to put a stop to such operations and saved children from further mutilation, 'onanism' continued to be anathematised in the same old way. In 1910 a Dr Sterian menacingly claimed to be able to identify 'the unfortunate manual-sexual' by his 'pervasive odour of semen' ('L'éducation sexuelle'). Ingmar Bergman, the Swedish film director, was born a parson's son at Uppsala in 1918. His memoirs describe how, at his elder brother's suggestion, he consulted an encyclopedia for advice on the subject of masturbation:

> There it stated in plain language that masturbation was called self-abuse and was a youthful vice that had to be resisted by all possible means, that it led to pallor, sweating, trembling, black rings round the eyes, concentration difficulties and equilibrium disturbances . . . In more serious cases the disease led to softening of the brain, attacks on the spinal cord, epilepsy, unconsciousness and an early death. With these prospects for the future before my eyes, I continued my activities with terror and enjoyment. I had no one to talk to, nor anyone to ask. I had constantly to be on my guard, constantly concealing my terrible secret . . . The night before my first communion, I tried with all my might to resist my demon. I fought with him until long into the small hours, but lost the battle. Jesus punished me with a gigantic infected pimple right in the middle of my pallid forehead.
>
> ('The Magic Lantern: An Autobiography', pp. 110–11)

Writing in 1956, the English cleric and broadcaster Leslie D. Weatherhead stated that for many of his compatriots, male and female, masturbation was their life's chief problem and the cause of numerous 'neuroses', but he warned against sanctioning the practice because it was sinful. In 1967 the French abbé M. Petitmangin urged that masturbation be resisted at all costs: it was as much of a vice as the practice of contraception by married couples. The 'grave sin' of masturbation was similarly condemned in 1975 by Pope Paul VI in 'Elucidation of Some Questions of Sexual Morality'. Now that physicians and pedagogues have gradually bidden the subject farewell, therefore, masturbation is safely back in theological hands. 'The masturbator forfeits God's love', wrote the pope, and masturbation is a grave sin 'even though it is not possible to prove beyond doubt that Holy Writ expressly condemns that sin as such'. Since papal pronouncements always carry more weight than the Bible in doubtful cases, the faithful need not be alarmed by its silence on the subject of masturbation.

Besides, the Church has received some unexpected support from the East – more precisely, from China, the very country that bans procreation as vigorously as the Vatican bans contraception. Hubert Dobiosch writes as follows of a study trip he made there in 1985 in response to an invitation addressed to the faculty of moral theology at Augsburg by agreement with the German Bishops' Conference, its stated purpose being 'to build a bridge to the isolated Church in China':

> Vigorous information campaigns are being conducted in implementation of the family-planning programme. Young people are strongly enjoined to sexual continence and given the following advice: 1. Early marriage is harmful and promotes excessive sexuality. 2. An overactive sex life leads to impotence. 3. Self-abuse results in impotence, brain damage, and myopia. 4. The following countermeasures are recommended: (a) studying the works of Marx, Lenin, and Mao; (b) doing gymnastics; (c) getting up early, etc.; (d) not sleeping on one's stomach; (e) avoiding warm bedclothes; (f) not wearing tight underpants; and (g) shadow-boxing, which is highly recommended and practised everywhere.
>
> ('Theologie der Gegenwart', 1986, 2, p. 106f.)

One-child China offers the Catholic Church a great missionary field for its gospel of continence, and the convenient fact that the Chinese are masturbating themselves into myopia promises to give its glad Christian tidings an additional impetus. The German bishops are far-, not short-sighted in regarding China as fertile soil for future cultivation. Where masturbation is concerned, this may be inferred from an article on Chinese sex education in 'Der Spiegel' (No. 13, 1986, p. 189): 'Self-abuse, warns the booklet "General Knowledge of Hygiene and Biology among the Young", "damages the health" ... "Excessively tight trousers" and "heavy bedclothes" are to be avoided.'

TWENTY-EIGHT

Homosexuality

The Greek and Judaeo-Christian creation myths are at one in representing every human being as incomplete, but they differ over whether the missing half of a man is a woman or another man. The biblical account of the Creation conveys the process whereby man and woman became 'one flesh' by stating that Eve was fashioned from one of Adam's ribs. This primeval relationship is not to be taken scientifically, nor does Genesis conflict with the theory of evolution because, like Adam, Eve evolved from an animal body. The biblical account of their original relationship is, in fact, a metaphorical expression of how profoundly man and woman belong together. 'This is now bone of my bones and flesh of my flesh,' says Adam when God brings Eve to him, and the account concludes: 'Therefore [because female sprang directly from male] shall a man leave his father and his mother, and shall cleave unto his wife: and they shall be one flesh' (Genesis 2: 23, 24). That is to say, they will in a sense resume the intimate physical communion in which they used to live when woman was still an integral part of man. Woman and man originally formed one physical unit; *that* is why she will again become one flesh with him and he with her – in marriage. Viewed in the light of man's and woman's oneness and its renewal in marriage, homosexuality appears unnatural by Jewish, Christian, and Islamic standards. Man naturally seeks to re-create that original oneness only with woman and woman only with man.

The Greek myth as recounted by Plato (d. 347 BC) in the 'Symposium', takes a different view. According to this, we were not originally constituted as we are now. There used to be three kinds of complete human beings, all of them spherical: one consisted of man and man,

290

another of woman and woman, and the third or heterosexual kind of man and woman combined. The gods punished our spherical ancestors by cutting them in half, and ever since then each half has striven to reunite with its pair. The Greek myth speaks disparagingly of the heterosexual category: 'Those men who are halves of a being of mixed sex, which used to be termed . . . a hermaphrodite, direct their love toward women, and most adulterers are of this kind . . .' After a brief reference to lesbians, the myth goes on to speak of 'those who are parts of a whole man' and thus 'pursue males . . . Such boys and youths are the very best of their kind, being by nature the most manly . . . One cardinal proof of this is that such boys alone, when they are full-grown, devote themselves to public affairs . . . They are naturally averse to marriage and procreation, and are compelled to engage in them only by convention.'

So the practice described as an unnatural vice by Christianity, which has sent many homosexuals to the stake in the course of its history, is characterised by Greek myth as 'natural'. Celibatarian churchmen 'averse to marriage and procreation' would have been regarded by the Greeks as classic examples of the male homosexual species. Clearly, 'natural' and 'unnatural' have not always meant the same thing to different people at different stages in history.

St Paul, a Jew, abominated homosexuality and accounted it a typically Greek vice. It was not an uncontroversial subject even among the Greeks, however, as the following incident shows. The Greek historian Plutarch (d.c. AD 120) wrote of a Theban 'lovers' battalion', an elite unit recruited from homosexuals on the principle that it was a good thing 'to post a lover beside his beloved' because one would fight his hardest to defend the other in time of danger. This Theban unit, also known as 'the Sacred Band', had been invincible until Philip II, father of Alexander the Great, defeated it at the battle of Chaeronea in 338 BC. 'When Philip inspected the dead after the battle and came to the spot where the three hundred lay, having all charged the enemy's spears and fallen side by side, he is said to have been amazed. And, when he learned that they were the band of lovers and beloved, he wept and cried: "May those die who suspect such people of having acted discreditably" (Pelopidas in 'Lives', 18). Philip would not have inveighed against critics of homosexuality unless they existed.

Seneca the Elder (father of the famous Seneca whom Nero forced to commit suicide in AD 65) expressed a contempt for homosexuals when describing their decadence in the following passage: 'The souls of these effeminates are filled with an unwholesome passion for singing and dancing. They imitate women in their mincing movements and devote themselves to obscene experiments. Such is the ideal of our young men. Pampered and highly-strung from birth, they are ever ready and willing to offend the modesty of others while paying no heed to their own' ('Controversiae', Preamble 8). The Stoic philosopher Epictetus (d.*c.* AD 135) wrote of perfumed and ringleted orators whose sex was in doubt ('Dissertationes', III, 1), and Aristophanes, the Athenian comic playwright, poked fun at homosexuals in the fourth century BC: 'Pale complexions, shaven cheeks, feminine voices, saffron robes, hairnets – one wonders whether one is confronted by a woman or a man' ('Thesmophoriazusae', V, 130f.). It is apparent, therefore, that not everyone viewed homosexuality with favour, even in ancient Greece.

Christianity, which inherited its abhorrence of homosexuality from Judaism, tried to exterminate homosexuals as soon as it attained secular power. A law enacted in 390 threatened them with death by fire, and Article 116 of Charles V's 'Peinliche Gerichtsordnung' (1532) decreed that they should be burned at the stake 'pursuant to common practice'.

All that Catholic Christianity had in common with the male homosexuality of the ancient world was the low regard for women typical of a warlike society dominated by men. In particular, it took over the Aristotelian idea that women were incapable of friendship – that friendship, the most exalted relationship open to adults, was possible only between men.

As we have already seen, the two great pillars of the Catholic faith, Augustine and Thomas Aquinas, made it clear that woman was given to man purely as a helpmate, but that 'man is a better aid to man' against solitude, i.e. better company. It was in keeping with its sexual pessimism that the Catholic Church should have desexualised homosexuality in its own ranks and then proceeded to nurture it into a male society disdainful of women.

Where more sympathetic churchmen are concerned, it would be fairer to say that they ignore women rather than despise them. Here is Pope John XXIII writing in his spiritual journal in 1948:

292

How well I remember, after more than forty years, the edifying conversations in the Bishop's residence at Bergamo with my revered Bishop Mgr Radini Tedeschi! Never was there a single reference to a Vatican official, from the Holy father downwards, that was lacking in reverence, affection or respect. As for women, and everything to do with them, never a word, never: it was as if there were no women in the world. This absolute silence, even between close friends, about everything to do with women was one of the most profound and lasting lessons of my early years in the priesthood; and I am grateful still to the kind and illustrious man who taught me this discipline.

('Journal of a Soul')

In this exclusively masculine environment, this womanless and totally isolated vivarium designed to preserve popes and their mentors from what they would regard as the beginning of their gravest blunder, an acknowledgement of humanity's other half – in this male-dominated ecclesiastical ghetto, in other words – women are merely objects to be ignored as a celibatarians' precaution against any assault on their chastity or invasion of their own secluded world. Such is their attempt to behave 'as if there were no women', their surrealistic endeavour to time-warp themselves back to the paradisal days when Eve had still to be created by God, and their infantile craving to seek refuge in a kind of male womb, that they have lost sight of the real world: the world of humanity, which is populated by men *and* women.

TWENTY-NINE

Moral Theology in the Twentieth Century

Sex is an aspect of human existence that has fallen prey in special measure to a very special form of theological science: the theological outgrowth or offshoot known as moral theology. Its biblical foundations are meagre in the sense that nothing of the kind exists in the New Testament, so it has had to achieve its ambition largely by dint of its own efforts. That ambition is, among other things, to provide 'Christian guidance on all of life's foreseeable contingencies' ('Lexikon für Theologie und Kirche', vol. 7, 1962, p. 613). Those engaged in such an endeavour were bound to feel rather neglected by Christ himself because his teachings did not take the form of 'a complete or systematic exposition or ethic of the coming of the Kingdom of God' (ibid., p. 618).

The Church's moral theologians remedied this doctrinal omission on Christ's part by amplifying, systematising and concretising his gospel in a way that exemplified one of their essential peculiarities, namely, a love of systematics and detailed casuistry. As time went by, casuistry became the moral theologian's most salient characteristic. Christianity deserted the light of day for the gloom of the confessional, where priests devoted more and more of their whispered inquisitions to the so-called sins of the flesh because they believed, pursuant to the Roman ruling of 4 February 1611, that such sins could never be trivial. The Council of Trent (1545–63) rejected Luther's dismissal of the nicely gauged difference between one sin and another and insisted that penitents should decribe the nature, frequency, and circumstances of their sinful acts. This whetted moral theologians' interest in precise moral standards and rules and encouraged confessors to interrogate their penitents in detail. From the sixteenth century onwards almost all religious orders published collections of case histories complete with commentaries and opinions formulated by a host of casuists, most of whose rulings hold good to this day.

Worthy of special mention here is a moral theologian whose name has cropped up several times in previous chapters. Alfonso Maria de' Liguori (1696–1787), founder of the Redemptorist Order, spent thirty years as a missionary and preacher before becoming a bishop and finally returning to a monastery. His voluminous work, 'Theologia moralis', had a decisive influence on the development of Catholic moral theology, and the Church has posthumously invested him with all the honours it can bestow. Beatified in 1816 and canonised in 1839, he was promoted a Doctor of the Church by Pius IX in 1871, who affirmed that he could find nothing in Alfonso's works that conflicted with the truth as taught by the Church. In 1950 Pius XII named him the patron saint of all confessors and moralists.

The official Redemptorist biography of Alfonso, whose 'realism' has been stressed in our own century by Bernhard Häring, a member of his order, provides us with the following vivid picture of his attitude to the opposite sex: 'As a bishop he granted audiences to women only in the presence of a servant, and on one occasion, to a very old woman, in such a way that she sat at one end of a long bench while he, with his back to her, sat at the other. When confirming women he would never touch the bare cheek when obliged to lay hands on them as prescribed by the Church, but only the confirmands' head-dresses' (cited in Karlheinz Deschner, 'Das Kreuz mit der Kirche: Eine Sexualgeschichte des Christentums', p. 325f.).

Alfonso's magnum opus has run through more than seventy editions and been parroted by hundreds of moral theologians, all of whom have helped to institutionalise a wretched theological ethic that not only presupposed the nonage of the laity but systematically inculcated it. Instead of developing and strengthening the exercise of conscience, Alfonso's theology split hairs and made sexual morality a science exclusive to celibatarians. Franz Göpfert wrote in 1906 that 'ordinary, uneducated people cannot distinguish between unchastity, sensuality, and immodesty' ('Moraltheologie', II, p. 346). Only the celibatarian arbiters of the confessional are capable of such discrimination, which would overtax the conscience of the ordinary individual, uneducated or not.

Häring, too, indulges in the same incomprehensible moral theologians' gibberish: 'Sexual excitement to which no direct consent is given, but which is provoked by culpably immodest acts, is a grave sin by its nature (*ex genere suo*). This means: it is a venial or a mortal sin according to the lesser or greater infringement of the order of modesty and the relation of this infringement of order to the sexual excitement' ('The Law of Christ', III, p. 294). Confessors should, of course, realise that they can ask too much of their penitents. Häring urges them not to insist that confessions be 'materially complete in respect of scientific distinctions'. How very wise of him. If confessors did *not* refrain from insisting on materially complete, scientifically detailed confessions, or on what they regard as such, they would have to stock up the confessional with iron rations enough for a good long stay!

Alfonso, as we have already seen, encouraged confessors to question the young – who are, of course, even more obtuse than their elders – about their sexual lapses. Children present a special problem. 'It cannot be denied,' wrote Göpfert, 'that children regard many acts as playful and mischievous without recognising them as grave sins, e.g. when they touch one another or look at or expose themselves to others in an impure[!] fashion' (Göpfert, op. cit., II, p. 346).

It was Alfonso, too, who perpetuated the demonisation of sex. Thanks to him the confessional continues to be haunted, even in the twentieth century, by the incubus and the succubus, the he-devil that lies on top and the she-devil that lies beneath. People still confess to having had demonic intercourse. Göpfert does, admittedly, warn against 'readily believing' such penitents (ibid., p. 365) and mentions in this connection that they may be insane or hysterical, but it is unfair to discredit the victims of an abstruse theology when accusations of insanity or hysteria should first be levelled at its authors and upholders. Although Göpfert himself did not consider demonic intercourse 'readily believable', he did think it believable. It is only now, as our century draws to a close, that theologians are ceasing to apply themselves to such chimeras, and that the belief in them is dwindling. Under the pressure of a more enlightened age, theology has thus been deprived of a once-extensive field of special knowledge.

Even in the twentieth century, the sexual casuistry developed by Alfonso provided sexual pessimists with a basis for wide-ranging studies of the extramarital sphere (within marriage they concentrated on 'conjugal abuse', alias contraception). Austere moral theologians found many a stone that could be turned to reveal an unchaste or immodest worm, for 'by unchastity is meant any form of sexual gratification that conflicts with the God-given purpose of the sexual instinct. It seeks pleasure alone outside the duty that is, pursuant to God's will, associated with the exercise of conjugal intercourse in marriage' (Fritz Tillmann, 'Die Katholische Sittenlehre', IV, 2, p. 117). Pleasure was like a red rag to such pleasure-hating theologians, though by 'pleasure' they did not necessarily mean its ultimate form: 'On the way to the consummation of the outward act are impure looks, physical contacts, embraces and kisses inherent in which is a strong inclination to proceed to extremes' (ibid., p. 122).

As long ago as the sixteenth century, moral theologians had devised a practical system whereby to classify the gamut of acts intermediate between looks and kisses, for which the umbrella term was 'immodesty'. Just as butchers divide carcasses into superior and inferior cuts of meat, so theologians divided human beings into superior, inferior, and condemnable parts of the body. Man's relationship to God and vice versa was dependent on how he regarded or treated his own anatomical components and those of other people. 'Because of their varying influence on the excitation of sexual pleasure, parts of the body are divided into modest (face, hands, feet), less modest (breast, back, arms, thighs), and immodest (the genitals and parts that very closely adjoin them)' (H. Jone, 'Katholische Moraltheologie', p. 189). In keeping with tradition, Göpfert referred to 'immodest' parts of the body as 'vile' and 'obscene' (Göpfert, op. cit., II, p. 366).

Ecclesiastically defined immorality can sometimes have dire results: 'Gentle contact with a female's hand can thus be a mortal sin if it occurs for impure ends.' So squeezing a girl's hand may only sometimes be mortal sin, but kissing her on the arm is 'in general a mortal sin, for one can conceive of no legitimate reason for so doing; but, if there is no legitimate reason, they [the kisses] are either lustful or at best very titillating'. Even touching another's hand should not be taken too lightly, however, because it is a venial sin under all circumstances: 'Contacts with the modest . . . parts, even if only fleetingly occasioned in frivolity, jest, or curiosity, are venially sinful. It is, therefore [only] a venial sin lightly and fleetingly to touch the fingers, hands, or face of a person of the opposite sex without evil intention or sexual desire or the risk of acquiescence in sensual pleasure, provided always that, if there is a stirring of sexual desire, one suppresses it and then desists from such an act' (ibid., p. 368). Göpfert cites a number of moral theologians, Alfonso de' Liguori included, who had taught this. On the other hand, he had previously stated in an earlier edition that 'To hold a female's hand lightly while dancing is either no sin or only venially sinful' (ibid., II, 1900, p. 336). Not being too sure which, he played safe and omitted this sentence from the 1906 edition.

In addition to sinful physical contacts there are sinful looks or glances, which are divided into immodest and very immodest. Immodest looks may still be immodest even when their focus of attention is modest in itself, but we shall not go into that here. Suffice it to point out, as an example of the systematisation to which moral theologians are addicted, that four factors govern their assessment of the danger inherent in such looks: (a) their object; (b) the observer's intention; (c) the observer's disposition; and (d) the mode of observation. In the opinion of the vast majority of moral theologians, the disposition of the person looked at makes no specific difference. When it comes to distinguishing between immodest and very immodest looks, it is obvious that the latter are directed at 'immodest' parts of the body – not necessarily unclothed: 'It is likewise a grave sin to see such things through a net or a very thin, transparent garment, for this tends more to excite lust than extinguish it' (ibid., p. 376).

Häring manifests the same moral spirit in 1967. He subdivides 'sins of immodesty' into (a) looks, (b) physical contacts ('our modern overcrowded means of transportation are also the occasion of anonymous flirtations'), (c) conversations, and (d) reading '('How serious our attention and concern must be in this area is evident from the motherly solicitude of the Church in forbidding evil books') (Häring, op. cit., p. 306f.). Häring's opening sentence reads: 'All acts of immodesty whose express purpose is sexual gratification or the provoking of sexual excitement outside married life become unchaste through that very purpose. Accordingly, they are very grave sins' (ibid., p. 306). Where (b) is concerned, however, Häring has some reassuring words for normal-minded Christians unable to avoid touching each other: 'But where true Christian charity and the spirit of helpfulness to others (the sick, for example) occasion and demand bodily contact, experience shows that normal persons have nothing to fear' (ibid., p. 309).

Where physical contacts, kisses and embraces are concerned, betrothed couples are permitted no more licence than the unbetrothed, meaning none at all, for, as Göpfert emphasises, (Göpfert, op. cit., II,

p. 372), 'betrothal invests an engaged person with absolutely no rights over the body of the other party'. Girls and young men may forge friendships 'only for a good purpose, in other words, early marriage . . . Intercourse [Göpfert means the social variety, not the sexual] should be restricted, that is to say, not too frequent and not too protracted. Greater frequency may be tolerated if marriage is to take place soon, say in one or two months' time, but the more marriage is deferred the less frequent such meetings should be. Greater frequency may be tolerated if the girl is never alone and always under careful supervision, less if the engaged couple are always alone together' (ibid., p. 373f.). Häring updated this in 1967 as follows: 'Although parental supervision in the old manner, which suited a closed society, is hardly feasible in today's dynamic, open society, sensible rules of conduct must be evolved even today. At the same time, Christians must clearly recognise that the modes of conduct customary in modern society have derived from ideologies incompatible with Christianity' (Häring, op. cit., p. 377).

Moral theologians perceived no such incompatibility during the Nazi era. On the contrary, National Socialism seemed to hold out the promise of support for many important aspects of Catholic moral theology, and the Church seized its chance with alacrity. Hitler's first personal interview with a Catholic prelate, Bishop Wilhelm Berning of Osnabrück, and Vicar-General Steinmann, representing Bishop Schreiber of Berlin, who was ill, took place on 26 April 1933. Berning's record of the meeting stated: 'The interview (which lasted an hour and a quarter) was cordial and businesslike. The bishops were delighted to note that the new regime intends to foster Christianity, raise moral standards, and prosecute the campaign against Bolshevism and godlessness with vigour and success' (Hans Müller, 'Katholische Kirche und Nationalsozialismus, Dokumente 1930–1935', p. 117). On 30 May/1 June 1933, the bishops' conference at Fulda issued a pastoral letter expressing 'gratitude to Hitler' because 'immorality' would no longer 'menace and ravage the soul of the German people'. To the German bishops, fighting immorality meant campaigning for 'chaste education of the young' and against 'swimming-pool excesses [i.e. the perils of mixed bathing]' (ibid., pp. 146 and 156). In August 1933, when Monsignor Steinmann greeted the crowds at the exhibition of the Holy Coat in Trier with a 'Heil Hitler' and was subsequently criticised in New York, he retorted that the German bishops regarded Hitler as a bastion against 'the plague of obscene literature' (Friedrich Heer, 'Gottes erste Leibe: Die Juden im Spannungfeld der Geschichte', p. 409).

Veneration of the Virgin and the Catholic ideals of chastity and celibacy all acquired a National Socialist tinge during the thirties, and the Catholic phobia about squandering sacred semen made common cause with the Nazi craze for racial purity. Bishop Berning, who advocated 'a return to the ties of blood, in other words, to genetic kinship' ('Das Neue Reich', No. 7, 1934, p. 9), regarded National Socialist blood-phantasies as an excellent growing medium for ecclesiastical celibacy: 'It happens again and again, thanks to the combined effects of a good biological heritage and a corresponding environment . . . that children from these families develop into priests and religious. They are in radiant contrast to those criminal families whose offspring fill the asylums and prisons' (ibid., p. 14f.).

German moral theologians were thus at one with the National Socialists in believing that the state must do something to combat the genetic peril. Fritz Tillmann wrote in 1940: 'In view of the great increase in the number of hereditarily diseased persons, the results of genetic research have led to the consideration of ways in which the birth of hereditarily sick offspring can be prevented. Education or prohibitions on marriage are clearly insufficient, given the mental incapacity and unreceptiveness of most such handicapped persons and their unrestrained sex life. It might, however, be possible to achieve the relevant aim by institutionalising them, though this would have to be for the whole term of their reproductive life' (Tillmann, op. cit., IV, 2, p. 415). Tillmann thus opposed sterilisation, but for reasons that make one's hair stand on end: 'The gravest moral objection to sterilization is, in fact, that it divorces sexual gratification from responsibility, which in the case of mental defectives, who very often possess an unbridled sex drive, can have disastrous effects' (ibid., p. 419).

Pleasure-hating celibatarians preferred the concentration camp to compulsory sterilisation. Cardinal Faulhaber has left a record of an interview he had in 1936 with Hitler, who advocated the sterilisation of the hereditarily sick, so-called, to prevent them from having handicapped offspring. 'The operation is simple, after all,' Hitler said, 'and does not render them incapable of working or marrying, and now the Church puts a spoke in our wheel.' Faulhaber replied: 'The state, Herr Reichskanzler, is not debarred by the Church from removing these *Schädlinge* [pests or vermin] from the national community in the interests of legimate self-defence and in conformity with moral law, but preventives other than physical mutilation must be sought, and such a preventive does exist: the internment of the hereditarily sick' (Faulhaber Remains, Item No. 8203).

Internment camps meant concentration camps, and these clearly came within the bounds of 'moral law'. Sterilisation, whether voluntary or compulsory, transgressed them because it permitted the enjoyment of sex while precluding procreation. Pope Sixtus V's 'lecherous eunuchs' of 1587 were not granted the right to marry until 1977.

Genetic considerations and ecclesiastical hostility to sexual pleasure combine to form an alarming amalgam in Häring's chapter on 'Responsible Decision':

> Genuine willingness to serve the Creator and Redeemer will dictate a choice of spouse most favourable to the building of a family and the formation of members of the Kingdom of God. *Eugenics* is progressively developing into an important science intended to provide information on which choice of spouse will naturally and most effectively conduce to the good of offspring. One's responsibility toward marriage and toward service to life utterly prohibits the choosing of a partner from whom, in all probability, only badly handicapped . . . children can be expected. A certain hereditary affliction . . . that gives rise to fears of sick and disabled but mentally normal offspring (e.g. haemophiliac, myopic, perhaps even blind and deaf) does not in principle debar a person from marrying, although this may be strongly advised against in serious cases. One experienced Catholic eugenist, for valid reasons, considers the marrying of persons afflicted with very serious hereditary diseases to be utterly irresponsible from the moral aspect . . . It is desirable that, prior to their betrothal, couples exchange certificates of hereditary good health issued by a doctor qualified in psychology and eugenics . . . The Church's prohibition of marriage between relatives (under current law extending only to the third collateral degree) fulfils a salutary eugenic function.
>
> (Häring, op. cit., III, pp. 337–8)

No one has anything against healthy offspring, which are every parent's ambition. The ancients, too, attached great importance to *euteknia* (a 'goodly brood' of children), as we have already seen, but it is misanthropic to forbid the blind and deaf and haemophiliac to marry or to 'strongly advise' them against it instead of leaving it to them to decide whether they want children despite their disability, or, if they do not, what form of contraception to practise when married. In adopting the human stud-farm approach, complete with certificates of hereditary health *à la* Häring, the Church ranges itself on the side of totalitarian systems. It did not, incidentally, occur to theologians until the nineteenth century that the Church had banned marriage between relatives for 'salutary eugenic' reasons, as Häring asserts. In the chapter on incest I showed that its real motive was merely a variant of the everlasting clerical hostility toward sexual pleasure and marriage.

Catholic moral theology has lost much of its reputation in very recent times, and its elaborate antisexual edifice lies in ruins. Many a human conscience has been warped by its insane demands, with their claims to religious validity and divine authority. It has burdened people with idiotic sophistries and sought to turn them into moral acrobats instead of making them more human and philanthropic. Operating on behalf of a 'supernature' remote from and hostile to humanity, it has suppressed human nature and human instincts so rigorously that the overstretched bow was bound to break in the end. Its theology is no theology and its morality no morality. It has foundered on its own foolish, presumptuous belief that it could deprive the individual of personal experience of God's will and replace the discovery of that will with a proliferating casuistic system. It has failed because of its lack of compassion – because it sought to subject human beings to its own binding laws instead of allowing them to obey God's commandments, which are a summons to freedom.

Karl Rahner rightly says of moral theology that the Church has, 'in both theory and practice, defended moral maxims with bad arguments because of questionable, historically determined "preconvictions" and "prejudices" ... This darkly tragic aspect of the Church's spiritual history encumbers it to the extent it does because the matters in question always or often intrude deeply into people's actual, everyday lives; because such false maxims, which were never objectively valid, imposed burdens on them ... which derived no legitimacy whatever from the freedom of the Gospel' ('Schriften zur Theologie', vol. 13, 1978, p. 99f.).

Moral theologians would be better advised to remain silent on the subject of sex, as the following passage from an article by H.J. Müller –

'Ehe ohne Trauschein' (Marriage without a Marriage Certificate) – exemplifies: 'There were times when, without realising that they were at fault, people transgressed objective norms in a way we now find inconceivable. One has only to think of the witchcraft trials . . . The same may be said of many young people's current attitude to sexual conduct. Even committed Christians among them cannot, so they say, understand why their carefully weighed decision to begin by living together outside marriage should be a sin.' Müller goes on to urge that strenuous efforts be made to dispel the darkness enshrouding their scale of values ('Theologie der Gegenwart', 1983, 4, p. 259). If moral theologians genuinely find the witchcraft trials of bygone centuries comparable with cohabitation in our own, the darkness enshrouding *their* scale of values must surely be denser by far.

Many couples who now regard themselves as married are not considered so by others (e.g. by Church or state). Others decline to marry because they feel that the cohabitation of man and woman is a personal matter requiring no civil or ecclesiastical attestation. It is clear that the forms and norms of marriage are currently in a state of flux. Many people complain that the institution of marriage is in danger, but their fears are unfounded. Marriage certificates may be in danger, perhaps, but they are a comparatively recent innovation.

How were marriages contracted in earlier times? Although many couples married in church, complete with wreath, veil and benediction, marriage often took the form of a stroll, a declaration of love, a proposal, and a simple 'yes'. Under Roman law, on which Church law was based ('consent constitutes matrimony'), the couple were then legitimately wed, with or without the moon as a witness. Marriages of that kind were termed 'clandestine', but their validity was not disputed. Although the Church insisted (from 1215 onwards) that the banns be read and published, this requirement often went unheeded.

Clandestine marriages were legally insecure, however. Many a woman swore that a rival's prospective bridegroom had already married her in secret, just as many a man who had tired of his church-wed wife invalidated their union by similarly laying claim to an earlier, clandestine, marriage. At Augsburg in 1349, for example, the authorities had to rule on no less than 111 cases of desertion, 101 of them brought by abandoned wives. Eighty of these petitioners had their pleas dismissed because marriage could not be proved.

Repeated attempts were made to dispel this legal uncertainty, for instance by Luther, who held that if a marriage had been contracted without parental consent – meaning, to all intents and purposes, paternal consent – the father was empowered to declare it invalid even if children had been born of it (Epiphany Sermon, Weimar Edition, vol. 10, I, 1; cf. G.H. Joyce, 'Christian Marriage: The Prohibited Degrees of Kindred and Affinity', p. 103f.). Luther's friend and fellow reformer Melanchthon, on the other hand, believed that a clandestine marriage, once contracted, could not be declared invalid by the father (Joyce, op. cit., p. 119). Reformed Protestants were most insistent on parental rights. The Anglican bishop Thomas Barlow (d. 1691) was in no doubt 'that a father hath just authority by the law of God and of nature to consider and judge what is good for his children and . . . to use . . . castigations and whippings too, to make them do their duty and obey his just commands' (ibid., p. 82).

In the sixteenth century the Catholic Church sought, unlike the Protestants, to defuse the problem of clandestine marriages. The 'Tametsi' ('even though') decretal of 1563 introduced the so-called obligation of form: 'even though' the validity of existing clandestine unions was not disputed, all future marriages had to follow a certain procedure: they would not be valid unless the ceremony was conducted by one's own parish priest in the presence of at least two witnesses.

This clerical solution did not commend itself to the Protestants, who championed the cause of parental consent. The 'Reutlinger Kirchenordnung', a Luther-inspired collection of rules governing religious ceremonies, had stated in 1562 that 'after the papal custom, many children marry behind their parents' backs', and that a marriage solemnised in church without the father's knowledge was invalid, 'for God's commandment of obedience to father and mother nullifies such a marriage vow'.

In ensuing centuries the Catholic Church made it clear (e.g. in the 'Declaratio Benedictina' of 1741) that it did not insist on the Catholic form of marriage for non-Catholic, e.g. Protestant, couples. Protestant marriages continued to be deemed valid without it, as they were prior to 1563.

In 1975 Pope Paul VI lamented 'the growing spread of moral decay, one of its gravest symptoms being the inordinate glorification of sex.' In celibatarian eyes, nothing can ever be graver than sex. The pope went on: 'Many today claim the right of premarital intercourse, at least in cases where this fulfilment, which they consider natural, is demanded by a serious intention to marry and a quasi-conjugal affection in the hearts of both partners. This applies in particular when the wedding ceremony is delayed by extraneous circumstances.' All such relationships, declared the pope, were 'unchaste'. They did not 'guarantee the sincerity and fidelity' that should exist between man and wife ('Elucidation of Some Questions of Sexual Morality', 1975).

This Vatican pronouncement was not only loveless and unjust but theologically slipshod. By indiscriminately condemning premarital relations between all couples as 'unchaste' the pope was contradicting his own canon law, which states that non-Catholic couples are subject to no requirements of form when marrying. In other words, Catholic canon law does not insist that they be married by a priest or a registrar; their marriage is validated simply by their intention to remain man and wife for good, in other words, by the 'quasi-conjugal affection' whose existence in the hearts of such uncertified couples the pope himself acknowledged.

Even where Catholic couples are concerned, however, the pope should have eschewed the word 'unchaste'. Although they have been subject to an approved form of marriage since 1563, ecclesiastical law (Canon 1116) also sanctions an extraordinary or 'emergency' form (affirmation of the wish to marry before two witnesses) in cases where the normal procedure prescribed for Catholics would entail 'grave disadvantages'. These may be of a wholly material nature. Canon 1116 could thus apply to students or pensioners, etc., who are prevented by extraneous circumstances from marrying in the conventional manner.

Even if the Vatican cannot bring itself to acknowledge the validity of such unions under Canon 1116, it might at least respect them instead of discriminating against them and describing them as unchaste. It is as unrealistic to believe that 'sincerity and fidelity' are automatically guaranteed by a formal ceremony as it is emotionally unobjective to ascribe unchastity to relationships which the Vatican itself admits may be 'quasi-conjugally affectionate'. It betrays a reluctance to accept that marriage is founded on the wish of two people to marry, and that all outward forms are historically determined and of secondary importance.

State intervention in marriage has been going on for a considerable time: civil marriages were first performed in the Netherlands in 1580 and have preceded church weddings in Germany since 1875. The Catholic Church attaches no importance to a state-issued marriage certificate; conversely, what the Church regards as marriage (e.g. under Canon 1116) does not constitute marriage from the state's point of view. Thus the form in which marriage comes into being has continually changed in the course of time. Since so many couples now reject the old forms, it behoves us to devise new forms and norms that pay greater attention to their wishes.

THIRTY

The Misdirection of
Mariology

Mary, the mother of Jesus, has always occupied an especially prominent place in the history of Christian theology and devotion. This is understandable, for her status as the mother of the Christians' acknowledged saviour has fascinated the faithful from earliest times. That a woman should play so outstanding a role in the ecclesiastical world of ideas was beneficial, too, because it prevented the Church from becoming an even more masculine institution and the world an even more male-dominated place. Women in particular have always regarded Mary as a refuge, a mother or sister to whom they could flee from a God who too often impressed them as a wrathful he-god.

But Mariology, or the ecclesiastical doctrine concerning Mary, was not evolved by women; it was evolved by men, and unmarried men at that, in other words, by those whose affinity with marriage was nil. Such men claimed that their unmarried state was superior, and that marriage was, relatively speaking, inferior. Marriage and its sexual concomitants have always lacked champions within the Church, never been regarded as other than morally questionable.

However, Mary was a married woman who bore a child – indeed, an unprejudiced reader of the New Testament will concede that she bore quite a number of children. Simply to accept this as it stands would be to credit Mary with a far from celibatarian, if not anticelibatarian way of life, so her New Testament image as the mother of several children had to undergo revision, as we saw in chapter 3.

The first step was to deprive her of all but an only son, Jesus. Her other children were taken away from her and pronounced to be the offspring of her husband Joseph by a fictitious first marriage. Later on, her surroundings were even more completely purged of the marital taint: her husband, too, had to be pure and celibate, so her children could no longer be foisted on him. Lest they detract from her virginal status, Jesus's brothers and sisters were transmogrified into his cousins.

Mary was even deprived of the birth of her one remaining son. She could not be allowed to give birth as other women do, because that would have precluded her 'virginity in birth' and, thus, her 'perpetual virginity'. Even today the Pope repeatedly stresses that Mary remained 'inviolate' – a celibatarian euphemism meaning that her hymen was not ruptured during childbirth. If this had occurred, she would have been physically impaired just as any other mother is physically impaired by the birth of a child and ceases to be 'as good as new'. If she was to remain 'inviolate', however, she could not give birth in the normal way.

This doctrine of 'virginity in birth', which cannot be abandoned without reducing the whole artificial edifice of Mary's 'perpetual virginity' to ruins, is a peculiarly crass example of the flights of fancy entailed by her transformation into a virgin. The traditional doctrine of virginity in birth states (a) that Mary's hymen remained intact, (b) that the birth was painless, and (c) that no afterbirth or *sordes* ('filth') resulted. Mary has been said to have given birth to Jesus as if emitting a ray of light, or the burning bush that is not consumed, or 'as spirits in general pass through bodies without resistance', or to have been transfigured in advance by his resurrection (M.J. Scheeben, 'Handbuch der kathol-ischen Dogmatik', II, 1878, p. 939). Setting aside the doubt cast on Christ's humanity by likening him at birth to a ray of light or 'spirits in general', it scarcely enhances a woman's dignity to turn her into a kind of supernatural film projector. Mariologists may, in their own terms, have bestowed something on Mary by drawing such a distinction between her and other mothers of children, but in feminine and human terms they have deprived her of an important attribute. Those who insist that a woman preserved her biological virginity in childbirth, and that the birth itself was a purely mental or spiritual process, should realise that they rob the woman in question of her very motherhood.

By depriving Mary of her motherhood, the doctrine of the virgin birth was intended to deliver her from the curse associated by celibatarians with the normal motherhood of all normal mothers. That curse, however, is merely a figment of the sexual neurotic's imagination. Like other Mariologists, Alois Müller regards a mother's physical impairment in childbirth as a special 'sign of the curse imposed by original sin'

('Mysterium salutis', III, 2, p. 464f.). Only Mary's parturition was painless, whereas all other mothers are subject to God's curse in Genesis 3: 16: 'In sorrow thou shalt bring forth children.' 'Eve was smitten by this painful curse upon her motherhood after the Fall' (ibid., p. 463), and all mothers save one have suffered from it ever since. Müller uses the word 'curse' with reference to motherhood no less than seven times on a single page (ibid., p. 464), but the more often Mariologists represent mothers as accursed, the more one suspects that the maternal curse, far from being divine, is a celibatarian invention of their own.

Mary gave birth painlessly for another reason contributed by Augustine, the author of our pleasure-hating sexual ethic: 'She conceived without carnal desire and thus gave birth without pain.' Theologians never tire of proclaiming this, even in our own century. Unlike Mary, every other mother is accursed: physically impaired, painfully chastised, and – last but not least – defiled.

The notion that Mary remained intact during childbirth is based largely on an account in the so-called Book of James or Protevangelium, an apocryphal book written in the second century AD by someone purporting to be James, one of the 'brethren of the Lord'. This forgery had an immense influence on the whole future development of Mariology. Although the Protevangelium was firmly rejected by the Western Church (as opposed to the Eastern) because it represented Jesus's brothers and sisters as Joseph's children by a first marriage, and because theologians, notably Jerome, were busy turning them into cousins, some aspects of the book were adopted nonetheless, e.g. the legendary names of Mary's parents, Ioacim (Joachim) and Anna (Anne). The Protevangelium's account of the examination of the intact hymen is less than delicate. Indeed, there are aspects of it that smack of theological pornography – of sexual fantasies cloaked in religious devotion.

> And the midwife went forth of the cave and Salome met her. And she said to her: Salome, Salome, a new sight have I to tell thee. A virgin hath brought forth, which her nature alloweth not. And Salome said: As the Lord my God liveth, if I make not trial and prove her nature I will not believe that a virgin hath brought forth ... And Salome made trial and cried out and said: Woe unto mine iniquity and mine unbelief, because I have tempted the living God, and lo, my hand falleth away from me in fire. And she bowed her knees unto the Lord ... And lo, an angel of the

Lord appeared, saying unto her: Salome, Salome, the Lord hath hearkened unto thee: bring thine hand near unto the young child and take him up, and there shall be unto thee salvation and joy ... And behold, immediately Salome was healed: and she went forth of the cave justified.

Such was the blunt instrument with which theologians knocked Mary's image into shape. Indeed, such was their eagerness to create a virgin that would match their celibatarian ideal of womanhood that they did not shrink from subjecting her to the indignity of a theological meat inspection. Despite this, Wetzer/Welte's ecclesiastical encyclopedia says of the Protevangelium that it 'intended to glorify the mother of the Lord' and stresses 'the dignity' of its account (1, 1071).

Having once submitted to this examination, Mary demonstrably possessed the attribute expected and demanded of her by male theologians: perpetual virginity. Unlike all other mothers, who were impure and violate, she was pure and entire. Theologians dumped their theological garbage on those other mothers in the devout belief that this would lend the mother of Jesus an even more immaculate appearance. By laying a perpetual curse on all women except the perpetual virgin, however, they circumscribed their view of womanhood and forfeited any understanding of it they might otherwise have gained.

Celibatarians strove to create an image of Mary that had nothing in common with that of other women. They succeeded, but at the expense of distorting a human face past recognition. Veneration of the one pure woman as opposed to the impure generality of women may have been an aid to them in their own womanless existence, which was often lonely, but it had a detrimental effect on a host of others.

Many people may well have hankered after the image of a queen of heaven, but many more would have preferred a human being, and all who might have encountered the image of a real person in a theologically less miraculous and more realistic Mary were cheated of that encounter by the doctrine of an incomprehensible and existentially meaningless preternatural prodigy. In so far as Mary is meant to set Christians a practical example, Mariology's lack of humanity has made it impossible for them to perfect their faith. How are they to discern the woman in Mary when the Litany of Loreto speaks of her as the '*mater inviolata*'? All other mothers are referred to as '*matres violatae*', meaning women who have been subjected to sexual violence, abused, sullied, polluted, defiled, and profaned.

310

Catholic theologians have stood Mariology on its head for long enough, and the time has come to right it again. What overturned it was the fact that it became a male province very early on, and a celibatarian one into the bargain, so the usual male reversals of the world and its values intruded on its sphere of influence. Traditional Mariology is unworthy of its name. It has become a kind of anti-Mariology in that it claims to emphasise a woman's greatness and dignity and paint them in glowing theological colours while crudely destroying all that constitutes feminine dignity in Mary the human being in particular and in all women in general.

It is a hard fate for a woman to have to lead an existence corseted and dogmatised by men. Mary has suffered uniquely in this respect. Everything connected with female sexuality, all that betokens the natural generation and bearing of children, have been denied her. She was not allowed to conceive her son by a man; he had to be sexlessly begotten on her by the Holy Ghost. She was not allowed to give birth to him in the normal way because she had to remain inviolate, nor was she allowed to have any other children because that would have entailed her physical violation. She was thus transformed into a kind of sexless creature, a mere semblance of a wife and mother restricted to her role in the redemptive process. The lords of creation allotted her an existence sufficient only for the fulfilment of that function; everything beyond it was taken from her. Of her wisdom, for example, Thomas Aquinas says: 'It cannot be doubted that the Blessed Virgin received the gift of wisdom in an eminent degree' ('Summa theologica', III, q. 27, a. 5 ad 3). However, this gift of wisdom turns out on closer examination to have been very limited, for 'she enjoyed the use of wisdom in contemplation . . . not in respect of teaching' (ibid.). Theologians wanted to teach people about her, not to be taught by her. We are not left wondering for long why St Thomas granted Jesus's mother a measure of wisdom too meagre to equip her as a teacher: teaching does not 'befit the female sex' (ibid.). Not even Mary has been exempted from celibatarian arrogance.

The truth is, celibatarians have invariably failed to see Mary as a human being and a real woman despite, or perhaps because of, their dogmatic training. They have taken a celibatarian view of her role in the redemptive process, furnished her in that role with abstruse and miraculous attributes, and hung her dehumanised picture in their austerely masculine world of ideas. One such bloodless male idea has

311

been recorded by Bishop Hermann Volk: 'Mary is not venerated and mentioned in the Gospel for her own sake, but rather because of her function and requirements in God's redemptive plan' ('Collected Works', vol. 2, 1966, p. 78). It would indeed be a celibatarian sin to venerate a woman for her own sake. Mary is important and worthy of veneration only as an instrument of God's grand design. Although theologians have entitled her Mother of God, the greatest dogmatic honour they could bestow, they have failed to perceive that a woman is more than a breeder of children to order. That applied as much to Mary as it does to every woman, and their failure to grasp the fact is as complete in her case as in all others.

It should be added that many Catholics now doubt the traditional doctrine of Mary's perpetual virginity, i.e. the assertion that she remained physically intact before, during, and after childbirth. More and more theologians are coming to recognise that 'virginity' is, in modern terms, a metaphor for the recommencement of history with Christ, and that to interpret the relevant New Testament accounts in a literal sense is to obscure the Gospel's true significance.

In view of modern theology's slowly dawning perception of the exclusively theological nature of New Testament accounts of the virgin birth, the Pope's unflagging insistence on Mary's miraculous biological attributes is just one more addition to the ever-growing heap of outmoded ideas on which he perches. That a supreme pontiff should uphold old doctrines is no novelty, given that popes are the last persons from whom theological progress can be expected. What is surprising, however, is that he has lately been supported even by those bishops whose theological research has contributed to the findings he rejects.

One example: John Paul II stressed in his encyclical 'Redemptoris Mater' (1987) that Mary 'preserved her virginity intact' and meant this statement to be construed in the thoroughly biological sense of an intact hymen, whereas Bishop Karl Lehmann, the current president of the German Bishops' Conference, adopted a far less papally biological approach in 'Vor dem Geheimnis Gottes den Mensch verstehen', the anthology he published to mark Karl Rahner's eightieth birthday in 1984. Lehmann's introduction pays tribute to theology professor Rudolf

Pesch for 'endeavouring to develop the difficult question of the "virgin birth" in dialogue with Karl Rahner' (p. 8), and he concludes by offering Pesch his renewed and abiding thanks (p. 138).

Here is the kind of assertion for which Pesch earned the praise and gratitude of the German bishops' current president: 'Rudolf Schnackenburg has stated, for example, that "If one weighs up the arguments for and against [the existence of] (later-born) siblings of Jesus, one must grant that the presumption of such siblings carries greater weight ... The oldest written testimony, Mark 6: 3, clearly supports this."' Pesch goes on to say that he himself came to a similar conclusion in his dissertation 'On the Question of Jesus's Brothers and Sisters' (p. 25).

So Schnackenburg and Pesch are inclined to assume that Jesus had brothers and sisters, and a senior German bishop has commended Pesch for thinking farther along those lines than many other Catholics.

But Pesch's ideas, as set forth in Lehmann's book, go farther still. He approvingly cites the Catholic theologian Gerhard Lohfink: 'The New Testament professes and proclaims that Jesus is the Son of God, but not that Jesus was conceived without an earthly father' (p. 26). In other words, the biological virgin birth is not a biblical article of faith.

In 1984, therefore, the president of the German Bishops' Conference not only took a non-biological view of the virgin birth in company with Pesch, Schnackenburg, and Lohfink, but commended and thanked such theologians for their progressive ideas. In 1987, on the other hand, he endorsed John Paul II's unreservedly biological interpretation of the virgin birth and stripped such theologians, whose theological, non-biological interpretation of the virgin birth he himself had endorsed in 1984, of their authority to teach.

Pesch's contribution to Lehmann's book was significantly headed : 'Against a Double Truth'. Despite this warning, Bishop Lehmann espoused one view of the virgin birth when publishing pieces by German theologians to mark Karl Rahner's birthday in 1984 and another when backing the Pope in 1987, the year of his election to the presidency of the German Bishops' Conference. He thus proclaimed two different truths about Mary's virginity, the first intended for professors of theology, the second for the Pope and the mass of the faithful.

313

SELECT BIBLIOGRAPHY

Aaron, J.P. and **Kempf**, R. *Le pénis et la démoralisation de l'occident*, Paris 1978

Abelard (**Abaelardus**), Peter *The Story of My Misfortunes*, tr. H.A. Bellows, Macmillan, London 1972

Bachmann, Walter *Das unselige Erbe des Christentums: Die Wechselbälge. Zur Geschichte der Heilpädagogik*, 1985

Badinter, Elisabeth *The Myth of Motherhood*, 1981

Ben-Chorin, Shalom *Mutter Mirjam*, Deutscher Taschenbuch Verlag, 1982

Bergman, Ingmar *The Magic Lantern: An Autobiography*, tr. Joan Tate, Hamish Hamilton, London 1988

Brandl, Leopold *Die Sexualethik des heiligen Albertus Magnus*, 1954

Browe, Peter *Beiträge zur Sexualethik des Mittelalters*, 1932
    Zur Geschichte der Entmannung, 1936

Castelot, André *Marie Antoinette*, Paris 1962

Denzler, Georg *Das Papsttum und der Amtszölibat*, vol. I, 1973; vol. II, 1976

Deschner, Karlheinz *Das Kreuz mit der Kirche: Eine Sexualgeschichte des Christentums*, 1974; 2nd ed., 1987

Franzen, August *Visitationsprotokolle*, 1960
    Zölibat und Priesterehe, 1969

Fuchs, Josef *Die Sexualethik des heiligen Thomas von Aquin*, 1949

Gascoigne, Bamber *The Christians*, Jonathan Cape, London 1977

Göbel, F. *Die Missionspredigten des Franziskaners Berthold von Regensburg*, 1857

Goldmann-Posch, Ursula *Unheilige Ehen; Gespräche mit Priesterfrauen*, 1985

Göpfert, Franz Adam *Moraltheologie*, vol. II, 1906

Häring, Bernhard *The Law of Christ*, vol. III, Cork 1964

Heer, Friedrich *Gottes erste Liebe: Die Juden im Spannungsfeld der Geschichte*, 1981

Hefele, C.J. *Konziliengeschichte*, vol. I, 1855; vol. V, 1863; vol. VI, 1867

Heinsohn/Steiger *Die Vernichtung der Weisen Frauen*, 1985

Hering, H.M. *De amplexu reservato*, 1951

John XXIII *Journal of a Soul*, tr. D. White, Geoffrey Chapman, London 1980

John Paul II *Letter of the Supreme Pontiff to All the Bishops of the Church on the Occasion of Holy Thursday 1979*, Catholic Truth Society, London 1979

  Familiaris consortio, Apostolic Exhortation to the Episcopate, to the Clergy, and to the Faithful of the Whole Catholic Church Regarding the Role of the Christian Family in the Modern World, Catholic Truth Society, London 1981.

  Redemptoris mater, Encyclical Letter of the Supreme Pontiff on the Blessed Virgin Mary in the Life of the Pilgrim Church, Catholic Truth Society, London 1987

Jone, Heribert *Katholische moraltheologie*, 1930

Josephus, Flavius *The Jewish War*, tr. H. Williamson, Penguin Classics, 1981

Joyce, G.H. *Christian Marriage: The Prohibited Degrees of Kindred and Affinity*, London 1948

Klomps, Heinrich *Ehemoral und Jansenismus*, 1964

Leibbrand, A. and W. *Formen des Eros: Kultur- und Geistesgeschichte der Liebe*, 1972

Lindner, Dominikus *Der Usus matrimonii*, 1929

Lüdicke, Klaus *Familienplanung und Ehewille*, 1983

Luther, Martin *Reformation Writings of Martin Luther*, tr. Bertram L. Woolf, Lutterworth, London 1952

Mausbach, J. and **Tischleder**, P. *Katholische Moraltheologie*, 1938

Moltmann-Wendel, E.(ed.) *Frauenbefreiung: Biblische und theologische Argumente*, 1978

Müller, Alois *Mysterium salutis*, vol. III, 1969

Müller, Michael *Die Lehre des heiligen Augustinus von der Paradiesche und ihre Auswirkungen auf die Sexualethik des 12. und 13. Jahrhunderts bis Thomas von Aquin*, 1954

  Grundlagen der katholischen Sexualethik, 1968

Noldin, Hieronymus *De sexto praecepto et de usu matrimonii,* Innsbruck 1911
  Abhandlung über das 6. Gebot und den Ehegebrauch, 1923
Noonan, John T. *Contraception: A History of its Treatment by the Catholic Theologians and Canonists,* Harvard University Press, 1986
Pastor, Ludwig von *Geschichte der Päpste,* vol. X, 1926
Paul VI *Humanae vitae,* Encyclical Letter 'On Human Life', rev. ed., Catholic Truth Society, London 1970
Pfeiffer, Franz *Berthold von Regensburg,* 1862
Pilgrim, V.E. *Der selbstbefriedigte Mensch,* 1975
Pius XI *Casti connubii,* Encyclical Letter on Christian Marriage, McNabb, London 1933
Plato *Symposium,* tr. W. Hamilton, Penguin Classics, 1967
Raming, Ida *Der Ausschluss der Frau vom priesterlichen Amt,* 1973
Ranke-Heinemann, Uta *Widerworte,* Goldmann TB, 1987
Riezler, Sigmund von *Geschichte der Hexenprozesse in Bayern,* 1896
Robinson, Henry M. *The Cardinal,* Macdonald, London 1951
Schmaus, Michael *Katholische Dogmatik,* vol. V: 'Mariologie', 1955
Shorter, Edward *The Making of the Modern Family,* Collins, London 1976
Simenon, Georges *Intimate Memoirs,* tr. H.J. Salemson, Hamish Hamilton, London 1984
Strack, H.L. and **Billerbeck,** P. *Kommentar zum Neuen Testament aus Talmud und Midrasch,* 1924–1961
Suenens, L.J. *A Crucial Problem,* tr. G. Robinson, Westminster Md., 1960
Tacitus, Cornelius *The Histories,* tr. Kenneth Wellesley, Penguin Classics, 1964/1984
Tillmann, Fritz *Die katholische Sittenlehre,* vol. IV, 2, 2nd ed., 1940
van de Velde, Theodor Hendrik *Ideal Marriage,* Heinemann, London 1928
Vasella, O, *Reform und Reformation in der Schweiz,* 1958
Vogels, Heinz-Jürgen *Pflichtzölibat,* 1978
Waltermann, Leo (ed.) *Klerus zwischen Wissenschaft und Seelsorge,* 1966
Walzer, Richard R. *Galen on Jews and Christians,* OUP, 1949
Wetzer/Welte *Kirchenlexikon,* 2nd ed., 1886–1903

INDEX